The Indus People

Saraiki Saga
and
Sufi-Sant Renaissance

The Indus People

Saraiki Saga
and
Sufi-Sant Renaissance

Girja Kumar

Vitasta

Let Knowledge Spread

Published by
Renu Kaul Verma for
Vitasta Publishing Pvt. Ltd.
2/15, Ansari Road, Daryaganj,
New Delhi - 110 002
info@vitastapublishing.com

ISBN 978-93-80828-85-5

First Edition 2013
Second Reprint 2019
MRP ₹ 995

Cover & Layout Design by Vitasta Publishing Pvt. Ltd.
Printed by Thomson Press, New Delhi

Dedication

To *Shyamji Maharaj* (1543-1623), the founder of the Gosain lineage and a pioneer of the Bhakti movement in the north-western corner of the subcontinent.

To my great-grandmother *Tikan Bai*, who confronted the menacing Gitchki tribesmen, who had taken her husband, *Diwan Udho Dass*, the all-powerful Nazim of the sprawling Makran region (bordering Persia), into custody in January 1898.

To roly-poly grandmother *Pokhribai Gosain*, resplendent in her dazzling and freshly washed white chikan-kurta and free flowing jet black ghaghara.

As a perfect gift to newly-wed granddaughter-in-law *Emly Johnson Gosain* (m. Abhimanyu Gosain) and equally to her mother *Jean Guenther*.

To my two-year-old great granddaughter *Riya* (nee Neha and Parmit Mehta).

Last but not the least, it is a thousand salaams to the dour Scotsman and Honorary Baloch, *Robert Groves Sandeman* and his loyal associates *Hittu Ram* and *Diwan Ganpat Rai*.

Contents

Acknowledgement ix

Preface xi

Section - I

Saraiki Memories

1. Baloch Highlanders 3
2. Remembering Sweet Home 25

Section - II

The Indus Lifeline

3. Rigvedic Sindhu 45
4. The Lion River 67

Section - III

Mahabharata Genes

5. The Indus Fraternity 97
6. Villains and Heroes 115
7. Role Model Women 127

Section - IV

Baloch Universe

8. The Progressive Highlander 143
9. Balochistan's Hindu Connection 169

Section - V
Social Identity

10. Khatri Caste 201
11. Sikh, Muslim, Arora and the Sarasvats 222

Section - VI
Linguistic Bonds

12. Saraiki and its Dialects 243
13. Unity and Diversity 261

Section - VII
Literature and Liberal Tradition

14. Baba Farid to Shah Husain 277
15. Bulleh-Warris to Sarmast 297

Section - VIII
Native Sufism

16. Sufis, Sants & Liberal Tradition 329
17. The Aesthetics of Sufism 345

Section - IX
Responsive Bhakti Movement

18. Pan-Indian Bhakti Movement 371
19. Bhakti Aesthetics 390

Section - X
Progressive Khalsa

20. Sikhism and the Sant Tradition 411
21. People's Religion, Protestant Movements 431

Footnote 445
Index 458

Acknowledgement

It has taken me five years to write this book. It has been a lonely journey in discovering India of another kind. I have made extensive use of the extant literature on the subject

My grateful thanks are to authors whose writings I have consulted. The list reads like a litany of names of the former British civil servants, with marginal contributions coming from contemporary Indian and Pakistani authors.

Aitzaz Ahsan, L H Ajwani, Alice Albinia, R I Bruce, Alexander Cunningham, H Longworth Dames, Bibek Debroy, O'Flaherty Doniger, A W Erstwhile, Jean Fairley, Kisore Mohan Ganguli, David Gilmartin, Shrivastava Goswani, G A Grierson, Robert T Griffith, Hamid Hussain, Tasvir Husain, Denzil Ibbetson, Ishwari Prasad, P Lal, Magi Liddchi-Grassi, MA Macauliffe, Edward Maclagan, A K Majumdar, F Max Milar, M Mujeeb, Mushabir Hasan, K A Nizami, Harjot Oberoi, Robert N Pehrson, Athar Abbas Rizvi, J Rosberry III, S R Sharda, Annemarie Schimmel, C Shackle, Shuja Ashfaq, V A Smirnov, Tara Chand and Thomas Henry Thoronton.

I have made extensive use of *The Encyclopedia of Sikhism*, for which I am beholden to its variegated contributors. I am also grateful to the National Archives of India for opening up the records of British India's foreign department to my scrutiny. It is very much hoped, one day some Indian scholar would take time off to scrutizize rich records pertaining to Balochistan, the Swat Valley and the expanding borders of British Imperial Indian in the north-west corner of the subcontinent to his/her benefit and of the country.

I am equally thankful to Prof Krishan Kumar for compiling the index.

Lastly, my thanks go to my ever-obliging and patient publisher Renu Kaul Verma, my editor Papri Sri Raman and production chief Alok Saini.

Preface

Time stopped ticking for our family in 1945, two years prior to the partition of India. We departed from our sweet home, not knowing that we shall never return. It was a semi-desert, with sand blowing across our faces and entering every crevice in our bodies, but we loved it.

The present book is a journey of self-identity and the discovery of India beyond political frontiers. It is a pilgrimage to a homeland no longer accessible to millions who migrated across the artificial borders. While it shall remain a personal odyssey and a voyage of discovery, this book shall also be a carnival of collected memories and a book of record for future generations. The idea is a civilizational concept of shared experiences through historical times.

Very soon the cobwebs began to clear up for me and political boundaries began to fade away. The earnest search for self-identity began in a state of divided loyalties between hometown (janmabhoomi) and the place of adoption (karmabhoomi).

My peoples' romance with their homeland began about 450 years ago, both in *miri* (state craft) and *piri* (dharmic pursuits). There were close connections with the Moghul court, Sikh rule and the Raj. It hurts to be non-entities in the affairs of the capital over the last seven decades.

Multiple Loyalties

The Saraiki loyalty has been a driving force for self identity for the natives of the Middle Indus Valley in recent years. We are too proud of our Saraiki identity. Although a late entrant, the Saraiki sub-nationalism has emerged with a bang. The creation of Saraiki identity has inevitably involved caliberated choice of a language (now termed Saraiki) as a symbol of this identity. There is no such thing as a Saraiki race. It is the language that subsumes self-identity for the natives. Thus language and culture have a common identification.

Saraiki was earlier known as Lahndi. It is one of the oldest Indo-Aryan languages, with its roots going back to the Indus Valley Civilization. It is essentially a Prakrit language and it came into its own after Sanskrit ceased to be the language of discourse by he 6th century BC. The Sanskrit language was born and bred on the banks of the Sindu-Indus river and its subsidiaries, the divine language was a Saraiki gift to the subcontinental civilization.

Saraiki Language

The real transformation in shaping the language took place with the advent of Baba Farid (1175-1265 AD), more popularly known as Faridu'd-din Shakar. He was undoubtedly the pioneer in laying the foundation of Saraiki literature, hitherto confined to the oral tradition and limited to recitations of folk tales and stories conveyed from mouth to mouth.

The rise of modern languages as understood today is owed to Baba Farid's writings in his native language Saraiki. The very fact that the sacred book of the Sikhs incorporated the poetry of Baba Farid among sacred writings is sufficient proof of the continuing dialogues between several communities of North India.

Literary Forte

There is a magical quality about the waters of the Indus and its five subsidiary rivers. The literary giants born and bred on the Saraiki soil invariably have the liberal Sufi connection. However, they are yet not widely appreciated. Bulleh Shah, for instance, had to wait for nearly a century before his kalam was recorded. They look so contemporary and modern and are much ahead of their times. Without exception, they were the protestants of their age and proclaimed their apostasy.

Saraiki literature is an expression of liberal thoughts at its secular best. Here were the pioneers of the Hindu-Muslim dialogues. They chose to be in constant touch with the leaders of the Bhakti movement. Sants and Sufis kept the lines of communication open in the most turbulent times of Medieval India via their sane and wise expressions. They spoke the people's language. They were social reformers and vehemently opposed to orthodoxy and these were reflected in their writings.

Sufi Vs Bhakti Identity

Religion is more of an experience than a code of conduct in the sub-continent. Personal God is one the greatest inventions of human ingenuity. The intellectual mix contributed to this. While the Bhakti movement travelled from South to North, the Sufi cult travelled in the reverse direction. They met half-way and the sangam of Sants, Sufis and Yogis resulted in the foremost exposition of the liberal tradition.

They were all instruments of social transformation. The modern Indian languages were a singular tribute to their native genius. The peoples' languages such as Saraiki, Punjabi, Sindhi, Urdu, Kashmiri and Hindi arrived on the scene.

The aesthetics of Sufi-Bhakti movement cults were expressed best through music, dance and drama. Indian classical tradition has deep roots in the same tradition. The Khyal, Quawali, Dhrupad and Baul music owed to the same culture of love and devotion and they were like a breath of fresh air during the times of sustained political and social turbulence.

Vadhera Indus

Among the multiple identities, the brand Indus stands out. The saga of Sindhu-Indus is unique in the civilizational history of the subcontinent. The Rigveda called the river Sindhu. The very name of India is derived from Indus. Everything is unique about the 'he-man river' (male river) from the beginning to the end.

Sindhu was revered as one of the gods during the Rigvedic times. Rigvedic gods were incarnations of natural phenomenon like rain, fire, wind and rivers. They were essentially secular beings. Even today there is no river in the subcontinent to match its wayward grandeur. Its destructive capabilities are well-known. Max Mueller has called it the 'constructive-destructive Sindhu'.

Its ascendancy has been recognized throughout historic times as a sacred river. There is an episode of The Mahabharatha in which the gentle Yudhishtira is advised to go 'where the Sindhu unites with the Ocean' near the Rann of Kutch in Gujarat, and further, he is told to visit Panchanada, where the five rivers of Punjab merge with it.

The banks of Indus are also dotted with Sufi Khanqahs. Those are properly known as river saints. Shah Abdul Latif of Bhet in Sindh has been pronounced as the Voice of Sindh and a Sufi of the highest order. He was a vocal exponent of Sindhayat or the Greater Sindhaco, the cause which motivated him to travel to Dwarka in Gujarat, believed to be the place where the Indus joined the sea during ancient times.

Mahabharata Identity

The Mahabharata has been called itihasa but it is no history in the ordinary sense of the term. It is a storehouse of historical events concerning the Saraiki people and can be applied as a benchmark for a careful reconstruction of Indian history.

Its geography is fairly accurate. The boundaries of various kingdoms in which ancient Punjab was divided are accurately aligned with river courses. The Sapta Sindhu rivers mentioned in the Vedas and the cities and towns mentioned in the great classic are real. Saindhava horses, which were imported from this part of the world, have been accurately described. The fondness, with which they are described, is amazing.

The Mahabharatha was a war between the kingdoms of the Indus basin arraigned on one side, and those of the Gangetic plains further east ward. The main supporters of the defeated Kauavas were six kingdoms of ancient Punjab. Contemporary hostilities too extend to the same lands.

Personal Identity

Caste has earned a bad name. It, however, served a useful purpose at that time. It was one's signature and identity. It helped to place one's geneology and personal history in context. It gave one an identity amidst the mass and provided security. It did serve useful historical, sociological and anthropological purposes.

It is possible to write an accurate sociological history of ancient, medieval and modern Punjab by mapping the close relations of Hindu (and Muslims) castes such as Khatriya, Khatri, Arora and Sarasvat Brahmins.

It is the hilly tract of Potohar plateau near Islamabad and Taxila, bordering the mighty Indus, which is believed to have given birth to present day Khatri and Arora communities. They spread their wings towards Multan and Sindh in south-west, besides making Lahore, the epicenter of their activities.

The Sarasvat Brahmins originated from the banks of the now defunct Saraswati river, and spread their wings all over the subcontinent. The Saraswats were the traditional priests of Khatri and Arora communities and were as liberal and unorthodox in their worldview as Khatris and Aroras. To their credit they were as iconoclastic as our Sufis and Sants.

No wonder, these communities have collectively made a substantial contribution to the intellectual, administrative and professional (industrialists) leadership of India and Pakistan. All the Sikh gurus belonged to the Khatri sub-castes. There are a plenty of Muslim Khatris known as Khojas in Gujarat and Punjabi Sheikhs in Pakistan. Prominent contemporary Punjabi Sheikhs include among other public figures Najam Sethi (Friday Times) and well known industrialist Mian Rafiq Saigal.

Conclusion

There must be a little bit of Sant, Sufi, Yogi, Baloch, Pathan, Kirar, Khatri, Arora, Sarasvat, ancient Khatriya, Buddhist, Hindu, Muslim and Sikh residing in each one of us. Equally their must be an iconoclast and apostate residing in the inner most recesses of our minds activating our moribund subconscious. There is also a little bit of jehadi bravado clamouring for attention in each one of us. The ancient Khatriyas and equally, our contemporary jehadis, are motivated to violent death and destruction to achieve mythical heavenly abodes.

Section - I
SARAIKI MEMORIES

1

Baloch Highlanders

THE ancient trade route from New Delhi to Kandahar and Persia passes through Dipalpur, Pakpattan, Multan, Dera Ghazi Khan and the Sakhi Sarwar pass. This route was employed by the kings of Kabul to import luscious mangoes from western Punjab. The mangoes arrived in Kandahar in good shape in about nine days. The town of Dera Ghazi Khan assumed significance for its strategic location along the right bank of the Indus River. Alexander Burnes called the town, along with Shikarpur, as one of the 'Gates of Khorasan'. Founded by Ghazi Khan in 1476, a small town earlier existed at the crossing point and was known as 'Pattan' before Christ. It came to be known as 'Pattan Mukam' after the Muslim invasions that began in Persia in 633 AD. It became Pattan Dera and was so known until 1484. Dera in Persian means residence. From 1484 to 1940 AD, people of the region called it 'Thera Dera Ghazi Khan' which finally came to be known as Dera Ghazi Khan.

The place boasts of a colourful history through its association with historical personalities like Muhammad-bin-Qasim, Babur, Akbar and, above all, Robert Sandeman, the founder of contemporary Balochistan. In essence it represents the Baloch spirit. Given its rich history, the place is also known as 'the land of saints' and the 'land of traders', 'the place for saints, brigands and armies', etc. Its very survival is dependent upon the mighty Indus, which is not a benign river. It has also been called the 'Terrorising Vadhera' (the bullying elder) for its infinite destructive potential year after year.

The Invaders

The name of Pattan Mukam is linked with several events of historical significance. Muhammad-bin-Qasim came calling in 700 AD, and his advance to Multan was blunted by the Vadhera-Indus. He marshalled several hundred boats, tied to each other bumper-to-bumper, in order to cross the river. They were filled with sand and stones, enabling his entire force to cross over to the other side of the river.

Ghazi Khan, the Baloch, the next important ruler in the region, died in 1486. Babur came in 1504, during his first invasion of India, as a mere brigand. This was prior to his triumphant victory march to Delhi, two decades later. He confined himself to the right bank of the river, making his foray into the Baloch lands of the newly-constituted Derajat territories. In his memoirs, he expresses surprise at the new vistas opening up before his very eyes: 'I had never before seen the country of warm temperature, nor the country of Hindustan. Immediately on reaching them, I beheld a new world. The grass was different, the trees different, the wild animals of a different sort, the birds of a different plumage, the manners and customs of the wandering tribes of a different kind, I was struck with astonishment and there was room for wonder.' He faced resistance from "the refractory Afghans" and erected "a minaret of heads" to teach a lesson to "death-devoted Afghans" and Balochis (Baburnama).

Babur confined his march to the right bank of the river, moving parallely. The territory was inhabited by Baloch tribesman and had little to offer to Babur except droves of cattle fattening on the islands and rich grasslands bordering the river. Even the meanest of the retainers in his army was able to pick up 'three or four hundred bullocks and cows'.[1] His first entry into India resulted in the devastation of the Derajat, where the tribal chieftains, Ismail Khan, Fateh Khan and Ghazi Khan had established three separate towns at 60-mile intervals. These towns were boat and ferry crossing points on trade routes from India to Afghanistan and Persia.

Traveller's Delight

The British were empire-builders in India by sheer compulsion. They were also keen travellers, bent on exploring new territories. North-west India opened to them consequent to the collapse of the Sikh empire. The Indus banks were also viewed by them as possible conquests awaiting their exploration. The Balochi were a new breed of people for them. Across the river, Dera Ghazi Khan, the trade entrepôt leading to Afghanistan and Persia attracted their attention. The 'Russian Bear had also begun to nose around in the region, sniffing expansion'.

Charles Masson jumped into the fray with a bit of assistance from the East India Company. He undertook journeys to Punjab, Afghanistan and Balochistan for twelve long years from 1826 to 1838. He found plenty of wild jungles between Uch and Dera Ghazi Khan. Thanks to the bounties of the Indus and canal irrigation, he discovered the rich soil with 'a vigorous cultivation' of grains and sugar cane. He also found plenty of games in the wild marshes fed by the river. 'Wild foul are so abundant in the western parts near the Indus, that at Fazelpur, a goose may be purchased for [one paisa], in value less than half a penny, and two or three ducks may be procured for the same sum. They are caught by a peculiar race called Mohanis, who furnish the fishermen and sailors employed in the Indus. The jungles abound in game, in deer and the wild hog, partridges, quails, bustards, pigeons etc, are universal'.[2]

Masson also visited the town of Dera Ghazi Khan, at that time in a state of decay. He was, however, impressed by 'the immense assemblage of date groves and gardens' surrounding the town, locally described as 'Dera phulan da Sehra' (flower-decked forehead). The Kasturi canal flowing through the eastern corner of the town was the 'Jewel in the Crown'. It was fringed with thickly-planted mango-trees, while ghats lined the parks, thronged by swarming bathers during summer months. Michael Edwards praised the old Dera Ghazi Khan, as 'one of the most lovely spots' in Punjab. He called it 'the city of palms'. On both sides of the Indus grew cotton, indigo and sugarcane.

Myths and History

In prehistoric times, the country between the Suleiman mountains and the Indus, with the total frontage (the entire length) at the base of the mountains of 180 miles, was believed to be a huge wasteland. The total frontage of the district along the river was 210 miles.

According to oral traditions handed down through generations, there were only three towns in the vast hinterland before the first Muslim incursions. The district was a part of the Sindh empire of Raja Daher who ruled over an overwhelmingly Buddhist population. Earlier, the district had been devastated by the Mongols, who continued their vigorous and destructive intrusions from 900 AD to 1600 AD.The destruction of the territory by the great Timur during 1399 AD is still remembered with dread and fear. Alexander the Great had also been there. Harrand and Khandpur had been thoroughly destroyed by him. The Huns, Tatars, Mongols, Afghans, Mughals and Persians had been there too. So had been Nadir Shah and Ahmad Shah Abdali. There were tragedies' galore and few events deserving celebration.

Humayun, during his flight to Persia in 1541, was given protection by the Raja of Amarkot in the district. Akbar was born at Amarkot and this was a reason enough to celebrate. Dara Shikoh, during his flight, had also been there, but he was refused permission to cross Pattan. The Saraiki inhabitants of the region have long memories. It is believed that they had claimed the defeated Raja Daher as their own and refused to adopt Muhammad-bin-Qasim, the Arab, as one of them. In their flights of imagination they believed that the Mahabharata war was fought in the Saraiki heartland. To them Sitpur is the ancient location of Hastinapur, the capital of the Pandavas. Similarly, Indraprastha and Khandaprastha, they believed, were located in the same district. For Saraikis, Mahabharata represents three Saraiki words: Maha (great), bha (free) and rat (bloody). In their subconscious lurks the great desire to claim the pre-Islam heritage.

Local Folklore

Harrand, Marri and Asni were said to be the only towns in the vast barren wilderness of the district during ancient times. Two of these towns—Asni and Marri–are connected with the tales of Raja Risalu, the Jat ruler of Sialkot and the local Raja Sirkap and his lovely daughter Kokala. 'Marri' in Saraiki means a high building, by which the town is still known. These towns are associated with several legends. One such tale is of romance, high drama, tragedy and betrayal. The Jat Raja of Sialkot was a Sial Jat. This heroic tale of good and evil is widely popular in the whole of Punjab. It flits across the province with locales in Sialkot, Dera Ghazi Khan and Multan. The legend is given another twist when it is linked to the famous character of Prahalad, both to Raja Risalu and Hiranyakashipu, who had denied the omnipresence of Vishnu, and was then killed by the Narasimha, or the 'Man-Lion' avatar.

In the Raja Risalu version of the legend, Puran is portrayed as the step-brother of Risalu, who suffers and bears physical torture for twelve long years. Mother Nature empathizes with him. The armless Puran is 'fed by birds and cared for by animals', and 'for the twelve years that Puran had been away, the Sialkot trees had borne no fruit, its birds had sung no song, and Sialkot's cows had remained painfully and fretfully without a calf'.[3] Through his sacrifices, Puran turns himself into a hermit (bhagat) and eventually returns to his father's orchard, and, low and behold, 'At once it begins to bloom, the birds begin to sing and cows start bellowing calls to milkmaids'.[4] At another plane, Raja Risalu, hearing of the charms of Kokala, the Marri princess, settles down in the town of Marri. The Sirkap legend is even linked with the ruins of Taxila. General Alexander Cunningham fixed the probable capital of Raja Sirkap at Amba Kalpi in the district of Lahore. Above all, the legend of Risalu reflects the indomitable spirit of resurgent Punjab and its women like Queen Loona, Princess Kokala, Saukhani, Sundaran and Chandni, who had a mind of their own and dominated the scene.

The Saraiki Heartland

Multan is the heartland of Saraiki culture and civilization. Dera Ghazi Khan is a peripheral footnote to it. A mere 90 kilometers separate the two places, but Multan is the key to the understanding of the entire Saraiki region. It is the principal city in Punjab; established towards the middle of the second century of the Christian era. It rivals Lahore in fame. It also has a notorious reputation of being a place full of dust, heat and graves. There is a famous saying about Multan in Persian. *Chuhar cheez hust, took jujat-i-Multan, gird, girda, garma wa goristan.* In translation, it means 'These four gifts has Multan, dust, beggars, heat and graves'. There is, however, more to its well-earned fame. It is a repository of the Rigveda heritage of India, its symbol the famous Sun temple. The Sun is the favourite god and the Sun Temple of Multan is a definite reminder of that ancient heritage of worship. It is strategically located on trade routes from the east to the west and the north to the south to Central Asia.

Every invader from the north passed through this harsh land. Alexander the Great was probably wounded in the vicinity of Multan. The city is as old as Varanasi. If Varanasi is the place of Siva (the seat of the Saivite cult), Multan is the Rigvedic fortress, but Multan is, in addition to that, the meeting point of Rigvedic gods like the Sun and post-Vedic gods like Vishnu. Multan is also associated with the noble soul of Puran Bhagat, who is considered a cult figure in Punjab. Multan is the heartland of several Sufi cults that subsequently spread throughout India. Not far from Multan is Ajodhan, or Pakpattan, the seat of Baba Farid. The place derives its modern name of Pakpattan, meaning 'the ferry of the pure one' from this. Timarlane or Timur marched to Pakpattan in 1398, but spared the place due to respect for the memory of Baba Farid. Thus, there is more to Multan than dust, heat and graves. Multan is one of the holiest cities in the subcontinent, both to the Hindus and Muslims alike.

City of the Sun Temple

The practice of worshipping the Sun ('Aditya'), which was started by Samba, the son of Krishna, at Multan still continues. The Sun remained the great object of worship in the famous Sun temple that once crowned the citadel.

It was converted into a mosque, and subsequently blown up accidentally by the lighting of ammunition kept in the premise by the Sikh rulers. It was earlier known as Kasyapa-pura and subsequently as Hiranya-Kashipu, after the father of Prahalad Bhagat, who was in conflict with his father as the two were worshippers of the Sun and Vishnu, respectively. The conflict led to the eclipse of the Sun god, and the gradual emergence of Vishnu as the predominant deity throughout India. It was also the era of the triumph of Magadhan sculpture and art. The Vishnu cult had humanized religious practices and hence its triumph over the Rigvedic tradition, manifested through impersonal objects like gods and goddesses. The incarnations became the most exciting innovation in depicting gods. It was imaginative to depict gods as Baman (dwarf), Narasimha (half-man and half-animal), Varaha (wild boar) as well as in human incarnations like Rama, Krishna and the Buddha.

Multan has been known by several names throughout its history which are indicative of its historical, cultural and religious evolution. Besides Kasyapapura (probably its earliest name), it is also known as Hansapura, Bhagatpura and Sambhapura. It got the name Kaspeira, because it was once a part of Kaspeirei, the vast empire which extended from Kashmir to Multan. Bhavishya Purana called it 'Adityasthana' or the 'First Shrine', a name given to the Sun temple. The Arab conquerors of Multan called it the 'Golden Temple' and Masudi, the traveller, called it 'a meadows of gold'. It was popularly known as 'Mula-tana'. The Arab became familiar with it as Mulasthanapura, which means 'heaven, ether, space, atmosphere, God'.[5] All of these names are applicable to the Sun. Mulasthana means 'The Temple of Mula', another name for the Sun. The Sun temple here was the rival of the Somnath temple in Gujarat at one time.

Mahabharata War

India, in the age of the Mahabharata, was divided neatly into the north and the east. Hastinapura and Indraprastha dominated by the Pandavas and the Kauravas stood the middle ground in this great divide of kingdoms. This was a historic divide between the lands of pan-Vedic civilization of northern India and the emerging post-Vedic civilization of the east. The divide was reflected in the great Mahabharata war: 'When the two sides face each other on the field of battle, they are more than evenly matched. Other than the Yadavas, the Pandavas have Panchala, Kashi, Magadha, Matsya and Chedi on their side. The Kauravas have Pragjyotisha, Anga, Kekaya, Sindhu, Avanti,Gandhara, Shalva, Bahlika and Kamboja as allies. At the end of the war, all these kings are slain and the entire geographical expanse comes under the control of the Pandavas and the Yadavas'.[6] (see map)

This was virtually a war to end all wars between the northern and eastern kingdoms. The Saraikis represented the Indus people from the kingdoms of Sindhu, Kekaya and Gandhara and were arraigned on the side of the Kauravas, thus, inviting self-destruction voluntarily. The Kaurava alliance was completely based on the support from all the five kingdoms of Sapta Sindhu, namely, Gandhara, Sindhu, Kekaya, Madra (Shalva) and Bahlika, besides the kingdom of Kamboja located in the same direction.

The political alliance of the Kurus with Saraiki and Punjabi people was based on blood relations. Queen Gandhari, blind Dhritarashtra's wife, was the princess of Gandhara. Her scheming brother, Shakuni was the prince. Gandhari's only daughter, Dushala, sister of one hundred brothers, was married to Jayadratha, the king of Sindhu. Shalya, the king of Madra (central Punjab), uncle of the Pandava brothers, Nakul and Sahadeva, was brought over to the side of the Kurus through deceit. There is a striking similarity between the names of the Bahlika kingdom and Bheeshma's brother Bahlika. The Mahabharata war weakened the Saraiki people for all times, thus opening the doors to a stream of foreign invasions. The Saraikis have not risen out of their slumber until this day.

The Sapta Sindhu kingdoms were natural allies of the Kauravas, when viewed in terms of their sheer geography. Gandhara was situated on both sides of the Indus with the historic cities of Peshawar and Taxila as its capital. Kekaya stood in the middle path on the left bank of Indus, below Attock and Kalabagh. A large portion of this kingdom consisted of the tract lying between the river Indus on the east and Jhelum (after its junction with the Chenab), and is known as the Sindh-Sagar Doab (Desert of the Indus). Part of the Jhang district lies in it. Queen Kaikeyi of Ramayana notoriety, hailed from here. Numerous queens of Bharata/Puru lineage came from the

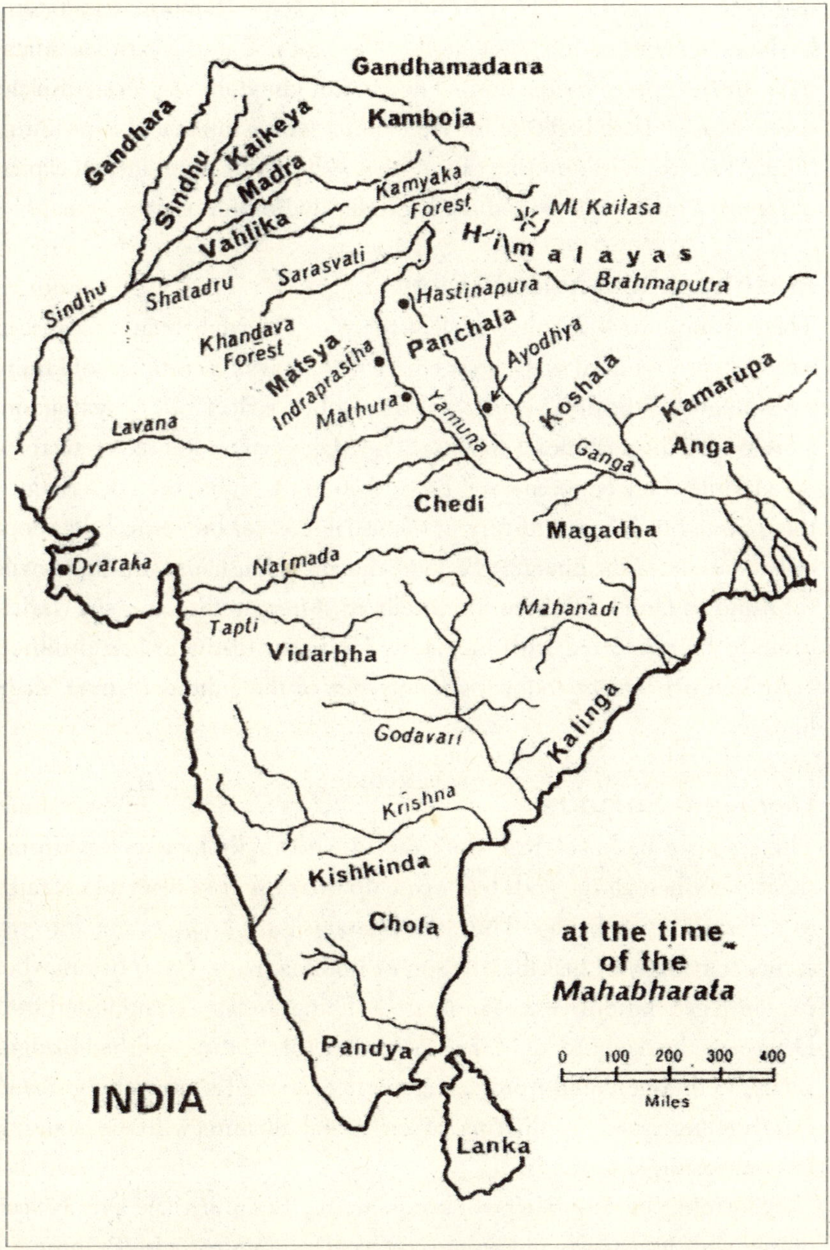

Source: The Mahabharata of Vyasa, condensed from Sanskrit and translated into English by P. Lal, Vikas, New Delhi, 1980.

land of the Heer-Ranjha romance. Queen Madri of Mahabharata belonged to Madra, situated on the right bank of the Ravi. Kamboja was located in the extreme north-east, as Gandhara was located in the extreme north-west (in the opposite direction). The Sindhu kingdom was located in the south-west on both banks of the river Indus, with Multan and Aror (Sind/ Sindh) located in its opposite extremities. While Aror is the ancient capital of Sindh, Multan epitomized the Rigvedic civilization of yore.

Flashback to Ancient Times

There is more to Mahabharata than the war. The Mahabharata has been variously pronounced as the great epic, a maha-kavya, a chronicle of Hindu mythology and the fifth Veda. It is also described as the Doomsday Epic and a prolonged dirge of moral collapse. The Mahabharata war has came to be dated somewhere between 3500 BC and 1000 BC. It has been described as the *itihasa*, but it is not history in the usual sense of the term. It has been called the epic of the Bharatas. Bharata, the son of Dushanta and Shakuntala (of Kalidasa fame), has been immortalized. After all, Bharatvarsha (India) came to be associated with his name. He had a distinguished pedigree, crystal clear from the following family-tree of the famous Bharata/ Puru lineage.

Devayani Episode

The epic is a flashback to history mixed with mythology. It was during the times when all the gods had made up their mind to descend on earth to redeem human beings. Thus, the Bharata/ Puru lineage came into the scene, starting with Daksha, the son of Brahma. King Yayati belonged to the tenth generation(see the family tree). Things became complicated with Devayani, the daughter of Maharishi Shukra (of the distinguished Bhrigu/ Bhargava lineage), boldly proposing marriage to the Kshatriya king. Yayati was thus enmeshed in a dharma sankat, moral dilemma with the Brahmin lass proposing to him.

She told King Yayati in no uncertain terms, 'Brahmins have already been united with Kshatriyas and Kshatriyas have been united with Brahmins'.[7] After all, no less than Daksha, the head of the Bharata/ Puru lineage was a

Family Tree

Bharata / Puru Lineage

1
Daksha
(son of Brahma)

10
Yayati - *m* - Devayani and Sharmishtha

11
Yadu (ancestor of Yadava)

11
Puru

14
Sarvabhouma - *m* - Sunanda

25
Dushanta - *m* - Shakuntala

26
Bharata - *m* - Sunanda

35
Ajamalha - *m* - Kaikeyi , Gandhari and 3 others

36
Samvarana - *m* - Tapati

37
Kuru - *m* - Subhagi

41
Bhimasena - *m* - Sukumari

43
Bahlika, Shantanu - *m* - *Ganga* - *m* - Satyavati, Devapi

44
Bhishama (Devavrata)

45
Dhritarashtra & Pandu - *m* - *Kunti* - *m* - *Madri*
- m - Gandhari

Duryodhana ←

46
Yudhishtira Bhima Arjuna Nakul Sahadeva

47
Abhimanyu - *m* - Uttara

48
Parikshit - *m* - Madravati

49
Janamajaya - *m* - Vapushrama

Abbreviation : m-married to
Note: Devapa is also known as Vaishampayana, Krishna Dvaipayana and Vedvyasa. He is said to be the narrator of Mahabharata.
Source: The Mahabharata, V.I.,tr. by Bibek Debroy

Brahmin himself. Since Yayati was still half-convinced, she sought a boon from her venerable father, 'Let no great sin descend on me as a consequence of mixed caste'.[8] The determined lady was finally united with King Yayati, and they gave birth to the Bharata/ Puru and Yadava lineages. The trio of Krishna-Arjuna-Duryodhana as well as Bharata have the Yayati/ Devayani blood running in their veins. And there is a Saraiki connection to.

Saraiki Connection

The great grandson of the great Yayati was King Ahampati. He was married to Kritavirya's daughter Bhanumati. She gave birth to Sarvabhouma, who defeated the king of Kekaya and abducted his daughter Sunanda. He was twelve generations removed from the Bharata lineage, after whom is named Bharatavarsha, that is India. Thus, the Kekaya princess from the Saraiki region mothered India.

The Bharata/Puru lineage continued for long. The twenty-fifth generation saw King Dushanta marrying both Shakuntala and Paramshiti. While Shakuntala's descendants, headed by Bharata, came to be known as Bharatas, Paramshiti's descendants were called Panchalas. The Saraiki connection was further strengthened by the time we reach the thirty-fifth generation, King Ajamalha of the thirty-fifth generation married another Kekaya princess known as Kaikeyi.

The Bharatas and the Panchalas fall apart by the time we reach the thirty-sixth generation. The Panchalas usurped the Bharata hegemony and made the Bharata king Samavarna flee for his life. Samavarna headed in the direction of Queen Kaikeyi's land of birth 'along with his wife, sons, advisers and friends. He then found shelter in the forests on the bank of the river Sindhu where the river extends upto the mountains. Facing a difficult situation, the Bharatas lived there for thousand years'.[9]

Pandava Connection

Finally, the Bharatas returned to their own land and once more became the dominant power. King Bhimsena, who belonged to the forty-first generation of Bharata/ Puru lineage, strengthened the marital bonds by marrying the Kekaya princess Sukumari. Their son King Parashrava, also known as Pratipa, married Sunanda and had through her three sons: Devapi, Shantanu and Bahlika. Shantanu was married to Ganga, who gave birth to the great Bhishma. Shantanu was grandfather both to the Pandavas and the Kauravas.

The Mahabharata traces the Saraiki connection up to the thirty-sixth generation of the Bharata/ Puru lineage, starting with King Sarvabhouma, up to Janmejaya, great grandson of Arjuna. Remember the thundering voice in the sky forecasting to Kunti, 'Arjuna will bring under his sway the countries of Madra, Kuru, Kekaya, Chedi, Kashi and Kishkinda, establishing the prosperity of the Kurus'.[10] The prophesy was fulfilled when the kingdoms of Madra, Kekaya, besides Sindhu and Gandhara fell into the lap of the Pandavas after the Mahabharata war.

Crossing the River

Indus has been called the 'Terrorizing Vadhera' due to its destructive capabilities. Varunadeva, the god of rain and waters, must have been irreconcilable in this particular manifestation. The Chinese traveller, Xuangzang (c. 645) knew it at his own cost: 'The River Sun-Tu (Indus) is pure and clear as a mirror... Poisonous dragons and dangerous spirits live beneath its water[...]. If a man tries to cross the river carrying valuable gems, rare flowers and fruits, [...] or relics of the Buddha, his boat is engulfed by waves'[11] Even until recently, travelling from Multan to Dera Ghazi Khan via Ghazi Ghat terminal was troublesome, time-consuming and irritating, due to the unbridgeable waters of the mighty Indus. It was also adventurous and unpredictable, with the choice of different means of transport like tonga, minibus, boat bridge, ferry, steamer and kanta (the sail boat), confronting the traveller. The local shuttle terminated at Mahamaddkot, on the eastern bank of the river. Three passengers, and a single driver who drove the back-breaking tonga with his muscles and stamina, along with the strapped luggage(of the passengers)over an unstable sandy track, with meshed-wire nets of two square inch laid on it, to provide stability to the kutcha track-and this was the usual experience here.

When the steel-coated tonga rim came into contact with the mesh-wire net, sparks flew. The outer rim and wooden wheels were constantly coated with water. The movement of numerous zooming and swinging tongas generated sand storms, the sandy air whirling from afar, above 100 feet or about, was a sight to behold. During the winter months, the river had to be crossed via a boat-bridge, clubbed through a flotilla of large boats lined up cheek-by-jowl. Now there was a 12 feet wide span bridge for vehicles and tongas to travel and cross the river. During the summer months, one had to change over to the steamer or kanta. The steamer took as much as four hours or more, because it had to search for deep waters to navigate. To travel in the kanta was any day more exciting, as it usually sailed during the early hours of the morning, in fact before dawn. It took another eight miles to reach the destination, while crossing into the other side of the river. Then, again, one more tonga was required to reach the ultimate destination of the town of Dera Ghazi Khan. In the early 20th century, the tonga carrying the postal mail was considered a prized one. It had the right to enter the precincts of the town ahead of the crowd. The presence of the policeman made sure that convention was never violated. In those days, travelling home was a back-breaking and exasperating adventure in itself.

Destructive Vadhera

The river begins to rise in May with the melting of the snows and continues to rise till the end of August. It brings in its train immense destruction year after year. The river fills its bed for as much as the breadth of nine miles. The river usually rises eight-and-a-half feet in the inundation period. During 1876, the river rose to 74.6y (yards/3 ft) at Attock due to the sudden bursting of a glacier-loaded lake in the Himalayas. The flooding of the river and its subsequent steep fall during winter months is accompanied by immense erosion due to the sandy nature of the soil. It does not possess a constant main stream for any length of time. It keeps changing its bed, creating massive islands (rich with grasses) or chakkars and creeks, which sustain the population of milk-yielding animals. The earliest river bed that can be traced was in the middle of the Sindh Doab, between the Jhelum and the Indus. The river then gradually moved towards the direction of the old town of Dera Ghazi Khan. At one time it flowed a dozen miles away from its borders. Eventually, it destroyed the old town of Dera Ghazi

Khan, thus decimating the beautiful and graceful town established by the Mirranis way back in 1476. It keeps shifting west due to the centrifugal tendencies of the earth to move in the direction of the northern hemisphere. However, during the geological age, the Indus flowed at the foothills of the Suleiman mountains.

Calamitous 1789

The most calamitous event in the history of the Indus took place in about 1789. The exact date is not certain though. It could be earlier, in 1784, when the unpredictable Vadhera decided to change its direction westwards.

The Nawab of Sitpur had constructed a new canal in the town. The river chose to shift into the bed of the canal. It broke the right bank and moved in the westerly direction. It brought about the destruction of the economies of the semi-autonomous region of Dera Ghazi Khan and the adjacent district of Muzaffargarh. The abrupt change in the direction of the river cut the canal system like slices. The Dhundi canal and other canal systems became headless, with no water flowing into them. The junction of the Chenab (and its tributaries), called Panchanad, shifted from the holy city of Uch in Muzaffargarh district. It shifted its junction with the Panchanad, about 60 miles downstream near Mithankot.

The renowned Sufi headquarters has a hoary past. It was founded by Alexander at the confluence of the Indus with other rivers of the Punjab, and came to be known as Askandra or Alexandra.

A civil disturbance, coinciding with the demise of the Khan of Kalat, took place between the Nahars of Sitpur, Daudpatras of Bahawalpur, the Langahs of Multan, and the Mirranis of Dera Ghazi Khan. The sequence of events is best described in the words of Robert Bruce:

'The heads of the Bisharat and other canals in the south of the district were completely carried away, while inundation which had never been known before, overspread the face of the country from north to the south'.[12] The results were devastating not only for irrigation, but also for the settled population on farms and in villages.The shift in the course of the river had brought out the worst in people. The entire southern part of the district was turned into a big sheet of water. The Baloch tribes were in the process of settling down on the plains. Peace had not returned to the cursed land in centuries. Incidentally, 'It was about the same period that the Balochis, who had gained a firm footing in the plains, commenced a series of wars and bloodshed which lasted for over forty years, and devastated the country'.[13]

There were also other actors involved in the developing drama. The Talpur Mirs of Sindh, the Durranis of Afghanistan and the Sikhs also drew blood and prepared the ground for the entry of the British in a not-too-distant future. The last of the Mirranis, Nawab Ghazi Khan Mirrani, died issueless in captivity in Sindh in 1775 AD. A couplet on his grave in Hyderabad says, 'Ghazi Khan left this world in a pathetic condition. He was away from his home, friendless and a victim of oppression'.[14] He was lucky to pass away about a decade or earlier, as if anticipating the calamitous event of 1789.

Baloch Universe

The Balochis are late entrants to the area, but they represent the ethos and spirit of the Derajat. They constituted about 40per cent population of Dera Ghazi Khan. Earlier, they were hill tribesmen practising pastoral herding, primitive agriculture and mass raiding. They were divided into tribes called 'tumuns', headed by tumundars, as they were called, 'the leader of the ten thousand'. The tribes had colourful names like Gurchanis, Mazaris, Legharis, Bugtis, Bozdars, Mirranis, Khosas, Khatvans, Nutkanis and Drishaks. Mirranis belonged to the Dodai stream who were the original rulers of Dera Ghazi Khan for about three centuries. Khetrans were possibly not Balochi. The language spoken by them approximated to Saraiki. Similarly, the Gurchanis traced their origin to a confederation of Rajput tribes occupying the Derajat before the British occupation.

An important section of this tribe was Dodai, from which have sprung part of the Gurchani tribe and the Mirranis of Dera Ghazi Khan, both now classed as Balochi, though not admitted to be pure Rinds.[15]

The Balochis migrated from Makran, where already several Indian communities like Jats and Rajputs ruled. Similar was the situation in Dera Ghazi Khan. The purity of the race is a myth at one level, but at another level, the Derajats and the Balochi are coterminous in the mind of local inhabitants. This myth was also perpetuated by the British rulers. They were simply fascinated by the Baloch tribesmen and managed to come to terms with them on a more familiar plane.

Original Roots

A martial race free from bigotry and prejudices, the original name of the Baloch was 'Blot' in Persia. They were variously called 'Balosh', 'Baloch', 'Bales' and 'Barosh'. They were fire worshippers free from religious prejudices, a total contrast with their counterpart Pathans. The Baloch came from the region of Aleppo, they migrated, through Mesopotamia, and southern Persia, to Balochistan and settled in Makran for several centuries. They slowly moved in the direction of the Indus Valley after settling down in the foothills of the Suleiman mountains. The towns of Dera Ismail Khan and Dera Ghazi Khan bear the names of Baloch chiefs, who founded them as the deras (encampments), as a tribute to their entrepreneural skills. The Rinds and Lasharies formed the vanguard of this Baloch lashkar in mass migration. A clarion call went to the Baloch tribesmen, some of whom settled in Balochistan and the remaining moved in the direction of the Derajat, with the Indus river beckoning the thirsting tribesman: 'Come, let us leave the barren land, let us spy out the running streams and sweet waters, and distribute them among us, let us take no heed of Chief'.[16]

Here was a bit of bravado and exaggeration in the assertion. Forced out of Seistan, settled in the villages and hills of Makran between the seventh and tenth centuries, they stirred into action under the inspiring leadership of the legendary Baloch hero Mir Chakar Rind. They moved in the direction of Sibi at the head of 40,000 warriors during the second half of the 15th century. Not too long afterwards, Malik Sohrab laid the foundations of Dera Ismail Khan during 1469 and the Mirrani family, led by Haji Khan Mirrani, founded the town of Dera Ghazi Khan in 1476. Thus, during the span of half-a-century were established two flourishing trading deras with their links in Central Asia. The Baloch leadership proved to be men of mettle in deciding to utilize the Indus water through a system of canal irrigation channels, especially in the district of Dera Ghazi Khan. The Mazaris tumundar excavated a canal known as Hamalinah, perhaps as early as in the sixteenth century.The Mazaris, along with the Drishaks, established their credentials by showing skills in canal construction and by utilizing the river waters for irrigation purposes. Nawab Ghazi Khan was to go much further by establishing a network of canals in Dera Ghazi Khan.

Baloch Characteristics

No strict religion was meant for the Baloch. They were believed to be only nominally Muslims. The Mullahas were a 'no', 'no' for them. There was no record of a Baloch mosque until the 1900. The Baloch did not observe Ramzan, because his chief did on behalf of the entire tumun. He earned a reputation for truthfulness. He dressed himself in white on all occasions. His love of freedom was notorious. The Baloch were lavish in their hospitality. They were frank and good-natured people. In their treatment of women, they were much more chivalrous than the Pathans. At all times of the year, Baloch women were found working freely and unescorted, in the hills. Every Baloch was supposed to be a camel man. He was as hard as a camel, rightly described as the 'Ship of Desert'. He was actually fond of horses.

Horse-racing was the Baloch passion. He must own a horse at all cost. If he cannot afford one, he shall be content with owning as many legs of a mare as he could afford. There are many proverbs underlying his love for horses. One of them goes like this, 'A man with his saddle on a mare has his saddle on a horse, a man with a saddle on a horse has his saddle on his head'. He has been called a 'thief' on account of his cultural passion, but taking cattle came naturally to him. The saying goes, 'God will not favour a Baloch who does not steal and rob', and 'the Baloch who steals secures heaven for seven generations of his ancestors'. The British had declared the Bozdar tribe as 'notorious cattle thieves'. Balochis' love of cattle was reflected in their acts of 'thievery'. A Baloch was also extremely superstitious. When a male child was born to him, ass's dung mixed with water was administered to him from the point of a sword, before he was given the breast. He was a nomad by nature and instinct and hence taught his newly-born a lesson or two about nature's instinct.

Limited Monarchy

The tribal organization of the Balochi was very special to him. The Tumundar heading the tribe conducted himself like a monarch. 'The tumun was a specimen of limited monarchy. The title was hereditary and it passed from one generation to another. He was the unquestionable boss in times of peace and war. The Baloch was docile by tradition and followed the leader to the last. The tribe was divided into phallis (sections) headed by headmen called mukhaddams, who were equally powerful as the tribal chief, and had a deciding voice in determining matters of peace and war. Every member of the tribe was bound to render military services to the chief, who in return shared the bounty of the loot with his tribesmen. The warfare between tribes inhabiting the foothills of the Suleiman mountains was a very common feature, before the advent of the British. The tradition of *chapaas*(raids), with small parties of tribesmen, in frequent marauding expeditions to murder and plunder, with the victims generally taken by surprise, was his distinctive trait.'

The finest example of the practice of limited monarchy could be found in the rule of Jamal Khan Leghari of Choti, who headed one of the most powerful of the Baloch tribes. The Legharis had been fortunately placed as the custodians of the Sakhi Sarwar shrine and the pass opening to the vistas of Balochistan. The Legharis had access to both, full torrents and canal lands. They also controlled the access to *kalapani* lands in the Barkhan valley that was adjacent to the Balochistan hills. Through marriage arrangements with the Khetrans, they also controlled trade from the Barkhan (Balochistan) region. Jamal Khan Leghari was also responsible for the expansion of Baloch investment in canals in Dera Ghazi Khan district in the early 1860s. He developed a remarkable, working relation with Robert Sandeman, who employed him on the Sandeman mission to Kalat as a go-between. His generosity to his co-tribesmen was legendary, which was equally matched by his hospitality to all and 'of all Chiefs of tribes the Choti Nawab is the first with the knife in hand… to kill the fattened kine, sheep and goats … that nothing should be lacking in hospitality'.[17] Bullocks, turning grinding mills, perpetually ground corn to match his hospitality yardstick. Jamal Khan Leghari has been called a 'native capitalist'. His grandson came to possess an estate of 114,000 acres of which, 12,000 acres were irrigated by canal water, and 2,500 acres by rodaki hill streams.

Primitive Instincts of the Baloch

The Balochi have been variously described as 'fierce', 'warlike', 'brave', 'bold' and of 'good physique'. The Baloch stands apart by his sheer physical appearance and his winsome physical charm. The British rulers were simply taken in by his childlike simplicity and they have left official and unofficial records as tribute to the community as a whole. Even the district gazetteer of Dera Ghazi Khan, prepared by British officials, is no less a lyrical tribute to the Balochi:

'The Biloch is tall and spare in appearance, temperate in his habits, with great powers of endurance, being capable of sustaining prolonged fatigue on very poor food. The face is long and overall, and the hair is long, the jaw is worn long in the style of the cavaliers of the time of King Charles I, the beard and whiskers being allowed to grow untrimmed, but the moustache being shaved in the orthodox Muhammadan style. Curls are common, but the hill men often wear their hair hanging down behind in unkempt shocks. They are frank, good-humoured people, thoroughly enjoying a joke and capable of a hearty laugh, in the characteristics of truth and honour infinitely superior to their Afghan neighbours. To their chiefs they are generally very docile and obedient, but towards others their bearing is proud, free and independent. They had at one time a deserved reputation for truthfulness, but they have now learned to lie, and the progress of their education in this respect has been most marked even in the last ten years, a woeful result of the application of English laws to people for whom they are unsuited. They are still as a rule, truthful, to their chiefs'.[18]

At another plane, a Baloch's simplicity and rusticity is shown by his treatment of the Hindu minority, who usually performed the role of trader-cum-accountant in the Baloch hinterland. 'He was considered an outsider and treated somewhat with respect and contempt at the same time. He was integral to his scheme of things, but considered marginal in his social existence. He was indispensable as a pet animal in this zoological wonderland'. David Gilmartin was to observe correctly, 'The subordination of Hindus was indicated by dress, but their protection was critical to Baloch honour'. As one British official put it in 1805, 'Amongst the Baloch the good treatment of Hindu traders and their families, through whom all monetary transactions are carried on, is a point of honour'.[19] Similar was the attitude of the Pathan towards the Hindu minority. The Hindu trader and bania, in this instance, Arora or Khatri, were too valuable to be sacrificial goats.

Nawab Ghazi Khan

The mass migration of Baloch tribes from Makran happened under Mir Chakar Rind. One of the fortune hunters in the vanguard was Sohrab Khan Dodai, who along with his two sons, Ismail Khan and Fateh Khan, wielded considerable local influence, to the extent of pressurising the Langah rulers of Multan in trans-Indus territories. The Langahs thought it wiser to assign a jagir to him beyond the Indus (in about 1469 AD), 'as a means of securing tranquility on the frontier'. The entire area which now constitutes the Dera Ismail district was assigned to him and his tribe to compensate them in requital of their military services. Malik Sohrab's sons, Ismail Khan and Fateh Khan, gave names to the respective so-called deras,, which came to be well-known as trading points. The other adventurer was Haji Khan Mirrani, who was accompanied by his famous son, Ghazi Khan. He grazed cattle for sometime at the site of old Dera Ghazi Khan, and liked it so much that he decided to settle down there. He started as a cattle merchant, but gradually expanded his area of influence and increased his fortune.

He also came to terms with the Langahs of Multan, the nominal rulers of the region, and from being satrap he turned out to be the master of the sub-regional state. All the Baloch tribes in the Dera Ghazi Khan district acknowledged the suzerainty of the Mirranis, who for fifteen generations ruled Dera Ghazi Khan, a town that turned out to be the pride of the region. The Mirrani Nawabs were either a Haji Khan or a Ghazi Khan, each giving his son his own father's name. Ghazi Khan passed away in 1494. The Mirrani dynasty came to an end in 1769, when the last ruler was taken prisoner by Mian Ghulam Shah, and he died in captivity in Hyderabad (Now Pakistan). Ghazi Khan was a statesman of the highest calibre, who governed with compassion and sense of justice, by combining political and economic leverage through encouragement of harmonious social relations.

2

Remembering Sweet Home

NAWAB Ghazi Khan encouraged the Hindus to practice their way of life. He built several canals, including Manaka canal, which ran for 80 miles in the middle of the district. It was built under the supervision of his revenue minister, Raja Manak Rai. His greatest contribution was laying the foundation of an important regional state of Dera Ghazi Khan, a jewel in the Mughal crown. Here was a classical instance of the Hindus, who constituted barely ten per cent population of Dera Ghazi Khan, hitherto engaged in commerce and trade, enterprises and government administration at subordinate levels. It was to the credit of Nawab Ghazi Khan that he involved them in all the walks of life, especially those possessed of entrepreneural skills. But prejudices die hard. The Baloch author of the Multan campaign used the term, 'dhoti-wearing Kirar'[1] as if it were the ultimate insult. This prejudice grew out of the fear of their infinite capacity and 'their mastery of accounting and orderly business habits to manipulate and milk Muslim overlords'[2] and simple Baloch folk. The 'Kirar' belonged to local Khatri and Arora sub-castes and they had the characteristics of the *banya* or Vaishya community. Thus, there was a love-and-hate relation between the two communities. It was, however, a relationship that worked for centuries.

'Kirar' Defined

Here were, however, zero social relations between the communities. Alexander Cunningham chose to emphasize the prejudices that overwhelmed certain communities. In the lower Punjab and in Sindh, the whole population included Hindus under the term 'Kirar'. In the upper Punjab the term 'Kirar' was used to denote a coward, and in Multan it was likewise an expression of contempt like that of a Hindu, as a trafficker. Professor Wilson identifies them with the 'Cirrhae of the ancients' and indeed Keretis was one of the five Prushtha–'as regions of the Hindu'.[3] The name Kirar is said to be synonymous with the Arora community, which constituted the majority of the Hindus in the district, but, otherwise a miniscule minority in the entire Dera Ghazi Khan district, except in a few places of concentration, in the towns. Generally it was a few families of Hindus who functioned as shopkeepers and village accountants. They were distinguished by their 'skull cap and dhoti'. By convention, they were prohibited to ride a horse or mare. Like Sancho Panza, the Kirar was noticed from a distance,riding a donkey, indeed a pathetic sight and a slur on the minority community.

The authority to establish the truth of the matter lay with the Multan Gazetteer of the Dera Ghazi Khan district (1883). 'The Hindus of the district have all the appearance of a downtrodden and subject race. They are called by the common name Kirar, which is applied to all the Hindus of whatever caste. The name Kirar is said to be synonymous with Arora,[4] who were allowed to ride nothing but donkeys. They were also forbidden to wear turbans'. Another official document of the same period has sought to confirm the impression. 'The Aroras were indigenous to western Punjab. The common name for an Arora was Kirar, a word completely synonymous with "coward"...the traditional caste occupation of shopkeeper, moneylender and village accountant. In Multan, they worked as goldsmiths, manufacturers of brass and copper vessels, traders and weavers'.[5]

Hindu Resurrection

Hindus came to be respected only after they started investing and took over the ownership of the agricultural land. A Hindu had to be a landowner to earn respect in the social hierarchy of the feudal order. There was considerable investment by the Hindus in canal irrigation to obviate the prejudices and overcome social handicaps. This is similar to the process of Sanskritization of the lower strata of Hindu society. Their investment grew with the advent of the British rule. Shikarpuri traders, recognizing the importance of indigo and cotton as commercial crops with tremendous export potential, poured in huge amount of capital to this sector. There was a working alliance of British administration, Shikarpuri capital and tumundari labour and enterprise, resulting in tremendous burst of canal irrigation. This did not, however, translate into the disappearance of social prejudices, because the two communities were unable to work out relations on the social front.

The adage attributed to Mao, 'Power grows out of the barrel of the gun' held true even then. The successful occupation of Dera Ghazi Khan by the Sikhs and the British had a transformational effect on the balance of power in western Punjab. The balance tilted in favour of the Hindus, who had now gained considerable say in political affairs of Dera Ghazi Khan. Nihal Singh, the head of the Sikh army, crossed the Indus and seized Derajat including the districts of Dera Ismail Khan and Dera Ghazi Khan, and placed the Derajat under the custody of the Nawab of Bahawalpur. This was passed on to Maharaja Ranjit Singh in 1819, who extended the rule to trans-Indus territories. He is believed to have visited Dera Ghazi Khan in person, and paid his respect to the local deity, Shree Gopinath Maharaj, by offering the golden plum and his studded sword. The mighty Vadhera, however, had her revenge on him. He lost a portion of his army while crossing the river. The lease of the district of Dera Ghazi Khan to the Bahawalpur ruler ended in 1830, and General Ventura of the Sikh army took over the direct administration.

Sikh Rule

There was a time when the Hindus of Dera Ghazi Khan had 'all the appearance of a down-trodden and subject race'–that is if one were to go by official records of British India. But, soon, it was no longer true. The Sikh rule transformed them. The Sikhs had a long memory and they found it hard to forget their centuries-old persecution. In response, they were equally revengeful. As a result, J Royal Roseberry III, did not fail to notice, 'nevertheless, the right of the despised, 'dhoti-wearing Kirars' (in Multan), openly in the driver's seat was quite without precedent'.[6] The Sikh officers of Ranjit Singh made their presence felt in the neighbouring towns of Dera Ismail Khan by having regular recitations of the *Guru Granth Sahib*, the holy book of the Sikhs.

It must have been unprecedented and unheard of a practise in Dera Ismail Khan and, to add insult to injury, the semi-independent Nawab of Dera Ismail Khan had to make concessions to Sikh sensibility,[7] Contrary to tradition, and, furthermore, within his sight, 'many of the Banyas were accustomed to attend and read from the Granth, which they always did aloud'. The Hindus were never allowed to celebrate festivals like the Holi publicly, but this practise was resumed during the Sikh rule, and was started in Dera Ismail Khan, during the visit of General Maha Singh, one of the officers of Hari Singh Nalwa.[8] The Hindus continued to hoard capital under the Muslim rule, somewhat invisibly. Now the secret was out, and 'the Hindus, always the principle inhabitants, felt themselves at liberty under Sikh sway to display their wealth, whereas under Mohammedan masters they were studious to conceal it'.[9]

Maharaja Ranjit Singh issued orders in Dera Ghazi Khan to prohibit *azaan* in mosques and no public prayers in mosques, and, prohibited cow slaughter. Several mosques were converted into Gurdwaras, this included the historic mosque of Nawab Ghazi Khan. The other two mosques converted into temples were mosques of Abdul Javar and Chita Khan. The famous Sun temple, converted into a mosque, was turned into an ammunition depot by the Sikhs, and it was blown up accidentally by the British during the last Anglo-Sikh war.[10]

Rise and Fall

Diwan Sawan Mal[11] (1788–1844) of the Chopra-Khatri sub-caste from Gujranwala, took over as the Governor of Multan in 1832 and his stewardship of Dera Ghazi Khan district had a transformational effect on the Hindu community. He encouraged the Khatris to migrate to Multan and participate actively in the administration of the region. He was a benign human being and a statesman. He was as progressive as Nawab Ghazi Khan, who preached and practised communal peace and harmony. He befriended the Baloch tribes and cultivated the local Hindus by placing them in strategic positions. Among his officials were *kaardars* (governors/agents) in the Dera Ghazi Khan district who included Jawahar Mal, Rang Ram, Launga Ram, Radha Krishan and Bahadur Chand. Launga Ram was also Multan's Governor at Dera Ghazi Khan.

Diwan Sawan Mal passed away in 1844 and he was replaced by his son, Diwan Mul Raj, as governor of Multan province. His rise coincided with the declining Sikh power and the rise of the British empire. Khatris in large numbers had migrated from eastern Punjab during the Sikh regime, at the invitation of Diwan Sawan Mal and they held numerous official positions in all walks of life. The names included Diwan Kaura Mal, Diwan Ladda Ram, Diwan Manik Rai, Diwan Hukam Chand Brahka and Diwan Ram Diyal. Launga Ram and Chertan Mal held the senior positions of *kaardars* of Mul Raj. They were his most faithful loyalists. Launga Ram was a brave soul and fatally loyal to Diwan Mul Raj, who was now under attack on a treason charge against the Lahore Durbar. Herbert Edwardes led the charge against Launga Mal, a follower of Diwan Mul Raj. He fought bravely and was eventually wounded, captured and put in chains, but he continued to communicate with Mul Raj by bribing his guards. He was hanged, but 'The kaardar "died without the least mark of trepidation, adjusting with his own hands the fatal noose"'[12] Chetan Mal, who was also confined to the fort of Dera Ghazi Khan, along with Launga Ram, was killed.

The British were waiting in the wings and took over Dera Ghazi Khan soon after the death of Maharaja Ranjit Singh. Herbert Edwardes was appointed the political officer on the Derajat frontier during 1848–49.

He was a soldier-diplomat-administrator. The Hindus did very well (for themselves) by favouring the British rule. They simply transferred their loyalty to British rulers. They came into their own with the advent of Sir Robert Sandeman on the scene. Diwan Tharia Ram was a *srishtadar* to him and after his retirement, his nephew Diwan Ganpat Rai and the son of his friend, Hittu Ram took over from him.

Goswami Cult

The next generations of brave souls were also highly regarded. They also came to possess large estates, thanks to their dual loyalty to successive Sikh and British regimes. The Diwans, like the Gosains, have continued to provide leadership to the minority community of Hindus, both in *miri* (state craft) and *piri* (spiritual matters), as the sayings of Sikh gurus tell us. For centuries together, the Hindus of Sindh and western Punjab confined themselves to the caravan trade with Central Asia. The Sikh rule was the most pleasant interlude for them, transposing them to the profession of ancient Kshatriyas, of running administration and fighting wars. The 'sword arm' of Hindu society had forgotten its true vocation, and it needed a jolt to be reminded of its true functions.

The Bhakti movement spread like a wildfire in western Punjab. Its epicentre was Multan, but it had equal competition from across the Indus, with headquarters at Dera Ghazi Khan. The Shyamji sampradaya of the Chaitanya Mahaprabhu cult and the Lalji sampradaya of the Vallabhacharya cult spearheaded the Vaishnava Bhakti movement, with inspirational leadership received from Vrindavan. The Bhakti movement upsurge coincided with the rise of the Mirranis in the 15th-16th centuries, who chose to build an entrepreneurial rapport with the Hindus. Nawab Ghazi Khan was a Chota Akbar. Shyamji Maharaj Goswami (1519–98), who had settled down at Ghali, was persuaded to shift to the newly-founded town of Dera Ghazi Khan. The Mirranis had also been persuasive in attracting some Shikarpuri Aroras to pioneer trade and commerce and invest in newly-constructed irrigation canals. The rise of the Bhakti movement in western Punjab is connected with the rise of the Khatris in the political field, and the Aroras in commerce and trade. That explains the emergence of Vaishnava Bhakti movement in this part of the world, and, indeed, in the eyes of the many, Vaishnavism is the cult of the Aroras, who constituted the majority of the Hindu population.

The spread of the Bhakti movement is attributed to the ground work done by the *Bairagis* in the Punjab. The Bairagis moved from town to town, and village to village, danced and sang their way to the heart of the common Hindus. The message of the Vaishnava movement was conveyed in the name of Radha and Krishna to the farthest corners of western Punjab. The local inspiration was provided by the shrine of Ganjamali in Multan city. Krishnadas Prabhu Ganjamali was the Goswami heading the temple during the times of Shyamji and Lalji. The founder of the sect was a Brahmin, who is said to have lived there some four centuries ago, and to have obtained the title from wearing a necklace (mala) of ganja seeds. He was a Gosain, a resident of Multan and a worshipper of Krishna; he is now looked upon by many of the Aroras as their guru, and his cult is closely connected with the Arora community. The Khatris, however, maintained an equilibrium by worshipping the Granth Sahib and Bhagavat Purana simultaneously.

Vaishnava Movement

Shyamji Maharaj and Lalji Maharaj belonged to different sampradayas of Vaishnavism, but their advent on the scene coincided. Shyamji or Shyam Das belonged to Dipalpur, equally famous for its association with Baba Farid of Pakpattan. He adopted Krishnadas Prabhu Ganjamali of Multan as his guru. He joined the mandali of Janardan Mishra, who also belonged to the Ganjamali circle. He moved to Vrindavan in his early teens in pursuit of his guru and stayed there for 12 years. Vrindavan made a deep impression on him. There were 4,000 big and small temples in the city of Vrindavan. There was also a Multan connection to it.

The famous Madan Mohan temple was built by Ramdas Kapur of Multan. It is believed to be one of the oldest temples in Vrindavan. Shyamji stayed there for 12 years, serving his guru at the Shringavat temple (Vrindavan), located adjacent to the Radha Damodar temple, on the bank of the Yamuna river, the temple initimately associated with and dedicated to Sri Chaitanya Mahaprabhu. It is considered an ancient temple and is made of redstone. The temple is known by this name, because it is believed that this was the place where Sri Krishna dressed Radha's hair into a coiffeur lovingly with his own hands, hence the name of the temple is 'Shringavat'.

Lalji Cult

Similarly, Lalji was a near contemporary of Shyamji, but had a different background. While Shyamji was a Khatri, Lalji was a Brahmin, a resident of Siwan in Larkana district of Sindh, born in 1551 and died in 1618 at Dera Ghazi Khan. He was named Tulasidas and moved to Vrindavan at a very young age. He was adopted by Vithalanatha, the son of the famous Vallabhacharya. Tulasidas grew up in Vithalanath's household, and was affectionately referred to as 'Lalji'. Vithalanatha had seven sons, all of whom were presented with a deity and allotted territories, called the seven main gaddis of the Vallabha sampradaya. Tulasidas was allotted the eighth gaddi to spread the message in Sindh and western Punjab. He then came to be known as Lalji and established a large temple at Dera Ghazi Khan in honour of the deity called Sri Gopinathaji.

Tulasidas, or Lalji was also addressed as and worshipped as Amar Lal. Shyamji and Lalji are highly regarded and their contribution is considered next to the Sikh gurus: 'The influence of these men in favour of the Hindu religions had been enormous and they had in all probability retained the hold of the trading community of the south-west from a virtual conversion to Sikhism or Mohammedanism. To be a Hindu by religion, was in these parts, almost synonymous with being a follower of the gurus. The Khatris and Aroras of the southwest were divided into Sikhs and Sewaks–the followers of Nanak and the disciples of the Gosains; and it was due to the influence of Shyamji and Lalji that the latter became numerous in numbers.'

Shyamji, the Cowriewallah

Goswami Dwarkadas blessed Shyamji and endow him with miraculous powers, and asked him to move to Dera Ghazi Khan. Krishna was believed to have given him two idols and told him, 'The Hindus of the western country of the Sindh are ignorant of their religion. They have no guru to guide them between good and bad. Go to the west and teach the Hindus the ceremonies of their religion and make them your disciples (sewaks). Your words will have speedy effect'.[13] Shyamji's disciples included Chabildas and Rangildas, besides Chandiya Baloch, and they are famously known as the 'two-and–a-half disciples'. While the two of them were Khatris, the third one was a Baloch, whom Shyamji had cured miraculously. He also used to wear a skull cap on his head. He lived a parsimonious life, earned money by sewing and selling skull caps.

He is seen totally absorbed in a contemporary painting— bent down by age, wearing white skull cap, and busy sewing his caps. He highly regarded the local Sufi saints like Sufi Din Panah, the patron saint of Nawab Ghazi Khan. He refused to accept gifts, except the cowries presented to him by his disciples. He put up the temple dedicated to Ram-de-Rai. His cowries were sold at 20 cowries per paisa. Thus, he came to be known as Shyamji Cowriewallah. His sayings have been lost, because those have not been recorded, except for a few of them: '*Dunya saka har koi–Sang na saka koi. Paise bajan Shyamdas–bas napucho koi*'. This means—'everyone claims to be relative, but nobody accompanies you. Money makes a ringing tone after death, nobody bothers about it otherwise'.

Obviously there is a mixture of the Braj bhasha and Saraiki languages in Shyamji's work. Thus, the Bhakti movement in western Punjab suffered from a handicap. The medium of communication of religious discourse was Braj bhasha and not Saraiki. Sikhism went forward due to its adoption of the Punjabi language. Vaishnavism failed to adopt Saraiki as its medium of expression.

Lalji Lineage

Like Shyamji, Lal Das would sew caps and sell them for his living. He shifted to Dera Ghazi Khan in Samvat 1641. Tulsa, the son of Aju Ram of Larkana in Sind, was a disciple of Vallabhacharya, as opposed to Shyamji, who was a follower of Chaitanya Mahaprabhu, but both of them gave their loyalty to the Radha-Krishna cult. They were eminently successful in spreading the Vaishnava cult among local Hindus. Wherever the traders travelled in pursuit of commerce, whether it was Balochistan, Sindh, Afghanistan, or Central Asia, the message of the Vaishnava cult was conveyed and readily accepted. Bhakti movement had by now travelled in all directions, in north and south, between Kanyakumari and Peshawar and Kabul. Blackstone idols of Navanit Piavre and Shri Gopinath, also known as the black pir, were familiar figures to the local Hindus. There was the make-belief story of Lord Krishna telling Tulsa to start his journey for the Indus, accompanied by the idol of Gopinath, trailing just behind him with the distinct twinkling of bells to assure him. Whereupon, Lalji set forth on his journey to Dera Ghazi Khan, turning once his back to look at the deity, who, subsequently refused to proceed further. The idol is said to have told him, 'You have stopped, and I am going no further'.

So Lalji decided to build a temple on the spot, which subsequently came to be known as the famous Sri Gopinath Temple of Dera Ghazi Khan. There is also another story about the deity with a broken arm located in one of the temples of Dera Ghazi Khan. The Gosain families were believed to be originally of the Arab stock of the Quraishi lineage, descendents of pujaris (preists) at the Ka'aba prior to the conversion of the temple into a mosque. Consequently, the priests departed after taking possession of the statue with the broken arm. In another version, Prophet Abraham appeared to have damaged the statue and rested his axe on it, and it remains as such even today. The statue was 'brought' from Mecca to Dera Ghazi Khan by the 'Gosain Arabs'. It is even asserted that the statue was brought to the local temple in 1501 and installed in it. The other shrines were also established in the region, variously called Nagraj (Dera Ismail Khan) and Sri Girdharji (Bahawalpur), besides the main temple of Sri Gopinathji. There were also Vaishnava temples dedicated to Krishna Lalji, Mahaprabhu, Sewak Lila Dhar, Banshi Dhar and the likes.

Kewalarama, the Saint

Kewalarama (c. 1588) was a grandson of Lalji and equally renowned for his saintly qualities and literary traits. He was popular both among Hindus and Muslims in Dera Ghazi Khan and Dera Ismail Khan. He was the most celebrated among Sri Lalji's descendants. He was popular as a local saint referred to as Bahariyawala, that is because his thalia (platform) was situated underneath a banyan tree called *bahara* in Saraiki. His famous thaliaat Bilot, near Dera Ismail Khan, is now cared for by a *mujawar* appointed by the local Mukhaddam of the Dargah of Pir Shah Isar Qattar of Bilot. Here is an instance of Hindus and Muslims worshipping at the same place seamlessly. Miraculous powers had been attributed to him. Kewalarama enjoyed debates with local pirs. He was believed to possess psychic powers so as to corner a tiger sent to frighten him. If he is to be believed, the tiger meekly sat down besides him. He has described this incident in one of his couplets:

> '*Kehra ko upavarha dhara, baithe Kewalarama. I*
> *Pache giri age salila, jugasana abhirama II*
> (i.e. Kewalarama sits in an alternative yogic posture using a tiger as a pillow with the mountains in the background and the river in the foreground)'[14]

The one fact, however, stands out clearly. There were tigers roaming freely in the jungles during the time of Kewalarama. There were certainly tigers to be found 150 years ago. His literary powers are not to be underestimated. Works attributed to him in the eighth Gaddi manuscripts have the 'chapa' (mark) of 'Kevala' or 'Kewalarama'. His literary output has been compiled under the title of the Rasa Mana Ka Paula and contains 550 poems. He is essentially a poet of the Brij Bhasha, with substantial elements of Saraiki and Khariboli contained in his poems. His poems are to be placed in the Sant tradition of Vaishnava poetry. Kewalarama was addressing a larger audience beyond western Punjab. The net result, however, was a constrained audience for him, the language best understood by Vaishnava sewaks of Shyamji and Lalji was Saraiki.

Sakhi Sarwar, Sultan Cult

The local Sufi pir, Sayyad Ahmad, popularly known as Sakhi Sarwar Sultan, had his dargah strategically located at Sakhi Sarwar pass at the foothills of the Suleiman mountains. No one knows when Sultan Sakhi Sarwar lived. He was an immigrant from Baghdad. His cult had spread all over the Punjab. Hindus, Sikhs and Muslims were all his committed followers. The semi-Muslim sect of Sultanias or Sarwarias was at one time the most popular local cult in direct competition with formal religions. The cult specially attracted the Balmiki Sikhs of eastern Punjab. Langha Bhai was a well-known figure in Sikh history. He was a follower of Sultan, 'his own prophet'. Literally speaking, Sakhi Sarwar means the 'Bountiful Master'. He was also known as Sultan (king), Lakh-data (bestower of millions), Lalanvala (master of rubies), Nigahia-Pir (the saint of Nigaha) and Ruhianvala (Lord of the hills). He became famous because miraculous powers were attributed to him. His dargah was located at Nigaha, at the foothills of the Suleiman mountains in Dera Ghazi Khan district. He was a liberal saint, unusual for the medieval times. He was especially fond of animals and the special protection he provided to them attracted many people to him.

He was a man with a difference, who practised his version of Sufism which approximated to humanism. 'He did not lay down any creed or doctrine for his disciples, nor any code of conduct or ritual. His followers, commonly known as Sultanias, thus had the freedom to retain their Hindu or Muslim affiliations. Hindus as well as Muslims visited the Pir's shrine at Nigaha'. Group gatherings called sang were led by *bharais*, where the drum-beating Muslim *pirbhais* acted as professional guides and priests at the local shrines known as *pirkhanas*. Members of a sang addressed each other as 'pirbhai or pirbahin (brother or sister-in-faith)'[15] The Jat community of eastern Punjab had embraced Sikhism in large numbers, but many of them continued to adhere to their former beliefs and practices of the Sultanias. According to Major Aubrey O'Brien, 'The great shrine in the western Punjab is that of Sakhi Sarwar...men, women and children, Sikhs, Hindus and Muhammedans alike, come from all districts in the Punjab. There are traditions to suit each and all the welcomed by the Muhammedan servants of the shrine'.[16]

Popular Religion

The largest number of visitors come to the shrine during the week-long Baisakhi fair in the month of April. A month-long fair is also held in Gujranwala district. Other fairs are Jhanda Mela (fair of the flag) at

Peshawar, and Qadaman ka Mela (fair of the feet) at Lahore. Indeed, Sultan was in direct competition with the established Sufi saints like Baha-ud-Din Zakaria and Shams Tabriz of Multan. Sayyad Ahmad gained immense popularity because he accumulated no wealth. He was known for his generosity in distributing his property to the poor, thus earning the name of Sakhi Sarwar, or the bountiful land Chief. Nigaha, located at the edge of the Suleiman mountains, was chosen for its excellent location. It has been said, 'that anyone with the least regard for his personal comfort would choose as an abode'.[17] The present shrine at Nigaha is on the high banks of a hill stream. It is reached by a steep flight of steps made at the expense of two Hindu rich merchants of Lahore. Within the enclosures of the shrine are tombs of Sakhi Sarwar, his wife and of the Jinn (apparation) whom he had held in his power. While his tomb is located in the west, a shrine to Guru Nanak is located in the north-west. On the east is a *thakurdwara*, the Hindu temple, and in the adjacent apartment is an image of Bhairon, who had functioned as Sakhi Sarwar's messenger, in carrying out his errands.

The present guardians of the Sakhi Sarwar number 1650, and it is said to be a fact that 'there are never more nor less than 1650 *mujawars* or descendents of the three original keepers of the shrine'.[18] The mujawars were Hindu, Sikhs and Muslim. Sakhi Sarwar went on to prove that religious boundaries were flexible. The categories 'Sikh' 'Muslim' and 'Hindu' did not have the same implications as today. The situation began to change with the advent of the Arya Samaj and the Singh Sabha movements, as well as the emergence of fundamentalist movements among the Muslims. To sum up, 'the Sarwar shrine was part of a region-wise multifaceted cultural system. People who worshipped the pir or took pilgrimages to his shrine did so for many reasons: to harness supernatural powers, to cure physical ailments and psychological problems, to learn about Islam, to resolve inter-personal conflicts, and to dramatize their needs. In the process of all this they confirmed and strengthened the cultural logic of their social world. It was a world in which members of different communities and people of diverse social backgrounds collaborated to face the uncertain and afflictions of human life, their medium being a popular religion.'[19]

Life-style: Mud Housing

The Dhingara canal situated on the eastern border of Dera Ghazi Khan was the only source of entertainment during the summer months for the poor and rich alike. The canal banks were 55 feet higher than the water surface with a declining steep and slippery 50 degrees. The banks were made of *chikni mitti* (literally made of slippery earth), when sodden with water, it was as hard as treated cement, but in reality it was soft as silk and slippery as the sliding surface, inviting to play local game called *ghisi* (the sliding surface). *Chikni mitti* and the Saraiki civilization shaped itself into the lethal combination of earth and river water. It was indeed the gift of the Indus to the Saraiki homeland. Perhaps, the tradition of building huts and mud houses goes back to the Rigvedic times.

Think of the rishis and munis sitting motionless and stern at the river-bordered ashrams in thatched mud huts, conceptualizing the four Vedas. Probably their huts were made of *chikni mitti*.

Wendy Denigar had doubt on that account, 'They lived in the area of the seven rivers (Sapta Sindhu), the five tributaries of Indus and the Sarasvati....The Vedic people left no cities, no temples, scant physical remains of any kind; they had to borrow the term for 'mortar'. They built nothing but the flat, square mud altars for the Vedic sacrifice and houses with straw and later, mud. Bamboo ribs supported a roof. None of this of course survived.'[20] The same tradition continues even today. Indologist Henrich Zimmer has drawn a graphic picture of the dwellings in a typical Rigvedic village. It was built of 'Columns.... Set upon firm ground, with supporting beams leaning obliquely against them, and connected by rafters on which long bamboo roads were laid, forming the high roof. Between the corner-posts other beams were set up, according to the size of the house. The crevices in the walls were grilled with straw or reeds, tied to bundles, and the whole was to some extent covered with the same material. The various posts were fastened together with beams, pegs, ropes and thongs'.[21] How were the huts locked? Probably these were fastened with a strap, as in 'the Homeric houses'?

Substitute the bamboo with palm-tree logs, ropes, pegs, mats and straw and you are transported to a typical Saraiki rural dwelling in modern times.

The stone and brick buildings were inducted by the medieval Mughal rulers. The *chikni mitti* constructions were environmentally friendly, inexpensive and affordable by rich and poor alike, emphasizing the egalitarian nature of society. Such buildings were rain-proof. They were built of ingredients which were freely available locally. You could scoop the earth and pull out from river banks the ancient art of *chikni mitti* that continues to be the hallmark of the Saraiki region.

The *chikni mitti* homes were made of mud walls and roof plastered with thatched material. Water was mixed with earth and whipped with bare feet to drive the bubbles away. Now the *chikni mitti,* after treatment, was perfectly usable as plaster for walls and roof surface. The foundation of the building was hardly one foot or so.Wooden girders for roof surface were made of local wood including palm trees and of other trees, locally available. Prior to its plastering, the roof was covered with mats made out of reeds growing aplenty on the banks of the river. Here was an ideal combination of local material including earth, water, tree trunks and reeds. Finally, the walls of the building were plastered with *chikni mitti* to give it a shining look. It was now rain resistant. The homes made of *chikni mitti* were cool in summer and warm in winter. *Chikni mitti* is to be distinguished from the *Multani mitti,* which was employed for medicinal purposes. Multan is as famous for *Multani mitti* as for a variety of other reasons.

Life-style: Hakims

Hakims in those days had no formal training, they learnt by practise and watching. Traditional skills, partly Unani and partly Ayurvedic skills, were passed on from one generation to another. It was a monopoly of the Arora community. Hakims had names like Mehta (Matta), Chawla, Nangia and Bhutani. Several local hakims had earned name and fame. The name of Gopal Das Matta stands out in this roll of honour. He diagnosed the disease by watching the urine of the patient with a mere glance. He was always dressed in spotless white and sat in his doctor's clinic, perched on a seven-foot high marble platform, with the patients queuing outside and awaiting their turn.From this vantage point, he would glance at another three-foot high marble pedestal stationed in the outside street, the urine poured on it. Hakim Gopal Das kept watching attentively and noted the peculiar colouring of urine in each case. In a jiffy he could identify the disease, and on a slip he would be able to prescribe the medicine. The compounder would prepare the medicine, and hand it over to the patient as quickly as possible. The total cost of the medicine would work out to a mere paisa (equivalent to 1/64th of a rupee). He would even discover early pregnancy by observing the urine from a distance. He had a long innings, serving his patients from 1840 to 1900 AD.

The tradition was continued by his nephew Hakim Gopal Mohan Lal. He specialized in discovering the disease by placing his three fingers on the pulse. There are so many tales about his diagnosing the disease by watching the patient from a distance.

Two other hakims, Hakim Ram Das and Hakim Sabu Ram Bhutani, were also related to the Matta family through marriage. Phatna Hakim earned name and fame by inventing the curative properties of sugar and gur (jaggery) mixed with herbal powders, 'This Hakim was known for his famous *Chataas*, which he prepared himself. He made a thick paste of either sugar or gur and mixed various types of herbal powders for different types of coughs.

Whether it was the ordinary cough with congestion in the chest, or bronchitis, or the whooping cough, very common there, or any other lung irritant, it was sure to be cured by licking fingers dipped in the *Chattas*.'[22] It was a different world altogether. Gulkand (dried desi rose petals) was the usual prescribed medicine for constipation and other diseases. The barber was the master surgeon, treating skin diseases like eczema with the help of his skillful surgery being done by cutting and cleaning.

Life-style: Foods

It was a different world altogether, and perhaps those were happier days in a manner of speaking. Flash back to 1837 of Dera Ghazi Khan, it was definitely a happy world in terms of food prices. The following table presents a comparative view of selected prices of food stuff in Dera Ghazi Khan during 1837 and 1945:

	1837	1945		
Product	**Weight**	**Price**	**Weight**	**Price**
Wheat	1.5 maund	Re 1	1 quintal	Rs 5
Rice	1.5 maund	Rs 2	X	X
Gram	1.25 maund	Re 1	X	X
Moong dal	1.25 maund	Re 1	X	X
Onions	—	X	1 quintal	Rs 1.75
Gur (brown sugar)	1 maund	Rs 3.50	X	X
Milk	—	X	8 litres	Re 1
Ghee	1 maund	Rs 8.50	1 kg	Re 1
Mustard oil	1 maund	Rs 4	X	X

Note: One maund is equivalent to 40 seers and one quintal is equivalent to 100 kilos, besides one kilo is the equivalent of 2.2 seers approximately.

Food was the flavour of the season and several shopkeepers became well-known as local brands. Dwarka Halwai earned a place of primacy on account of his kachauries, halwa, katlamas and samosas, and so was Kanhaiya Kheerwallah known for his milk products like rabri and malai, mostly made of cow milk. Sonu Gulgulewallah earned fame for his piping hot gulgulahs or mustard-oil pakorahs, served with delicious chutney. Rijhu Dalwallah was famous for his fried dals, 'Dal tati, Ghieu di ghatti' (hot and ghee saturated) as the local savory, based on grain and moong pulses. Pokhar Papparwallah stands out from the rest, because his pappars were made not only of pulses, but also made of almonds, pistachio, pepper and malai (milk fat). Those were also exported.

There were very few opportunities for entertainment at Dera Ghazi Khan. Swimming in the local canals during summer months and entertaining friends and family members was the main preoccupation of the male members of the community. The local theatre with Parsi-version plays was another source of entertainment. For the rich, it was the dancing girls, locally known as *kanjris* who provided relaxation and entertainment. For the house-wife it was preoccupation with the family, which perhaps brought her some relief when she sang devotional songs at the wheat mill in praise of Radha and Krishna. What brought the family together was the breakfast food, fetched from the bazaar by the head of the family and shared together. This was repeated day-after-day as a regular ritual by many households.

Thus, food was the main preoccupation and perhaps the only source of entertainment, and thereby, many local halwais were household names in Dera Ghazi Khan. Perhaps the morning ritual started with a visit to the shop of Dwarka Halwai that was constructed of thatch work. His kachauries were famous, and those were out of the world. The early morning trip to Dwarka's sweetshop was a habit and compulsion. His large kachauries were available for a rupee in 16 pieces and the smaller version was available for the same price in 32 pieces. Those were delicious and, indeed, practically out of the world. Equally, his malpuahs with halwa were irrestible. Those came for the same price. This delictable breakfast finally ended with a glass of lassi made of cow milk curd in ample dozes. Those who economized could live on chawal-moth boiled and those were available for one anna per patta. Come to Block No. 6 for mustard-oil sizzling pakauras. Or, one could content oneself by savouring papads at one paisa per piece, and those came with achar made of arabi and carrot. The taste in the mouth lingers on after six decades have passed by. The loud belch in the end spoke for itself.

Section - II

THE INDUS LIFELINE

3

Rigvedic Sindhu

INDIA and the Indus are like inseparable twins. Though separated in history on occasions, they are culturally united in our consciousness. The very name of India is derived from the River Indus. Rigveda called it Sindhu. While mountain passes like the Khyber formed the geographical frontier of the subcontinent, there are many who consider the river as the real protector guarding its frontiers. One of the several literal meanings of the Sindhu is actually this. Neighbouring tribesmen, speaking Iranian dialects, prounced the 's' as an 'h', and as 'h's were dropped for the ease of pronunciation, Hindu became Indu. Enter the Greek influence.The river became Indus and the people were Indoi. Subsequently, were born the Indus and its cognates–India, Hund, Hindu and the Indies.

The whole world rejoiced in naming the mighty Indus, and it was only then that the great religion Hinduism and the 'mysterious' country called India entered the scene. While others were engaged in the 'christening' ceremony, the host, that is India, was marked absent. It must not have been aware of the naming ceremony and the significance of the landmass politically.

River Saga

The saga of Sindhu/Indus is unique in the civilizational history of the subcontinent. From the table watershed of Mount Kailash in Tibet flow four rivers of the subcontinent. Sutlej, Brahmaputra, Ganges and the Indus. The sacred Kailash is also called Kangri Rimpoche,which is also a pilgrimage centre of four faiths closely related to each other: Bon, Buddhism, Jainism and Hinduism. The Indus started its historic journey from Tibet via Ladakh (Kashmir), Baltistan, Gilgit, Swat Valley, North-West Frontier Province (Pakistan), Saraiki landmass (Northern and Southern Punjab), Sindh, before finally falling into the Arabian Sea. It traversed over a distance of 1,988 miles, with the total drainage area exceeding 450,000 square miles, with an annual flow of 207 million cubic kilometers.

Everything is unique about the river from the beginning to the end. River Indus and the Tibet plateau are more ancient than the Himalayas and the Indian subcontinent in geological terms. The river is believed to be originating from the unpretentious 'Lion's Mouth'. The Tibetans call it Senge Khabab. 'Come summer and come winter', the same amount of water is released from the ground. Very soon it is joined by its first tributary, the Kla-Chu which is ten times the size of the main river.

The Tantric Mahaguru, Padmasambhava, was a native of Swat Valley ('Uddiyana'). Popularly known as Guru Rimpoche (rhyming with Kangri Rimpoche), he trekked to Ladakh and Tibet via the Indus river during the 8th century. The landscape of Ladakh, where we find the monasteries known as the treasure-houses of Tibetan art, is dotted with his distinctive footprints. He was the founder of Tibetan Buddhism. He is also known as the Great Master of Uddiyana, the Second Buddha and the Precious Guru.

Aryavrata Discovered

The beautiful Swat Valley seems to be the great dividing line between

Buddhism in the east and the Rigvedic Aryavrata in the west. The Uttarapatha that diagonally cuts across the Indus from Pushkalavati (Peshawar) to Takshashila (Taxila) via the ancient Hund and contemporary Attock was the dividing line between the two great faiths.

Emperor Babur was purported to have said: 'Once the water Sind (river) is crossed, everything is in the Hindustan way' (circa 1526 AD). All the conquerors must have crossed into mainland India near Attock or its neighbourhood in the ancient Hund. It is here that the plains of India were sighted for the first time. The Aryans too could have crossed into mainland India about here and spread themselves on the banks of the river, all the way to 'the Panchanad' (the meeting point of five rivers of the Punjab with the Indus) near Mithankot bordering Sindh province. The probable date of the vast concourse of Aryan tribes pushing their entry into the Indus valley has been estimated at about 1500 BC. They may not have crossed into the Sindh province, the bastion of the Indus Valley Civilization, then in probable decline. They, however, spread themselves comfortably around its five subsidiary rivers and reached as far south as the now-defunct Sarasvati.

Medieval historians were in awe of the Indus and its subsidiaries. Those were designated as 'the seven dreadful rivers' (with the identity of the seventh river not known). There were contrasting views. The Aryans viewed it otherwise. The Rigveda (Circa 1200 BC) is never short of praising the divine river as the harbinger of milk and honey through its waters. The Rigveda has been termed as 'the record of passion and obsession' of the Vedic sages.

Obsession Magnifique

These sages had the utmost passion, love, affection and high regard for their beloved Sindhu. The river was their patron saint who provided them with their day-do-day needs and protected them from enemies. Sindhu was also revered as one of the gods. The following hymn from Rigveda illustrates the instance. 'With nourishing waves it rushed forth, a firm stronghold and brazen fortress for us; like a fighter in his chariot, the stream flows on, overtaking all others. It alone among the rivers flows with pure water from the mountains to the sea; with regard for riches, for many men, it brings fitness and a refreshing draught to their dwellers on the shore'.[1]

The Rigvedic people must have lived very simple lives. The river was above everything else in their lives, they found sustenance mainly from it. It must have been a rural society with no urban pretensions. Defence from enemies also seemed to be the uppermost consideration of the society. Probably, the Rigveda also looked beyond the plains of the Punjab. Does it also refer to snowbound tributaries of the Sindhu? Could it be the Swat river, a tributary of the Kabul river, which in turn is a tributary of the Indus river, that it speaks off? The descriptions could also apply to rivers flowing through Tibet, Ladakh, Baltistan and Gilgit. The end of the winter and the advent of spring is a welcome sight because the rivers (and rivulets) are at their best during that time.

Spring and Summer

With the melting snows, the rivers come into their own; the peasants get ready to sow the resurgent fields. The following hymn probably concerns this kind of situation in a cold and mountainous region: 'The rivers having pierced the air with a rush of waters, went forth like milk cows ... exuberant with their full udders... their water mixed with butter and honey'.

'We solicit from you, waters, that pure, faultless, rain-shedding, sweet essence of the earth which the devout called the beverage of Indra'.[2] The world of Rigveda is an uncomplicated one consisting of river and rain waters, cows, milk and honey. Soma is said to be the favourite drink of the gods, but the ordinary mortals are equally delighted to be savouring pure water, milk and honey. The sheer joy coming from the change of weather is not to be missed. The exuberance is captivating and hence is the cause for spring celebrations. In the plains, the summer months followed by the monsoons are the most welcoming period.

Rigvedic Gods

Rigveda is the most ancient text of all times. It is also the most authoritative text, reinforced by religious sanctions. It has, however, no written text. It was memorized and conveyed in the oral tradition from generation to generation.

The ancient rishis (sages) and poets constructed it hymn by hymn, over several centuries. The probable early date is said to be 1200 BC. It must have taken one thousand years to compose the entire Rigveda. Most of the hymns were composed on the banks of the Sindhu. The rishis, who also could have been poets, must have lived in their ashrams located conveniently on the banks of the river. Indeed, the river prompted them to be inspired to recite hymns and communicate them widely through the word-of-mouth, until the entire chain of ashrams across rivers resounded with Rigvedic hymns. Thus was the Rigveda born.

Rishis lived in natural surrounding. They were children of nature. They lived with nature and counted its blessings. They were also aware of its destructive capabilities. While they stood in awe of it, they were simply dazzled by it. The communities were scattered on the banks of the Sindhu and its five tributaries and the now defunct Sarasvati river. They owed their very existence to the river for water supply, the fauna and flora, the means of transportation, the renewal of land through flooding and its role as the natural wall of physical protection. The Indian civilization, Sindhu and the Rigveda are intertwined as a single whole.

The Rigveda comprises ten books or Mandalas. It consists of 1028 hymns in all. It is a composite work contributed by several rishis. The highest regard is given to the rivers for bringing 'divine waters' from the Himalayas to the plains. Sindhu is especially singled out as a divine god. The Rigvedic gods cover the whole range of natural phenomenon. Gods of Rigveda are related to natural phenomenon like Agni (fire), Aditi (dawn), Indra (Thunder) and Sindhu. Sindhu is viewed simultaneously as water, flood, sea and ocean (samundra).

There is a special relation between Indra and Sindhu. Sindhu god is the closest ally of Indra because it controls rain, water and floods. Indra controls waters which are in turn received by rivers. Indus has also a special status as a male god, with tributaries joinining it at intervals. The rest of the rivers are feminine. The river Indus thus stands out. There are also occasions when the river is addressed as a feminine god. Its motherly instincts are highlighted, when the river Indus is referred to as 'the most motherly'. In one instance it is described as a daughter.

Rain God Indra

Sindhu controls water and releases it at will after parched summers. The river Indus and its subsidiaries are at Indra's sufferance. Max Müller has sought to establish the association by analysing the grammatical root of the word 'Indira': 'The derivation of the Indira, a god who is constantly represented as bringing rain from the root which yielded ind-u, rain drop, is beyond the reach of reasonable criticism... There can be no doubt that in the mind of the Vedic poets, ind-u and ind-ra were inseparably connected'.[3]

Whether the linguistic root indu has any connection with the Latinized term remains to be proven. What about the Sanskrit word for Indus, which generally means 'river, stream and sea', taken probably from the root 'to keep'? The fact, however, remains that most of the functions Indra (thunder) performed are duplicated, though secondarily, by the Sindhu river. The very names 'Sindhu' and 'India' are aligned to god Indra. The very word 'India' is a by-product of this interplay. The name was applied to the subcontinent by the British for the first time soon after their advent to India. It has gained universal currency since then. The terms Sindhu, Hindu, India and Indus are now deeply ingrained in our psyche due to foreign influences. The word Sindhu has its charm and ought to be given currency in future in place of the prosaic substitutes like Indus and Sindh.

Rigvedic Hymns

Rigveda mentions the term Sindhu 176 times, of which 95 times it is in the plural. The same term is applied in Rigveda as specific to Indus, as well as employed interchangeably as a generic concept representing the totality of rivers. There is an additional luster attributed to the Sindhu due to its divine status, the reference made time without number.

'This prayer may Varuna grant, and Mitra, and Aditi and Sindhu, Earth and Heaven' (Hymn 41; Book VI). In the same book is to be found a direct supplication to Sindhu. 'Sindhu, the sea, the region and the firmament, and the ocean' (Hymn 96; Book VI).There are several hymns, in which its roar is lifted up to the heavens. In one particular hymn Sindhu is seemingly raised to the status of the Sun god. 'Sindhu hath yielded her car, light rolling, drawn by steeds and with that car shall win booty in the fight' (Hymn 75; Book X). Two things are worth noting. The Aryan tribes must have been engaged in constant warfare, in which winning the booty was the highest mark of achievement. In this particular instance, Sindhu is addressed as 'she'.

Sindhu Celebrated

Rigvedic rishis/poets miss no opportunity to sing hallelujahs in deference to the divine river. They must have viewed Sindhu with wonder and the wonderment has continued. There is no end to their love affair with the river. There is nothing to beat hymn 75 of Book X of the holy book. The singers are cajoled to sing the hymn repeatedly and it is appropriately titled as 'The Rivers':

> *The singer, O ye Waters...,*
> *shall tell your grandeur forth that is beyond compare,*
> *The rivers have come forward triply, seven and seven,*
> *Sindhu in might surpasses all the streams that flow.*
>
> *Varuna cut the channels for thy forward course,*
> *O Sindhu, when thou runnest to win the race,*
> *There speedest o'er precipitous ridges of the earth,*
> *When thou art Lord and Leader of these leading floods.*
>
> *His roar is lifted upto heaven above the earth,*
> *he puts forth endless vigour with a flush of light,*
> *Like floods of rain that fall **in thunder** from the cloud, so Sindhu rushes on bellowing like a **bull**.*
>
> *Like mothers to their calves, like milchkine with their milk, so Sindhu, unto the roaring rivers run. Thou leadest as a warrior king thine enemy's wing what time thou comest in the van of these swift streams.*[4]

Grandeur Indescribable

Even today there is no river in the subcontinent to equal Sindhu's grandeur.

TheTibetans call it the 'Lion River'. It roars like a lion all the way, especially during the summer months. No artificial barriers like sand-laden banks, river islands and precipitous ridges can ever match it. It has youthful energy unequalled by its rivals. It has truly been called 'the lord and leader of spring and summer floods'.

It's comparison with a bull is appropriate, because the entire Rigvedic economy depended upon bulls/cows and horses/mares. The bellowing of an angry bull has to be multiplied million times to match the roar of rushing and angry floodwaters during summers. The roar keeps resounding in the ears of the present author, even after a lapse of seven decades and past long-forgotten childhood memories. It is an experience to be experienced once in a lifetime. The quiet and calm Ganges flowing past the ghats of Varanasi appears to be a lamb in comparison.

There are at least twenty subsidiaries that join Sindhu in its entire course from the Tibetan plateau. Their joining has been compared to 'milch kine' (cow) making its offering as oblation. The subsidiary rivers are too anxious to merge their identity. Since they also carry 'divine' water from the Himalayas, it helps Sindhu to turn into 'a vast samundra (sea). Here is a sight for gods to see when silt-ridden Kabul flowing from the west, merges with the Indus river from the east with its icy-blue with glacial mountain snow-melt waters. The brown and blue waters run parallel to each other and merge only after travelling a distance. Seemingly the magician in the river must be working overtime to dazzle with a Pandora's box of magician tricks'.[5]

'Seven Rivers Triply' Explained

There is an obscure reference in (Hymn 75; Book Ten) that remains to be clarified: 'The Rivers have come forward triply, seven and seven'. Scholars have interpreted it differently. Rigveda does not help in the matter. Mercifully it is not the only obscure reference. It leaves a scope for sociological imagination.

This particular hymn has also been interpreted differently. H H Wilson was of the view that the seven rivers flowed through three worlds: Earth, Sky and Hell. This must have been the limits of the Rigvedic universe. Max Müller and Muir have different interpretations but seem to be in mutual agreement. To them 'Each set of seven streams' and 'By seven and seven' have meant 'three-fold courses' and 'a three fold course'. The great classical scholar Sayana is of a different view. To him twenty-one rivers meant 'two other sets of seven each being added to the seven chief rivers of the Punjab'. This line of argument seems plausible. This particular hymn, however, mentions no names of any subsidiaries except for the Punjab subsidiaries. Could it be other rivers like Kabul, Kurram and Ghumal? The list is endless.

Favour ye this my land,
O Ganga, Yamuna.
O Sutudri, Parsni and Sarasvati
With Asikni, Vitasta, O Marudvidha,
O Arjikiya with Susoma hear my call.

First with Trstama thou art eager to flow forth,
With Rasa, and Susartu, and with Setya here.
With Kubha, and with these, Sindhu, and Mehatnu,
thou seekest in thy course Krumu and Gomati.

Ganga and Yamuna

Obviously, there is a poetic license to be found in these hymns called the 'Rivers'. It looks like a gathering of rivers even beyond the boundaries of the traditional Punjab. It appears to be a pan-Indian gathering to honour the father Indus. The Punjab subsidiaries are all there except for Beas which is not identifiable in the list. Sarasvati is also there. It appears as often in Rigveda as the mighty Sindhu. Kubha, Krumu and Gomati are also mentioned. Probably those were 'unimportant effluents of the Indus'.

The Ganges is mentioned specifically along with Yamuna for the first time and the only time in Rigveda. There is also another reference elsewhere, which, in all probability, alludes to the name of a woman going by the name of Ganga. It is considered a distant river in the scheme of things in Rigveda. The very fact that only one reference is to be found, that too in Book X, is significant. Considering the fact that Rigveda was not recorded in a single day but completed over centuries.

Book X being the last, in chronological terms, explains the logic when the Ganges made its appearance at a very late stage. The Aryans must have continued to expand eastwards relentlessly. Here is a striking contrast between the Vedic age and the Epic period. While Sindhu takes central stage during the earlier period, the Ganges takes over in the later period. There should be no doubt about Sindhu occupying the centre stage in the Rigvedic scheme of things. It helps to understand that Rigveda is not a work of history. It is a poetic work which helps in understanding history, as it helps in coming to grasp with folklore, social anthropology, social psychology and religious practices.

Male God

The mighty river is represented to possess all the male attributes like tendencies to dominance, impatience and irrepressibility. The contrast is striking. The male dominance thus finds sanction in the Rigvedic milieu. There are also exceptions, when Sindhu enacts a female role, as in :

> *Flashing and whitely gleaming in her mightiness, she moves along her ample volumes through the realms. Most active of the active, Sindhu unrestrained, like a dappled mare, beautiful fare to see.*
>
> *Rich in good steeds is Sindhu, rich in cars and robes, rich in gold, nobly-fashioned, rich in ample wealth.*
>
> *So have I praised...Its power, mighty and unrestrained.*
> *(The River. Hymn 75; Book X).*

Here was a complete sexual transformation and so sudden as to be inexplicable. The male characteristic of 'mightiness' is attributed to the 'She Sindhu', as well as there is a tribute to 'her ample volumes', and, above all, Sindhu is compared, to 'a dappled mare' dazzling with her 'beautiful fare to watch'.

Mother Goddess

The mighty river is compared to a 'dappled mare' with striking spots of colour spattered all over her body. It was usual for the Rigvedic Aryans to harness their rathas with dappled mare. Mares rather than horses were suited to such occasions. Notwithstanding the female characteristics, it connotes power 'mighty and unrestrained', a reminder of the Indian tradition, best personified by the image of half-man and half-woman (Ardhanarishwara) carved on the niches of the famous Kailash temple (Ellora).

At another level, the title of mother given to the mighty Indus is not surprising. Mothers are generous by nature; prone to give away in one-way traffic. Since Sindhu is considered to be the divine mother, its generosity is said to be proverbial. The waters of Sindhu and Sarasvati have been endowed with the quality of divinity. Indeed, river waters in general have also been blessed with the same miraculous powers. What can be more divine than life-giving waters? No wonder Hymn 23 (Book III) singles out the Sindhu-Sarasvati waters in particular. They are said to be doubly blessed. Justifiably, Sindhu assumes the role of mother because its beneficiaries are doubly blessed. What could be more blissful than the role of divine mother? Imagination runs riot in another instance, when Sindhu is compared to a young girl as the embodiment of innocence and with quality of mercy. Sindhu has thus been shown as three-in-one: father, mother and daughter. It is not mere poetic license, but an expression of gratefulness for Sindhu's infinite generosities and benefits to people.

Sapta Sindhu

Rigvedic civilization was founded, developed and firmly established in the land of the seven rivers. It had its initial beginnings on the banks of Sindhu and gradually expanded eastwards. It is thus a misnomer to limit it to the boundaries of five rivers. There was also a joker in the pack. The Sarasvati determined the farthest limits of the Rigvedic civilization eastwards. Sindhu provided the concept cover, for the five rivers like 'mothers to their calves', 'unto thee roaring rivers run', merging their identity into the Lion River, or, better still, the Father River joining at Panchanad until eternity.

Current Name	Ancient Name
Jhelum	Vitasta
Chenab	Askini (Chandrabhaga, Ascesinesor)

Ravi	Parusni (Iravati)
Beas	Vipac
Sutlej	Catudri

It makes it six in number inclusive of Sindhu. Sarasvati is the last entrant. It is a river with a difference. It is considered number 2 in the Rigvedic hierarchy, headed by Sindhu. It did the disappearing act about 4,000 years ago due to the tectonic changes in the upper Himalayas. It, however, was in the mind of the believers as a living monument. It followed a course independent of the Sindhu. It also did the disappearing act in the Rajasthan desert. There is a mythological memory of long standing which places its delta at the foot of the Somnath temple, in obeisance. The ancient delta of Sindhu is also presumed to be located there. Sarasvati has another independent status of being the 'Goddess of Knowledge' and 'Enlightenment'. She is, however, a full member of the Sapta-Sindhu family.

Sarasvati River

There are supplications for all the rivers to come together in a show of unity. The rivers in unity are addressed as Mother Goddess, yielding riches in their generosity. Hymn 64 (Book IV)

> *Let the great streams come hither with their mighty help, Sindhu, Sarasvati and Sarayu with waves. Ye Goddess Floods, ye Mothers, anointing all, promise us water rich in fitness and in balm*

There are as many references to Sarasvati as to Sindhu in Rigveda, especially in its Book VI.

The word Sarasvati appears in three contexts: 1) the invocation of Sarasvati all by itself; 2) in association with the five rivers of the Punjab and Sindhu as an integral part of Sapta Sindhu; and 3) as the goddess of knowledge, as Sarasvati. Its multiple roles are a matter of confusion to the ordinary folk. The mystery of multiple roles continues to remain unsolved.

Goddess Sarasvati is said to be the 'Divine Speech'. She is also addressed as the 'Goddess of Word'. In literal terms saro and saros mean knowledge, and, therefore, Sarasvati is considered the embodiment of knowledge.

Sarasvati also means 'She of the Stream, the flowing movement'. Sri Aurobindo has sought to reconcile the irreconcilables by viewing the Sarasvati both as river and as 'the goddess of inspiration'.

How come one of the Sapta-Sindhu acquired special 'psychological power' and stood out from the rest? After all, all the seven rivers laid equal claims to dispensing 'divine waters'. There is no rational explanation. It may be explained in a historical context. Rigveda was constructed over a period of several centuries as an instance of collective memories. The explanation lies in the growing importance of the Sarasvat Brahmins, who trace their true lineage to the Sarasvati river.

Sarasvati, as one of the Sapta Sindhu, used to flow between Sutlej and Yamuna. It began from the Himalayas and ran through present-day Haryana and Rajasthan. Sarasvati dried up completely by 1900 BC, as confirmed by archaeological and hydrological-cum-radio carbon datings. It is possible to trace its dry course throughout accurately. It must not be confused with the Ghaggar river. It also needs to be emphasized that it did not join with the five rivers of Punjab and Sindhu. Yet it continues to be associated with the six rivers, because its boundary constituted the outer limits of the Rigvedic civilization.

The euphoria expressed for Sarasvati does not match that reserved for the mighty Indus, but it achieves almost the same proportions. It is also called the 'Divine Sarasvati' besides being addressed as, 'O Blest Sarasvati' and 'most divine of streams'. It is twice blessed, because not only all the sages bless her, but she is also 'seven-sistered and three-fold sourced from Heaven, Hell and Earth'. Additionally she is required to be invoked in religions rituals.

Rigvedic Environment

Rigvedic gods were secular beings. They have hardly any spiritual pretensions. They represented various dimensions of wonderful nature, which were also practical in meeting with the day-to-day and essential needs of human beings. The Rigvedic man lived a pastoral life, depended entirely on land, water and nature in general. Cows, bulls, horses and mares were his essential companions. He did not have a settled life. Floods were his welcoming companions. The huts destroyed by annual floods was replaced in no time. The overflowing flood indicated the end of dry season and the advent of monsoons. The god Indra opened his floodgates, enabling plentiful waters to flow in the parched land.

Floods brought clayey soil in its train. It spread over several kilometres on both sides of the banks of the Sindhu. The spread of 20 kilometres on each bank was a matter of no surprise. It was like virtually spreading natural fertilizers on each bank. Grass grew in plentiful, providing natural fodder to domesticated animals like cows and horses. Psychologically, it helped matters because the beneficent nature was interchangeable with the Rigvedic gods. Rigvedic gods were benign and their rivers were beneficent. These feelings are best expressed in the following hymns devoted to Sarasvati.

Hymns in Praise

HYMN 61 (Book VI)

May the divine Sarasvati,

....

... Thou who art strong in wealth protect us well

ye, she most dear amid dear streams,
Seven sisters, graciously inclined,
Sarasvati, hath earned our praise.

....

Seven-sistered, sprung from three-fold source.

....

Sarasvati ... must be extolled by every sage.

HYMN 66 (Book VIII)

So may Sarasvati auspicious send good luck, she is rich in spoil, is never niggardly in thought.

HYMN 25 (Book VIII)

... The Sindhu of the floods...

Sarasvat Brahmins

According to Colebroke, 'the Sarasvata was a nation which occupied the banks of the river Sarasvati. Brahmins who are still distinguished by the name of their nation, inhibit chiefly the Punjab or Panchanad a west of the river from which they take their appellation through the southern and western parts of Hindustan proper and is probably the idiom to which the name of Prakrit is generally appropriate'.[6]

Sarasvats are the elite among the Brahmins. They are now credited with the authorship of the Prakrit language. They probably made substantial contributions to the development of the Prakrits by making the Prakrit language the medium of the masses. Saraiki, Punjabi and Hindi Prakrits could have owed greatly to their intellectual capabilities. Sarasvat Brahmins are the only survivors of the Sarasvat community. They are worthy leftovers of the Rigvedic civilization.

They are like the Jews, to be found in several parts of India. They are to be found in northern states including the Punjab, Sindh and North-West Frontier Province; they have also migrated to southern India. They are concentrated on the western coastline with Mangalore as their epicentre. The Sarasvats are the principal priests of communities in the Punjab and Sindh. They are principal priests of the Khatri community as well as of the Bhatia community of Rajasthan and Sindh. Chitapore Mangalorean Brahmins are looked upon with much respect and awe in their local communities. They have physical features which mark them out distinctly. Among our contemporaries, Nandan Mohan Nilekani, KV Kamath, Girish Karnad and Shyam Benegal are from the Chitapore Mangalorean Brahmin community. The route this particular community must have taken to migrate should be of historical interest.

Sarasvat Brahmins of the Punjab are officially designated preists of the Khatri community, going back to the farthest past. Here is an illustrative list;

Khatri Caste	**Purohit (Sarasvat Brahmin)**
Khanna	Jhingran
Kapoor	Kapuriye
Sethi	Sudan

Mehra/Malhotra	Jaitley
Kohli	Dutt

It is now possible to work out permutations and combinations. The protocol would have required Sanjay Dutt to preside over family functions of the Prime Minister of India, Manmohan Singh, a Kohli Khatri by birth. Arun Jaitley, purest of the pure Sarasvat Brahmin, should be searching for a Mehra/Malhotra to accept him as his priest. So would Najam Sethi, former Editor-in-Chief, Friday Times (Lahore) be thirsting for a pure Sudan Sarasvat Brahmin to adopt him as his family jajman.

Constructive-Destructive Power

Max Müller was not the first to note the constructive-descriptive capabilities of the Indus. He was indeed very perceptive and compared the potentialities of the river with 'the endangered humanity of the divine'.[7] It has also been raised to the status of the divine in the past and in contemporary folk literature. Sindhu has, thus, assumed the status of the Hindu trinity of Brahma, Vishnu and Siva, the respective gods of creation, sustenance and destruction.

Rigvedic Aryans were able to come to terms with it. They had very simple habits. The urban habitats were few and far in between. They lived in rural communities or ashrams on the banks of the river. Horses, mares, cows and bullocks, cotton clothes, gold and silver ornaments, woolen garments and simple food must have constituted their entire world.

Horses and cows were their status symbol. Floods were an annual feature in their lives. They were clever in harnessing the deficiencies to their advantage. They had come to realize that the river could turn destructive rather frequently. They had learnt to come to adjust with its assets and liabilities. This fact has been noted carefully by many perceptive observers. Alexander Hamilton was not the only one to realize this predicament of those who lived in the river basin. He was, however, the most perceptive of all. He travelled down the Indus and published the account in his *A New Account of the East India* in 1727. It must have aroused much interest in Indian affairs in his home country.

He viewed the Indus like a magician with a bag full of tricks. According to him, two Rigvedic gods, Sindhu and Indra, conspired to bring about the situation; come every summer, the tricks were repeated with monotony, the summer months were the most crucial. The annual ritual coincided with the melting of the snows in the Himalayas. The outflow was guaranteed year after year. Kalidasa's *Meghdoot* could not have been conceived on the banks of the Sindhu river, because the monsoon clouds were marginal to the scheme of things. The whole philosophy was propounded scientifically by Alexander Hamilton:

'[Peasents] never know the misery of Famine, [as in other parts of the country], for the Indus overflows all the Low Grounds in the months of April, May, and June, and when the floods go off, they leave a lot of slime on the Face of the Ground, which they till early before it dries and being sown and barrowed, never fails of bringing forth plentiful crop'.[8]

The river Indus changes its course frequently. It cuts across the clayey soil like a tailor cuts the cloth smoothly and leaves large swathes of cloth like open spaces. Naturally those turn into islands. In course of time these islands grow rich grasses which get turned into nature's fodder.. The ancient Aryans loved their horses and cows and these river islands became nature's munificent gift, as pasture lands. No wonder the grateful Aryans viewed Sindhu as a fertilizer, besides giving it other benign titles like father, mother and the watchman. Truly speaking, the Aryans had a continuing love affair with the Sindhu. There was a negative fallout due to perpetual meanderings of the river. Boundaries between communities and tribes became indeterminate on a regular basis. Rigevda is full of perpetual tribal warfares. The change in the river boundaries must have been the main cause.

Sindhu is not only Vishnu and Brahma, both creator and sustainer, but equally a Siva in his destructive capabilities. At least thirty destructive floods occurred between 1857-1910 for which the records are available. In Sindh they call the Indus 'Purali', that is capricious. Alexander Hamilton noted its 'shifting and treacherous nature'. John Wood in his survey of the river in 1836 called it 'highly unstable, subject to frequent flooding and change of course'.

Attok Effect

The Siva dance performed by Sindhu is best seen as it enters the plains from the hills near Attock, forcing itself into a narrow gauge with 'dashing waves' turning 'the bile of fish into water', and breaking 'into fragments the rocks and black boulders upon which they beat'.[9] Alexander Burnes is one of the most adventurous of travellers recording and experiencing the Indus saga. For that reason, he has rich names like 'Indus Burnes', 'the modern Alexander' and 'the Sikander Sane' (the equal of Alexander). He decided to savour the ferocity of the Indus at Attock by experiencing it himself by descending into the whirlpool:

'In the gorges below Attock, the river, pent in between high cliffs, and seen with jagged rocks, was in places as much as thirty fathoms deep; sluicing down at nine miles an hour - the water foamed and raged, piled up as sharp angles of its course and then abruptly dropped, sometime as much as eighteen inches. At the sound of broken water ahead, the boatmen knelt to pray, and then leapt to their oars. The "passage was fearful enough in some places, sometimes the river ran in a rocky channel and detached cliffs stood up in the middle of the stream like basaltic pillars, having marks upon them which indicated the rise of the river of fifty and sixty feet above its bed'.[10]

Yet history was made at Hund and Attock repeatedly over centuries. After the Khyber pass, Attock was a gateway to India. Attock was the highway on which Buddhism travelled beyond to Central Asia, East Asia and China. There was also a negative edge to the Sindhu through historical times. It was never a gentle river throughout its course from the Tibetan plateau to the Arabian Sea. It is even believed that Buddhism in Swat Valley was destroyed due to the decimation of a chain of monasteries in that part of the country. It came to pass due to the rampaging floods of the Indus river. The famous Chinese traveller Xuanzung called it a 'dark and gloomy river'. He had a grudge against the Indus. While returning to China with 72 horses loaded with 520 sutras (holy texts) and rare botanical collection, his flotilla of boats was lost while crossing the Indus. It was natural for him to have no kind words for 'the River Swato' (the Chinese name for the river).

Mother Nature's Mayhem

Rivers are an integral part of mother nature. Like nature, they are neutral between constructive and destructive tendencies. There is no life and death in nature. It is a cycle whose direction must be determined by choices to be made by man. Similarly, destructive-constructive tendencies of rivers are a choice to be made by man. The best option of dealing with the river is by not placing man-made hurdles in its path. Dams and canals are man-made hurdles and obligate self-destructive responses from 'self-respecting' father Indus, left with no choice but to respond in punishing terms in time of its choosing.

There is a lesson to be drawn from the situation–that a valuable natural resource is an environmental hazard for mankind. In other words, rivers, like nature, are human-friendly, so long as man plays by the rules of the game. Rigvedic people played by the rules of the game laid down by the sacred Sindhu. Everybody lived happily thereafter, so the story goes. The pact between man and nature is a solemn one. It shouldn't be violated at any cost.

Chishti Silsilah

There is something to the waters of the Indus that evokes feelings of sufiana devotion, reverance and accomodation. The banks of the river are dotted with a chain of khanqahs of the Chisti Silsilah in Sindh,Bawahalpur and the Saraiki districts of Punjab. The Chisti saints like Khwaja Nur Muhamed of Mihir were largely responsible for the spread of the liberal-oriented Chisti Silsilah, so much so that it eclipsed the other mystic fraternities in the 18th and 19th centuries. The tradition of liberal thought bordering on apostasy must have inspired Khwaja Ghulam Farid of Bawahalpur who sang in praise of immortal heroes like Shams Tabriz, Sarmad and Mansur not hesitating to lay down their lives in the cause of their convictions. The popularity of Sufism could also be attributed to the predominant Baloch ethos of the land. The Bhakti and Sufi movements spread their wings together in the true spirit of secular accomodation. It was in the same spirit that Warris Shah denounced the 18th century foreign invaders in the following unequivocal terms:

'Aj mili Punjab Kandaharianun
Sara mulk kharab Punjab vich........
(Today the Punjab is at the sufferance of the invaders from
Kandahar, Here is the tragedyof the spoilt land)

Folk Tradition

The final judgement shall rest with the common people. Folk tradition has a different concept of the river. Hindus and Muslims alike worship the Indus and have adopted it as a part of their life. In fact, what has united the Hindus and Muslims on the same platform, especially in Sindh, is the river. Hindus worship the river as Jhulelal or Uderelal. Muslims call it Shaikh Tahir. Everybody calls it Zindapir (living saint). To the Hindus of Sindh, Zindapir is 'the river god', a personification of the Indus. To the Muslims he is a Sufi pir, who communicates with his worshippers person-to-person by participating in their sorrowful and joyful moments. The Hindus and Muslims have shrines located check-by-jowl on a river island near Sukkur town.

There are several Sindhu munajats or popular hymns which are recited widely. They have a litany common to them. The river Indus is praised as a beneficent stream, more so, because its fury is exhausted by the time it reaches its tail-end in Sindh province. It is singled out as the river-god with 'thousands' weeping and praying 'at thy threshold'. He is praised as the 'verdant lord', 'owner of daily bread', 'O friend', 'thou the selfless', and 'being great in learning'. The Sindhu is also upgraded to the status of Goddess Sarasvati for its learning capabilities. The river-god is even raised to the status of the deity on occasions. Here the Sindhi munajats echo the Rigveda. The old tradition continues and finds echo in contemporary times. Here is a specimen of a Sindhi munajat or hymn, often recited in honour of the Indus:

O thou beneficent stream!
O Khizr, Thou king of kings!
O thou that flowest in thy power and might!
Send thou joy in my heart!

I have sinned times innumerable;
Pardon my transgressions!
Thousands weep and pray at thy threshold
Send thou,…

Intercession becomes thine exalted rank,
Bright are thou, and bright is thy look,
Above thee there is no (earthly) power.
Send thou,…

O river of daily bread, send it to me!
Give my heart parity and truth!
Difficulties surround me,
Send thou,…

O Sultan! O verdant Lord!
Aid thou the weak one!
Thou knowest my case
Send thou,...

Make my foes my slaves!
Destroy my obstinate enemies!
And thou the selfless!
Send thou,…

Thou art great in learning,
Fearful and lordly.
A worker of miracles, a brave benefactor.
Send thou,…

(Through thee) all the sorrowful are joyful,
All the hungry are fed,
All the weak are strengthened.
Send thou,...

Thou art our aid, our stream, our horseman,
Thou takest our boats to shore,
Thou art our defence in time of need.
Send thou,…

Be with me in all things,
Give me power before men,
Support me in difficulties,
Send thou,...

O friend! I bear thee in mind,
Thou corner-stone of the weak!
Hear the prayer of Eesav!
Send thou joy to my heart!"[11]

There is also a marked difference between the Rigvedic man and our contemporary man.The former does not feel helpless, because the river-god is only an accessory to him. But in contemporary folk tradition, there is a considerable element of helplessness displayed by human beings. This is a marked difference in the two traditions. While the Rigvedic man is wonderstuck at his environment, his contemporary counterpart is worshipful and frightened in his outlook. Unfortunately, this is a qualitative difference between the two situations

4

The Lion River

THE Indus river is called Sengo Tsampo, which, when literally translated into Tibetan, is the Lion River. Jean Fairley travelled for two years, faithfully following the trail of the river and named it the Lion River. The river flows effortlessly from underneath the source, shaped like the Lion's mouth, and so the argument goes, 'of all these names the first (that of the Lion River) seems the most apt, for the Indus is a lion throughout its course. It is beautiful, powerful, unpredictable and dangerous. Sometimes, of course, it can be gentle above its woodlands, shallows of the poplars rustle...But for the most part, both in time and pace the Indus is cruel, and as ruthless and cunning as any lion'.[1]

Universal Acclaim

The reputed British traveller, Richard Burton had a different view. He called it 'the noble Indus'. Annemarie Schimmel has called it 'the river of poetry'.

The renowned Sufi poet Shah Abdul Latif says 'Every wave is filled with rubies, water perfumed with musk, from the river waft airs of ambergris (perfume)'. Atharvaveda speaks of the miraculous medicinal qualities of the Indus and its tributaries as they come down the Himalayas to distribute their abundant largesse:

They flow down from the Himawat,
They get united in the Sindhu river.
Those divine waters give me medicine to
Strengthen my heart.

The great Sanskrit scholar, Max Müller, begged to differ by occupying a middling space. He called the river 'constructive-destructive'. The Indus could as well be termed the Father River, Mother River and the Sacred River. The fact, however, remains that it has been recognized as the oldest river in the subcontinent, and it is definitely older than the Himalayas. It also seems to be the favourite river of the Rigvedic Aryans as it is of any contemporary Tibetan, Ladakhi, Baltic, Gilgitan, Swati, Pathan, Potohari, Saraiki, and, above all, of the Sindhis. It is worshipped by all of them.

Rigvedic Times

The oldest name of the river-Sindhu-is the favourite of the Rigvedic people. It is variously interpreted as 'divider, keeper or defender'. Atharvaveda called it 'saransh', which literally means 'flowing forever'. The other literal meaning of Sindhu is the 'root'. In fact, we must travel back in time and transit from the Rigvedic times to the Indus Valley Civilization (hereinafter referred to as IVC) to trace the origins of the word 'Sindhu'.

The Indus Valley was the earliest cotton-growing area of the world. It is equally true of the present times. The word Sindhu connoted cotton for the ancient Babylonians: 'It is even possible that Sind derived its name from being the main cotton producing area of the region at that time. It was also ascertained that the linen worn by the Egyptian Pharaohs was Sindh cotton. It is postulated that in those days, Egypt imported cotton from the Indus, and it was at a later stage that the Egyptians started producing their own cotton'.[2]

Kailash Mountain

One must travel back in space and time to chase after Sindhu. The Indus was born about thirty to forty million years ago following the birth of Kangri Rimpoche (the sacred Kailash Mountain).

The Kailash Mountain is equally sacred to the Hindus, Buddhist, Jains and the Bon Tibetan faith. To the Hindus it is the abode of Shiva and Lake Mansarovar. For the Buddhists, especially to the followers of Lamaism, it is the centre of the earth termed 'the navel of the earth'. It is also equally sacred to the Jains for being the place of enlightenment of the first Tirathankaras. To the Tibetan Bons, it is the abode of sky goddess Supairwen. Bon text has an entire vocabulary of names for the Kailash Mountain: 'Water's flower', 'Mountain of Sea Water', and 'Nine Stacked Swastika Mountain'. Whatever you call the Kailash mountain, one must follow the Tibetan example by calling it Kangri Rimpoche. It truly rings a bell in your ears, equally so in the English language when translated as the 'Precious Snow Mountain'.

Lion's Mouth

To their credit the Tibetans must be the masters of word play. Compared with the vocabulary coined by the Tibetans for the river, our historical terms like Sindhu, Indus and Sindh ring prosaic and without much rhythm. Kangri Rimpoche has an operatic ring to it. So does Sengo Tempo ('the Lion River') in Tibetan for the Indus. The Tibetans have coined several wonderful terms for the river and its source. The source of the river means 'Lion's Mouth' in English. The actual Tibetan word for it is 'Senge Khabab'. Wait a minute! That is because the Tibetan vocabulary is more colourful. It holds one's attention. The 'Lion's Mouth' must have a tail. Have you heard of a lion without a prominent tail? The source has a 'Lion's Tail' picturesquely called 'Senge Nama'. Since 'Lion's Mane' must precede 'Lion's Tail', we have the 'Lion's Mane' in 'Senge Ure'' ('the Lion's Mane'). What about the claws? A lion without claws is worse than a fox minus its high IQ and proverbial cunningness. Hence, you have 'Sengo Nombo' with its claws. So our Senge Tempo has 'Senge Khabab' ('the Lion's Mouth) as well as 'Senge Ure' ('the Lion's Mane'), 'Senge Nama' ('the Lion's Tail) and the 'Senge Nombo' ('the Lion's claws). Only a sensitive artist would have conceived of a 'Lion's Mouth' with its physical limb formations in a rock with bubbling water. Thus, our Lion River has claws, mane and tail as a warning signal for those concerned.

All credit is due to the young British travellers Alice Albinia (*Empires of the Indus*) who walked all the way to the source of the river, accompanied by her Tibetan companion Karma, who has provided us the following graphic description: 'But we follow the stream up to the top of this gentle hill and there it ends, in a pale rock face at the foot of which water bubbles from the mossy earth.'

'This is the Lion's Mouth', says Karma, pointing to the rock face as he translates 'Sonamtee' into Hindi. He points to the hill behind, 'That is Senge Ure, the lion's mane'. His finger moves west. That is Senge Norboo, its claws. That is Senge Nama, the lion's tail'.[3] The mystery about the source remains unsolved so far. Here again the Indus river proves to be different from the rest of the crowd.

Nanga Parbat

The famous Chinese pilgrim Xuangzang called the Indus 'Sun-tu'. The other Chinese names for the river are 'Shiquanha' and 'Yindu' (rhyming with 'Hindu'.To the people of Karakoram and the Himalayas, it is the eastern river, because it comes from Tibet and then Ladakh, where it is commonly known as Sengo Tsampu ('The Lion River').

It flows west for 1000 kilometres, from Tibet, and then suddenly it is forced to turn south when faced with the Nanga Parbat. The turning point is contrasted with two formidable rivals confronting each other. The Indus here changes its direction.

The view is dramatic because on the one side it is possible to look down upon the river with one sweep of the eye, and, on the other hand, one is dazzled by an eye-popping stare at the 26,000 ft. high Nanga Parbat. The Nanga Parbat stands alone, dwarfing low hillocks. Contrast it with the trough of the Indus at the steep fall of 500 feet below. The Nanga Parbat is believed to be the Mount Meru (the abode of gods) of the Rigvedic people. Both, the mountain and the river, are seemingly protected by heavenly forces from above.

Just as the river Indus is known for its constructive-destructive tendencies, the same is said of the Nanga Parbat, which literally means 'the Naked Mountain'. As the Indus stands unrivalled among its twenty odd tributaries, equally the Nanga Parbat has no other peak that reaches within 10,000 feet of its crest.

Phrases like 'a perpetual delight', 'vision of soft pure white' and 'too ethereal for earth' have been employed for the Nanga Parbat. The mountain gives 'a feeling of impossibility' so much so that human beings have no choice but to reconcile themselves to a feeling of 'one didn't matter'. Many of the sentiments equally apply to the river as well. What makes it fascinating is to realize that both of them have destructive-constructive tendencies which make them all the more fascinating.

Baltistan and Pathan Lands

Rigveda may have compared the Indus to 'speckled as a mare, beautiful as a handsome mare', but it turns out to be contrary, being the most turbulent river passing through Baltistan and Gilgit. 'It has to be viewed near Skardu in its true Kali incarnation, framing an oval basin 7,500 feet above sea level, some twenty-miles long and eight miles wide, enveloped by rocky mountains 17,000 ft high, with the Askandria Fort, standing isolated in the middle 'like the Rock of Gibraltar'.[4]

The Baltis have no love lost for the mighty river. The Indus is recalled with considerable fear and awe as Gemtsuh (the Great Flood). The other Baltic name for it is Tsuh-Fo ('the Male River'). They must have had long memories because it is the same description of the river given by the Rigvedic people.

When it enters the plains, the Indus gets ready to cross the Pathan lands. Following the Tibetan tradition, it is called by Pushtu-speaking people 'the Sher Darya' ('the Lion River'). Breaking out of the jackboot of the mountains, rich in tributaries and flowing parallel to the borderlands of Swat valley, it heads towards Attock to merge with yet another tributary. Its blue-water is contrasted with the brownish and dirty waters of its tributary from Kabul. The contrast in colour is very sharp, very similar to the contrast seen at the Sangam (merging place) at Allahabad. The Pathans are fond of calling it 'Nilab' ('the Blue River'). They have also named it 'Abasin' ('the Father of the Rivers'). Khushal Khan (the national poet of the Pathans, imprisoned by Emperor Aurangzeb) wrote longingly of his home river Kabul (or Landai) and the Indus in the following nostalgic words:

> *Gentle breezes, bear my greeting,*
> *Past the silver stream of Landai,*
> *To Surai, Surai my home.*
> *Father Indus hail him loudly,*
> *As across his flood ye go,*
> *But to Landai, gentle breezes,*
> *Softer salutations blow.*
> *Ganga, Jamuna, how I hate you,*
> *Sluggish rivers of the plain*
> *Would that I were home again,*
> *Once again to drink of Landai –*
> *Hell must one day loose its chain'.*[5]

Khushal Khan loved his Landai and its breezes and waters, but it has no comparison with the blue 'divine' waters of the Indus.

Attock the Entrepôt

Attock is the dividing line between the hills and the plains. Here the river becomes sluggish and spreads itself wide. Now it enters Kalabagh and all along travels through the plains on its way to Sindh province and reaches its final destination to the Arabian Sea. It becomes too capricious by changing direction at its will. During floods it may spread twelve miles across in either direction, whereas it turns into a narrow creak during dry season. The triangle of land, with apex resting in the south at the 'Panchanad' between Indus and Jhelum-Chenab, has been called the Sindh Sagar Doab. It has been named 'Desert of the Indus' or 'Thal Doab'. For many years it was considered useless except for breeding horses and milch cows (possibly of the Rigvedic vintage). Babur, during his first expedition, confined himself to trans-Indus. He found it a wasteland, but managed to steal horses, bullocks and cows and took them back to Ghazni. The river belt happens to be the poorest and the people inhabiting those lands to be its worst victims.

Liberal Traditions

Kalabagh to Panchanad is considered to be the middle ranges of the Indus. This is the territory of the Rigvedic people. Sindh province constituted one of the final points of the river. It is the land of the Indus Valley Civilization. Here the river is treated respectfully and viewed as 'Vadhera' (elder brother) throughout this territory. Here alone the river has been totally integrated in people's way of life. Here alone Hinduism and Islam have come to terms on a liberal plane.

This is the land of the saints. Multan, Pakpattan, Sakhi Sarwar, Dera Ghazi Khan, Sukkur, and Jhuch are, among others, places of pilgrimage for the followers of Muslim, Hindu and Sikh faith, alike. It is the headquarters of the Vaishnava Bhakti movement. Here Sikhism has come to terms with Hinduism in Hyderabad, as has Hinduism with Islam (Sindh). Jhuch is the epicentre of radical social reform movements of the Sufi brand. Islam practiced here was of the liberal kind. The Sufi and Bhakti cults in Sindh have come to terms with each other. The river Indus is the fulcrum around which many religious practices have evolved. The river Indus at Sukkur is an ideal example of the same. To the Sindhis, the river is the beginning of the world and it is the end of the world for them. After all, the sub continental civilization made its mark with the dawn of IVC. Certainly, there is no life for them beyond it. It is also called 'Purali' meaning capricious in Sindhi. The poets have called it 'Mehran'. It is even called 'samundar' (sea or ocean), because it spreads itself wide in its lower marches. It has been referred to as the 'Fresh water sea' at the delta end.

The list of the uses the river can be put to is inexhaustible. It is also called, 'International Flyway Number 4', the ornithologist's description of the Indus pathway for millions of migratory birds, who travel regularly every winter from colder climates and follow the path chalked by the river and its tributaries. It is such a colourful mélange of sea, river, marsh, mangrove, desert, hill, forest and mountain birds. 'Come one and come all' is the message for millions of birds to the annual conclave presided over by the Indus year-after-year.

River Tributaries

The tributaries of the Indus form a vast network and they represent practically all territories through which the Indus travels. There are no tributaries joining the river from the side of Sindh or Balochistan. The land between two rivers in the Punjab is called 'Doab' (literal meaning: 'two waters or rivers'). This practice was introduced by the Mughals for the convenience of revenue collection. In practice, it also indicated marked cultural divisions. The demarcation is as follows:

- 'Bist Doab' - Area between the Beas and Sutlej.
- 'Bari Doab' - Area between the Beas and Ravi.
- 'Rechna Doab' - Area between the Chenab and Jhelum.
- 'Sindh Sagar Doab' - Area between the Indus and Jhelum.

During the geological times the rivers in Punjab did not flow into the Indus. They used to flow east in the direction of the Ganges. The Sutlej, which also arises from the Kailash mountain ('The abode of Lord Siva'), used to flow into Ghaggar–Hakra during the Harappan times. Several rivers have kept changing their location, which definitely includes the Indus. At one time Ravi and Chenab used to flow near the city of Multan. There is also a strong belief about the Indus joining the Runn of Kutch as its final abode.

Dreary Climate

The mid-Indus extending from the Potohar plateau in the north and Thatta port, south of the Sindh constituted the heart and soul of the Indus ethos. From the time of the Rigvedic Aryans, Attock and Hund in the Potohar plateau were the essential points of contact with the outside world, leading all the way to Patliputra (Patna).This was at one point the centre of another great civilization, and, it led us in the direction of Greece, Iran, Central Asia and China. The mid-Indus has been responsible for giving birth to several great civilizations, which indeed constituted the very foundations of contemporary India. Rigveda has sung hallelujahs in praise of 'Sapta Sindhu' bhumi (land).

The very first impression of the lands are most disappointing. The rivers are the only sign of life in an otherwise dreary landscape. It is full of sandy dunes criss-crossed with marshy patches. The summers are long and endless. Everything dries up and plant life barely manages to survive, except the frugal palm and kikar trees. Camel alone has adjusted to the climate and provides an easy means of communications. The land comes into life after the rains, begining in late July every year. As it was noted by a perceptive observer, 'you could lift the heat with your hands, it sat on your shoulders like a knapsack, it rested on your heads like a nightmare'.[6]

Let the last word rest with Humphrey Templeton, who was posted to Bahawalpur town (on the bank of the Indus) midway between Multan and Sukkur and recorded the experience of his first summer: 'The temperature was already mounting towards 110°C. Hot winds laden with sand blew in from the desert. I stand in despair while the dust storm raged, with a thick layer of sand which penetrated the ugly red-brick bungalow through the chinks and gaps in the door and windows. There was no sanitation. A sweeper carried a pail from the home and dumped the contents over the garden wall into an open pit. Four months of fierce dry heat was succeeded by four months of oppressive humid heat, with always the promise, never the relief of rain. I had gone to bed in the garden when the thermometer showed 96° and woke up in the middle of the night with it up to 108° and dust storm getting up. I have lain in bed on a roof on the edge of the desert on a still night with no breadth of wind, when in ten minutes a dust storm had rolled up and only weight was preventing my bed being hauled off the roof into the courtyard below'[7]

Rivers and Civilization

There must be close connection between hot climate deserts and waters that explains the rise of great civilizations in ancient times. The great medieval traveller, Ibn-e-Batuta (1333 AD) found an answer in destructive–constructive character of the lifeline rivers. Max Müiller has been a forceful proponent of this theory. Ibn Batuta has found striking similarities between the two great rivers–the Nile and Indus–and equally the two great civilizations of India and Egypt: 'He was astonished to find that when the Nile's inundation waters spread far and wide to peak periods and summertime flooding, the people readily abandoned their homes and hearths to temporarily settle in safer places. As the water receded in the late autumn, the people joyously resettled, renovating their old abodes and busily cultivated the enriched freshly irrigated lands as far as the river water spread'.[8]

The water, clay and mineral-enriched river soil proved to be an effective fertilizer enriching it perpetually. Even today, the Indus spreads itself as wide as ten to twelve miles on each bank during summer months.

'Challenge and Response' Theory

Here is another demonstration of Arnold Toynbee's theory of 'Challenge and response'. Ibn Batuta further reinforced the theory by comparing the situation of three great civilizations of (a) the Sindh Valley, (b)the Nile Valley and (c) the Euphrates-Tigris Valley of Mesopotamia, which emerged simultaneously in the third millennium before the birth of Christ. In fact, the four rivers associated with these three great civilizations gave birth to them.They also happen to be the ' global centres for the development of human civilization'. The great civilizations were in constant touch with each other to their mutual benefit. Unfortunately, none of them have left any written records, yet monuments, buildings and sculptures left by them speak eloquently about their past contacts.

All these great rivers are unpredictable and devastating to the extreme. The Indus river assumed the form of Lord Siva, the god of devastation. Near Attock, for instance, the dashing waves struck rock with devastating effect and turned 'the bile of fish into water'. No wonder, Xuangzang believed that 'the poisonous dragons and dangerous spirits lived beneath its water'. The medieval historians were in constant dread of the 'seven deadly rivers of Punjab'. The brave Pathan Khushal Khan was undoubtedly given a few anxious moments by the mighty river as expressed by him in a verse:

'Most cross the Attock ferry, trembling the while with fear, For Indus takes his tribute from pauper, and prince and poor'.

Unfaithful River

'Darya Chanha kalai leve te sona deve',
Darya Sindh sona leve tahe kalai deve'.
'The River Chenab takes away tin and gives gold,
The River Indus gives tin and takes away gold'

There are also a few harsh words for the loving river in the Saraiki folk tradition. There is another couplet which is more devastating in its effect:

'Draya Sindh kanjri vangu he'
'The river is like a prostitute'.

Buddhism was at its height in the Swat Valley (Uddiyana) and the Sindhu's devastating floods of the 7th century destroyed numerous monasteries, practically shutting out Buddhist thought, philosophy and religion.

During 1790 there was a major shift in the course of the Indus, when it moved to a more westerly direction, shifting its junction with the Chenab river near Mithankot. Thus, the entire Panchanad sought another address. An entire canal system was left destroyed. It led to a series of bloody feuds and, in particular, it resulted in the 40-year conflict between the Balochi tribes of Dera Ghazi Khan and other communities. The entire western Punjab was bloodied due to the havoc by this worshipful river. Those bloodied by the river had been the greatest beneficiaries of its canal system. Talpur Mir, the Nawab of Bahawalpur and the Durranis were equal participants in this 40-year mayhem.

According to records maintained about the Indus river since 1812, there have been floods practically every second or third year. Great floods occurred in 1812 and 1833 and again in 1841, when a pent-up lake gave away in the Himalayas with a glacier pounding its force into the river. In 1856 there was another great flood.

Floods Galore

The town of Dera Ghazi Khan was considered the pride of the Mirranis, who were the torchbearers of progressive Balochi tradition. The Indus was the lifeline of Dera Ghazi Khan district, but its chronology of floods make for interesting reading. The unfortunate people of this land were constantly confronted with mini floods from the 1790s, on a yearly basis. Records are available for 200 years to confirm. 1812, 1833 and 1841 are considered the years of the Great Floods. 1841 had floods with water rushing down at a velocity of 11 miles per hour. It was explained by the pouring of waters on account of the pent-up bursting of a glacier in the Himalayas. The 1856 flood was another one to remember; the civil town and cantonment of the town were washed away entirely. The local people calculated these dates from the year of the 'Devastating Flood'. At one time, the river flowed twelve miles away from the town, but in no time it crept to the suburbs of Dera Ghazi Khan.

By 1872, it was just three miles away from the borders of the Mirrani town. The cantonment had once again been destroyed in 1878. The river had risen by 54.6 feet at Attock during August 1876, flooding the countryside down to Mithankot. With the river threatening the town constantly, stone embankments were built during 1889–91 to provide protective cover to the town. The very next year the man-made ramparts were under threat. The Vadhera was showing guts by attacking the northern end of the town. There were untimely floods during 1901. Two of the three protective dykes were punctured. The river brought silt 12 to 15 feet deep at the site of the destroyed dykes, thus providing an illusory protection. The graceful Kasturi canal and its date palm and mango groves which were pride of the town at one time had disappeared altogether. Come 1910, the year of the reckoning, the process of erosion called Dhaa started. It became the constant refrain of the river, with loud threatening and deafening noises. The threatening waves of the angry Vadhera lashed at the outer walls of the temple of Gopinath. These held for some time, giving a false sense of security to the believers. The year 1911 was crucial for Dera Ghazi Khan and proved to be its nemesis.

Nature's Prisoner

The two important towns of the Derajat, Dera Ismail Khan and Dera Ghazi Khan, on the western banks have been this river's vicarious victims. The Derajat is famous for it saints, robbers, traders, heat and floods. Dera Ismail Khan was destroyed completely by flooding and a new town had to be built. Dera Ghazi Khan was known as 'the City of Palms', 'Dera Phulan de Sehra' ('the Crown of flowers') and its canal promenade was completely destroyed during 1910 and it was entirely rebuilt 15 kilometres away. Still there are no complaints by the fate-resigned local people because the Indus is considered their lifeline and 'annadaata' ('breadgiver').

There is a scientific explanation by the chief engineer of the Indus river project for the way-wardness of the Indus. The destructive/constructive power of the stern Father River is to be notionally explained in the following engineering jargon: 'Sun, frost, moisture and wind contending among the mountain tops; split off immense fragments of hardest rock from the massive bulwarks.Gravity seizes them within its grasp. They are dislodged from their places, they slide, they roll, they bound through the air with ever increasing velocity and plunge downward in wild career, the avalanche of rocks, scouring and pulverizing the mountain sides, sending up clouds of snow and rock dust till they find a resting place...Under the action of heat, cold, moisture, wind, the avalanche and the glacier mounts are ground to powder. The ponderous mixture of solid and semi-solid move with all the freedom and facility of a liquid but with greater devastating power.The rock-packed banks of the river crumble into the rushing torrent and large boulders topple into it and join the mad procession'.[9] It is a mad, mad world, with human beings only bit players.

Fauna and Flora

Fauna and flora of the Indus Valley is not very exciting, but somewhat interesting. The four animals and plants for which the region is known are:

1. Water fowl (bird),
2. Date palm (tree),
3. Camel (animal), and
4. Indus valley dolphin (mammal).

The river valley is not distinguished for its wild flowers. Emperor Babur was charmed by the spread of a field of wild tulips growing on the banks of the river near attoch it must be one of the rarest recorded description of flowers discovered near the banks of the river.

As Kerala is associated with coconut palm, so is the Sindh valley with date palm. The land is entirely covered with date-palm trees. It is a sight to watch in summer months, when palm trees are lush with multi-coloured dates of all hues and sizes. They come in yellow, brown, green, blue, red and indeed in all kinds of pleasing colours. Date palm trees in singles and groves break the monotony of the otherwise dull landscape. Date palm has many uses. The fruit, stems, fruit stone, branches and leaves have their uses. Date palm must have been imported from West Asia and probably brought by the Arabs after the Muslim invasions of India. Sindh and Multan belt are its epicentre. It is known as the 'Land of Date Palm'.

It is also the symbol of Islam. The green colour connotes peace. Indeed it is the religious flag of Islam. It also symbolizes the brotherhood of Islam, especially on the occasions of breaking of *rozas* in the late evenings during the Ramzan. Date palm is the essential content of the daily menu during the holy month. It is a welcome food for the poor during summer and winter months. It is also the foremost symbol of the lower Indus valley. It is eaten wherever the Saraiki and Sindhi languages are spoken.

Camel

The Saraiki language has a musical rhythm about it. Equally the cries of animals have a musical twang, appealing to the ear. Not to be forgotten that the Multani *Kafi* is accepted as being essential to the classical repertoire. Seven cries of common animals are listed below--those probably formed the foundation of early classical traditions. All of them, except for one word, end with the rhythmic 'K'.

Word		**Meaning**
Hinak	-	Neigh of horse.
Hing	-	Bray of donkey or mule.
Bak	-	Bleat of sheep or goat

Dhikh	-	Bellow of cow.
Garhk	-	Bellow of bull
Bok	-	Cry of he-goat or ram.
Minak	-	Gentle beat of she-goat
Burkh	-	Bubble of male camel[10]

Along with date palm, camel is another distinguishing feature of this part of the world. Camel is an ugly animal, but it has many uses. It keeps marching endlessly for days and weeks together. It munches constantly with its ugly but glistening teeth in perpetual motion. It has a crooked hump and bent back. It is slow-moving, with a head too small for its large body. The Camel is, however, a gentle soul, except when he is provoked. For centuries, trade has been carried on between Afghanistan and the Derajats by the 'Powindahs' (Afghan traders) with the camel as their only means of communication. Camel also emerges from nowhere in folk tales like 'Heer Ranjha'.

The Saraiki language has also many names for the camel. The male camel is called utth, the female of the species is called Dachi. The one-year, two-year, three-year, and four-year-olds are called Toda, Mazat, Tirhan and Chhatr, but a camel from one to four years has a colourful name, Lihak. The camel is called by different names determined by the number of teeth it possesses. While a useless (old) male camel after 13 years is called Khamba, the female counterpart is called Jharot.

Flyway No. 4

'Come one and come all', is an open invitation to birds from all over the world–from the rest of Asia, continental Europe, East Africa, Siberia, and even as far as the Antarctica to winter enclave in the Indian basin. At least one million birds, in particular, waterfowl have been following the trail for thousand years. Their largest number enter from northerly and north-westerly direction from four passes in the Suleiman mountains following the human trail. Then they follow the tributaries of the Indus like Kabul, Kurram, Chitral, Swat and the Jhelum, landing on and around the Indus basin.

The waterfowl constitutes the largest number, but the entire flock consists of at least 120 species. A large number of birds settle down in water depressions known as dhands and dhones in the Indus which get inundated during the summer season. Come summer, they fly back to their original homes. The Wilson's Storm Petrel comes a distance of 11,000 km and returns to its original home of the Antarctica in the South.

This enclave of birds includes waterfowls of all hues and colours. You name it and you find birds of the seas and rivers, from marshes and deserts, from ranges of arid hills and forest-covered mountain systems and from intensely cultivated plains, and plateaus with sparse vegetation. They come from far and wide. Name any variety, it is all there: pelicans, herons, egrets, swans, cranes, gulls, kingfishers, terns, ducks and geese. These birds are a boon for the people living in the Indus hinterland. The ecology of the basin is kept in balance due to their ceaseless activity. They are the true cleansers of the world. The migratory birds also add to the aesthetics of the place. The hanging nests of the weaver bird are found in abundance. The water fowls also add colour to the landscape. The singing birds add to the cacophony. Here is also a meeting ground provided by migratory and domestic birds. This distinct flyway has been named as Flyway No. 4. It covers the entire Indus water basin. It also acts as the 'Green Route', through which millions of water fowls travel year-after-year by sheer instinct. It has also been called the Great Caravanserai for Eurasian Aerofauna Travellers. They follow the Indus valley in search of food and shelter. The hospitable climate is welcoming to them. The Indus valley is also a staging, watering and breeding ground for birds.

Domestic Birds

Among the domestic birds, a note may be taken of: Bulbul, Magpie Robin, Black Partridge, Indian Skimmer, Parakeet and Koel. Bulbul remains the favourite of poets and lovers. It is a symbol of unfulfilled love. Bulbul couples are devoted to each other as any lovelorn couple. It occupies a place of honour, 'as the songster, a wailer, and an innocent query of the netter of birds'. It's voice is appealing but it has a limited repertoire. Besides, they are quarrelsome by refusing to give or take quarters.

Compared with the Bulbul, Magpie Robin is the most 'dignified bird welcome in the garden, besides being the best songster among domestic birds. The River Tern is definitely a graceful bird skimming the surface of water, splashing its wings, thus confusing its querry, eventually picking up fish, swallowing the head first, and flying off as if nothing happened. The Black Partridge, known as 'Kala Teetar' in Urdu is a pet and also singled out as delicious meat. The devout Muslim address the birds, 'Subhan-teri-qudrat' ('Praise to the Allah for its creation'). Emperor Babur addressed the Black Partridge as 'Sher-dream-Shahrah' (milk and little sugar). To a grocer, it is no more than 'lay-noon-tail-adrak' ('Buy salt, oil and ginger', in other words, cook as a meal).

The other two favourite birds are Parakeet and Koel. Parakeets are completely domesticated birds, which have even learned to mimic human beings. They learn to speak a few familiar words repeatedly. The favourite phrases taught to them include 'miya mithoo' and 'tota chasham' (having the eye of a parrot). Parakeet is a favourite bird and found in rich and poor families alike.

Koel has a distinguishing two-syllable whistling shriek, 'Koel-ko-el' or 'ku-oo-ku-oo' can be heard all over the countryside and home gardens with groves of mangoes. It finds its resting place or 'dera' on banyan, pipal, ber and mulberry trees. Crow is a notorious trickster, but Koel matches her in this department and lets the crow incubate her own eggs. The bird's life is an essential panorama around the Indus river.

Fresh Water Dolphins

Here is a tale truer than fiction. The Indus is several million years old. It used to fall in the Tethys Sea, way before the Himalayas and Indian subcontinent ever existed. The marine dolphins used to travel to the Indus to lay eggs. It was an annual ritual. Suddenly there happened the epoch-making tectonic upheavels upsetting the geological balances. The poor marine dolphin was trapped in the river system. It was forced to adopt itself into the fresh-water dolphin. Thus was born the dolphin that turned the river Indus into a unique brand. It is one of four fresh-water dolphin in the world. The evolutionary story of adaptation of marine into fresh-water dolphin is in the Indus.[11]

The river dolphin is fated to furrow a lonely furrow in its murky atmosphere. Visibility in the river system is restricted to no more than 2 to 4 cms.

The Indus river dolphin is a part of the world heritage and cause for much celebration. It remains an endangered species. There are no more than a few hundred river dolphins to be found now. The construction of the Sukkur Barrage Dam (1932) is the cause for worry. It prevents the dolphins from moving freely.

What makes it so unique? The sudden atmospheric changes called for a heavy price from the dolphins. It found itself trapped in the muddy waters of the newly-forming river system. It lost its eyesight, but through the evolutionary process, it learned to live without its sight. Indus river dolphin (biological name:Platanista Congestica Minor) has developed a sharpened faculty called 'echo-location' for the ease of hunting and navigation. It is able to detect matter via sound waves.

Palla Fish

Palla fish is a close competitor to the river dolphin and definitely exceeds in its popularity among the common folks. It is no other than the Bengal Hilsa. Essentially a sea-water fish, the reproduction urge makes it turn towards the direction of the river. The compulsive urge makes it travel hundreds of miles inside for breeding and food. It is believed to travel in a straight line and turns back when faced with an obstacle. The construction of Sukkur River Barrage has interrupted its free run, which has now been reduced exactly by one-third of its previous travel run to Multan.

Its technical name is Tenualosa Illisha.

The hilsa or palla fish, as known to Sindhis, has been adopted by them as 'the ancient symbol of a "riverine paradise"'. Zindapir island near Sukkur is a national shrine for both Hindus and Muslims. There is a long-held belief among the pilgrims here that the palla fish travels all the way from the sea to say prayers at the Zindapir and pays respects to the river god. Could it be credible, because Sajjad Nashin claims 'until recently, palla fish would swim up the river from the sea in order to salute the panoply of Indian river saints at Sukkur'.[12]

The fauna and flora of the Indus has a fascination of its own due to its biodiversity. Imagine more than a million waterfowl wintering at the reservoirs of the river and its associates by following the Indus Flyway 4 by sheer instinct. Equally fascinating is the story of the river dolphin adapting to a different environment and thus surviving for countless millennia. Equally are to be singled out date palm and camel as the very foundation of life in the river basin.

Sindhu Steeds

Horses and not camels were the flavor of the Indus region during ancient times. Camel is not native to this country. It is a foreign import from Mesopotamia and other Arab lands. Horses from the Sindhu region are frozen in time in the great classics of the Rigveda and the Mahabharata. These references are not merely generic to horses but they are specific to the Indus region. The Sindhu steeds, probably bred in Sindh Sagar or the Thal desert(in Pakistan Punjab), were imported by numerous kingdoms in the east, west and south of the subcontinent.

The Rigveda is fulsome in praise of the Sindhu steed. There are repeated references to "rich in good steed is Sindhu", or "Sindhu has yoked her car... drawn by steeds", or the roar of the racing Sindhu drawing the attention of the gods, or comparing Sindhu to ebullient horses, or as "they kissed the ground" or "the horses lightly touched the ground as they ran", in it.

The Sindhu river is addressed by several names in the great classics. It has been called, 'the runner' and 'the horse', 'the mother' and 'the child of the mountains'. It has also been compared to a beautiful mare – 'a sight to see' – in Hymn 75 of Book X of Rigveda, 'sparkling, bright with mighty splendour' and 'the quickest of the quick', 'roaring as it runs'. The rishis who contributed their poetic might to the Rigveda must have been romantic at heart,

Mahabharata Flavour

Mahabharata produces enough evidence to support the case for the renowned steeds of the Sindhu region. The ancient tale of love, separation, struggle and eventual union of Nala, the brave king of the Nishadas, and the beautiful princes Damayanti of Vidarbha, spans a substantial part of the Indralok Abhigamana Parva of the Mahabharata. The union of the two lovelorn is made possible, thanks to the quick-footed steeds from the Sindhu region belonging to king Rituparna of Ayodhya. Those steeds were trained by horse-trainer King Nala under the assumed name of Bahuka. They were required to travel long distance between Ayodhya and the city of Kundira, the capital of Vidarbha, in a day. The horses were equal to the task, much to the credit of the land of their origin. Bahuka harnessed four Sindhu horses to the royal chariot and made sure, they made it. The horses chosen were 'lean' but 'energetic and stray', 'born in a noble lineage', 'of good conduct' and 'they were bereft of inauspicious marks'. 'Their nostrils were wide and their jaws were big. They were from the region of the Sindhu and were as swift as the wind'[13]

Pandava Connection

Yudhishtira, the eldest Pandava, described as 'the lord of kings and bull among the Kuru lineage', decided...to assume the title of the 'universal emperor', or, in other words, 'A consecrated king who wished to achieve the characters of an emperor'. He dispatched his four younger brothers in various directions–north, south, east and west to assure compliance by other kingdoms. Accordingly, his younger brother, Arjuna, ('Kounteya, bull among men') headed towards the north. He was eminently successful in his mission, and he 'conquered the inner mountains, the outer mountains and the upper mountains' in and around the Indus territories. He defeated his enemies and subdued numerous kingdoms. He also extracted symbolic compensation from the subjugated kingdoms including 'eight horses that had the colour of a parrot's breast. There were some others the colour of peacock and still others that had both the colours'.[14]

Horses and more horses were the flavours of the times; they were perhaps considered worth fighting a war by the Pandavas. Yudhishtira, the incorrigible and compulsive gambler, had also no hesitation in placing his estates in the Indus region at stake, 'O Soubala (Shakuni)! I have many cattle, horses, milch cows, sheep and goats, of many species, to the east of he Sindhu. O king! These are my riches that I will play you for'.[15] He lost the bet as usual.

Thus horses were not only ingrained in the mind of the succeeding generation of the Baloch, but they were in the consciousness of their predecessors of distant yore like the Pandavas, and equally they were in the consciousness of their Nishada predecessors like King Nala. More definitely, horses come out as the flagbearers of the Saraiki homeland.

Indus in History

Four great civilizations were founded on the banks of the Indus, which in turn constituted the very found ation of pan-Indian civilization and culture: (1) Indus Valley Civilization; (2) Rigvedic Civilization; (3) Epic Age, and 4) Buddhist Renaissance. Those are listed in a proper sequential order. There is a spatial movement from south to northerly direction. The epiccentres of these civilizations were Mohenjodaro, Multan and Taxila respectively. The epicentre of the Rigvedic civilization is, however, not known. There were probably several epicentres due to the decentralized nature of the polity. The Indus Valley Civilization was centered around Mohenjodaro on the east bank of the river Indus, bordering the dusty and dry Balochistan. It was the epicentre of one of the most striking urban settlements of its own times. The imagination employed in designing its architecture and urban planning is mind-boggling. The Mohenjodaro civilization speaks with thousand tongues. Over 800 sites are known to exist in the entire river basin–south, north, east and west. Several sites have been discovered as faraway as the Potohar region, bordering Jammu and Kashmir.

While the epicentre of the Indus Valley Civilization was in Sindh province, the Rigvedic civilization which followed it was confined to Sapta Sindhu boundaries, lying between the Indus on one side and the Sarasvati river on the other. It definitely did not extend beyond the Panchanad. There is no recorded evidence to establish relations between the Indus valley and Rigvedic civilizations. There is, however, no dispute about the former preceding the latter, or occupying different spatial and temporal locations.

There is also another marked difference between the two civilizations. While the Indus Valley Civilization was urban dominated, the Rigvedic civilization was rurally oriented. There is no record of monumental structures and cities in the Rigveda. Rishis, Munis and sages were resident at their ashrams usually located by the side of the rivers. The scholarly discourse was orally communicated with no recorded words. The Rigvedic scholar had no use of recorded knowledge and hence no written records could be located. Intellect was their strong point. It required no paraphernalia of city-bred academic institution whereas Mohenjodaro remains to be deciphered.

Rigveda does not provide much evidence to find the connections. It is a matter of speculation as to why the Rigvedic civilization did not cross into Sindh properly. It was definitely Sindhu-river centric. This is a matter of conjecture, but history does not live by intelligent conjectures alone. It also remains to be investigated, why the civilization showed distinct tendency to travel south, but not westwards. There must be compelling reasons for this phenomenon, but this eludes the present day historians. It is equally true, civilizations are volcanic by nature, surfacing suddenly and violently and then disappearing. Another Alexander Cunnigham needs to be born to unravel the mystery. Along with him should be born another Frederich Max Müller to have another look at the Rigveda. The invasions, which were frequent in this part of the world, must have disturbed political and social balances. There is also a positive side to it. The invasions were definitely destabilizing, but in the long run those provided the much-needed stimulus for a change. The process of rejuvenation tends to be accelerated due to sudden and tectonic destabilizations at regular intervals.

'Adyasthana'[16]

The Aryans did not disappear but became the ruling class expanding to the farthest east and the Rigvedic Punjab. Multan, however, continued to be the centre of attention during the epic period, with a difference. It indeed constitutes the third phase in the evolution of our cultural framework for the Indic civilizations. Even the name of Multan speaks for itself. 'Mulasthan' was the most important centre of Sun worship indicating its connection with nature -worshiping Rigvedic Aryans, as it was to be the epicentre of Sufism in later times. The remains of the Sun temple still remain. The famous temple has crowned the citadel of Multan. The Chinese traveller Xuanzang was impressed by the magnificent temple with a golden statute, with offering from kings all over the country. At one time, it was considered the Varanasi of the north.

The temple was called the 'Adyasthana', or the 'First Shrine'. The temple and the city of Multan are a living monument to the Rigvedic civilization. Yet it is a closed chapter of Indian history. One needs to be reminded that the Rigvedic Aryans were worshippers of nature and natural phenomenon and the Sun symbolized this relationship. Multan was originally called 'Casyapa-pura', founded by Kashyapa, the father of 12 sun-gods, thus establishing a close connection with the Sun. The second name is 'Hansapura', named after the son of the original founder, who is famous for denying the omnipresence of god Vishnu (a post-Vedic god). Vishnu is an epic-level god as opposed to the Sun god of the Rigvedic vintage.

The third name is that of 'Prahaladpura', named after Prahalad, son of Hiranyakashipu. Prahalad is a folk hero even today. He was, however, a worshipper of Vishnu. Multan is also known as 'Sambhapura', named after Sambha, the son of Lord Krishna (of Mahabharata fame). He, however, worshipped the Sun god, because he was cured of leprosy by the sun. Hidden behind the fact was an ongoing conflict between the epic god Vishnu and Sun god, as is the running theme of the Puranas.

The city was called 'Adyashana', named after the sun god. The other name for it is 'Mitra'. Alexander's historians have named it 'Mula' which rhymes with Multan. Ptolemy has called the city 'Kaspeira' and Herodotus addresses it as 'Kaspaturas'. It is also called 'Malasthanpura'. Finally, the city came to be known as Multan, drawn from the root term 'mul'. It also means radish.

Indus Valley Civilization, Rigvedic Civilization and the Epic Age (of Multan,), are to be viewed in unity. Those constitute a triangle still mystifying and buffeted by confusing signals, and opens up new areas for debate and discussions.

Buddhist Renaissance

There is light at the end of the tunnel in the fourth phase which concerns the Buddhist age of enlightenment on the banks of the Indus, at Taxila, in extreme north-west next to the ancient town of Hund and Attock. Both were considered the crossing points and 'bridges' of the Indus. Taxila, Hund and Attock are strategically located on the Uttarapatha (the northern road) linking Central Asia and Mainland China with Patliputra, the roadway traversed by invaders and traders and scholars alike. Buddhist monasteries and libraries existed on both sides of the Indus.

Equally, it is not to be forgotten that Taxila was situtated at the cross roads of ancient Sindhudesh (Saraiki homeland) and the Gandhara geographical junction

The fourth phase is a unstated continuation of the third phase. Multan in its own time was the centre of trade, religious and spiritual sanctity and the heartbeat of intellect. So it came to be true of Taxila, a centre of political institutions, flourshing trade centre and intellectual debates and discussions. Taxila has also been exposed to ideas from abroad.

Some of the finest minds that India had produced were associated with the famous Taxila university, both in case of students and teachers. The university had on rolls students like Chanakya, author of the Arthashastra and the master of political strategy and tactics, Panini, the famed grammarian, Vishnu Sharma, author of the Panchatantra and Charaka, the author of the texts on Ayurvedic medicine.

It was said to be a university with distinguished teachers like Panini and Chanakya. The Gandhara art is world famous with distinct Hellenic influences weaved into the Indian artistic tradition. While Taxila was no doubt the foremost centre of Vedic and Buddhist learnings, its surrounding of Gandhara and Swat (on the western bank of the river) were known for their facility to speak Sanskrit fluently, Uttarapatha was the renowned market place for the exchange of ideas.

The catalytic agent in this transformation was Ashoka the Great (died: 232 BC), who left a legacy for perpetual celebration. He changed the nature of the dialogue. He went back to the days of Indus Valley Civilization by adopting a written script as the means of communication with the large mass. He must have been an advocate of universal literacy, and for that purpose he selected the people of north-west bordering the river Indus as his channels of communication. He gifted a script to India called the Brahmi script.

On the assumption that the written words are the true message, he installed edicts all over India. He chose builders, sculptors and scribes to install the edicts as far as south India with their famous signatures in Khorashti script to immortalize them. Those who had drunk the water of Indus by following the traditions of rishis, munis and sages, their ancestors of the past, were being treated as gurus for generations to come. Those were indeed golden years for Buddhism as practised in that part of the world. This phase came to a glorious close on the eve of the advent of Islam in north-west as the chakra of dhamma and history turned away from the river Indus and north-west India. Taxila flourished between the 6th century BC–5th century AD. It was closely connected to the two provinces of Uttarapatha, namely, Gandhara and Uddiyana (Swat).

Living Traditions

Living tradition is folk tradition with wisdom to be discovered in repeating itself. In fact, creativity is nothing, but endless repetition with a mind of its own. You need to go back to your past to chalk out your future. History is indeed an open book, as well as a living example awaiting to be emulated. There is so much to be learnt from the pattern of Harappans, textile weavers of Mohenjodaro and the Mohanas of Sukkur and Ghazi Ghat, who perpetuated the Indus Valley Civilization traditions by repeating it in day-to-day life.

The Indus boat-people were called 'Mohanas' in the entire lower Indus basin. This also goes by the name of 'Mallah', 'Mirhab' and 'Mirani'. He was part of the living tradition (going back to the Indus Valley Civilization). Mohanas spent all their lives on their wooden sailing boats which they plied all the day to carry passengers and loads. Their families lived either on the boats or by the river banks in makeshift cottages. The shape of the boats and practices in general has not changed much since ancient times. Given the choice they will prefer living all their life in the same manner.

The peasant of the lower Indus basin is very conservative in dressing in the same manner as his ancestors. There is a famous sculpture of a Sindhi peasant found at Mohenjodaro as an exact replica of his present-day progeny:

'The sculpture of the bearded man...wears a shawl engraved with a trefoil pattern and encrusted with traces of red pigment–a garment similar to the red and indigo *ajrak*, a hand-printed scraf worn by every Sindhi peasant'.[17]

Practice must have its practical uses, but unfortunately it has been followed without attempts at innovation. The reference to indigo is to be noted. The colour has been a native of the subcontinent and cultivated indigenously for centuries together. The two great trees of India, namely, 'peepul' and 'neem' were natives of the Indus Valley Civilization. So is the red brick which is a hallmark of building constructed all over India in present times. Even present-day Mohanas sail in the boats as those of their ancestors. The bullock carts 'plying on old [rough] tracks for grain and fodder transportation are the same as used by Indus people'.[18] The logic in this case is fallacious. The rough tracks in the countryside have not changed. They call for change in attitudes to match the requirements of infrastructure to improve bullock carts.

Even the women have refused to change. Compare the bangles worn by women residing in villages surrounding Mohenjodaro. Compare the two situations and you will find hardly any change over millennia. It is equally true of patterns which look so colourful and charming, with nearly the same type of motifs painted as in prehistoric motifs. Have a close look at the famous figurine of the dancing girl. She is a sure model for contemporary dancing girls, loaded with bangles.

All this stuff must have evolved after thinking over centuries and experimented upon, to snuff out the rough edges. Lots of out-of-box thinking must have contributed to the ultimate designs. Imagine the craftsmen of old times rising from their graves, who start giving lessons to craftsmen with stress on innovation. Those craftsmen are now dead souls, but they have left a trail of living tradition for the contemporary and future generations. The dead don't speak, but they live through their immortal products and by being interpreted properly.

River of Poetry

The last word shall rest with Annemarie Schimmel who has called the River Indus, the 'River of Poetry'. She is a true student of Sufism and has compared the Indus to the almighty god. Indus was, indeed, the living god for the people of the lower Indus. This was true of the Hindus and Muslims alike. While it was a 'Living Pir' for the Muslims, it was worshipped as the 'River God' by the Hindus. Perhaps there is no rational explanation for the beliefs. It is possible to view the river in secular terms with spiritual indentures:

"The Indus has many faces. It was the source of healing; sacred water in ancient times: it was a symbol for the overflowing Divine Grace among the Sindhi Sufis, or the destructive power to which Sohni met her end and yet, in Shah Latif's interpretation even this fact points to the divine ocean in which the soul should be finally annhiliated, for, as Rumi says, when 'the wave comes, that remembrance of the Primordial Covenant between God and man' (Sura 7:172) it shatters the fragile boat of human existence. In modern times, the poets, far from using religious symbolism, express the hope of taming the river in order to ameliorate people's lot, and at last the poets are faced with the constant danger from the Indus despite the technical progress, so that the river seems to no longer reveal Divine Grace.[19]

The profound statement refers not only to Rumi's thinking, the Koran and Vedanta philosophy, it also places the thinking of Shah Latif, Sarmad, Baba Farid, Bulleh Shah, Warris Shah, the Sikh Gurus and the Vaishnava Bhaktas in the same class by speaking through the voice of River Indus. It also speaks for the Buddhist monks who at one time inhabited both the banks of the Indus in Gandhara and Uddiyana (Swat).

Annemarie Schimmel is a modern Sufi poetess involved in deciphering Sufi verses. According to her, Indus can be referred to as the divine grace and the divine wrath, simultaneoulosy, by placing them on the same pedestal. It has been rightly said that the Indus gives both 'dukh' and 'sukh' to those who seek its grace. The Indus is constantly in the neutral gear. It must be like the god almighty himself, contrary to what the ordinary folks are made to believe. For that reason alone, it is believed that it is best to avoid confrontation with god, and river (and the mad dog) for our well-being. They are supplicated, respected, honoured and worshipped from a safe distance.

Section - III
MAHABHARATA GENES

5

The Indus Fraternity

IMAGINE the wars between India and Pakistan in contemporary times, and then transpose yourself to the Mahabharata war. It was a war between the kingdoms of the Indus basin arraigned on one side, and those of the Gangetic plain on the other. It was also north-west confronting the east of the subcontinent. It heralded a civilizational shift from the lands of the Vedas towards the east, towards the subcontinental landmass.

It was also a war of ideas and class war to some extent. The rise of the Jogi sects, Jainism and Buddhism, enthralled the masses. They had tremendous populist appeal. They questioned the domination of ritual performing, caste-based classes. The absolute authority of dominating classes like the Kshatriyas and Brahmins was being challenged for the first time. There was a dearth of new ideas emerging from the east. The east wind had begun to prevail over the north wind, both in terms of power and ideas. The northern kingdoms had begun to play a peripheral role in the affairs of the subcontinent.

The Mahabharata war made the Rigvedic lands of the Indus region a mere appendage. A host of foreign invasions over the subsequent centuries, detached the north from other parts of the subcontinent. There are, thus, historical reasons to justify the hostilites between India and Pakistan. The main supporters of the defeated Kauravas hailed from the north-west region. The six kingdoms included Gandhara, Sindhu, Kekaya, Shalva and Bahlika besides Kamboja. These six ancient kingdoms constitute the entire territories of contemporary Pakistan. The Pandavas had their main supporters in Panchala, Kashi, Magadha, Koshala, Chedi and the Yadavas, all of them being the lands east of the Sindhu, within mainland India. The Kauravas and the Pandavas are no more, but the succeeding generations have harboured the hostilities through several millennia.

Authentic Classic

This raises the larger question of the authenticity of the Mahabharata. Did the events mentioned in the classic come to pass? Did the characters like Arjuna, Krishna, Shakuni and Jayadratha mentioned in it exist in real life?

There are differing views on the subject. No doubt, there exist exaggerated images of characters and events in it. The epic is not history in the classical sense of the term, but it is more authentic than the other epic, Ramayana. Its characters behave more like normal human beings. Even its gods and goddesses have foibles common to the ordinary human beings. It symbolizes the spirit of India's past and its present, and it shall continue to be Brand India in the future as well.

The Mahabharata belongs to the oral tradition and was not recorded for a long time. It was conveyed by word-of-mouth in actual practice. It is a voluminous work of nearly 100,000 shlokas or couplets. It is believed to have been compiled by various authorities over a period of about a thousand years. There are considerable interpolations in it. The word 'Jaya' was the title of the original and shorter version of the Mahabharata. It was originally believed to be composed by the Kshatriyas of Potohar region, near Islamabad. Taxila, the famous seat of learning, has its locale there. It was the celebration of the Pandava hegemony over the lands of the Bharatas. No wonder, Gandhara and the Sindhu heroes like Shakuni and Jayadratha come out very badly. They were painted as unrelenting villains. Shakuni alone has been held singly responsible for the destructive Mahabharata war. Besides, they were on the side of the defeated Kauravas.

Interpolations Galore

The maximum amount of interpolations was done by the domineering Brahmins, who had gained strength and prestige after the practical decimation of the Kshatriyas, especially by the Bhargavas, the descendants of Bhrigu Rishi, who took over. They also introduced gods and goddesses who descended frequently on earth to interfere and arbitrate as well as take sides with human beings. The Bhagavat Gita was their ideological flag-bearer. It was probably interpolated into the main text. Obeisance is paid in particular to Krishna and Arjuna as the incarnations of gods Narayan and Nara. Krishna was the favorite god, upgraded to the status of God Almighty. The Pandava brothers were born out of *niyoga vivaha* (temporary liaison), but in the interpolated version, they were painted as resulting from liaison with super gods like Sun and Dharma.

When reduced to the bare minimum, as a powerful story of conflict between the cousins, the Mahabharata is an unparallel record of human beings in conflict situation, but rising above it in the final end. The Mahabharata is not a religious treatise. That is why it has been called Smriti (recorded) and not Shruti (the word of God). It is not history in the contemporary sense of the term. No doubt, it should be possible to reconstruct the history of the Indus region in its hoary past by picking and choosing through careful reading of this classic. It is no doubt stronger on geography than history.

Reconstructing the Past

Since the centre of gravity of the Indus civilization had shifted east by the time of the Mahabharata, with Hastinapur and Indraprastha (modern Delhi) as its epicenters, Indus, the favorite river of the Vedic people, received much less attention than the Ganges. In the Tirtha-Yatra Parva, Yudhishthira is advised to visit Dwarka in Gujarat, to pray where the Sindhu and Sarasvati rivers united with the ocean in his time. It has been termed as the 'king of tirthas'. Remember its echo in the poetry of great Sufi Sindhi poet Shah Abdul Latif? He was an exponent of 'Sindhyat' or the Greater Sindhko visiting the Runn of Kutch, where in mythical times, the River Indus was believed to have joined the sea(the Tethys, later the Arabian sea). The wise Yudhishthira was also to go on pilgrimage to the Panchanad (the sangam of five rivers of the Punjab with Indus).

There are numerous citation in the classic, to establish the identity of Sindhudesh within Jambudvipa, Bharatavarsha or the Indic framework. There are paens sung in praise of the Saindaha horses, imported from the Indus region. Maximum number of Saindaha horses were the casuality of the Mahabharata war. There was the mention of importing 30,000 Brahmins who settled in ancient Sindh at the instance of Queen Duhshala. Eventually, they came to dominate political and social life of the region. They were overthrown by Arab invaders during medieval times due to their tyrannical behavior with their subjects. It is, thus, possible to go back and forth in history by careful reading of the Mahabharata.

Eternal Sindhu

The Indus river, known as Sindhu to the ancients, was the centre of the world around which the history and geography of the Indus people remains entangled. The ancient inhabitants were known to be the Sindhu-Sauvirahs (also spelled as Sovira, Souveera and Sauvirah). The region has been described as Sindhu-Saindhva.

The ruler of Sindhudesh during the Mahabharata times was King Jayadratha. He had been described variously by different designations, but all of these were a play around the term 'Sindhu'. Even the horses imported from the region were called Saindaha horses. The term predated the Rigvedic times, and probably originated among the predecessor non-Aryan communities. There was also a mention of the Sindhu-Sauvirah in other ancient classics, like the Ramayana. This play upon the term 'Sindhu' is repetitive in the Mahabharata. Jayadratha has been described as 'the king of Sindhu and Sauvirah' as well as 'the king of Sindhu, Saivira and Shibi'. He is also described as 'the king of Saindhava', and 'the head of Saindhava Kshatriyas'. No river in the world, not excluding the Ganges, is in the consciousness of the people of the region as the Indus river through historical times. The tradition underlies the important recognition given to the aboriginal residents known as Saindhava. It also establishes the truth that the term 'Sindhu' is pre-Aryan. The interplay of Souvira-Sindhu goes to prove that due recognition was given to the federal structure of the kingdom composed of Souvira, Sindhu and Shibi (modern Sibi or Sivi is situated deep inside Balochistan) regions. There was a high degree of continuity in state structure, considering that Jayadratha claimed to have been 'born in the 17th noble lineage'.

The Saraiki Connection

The Mahabharata is the most relevant *itihasa* of all times for all seasons. The Saraikis may take an inspiration or two from the great classic to discover their own roots. How about substituting the contemporary term 'Saraiki' with the ancient term 'Sindhu-Saindhava' as the mark of identity for the Indus people? The mother term 'Siraiki' is totally inappropriate. It is a mere dialect, spoken by Punjabi and Baloch migrants settled in north Sindh, also known as Siro-(literally head) Siraiki language of the up-river (north Sindh). It requires serious and urgent consideration by the promoters of brand Saraiki.

Past into Future

Thus the probe into the ancient past proves to be a useful exercise. The three chapters on the Indus people are an unintended tribute to the remarkable personalities of Shakuni, Jayadratha, Gandhari and Duhshala. At least two of them have been tarred as villains of the Mahabharata. The great classic is a partisan story, portraying the Pandavas as the honourable ones, compared with the disgraceful Kauravas. Shakuni was as great a diplomat as his rival Krishna, ranged on the other side. Both of them were, however, not above board.

Similarly, Jayadratha was a remarkable ruler of a vast kingdom and allied with were at least ten other associate kingdoms. He was number 17th in his lineage, stressing continuity and stability in his kingdom. The Sindhudesh has been described as rich and prosperous, besides trading across the oceans. The two women, Gandhari (mother) and Duhshala(daughter), were remarkable characters as well as worthy consorts with capacity for fair and objective judgment of turbulent events taking place around them. They could be considered worthy candidates as role models for the present-day Saraiki movement. They shall also rank among distinguished women of ancient times, having left their footprint on the pages of India's ancient history.

The Mahabharata is popularly attributed to Maharishi Vyasa, who had his pupil Vaishampayana record his words faithfully for future generations. Actually, it was a collective effort spread well over a thousand years to communicate it orally. It is a thriller for all times and an unwinding symphonic poem, composed of multiple notes of discontent woven into a harmonic whole. The Indus people were also represented in this musical symphony, with even the Saindaha horses in the chorus. Eventually, it has been turned into a black comedy of all times. Above all, it is, essentially, a secular classic debating the core competency of the concept of dharma as the arbiter of human existence. The Indus people have yet to recover from the shock. Here goes the story:

Indus People

The Indus people residing on both banks of the Indus river were the true legates of the Bharatas, the ancient people of northern India. They were major players in 'the war of the Bharatas'. In other words, Mahabharata was their playground. It was a tragedy waiting to hapeen in the 'home of the Vedas' or 'the land of the seven rivers'. The Mahabharata war is dated anywhere between BC3500-1000. The text was composed between 300 BC and 300AD. It was possible to trace the genealogy of the Bharatas backwards to King Yayati, the common ancestor of the Yadavas, the Kauravas and the Gandharas. King Yayati was Bheeshma ancestor, twenty-nine generations before him.

The Indus people resided in Gandhara (with its capital situated in Kandahar) on the right bank of the Sindhu. They were also settled in Sindhudesh on its left bank, presently the homeland of the Saraiki people. The respective boundaries of Gandhara and Sindhudesh shrank and expanded with the flux of time. Pushkalavati (Peshawar) and Takshasila

(Taxila) were prominent cities of Gandhara located to the right and the left of the river. Those cities are believed to have been founded by the son of Bharata of Ramayana fame. Gandhari was the daughter of King Soubala of Gandhara. It is said that there would have been no Mahabharata without the machinations of prince Shakuni of Gandhara. Similarly, Sindhu-Sauvirahs, original inhabitant of Sindhudesh, were an important ally of the Kauravas as the Panchalas were of the Pandavas. Their king, Jayadratha, was son-in-law of Dhritarashtra and Gandhari, and husband to their only daughter Duhshala. Duhshala's grandson was a potential claimant to the throne of Hastinapur as well.

Gandharan Panorama

Gandhara has been recognized integral to the land of the Bharatas since ancient times. It has been referred to in the Vedas. It has the Bharata blood connection through King Yayati. Gandharans were said to be the best horsemen in their times. Gandhara was the opening to the world. Somehow, they have remained different from the rest of us. Arjuna spoke for all of us during his first visit to Shakuni's land, 'even from a distance, behind each rock I sensed a hostile presence'[1] Herodotus had made a note of it, while writing about the vast Persian Empire of Darius I (BC 521-485), divided into twenty satrapies. Gandhara was his 19th satrapy, while the 'Indians', the residents of the Indus valley or Sindhudesh formed 'the 20th Satrapy'. To be fair, the epic gives us contradictory signals about them. It does not hesitate to praise them for their 'valour, antiquity and learning', but at the same time, it portrays them as 'low, degraded and barbarian people' (XII.200.4.0). Karna goes to the extent of calling them 'sinful'.

Arjuna Speaketh

Arjuna provided some warped but fairly accurate image of Gandhara of ancient times which appear peculiarly contemporary. He was on his journey of discovery, accompanied by the Ashwamedha (sacrificial) horse, immediately following the conclusion of the Mahabharata war, to affirm the Pandava hegemony over the lands of the Bharatas. He saw a vision of 'treachery' and 'hostile presence, lurking in every nook and corner', and he was so overwhelmed by the 'fever spirits' in the prevailing atmosphere of Gandhara that he had refused to believe that the Gandharans belonged to 'our Vedic living'. One of the Gandhara principalities was known as Ikshvaku, thus claiming the Gandharan connection to the lineage of Rama of Ramayana fame.

Arjuna had to face a cavalcade of about 2,000 Gandharan horsemen sweeping him off his feet, 'screaming and shouting, brandishing their whips' and slashing right and left, playing the 'unAryan ritual' of handling a mangled caracas of a bloodied lamb, and subsequently celebrating with a communal meal of 'stewed mutton, which to (Arjuna's) great discomfort, was served in a communal dish. The men around (him) plunged their dusty fingers into the meat, then ate and sometimes licked their fingers to prepare them for the next foray into the dish'.[2] The past, present and future truly merged in the land of Gandhara. Such events had happened in the past, are happening today and shall repeat themselves in the Gandhara that is eternal, motionless and repetitive. That is the Gandhara of Shakuni for you.

Sindhu Saindhava

They were more like us. The Sindhu Sauvirahs were the ancient inhabitants of Sindhudesh. They are not mentioned in the Vedas. Presumably, they are believed to be pre-Aryans, and identified with the Panis of the Rigveda. We are also not sure if they were the ancestors of contemporary Saraikis, now inhabitants of Sindhudesh. We, however, know for sure that they monopolized inland and sea trade. They were for sure the ancestors of present-day Sindhi traders. Panini mentions them as a tribe. Buddhist literature mentions Roruva(_ka), which is identified with Aror in modern Sindh as the Sauvira capital.

By gleaning the vast spectrum of the Mahabharata, it is possible but just barely, to shrift information about the state of the Sindhu-Saindhava kingdom. Jayadratha has been addressed as heading the Sindhu army consisting of the Sivi, Souvira and Sindhu tribes returning from Hastinapur and proceeding to the Sindhudesh kingdom, capital of Souvira. On his way to his capital, he headed towards Madra to get married to cement his bonds with the Shalva kingdom. He was also accompanied by his powerful allies including King Katishkaya 'the king of the Shibis', the prince of Kuninda ('of the mountains') King Kshemankara of Trigarat and the son of Soubala of Gandhara, who was himself the king of the Ikshvaku.

Jayadratha has been described as the king of 'Sindhu and Souvira' presiding over 'the Saindhava and the Souvira hosts'. He is also mentioned as the head of the Saindhava Kshatriyas. He is equally described as a powerful king heading a confederacy of several neighbouring kingdoms. His father, King Vriddhakshatra, was widely regarded and respected in the entire Bharatavarsha. His Saindhava warriors were 'all fierce in battle'. Son Jayadratha had expanded his sphere of influence by working out a marriage alliance with the powerful Kauravas and the neighbouring Gandhara. He prescribed over lands which have been described as rich and prosperous. Jayadratha was also very proud of his pedigree and boasted, 'We, too, … belong by birth to the seventeen high clans, and are endowed with the six royal qualities'[3] [The six acts of a king are 'peace, war, marching, halting, sowing dissension and seeking protection'.]

Portrayal of Jayadratha

There are varying views about the character of Jayadratha and hence it is difficult to come to a balanced judgment. The protagonists for and against are divided down the line. At one moment Krishna addressed him as 'the heroic ruler of the Sindhus', but in another context, he has been described as 'the wicked-souled wretch'. Bheema had no doubt about Jayadratha being 'evil-minded', 'the sinful wretch' and 'the wicked king Jayadratha'. Even the gentle Yudhishthira called him 'the preceptor of evil deeds', after his failed attempt to kidnap Draupadi while crossing the Kamyaka forest. Draupadi, who suffered humiliation at his hands, had the last word on him. She called Jayadratha 'the crab that was conceived for his destruction'. There is also enough evidence to contradict the negative image. On his very birth, the divine voice predicted for him his future, 'as one of the foremost rulers of Kshatriyas', who would 'always be worshipped by heroes'. He had also received a boon from the three-eyed Siva, to be almost invincible in battlefield. He came to be known as 'the ruler of the Souvira' and 'the famous king of Sindhus' of great beauty of person, possessed of black-shinning locks. His standard had the device of a large boar in silver. At one time, Draupadi had tried to placate him, but managed to depict him also as unbiased. In the Draupadi Harana, she addressed him as 'O Sauvira' 'the ruler of the Suviras' and 'the king of Sindhu and Sauvira' and other countries, besides addressing him as 'solo ruler (of) the rich countries of Saivira, Sivi and Sindhu' and other neighbouring territories. This goes to establish his identity during the times of the Mahabharata. He has also been variously addressed as 'the famous king of the Sindhus', 'the king of the Sindhus', 'the king of Saindhava' and 'the Saindhava' in the Mahabharata. There is also no doubt from reading of the epic that Souvira was the preferred term as compared to Sindhu in popular parlance.

Sindhu Horse

Saindaha is described as the breed of horses and salt, special to Sindhudesh in the epic. To the east of Kalabagh on the Indus river, the triangle of land widens in the south between the Indus and the Panchanad (merging point of its five tributaries). For centuries together, it has been called the Sind Sagar Doab. It has been good enough for the breeding of horses for several millennia. Little else grows there except acres of wild grass. Most of the horses for the Mahabharata war must have come from the Sindh Sagar Doab and Kamboja in the extreme north of Gandhara. The horses of Bahlika (Central Punjab) have also come for praise. For instance, the Pandava brothers pursued king Jayadratha through the forest of Kamyaka, and after capturing him, headed towards their hermitage riding 'excellent' chariots, 'yoked to Saindhava steeds that had the speed of the wind or a storm', so it is graphically described in the Draupadi Harana of the great classic.

Horses have been idiolized in the vedic tradition. The Ashwamedha horse is considered the personification of Parajapati, the father of all creatures on earth. Ashwin the twin rulers of the horses in heaven, are considered the 'lords of the joyous elevation and the vital power'. Nakula and Sahadeva, the youngest of the Pandava brothers, are considered incarnation of the Ashwins. Horses also have a yoga connection. They are metaphors for senses that must be disciplined, or 'yoked through sort of spiritual and physical discipline such as yoga, a word whose basic meaning is 'to yoke', as in 'to yoke' horses to a chariot'.[4] It also symbolized power and aristocracy of the Kshatriyas as the ruling class.

Arjuna loved white horses as much as he distrusted human beings. He was known as Shwetavahana, 'He of the white horses'. His related names were Shwetavana, Shwetahaya and Shwetaseva. He explained the designation in his own words in the Mahabharata, 'while I fight in battle, white, golden-harnessed horses are yoked to my chariot. Therefore, I am He of the White Horses [Shwetavahana]'

Saindaha horses have been considered superior in their speed and swiftness since historical times. In the Ramayana, Rama dispatched his vanaras (monkeys) all over the place including Sindhu-Sauvirah praising its 'remarkable swimming horses'. The Mahabharata has testified to their distinctive qualities time without number.

So have the Jatakas reaffirmed their distinctive features. Even during the times of Buddha, the Sindhu horses continued to be famous. He went around his home town Kapilavastu in a chariot. It has been mentioned that his four horses of lotus colour had been imported from Sindhudesh.

The Saindaha horses are considered auspicious for the distinctive avatar (whorls). Six spots are considered special for the prized horses and those are indeed their signature. Those spots are to be found on their chest, forehead, sides, male organ, back and eyebrows. A horse having one avatar on his body, two each on the side of the chest and one on the back was considered the most auspicious.

Colour of the horse is equally prized as whorls on his body. The four horses of the chariot driven by Krishna were of the type called Savija, having green colour like parrots, Sugriva, with red colour like palasa, Meghapushpa, having the colour like shining clouds and Valahaka with white colour. The Pandavas and the Kauravas had horses with the colour saranga, a tricolour consisting of white, blue and red. Arjuna had a preference for white horses. The horses of parrot-like colour were gifted to Arjuna during his Ashwamedha sojourn to Kamboja. 'On his return from Hastinapur, Jayadratha was accompanied by twelve princes from Souvira, with chariots yoked to red Saindhava steeds with 'the speed of the wind or a stream'. The Saindhava princes returning from sojourn in Hastinapur were driven in red-colour horse chariots. The 18 akshavhnis (armies) during the Mahabharata consisted of supposedly an exaggerated figure of about 1-1.8 million cavalry horses. The extent of decimation may be gauged from the figure of 600 horses remaining in the entire Kaurva and Pandava armies in the middle of the last day of the war. Not only the entire Saindhava army was destroyed, there were equally heavy losses of the famed Saindaha horses in the Mahabharata war. The relief for the Pandava army came on the eve of the Aswamedha Yajna, when Kamboja offered so many horses to replace the decimated cavalry. Never again was Bharatavarsha to recover, to defend itself from foreign aggression, due to lack of quality horses.

While lamenting over the demise of Dronacharya, King Dhritarashtra recounted his numerous accompolishments and went on to sing lyrical paen to the Saindhava horses of distinctive crimson hue attached to his golden chariot. One wonders whether the Saindhava horses were the hidden secret of Drona's achievements as the supreme Kaurva commander during the Mahabharata war. 'How could he have been killed? His large Saindhava horses were crimson. They were garlanded in gold. They were fleet as the wind and were yoked to his chariot. They were beyond reach of all sounds of battle. They were powerful and neighed in joy. Those Saindhavas were controlled and were trained in bearing. They were firm in the midst of battle and never suffered from distress or exhaustion. They withstood the trumpeting of elephants in the battle and the sound of conch shells and drums. They tolerated the twanging of bowstrings and the shower of arrows and weapons. They had conquered their breathing and had conquered pain and they assured victory over the enemy. Those fleet horses quickly bore the chariot of Bharadvaja's son. How could they be overpowered? They were yoked to the golden chariot and controlled by the foremost of men. O son! How could they not cross that Pandava army? He was mounted on a supreme chariot decorated with pure gold'.

Indus Brotherhood

While the Saindhavas and the Gandharas were major players during the time of the Mahabharata due to blood relations and on account of political alliances, there were also other major and minor players. The ancient

Punjab was not only the land of Five Rivers, it was in reality the land of Seven Rivers. The Indus River was no doubt the greatest cementing factor. While Sindhu (Indus) and Sarasvati (now defunct) rivers were located on the peripheries, the other five rivers were mere adjuncts to them. This entire belt was also the land of the Vedas. Both Kekaya and Madra kingdoms were famous for learning and scholarship. Bahlika was the original home of the Kauravas and the Pandvas. There were too many uniting factors in the situation. Geography, history, culture, ethnicity and religions as well as tradition united them. The Mahabharata was the end of the era for the Indus community. The Kambojs were inhabitants of Kafirstan, Badakhshan and the Pamir region. The following chart provides a bird's eye-view of the Mahabharata times.

Indus Community Chart

S. No.	Kingdom	Ruling King	River Junction (Traditional Names)	River Junctions (Contemporary Names)	Doab1
1	Gandhara	Soubala / Shakuni	Sindhu (right & Left banks)	Indus (right and Left banks)	x
2	Sindhu	Jayadratha	Sindhu -Vitasta -Chand-erbhaga	Indus-Jhelum-Chenab	Sindh Sagar
3	Kekaya	Vrihaksha-tra	Vitasta-Chander -bhaga	Jhelum -Chenab	Chad
4	Madra	Shalva	Chanderbhaga -Iravati	Chenab -Ravi	Rachna
5	Bahlika2	Bahlika	Iravati -Vipasa	Ravi -Beas	Bari
6	Bahlika	Bahlika	Vipasa -Shatadru	Beas -Sutlej	Bist
7	x	x	Shatadru -Sarasvati (right bank)	Sutlej -Sarasvati	x
Ancillary Kingdom					
8	Kamboja	Sudakshina	x	x	x

1 Literal Meaning : Two waters or rivers (traditional name for landmass between two / three rivers)

2 Its boundaries coincide with the presentday Haryana.

3 Now a defunct river.

Other Kingdoms

The Indus brotherhood or community was the Kshatriya mafia that ruled and reigned over the entire north India not only during the Mahabharata period, but indeed the pure-breed Kshatriya Bharatas have dominated the scene since the times of king Yayati, nearly 30 generations preceding the great Bheeshma, the common ancestor to Pandavas and Kauravas. It has been truly said, 'You, can tell a Kshatriya from the swagger in his gait'. The rest of the world consisted of Mialechchas (literally foreigners. It also included the natives) or Yavanas (who did not speak Sanskrit. Greeks and Ionians or non-Aryans were included), who were no less barbarians, and those to be pitied for not knowing Sanskrit. In fact, the Bharatas, like the jihadists, believed in death as their destiny, because those who died in battlefield like Duroyadhana, went straight to heaven and were welcomed by nymphs or Apsaras. Thus, death in battle was welcomed by the Kshatriyas. The Gandharans, the Sindhus, the Kekayas, the Madras and the Bahlikas were the true mafia of their times, not only joined by blood ties but equally enjoined to maintain centuries-old exploitative Kshatriya hegemony.

Bahlika and Madra Connection

There was no doubt that several of the rulers were men of honor. King Bahlika stands out among them. The Bahlikas are ancient people who find mention in the Atharvaveda. Probably they were named after prince Bahlika, who was the uncle of Bheeshma. The Bahlika kingdom lay between two doabs of Ravi-Beas and Ravi-Sutlej. The Kuru royal family are believed to have migrated from Vahlika / Bahlika country. Bheeshma always spoke of Bahlika with much affection and indeed almost 'fatherly veneration' (XII 44-47) King Bahlika was the eldest prince on the battlefield. He was affectionately called the Great Grand Uncle and Bahlika the mighty. He was killed by Bheema on the battlefield. The horses of Bahlika have been praised for their breed. Bahlikas were also a prominent element in the population of the Punjab; the surnames of several sub-castes like Bahl, Bhall /Bhalla and Bhullar bear striking similarity to that word.

The next kingdom of Madra lay between river Chenab and Ravi. The ancient town of Lahore lies at its southern periphery. Once it was considered a centre of Vedic learning. Panini parceled the Madras into two divisions between Ravi and Chenab on the one hand and Chenab and Jhelum on the other, thus extending its boundaries to its neighborly kingdom of Kekaya. The kingdom of Madra was at that time ruled by Shalva, 'the auspicious one'. Madri (the mother of Nakula and Sahadeva) was his real sister. He belonged to the lineage of Saoubala, which probably had the Bahlika connection. Thus Gandhara, Madra and Bahlika were related and linked through royal connection. Shalva is addressed as "Bahlikup umgava" and his sister is also known as Bahlika. Shalva was an old man at the time of the Mahabharata war. He has also been called, 'the vainist monarch on earth'. He was tricked into fighting on the side of the Kauravas by Duroyadhana against his nephews Nakula and Sahadeva. He was Karna's charioteer but hated 'the vein-glorious' son of Suta (the caste of charioteers and bards.)and eventually led him to his death. He was the Kaurava commander on the last day of the war and was killed by Yudhishthira.

Other Clans

The next door neighbor to the Madra kingdom was the kingdom of Kekaya. It is sandwiched on the other side by the mighty kingdoms of Gandhara and Sindhu. It is an ancient kingdom with deep Bharata connection. Several queens of Bharata / Puru lineage belonged to Kekaya. Queen Kaykeyi of Ramayana notoriety was a Kekaya princess. King Ashvapati of Kekaya was well-known for his Vedic knowledge. He was considered on par with King Janaka for his scholarship, wisdom and deep knowledge. Bharatas, when defeated by their rivals Panchalas, retreated to Kekaya and are said to have ruled Kekaya for a millennium. They also have a deep Mahabharata connection. Five brothers of the Kekaya prince broke rank with him by joining the Pandava side. The main Kekaya army was on the other side. Kekaya is also singled out for the generation of unorthodox ideas. It was open to new ideas which travelled both from easterly and northerly directions. In subsequent years, it became the headquarters of the unorthodox Jogi or Yogi cult. Ranjha of Heer fame turned a Jogi due to the same influence. Thus, the entire Indus community composed of Gandhara, Sindhu, Kekaya, Madra and Bahlika kingdoms was on the wrong side of the history.

Mahabharata as History

The Mahabharata has been described as *itihas*. It is not history in our sense of the term, but a chronicle which literally means, 'this is indeed what happened', as viewed by subjective observers of the scene.

It is extremely partisan, being the victor's account of developments. The bardic tale travelled from mouth to mouth for well over thousand years. The Pandavas won and the Kauravas lost the war. Originally it must have been a straight account of the Mahabharata war attributed to Kshatriya authorship, with subsequent embellishments by Bhargava Brahmins out to score a point or two. Krishna the diplomat and war strategist was their hero, upgraded to the status of God. It was also indicative of the civilizational shift from the Vedic lands in the north-west to the easterly direction.

The Vedic tradition had been nourished by the ancestors of contemporary Saraiki-Punjabi people who had constituted the Indus community. Not only had the political power shifted, but civilization also moved in the direction of the Yamuna-Ganga Doab. The Ganga (Ganges), replacing Sindhu (Indus) had come to symbolize Indian values. The Mahabharata war was fought for a cause. No wonder, the entire Indus community was found on the side of the Kauravas in defense of traditional ancient vedic values. Gandhara and Sindhu kingdoms were found on the side of the defeated Kauravas. The Mahabharata war was the end of the road for the Indus people in particular, and the Indus community on the whole. New ideas like Buddhism and yoga started travelling backwards.

Collective Unconsciousness

The Mahabharata war took place several millennia ago, but it still remains in the consciousness of the Indian people. V S Sukthankar, the editor of the definitive edition of the classic, asserts in no uncertain terms, 'the Mahabharata is the context of our collective unconsciousness'.[5] In other words, 'it is our past which has prolonged into the present'. We are it : I mean the real We'. It has been variously defined as the 'doom narrative', 'tragedy of historic proportions', 'vision betrayed' and 'a grand tale of pyrrhic victory' and last but not the least, 'the end of a yuga (age)', for, the Indus people are suffering its after effects till today. The defeated are usually looked down upon. So were they the special victims of the scribes or traditional bards known as Sutas, painting the vanquished in the darkest colour? There was no place for the vanquished in the epic. That is the Mahabharata for you.

There is also another way of looking at things. There were the heroes and villains of the Mahabharata war. This is one way of doing the cost accounting in terms of gains and losses. Gandhara and Sindhu kingdoms were the main props of the Kauravas. The Indus people were in the frontline and consequently suffered heavy losses in terms of men and material. King Shakuni and King Jayadratha were considered the villains of the piece. Shakuni, in particular, got severly belabored as the person jointly responsible with Duryodhana as the progenitors of the great war. The existing version of the epic has to be taken with a pinch of salt. It is entirely the victor's version of the event. In fact, Shakuni was a diplomat par excellence, who matched his wits with Krishna, envoy extraordinary of the Pandavas. Shakuni has got booted, because he has been found on the wrong side of history. He is much sinned against than sinning.

Women Extraordinary

It is, in fact, the women who come out the best in the end. Gandhari, daughter of King Soubala of Gandhara and Shakuni's sister, comes out on the top. She was too majestic and remained so in all moments of crises. Notwithstanding the silken blinds, she continued to maintain the aura of the queen of Hastinapur. Here was a tragic figure who rose above the tragedy. Another noble lady happened to be Duhshala, queen of Sindhu, daughter of Gandhari. The tragedy of the Mahabharata was writ large on her face, but she filled the wounds of war to her advantage by her noble example. Duhshala was a minor character in the epic, but she was eminently successful in turning the tide in her favour through her subtle diplomacy. She won over the conquering Arjuna to her side, reminding one of the adroit handling of Alexander by the vanquished Porus. Equally majestic was the Gandhara queen, the widow of Shakuni, who reached across to Arjuna in the most strained circumstances. Let these five contrasting characters speak for themselves, celebrating the majesty of the Indus people caught in tragic circumstance over which they had no control.

6

Villains and Heroes

Shakuni the Gambler

Shakuni belonged to a distinguished pedigree. The Gandharans traced their genealogy to the common ancestor shared with the Pandavas / Kauravas and Yadavas. His father Soubala, King of Gandhara, was a disciple of Prahalad and known for his saintly disposition. Gandhari, the famous queen of Hastinapur, was his sister. Both of them had grey mountain eyes and they were 'straight and beautifully shaped'. He had an aquiline nose, which spoke for his character a great deal. He had six brothers. His elder son Uluka carried Duryodhana's message of war to the Pandavas. Shakuni carried the burden of a curse from his very birth, 'through the curse of the gods, the son of Gandhara became the enemy of the gods, the son of Gandhara became the enemy of virtue and a destroyer of beings'.[1]

He carried the bad reputation of being a 'cheat', 'wicked person' and also a 'scoundrel' who possessed occult power. There were numerous rumours floating around him, 'they say the dice he used were made from the bones of his father. His father had been put in prison by the Kauravas. They say his father told him that the dice game would be the beginning of the end of all the Kauravas'.[2] The old man also made the following gratuitous remarks, 'Mind you, with all respect to my lords, the Kshatriyas actually do some nasty things'.[3]

Dice Diplomacy

The Mahabharata is chockfull of all kinds of colourful epithets reserved for Shakuni. He was, however, as skillful in diplomacy as he was master of playing the game of dice. It was fascinating to watch him in supreme concentration. He was the main adviser to his nephew Duryodhana in his diplomatic games, as much as he employed dice to corner Yudhishtira and the entire lot of the Pandavas to surrender totally, without firing a single shot. He attacked the Pandavas at their weakest spot, 'I know their heart'. He led the myopic Yudhishtira to his doom by making him say his famous but pompous words, 'O king! O Soubala! I will make the beautiful Droupadi / Draupadi of Panchala, slender of waist, my stake. Let us play'.[4]

There is a striking contrast between the three main diplomat protagonists of the Mahabharata. While Yudhishtira employed dharma as his main instrument of diplomacy, Shakuni used pure diplomatic skills to achieve his purpose, Krishna stood in the middle by admixing diplomacy with dharma as the occasion arose. Yudhishtira reminds us of Mohandas Karamchand Gandhi and Jawaharlal Nehru. Krishna shall find his match in history among the best of the lot like Mao Zedong, who mixed ideology with diplomatic skills and threats adroitly. Krishna scored over Shakuni hands down, but it did not detract from the merit of Shakuni who came out the second best. The Mahabharata war must have been won and lost in the minds of Shakuni and Krishna.

Malevolent Character

The Dyuta Parva of Mahabharata makes the most fascinating reading with Shakuni's diplomatic skills coming to the fore in his dialogue with Duryodhana. He advised his nephew to conquer the Pandavas by means other than war, by delivering a thousand cuts on their body politics, and thereby assuring him, 'I will not fight in front of armies', and be it known to all, 'that the bow and arrow are (his) dice', and 'the heart of the dice is the string of my bow',[5] thereby scoring over the whole lot of Pandavas and their mentor Krishna by stunning them to total defeat and resultant surrender. Shakuni has been described as 'the valorous Soubala', but his skills lay elsewhere. Step by Step he led Yudhishtira to stake his kingdom, and further boasted to him, 'through handling the dice, one can defeat the enemy'.[6]

Shakuni dared to give a lesson or two to dharmic Yudhishtira in elementary diplomatic rules of the game by telling him, 'The learned triumph over the non-learned only through trickery. That is how the wise triumph over the stupid but people don't call it trickery'.[7] Shakuni's words of wisdom have a contemporary ring about them. It reminds you of Mao Zedong lecturing Jawaharlal Nehru and V K Krishna Menon in basic norms of diplomacy. It makes you think of Shakuni having been born and reborn throughout the ages.

The Crafty Cheat

The people of Gandhara were considered the best horsemen in the world. Shakuni, however, had earned an unsavory reputation which did not bring credit to his countrymen. Arjuna, during his first visit to Gandhara after the Mahabharata war, had a feeling of treachery, keeping Shakuni in his mind, 'and even from a distance behind each rock' (he) sensed 'a hostile' presence.[8] He went to the extent of saying that the Gandharans did not 'belong to our Vedic tradition',[9] conveniently forgetting that the Gandharans had the same blood running in their veins as the Pandavas and the Kauravas for umpteen generations.

Mahabharata reserved its unkindest cuts for Shakuni. He had the curse of gods hanging over his head from his very birth. He had been variously described as 'crafty cheat', and no less 'a cunning old rascal' and 'lying, cheating scoundrel', who was 'the enemy of virtue'. He had been described as 'unusual' with grey mountain eyes and hooked nose, thus standing out from the rest of the crowd. His weapons were unusual too. Those were 'his wit and his tongue'. The son of the king of Gandhara 'became the enemy of virtue and destroyer of beings'[10] in prediction for him. He was a smart guy who tried to please everybody all the time. It did not work in actual situation, because he was not taken seriously for what he said or promised. Bheeshma Pitamah spoke for all when he wished Shakuni to get back to his mountain retreat. He was loved by nobody and feared by all. Here was a backhanded tribute to his anti-charismatic personality.

War Clouds

Practically everyone of the Pandavas, and many of the Kaurava maharathis (commanders), held Shakuni responsible for the war. The youngest of the Pandava brothers, Sahadeva, was assigned the duty of dispensing off Shakuni during the final day of the war. Bheema held him responsible as 'the cause of all our battles, your poisonous Shakuni'.[11] Sahadeva taunted to remind him that he had 'a cheating gambler's debt to pay with compound interest'.[12] Was he the only guilty party? The rogue's gallery included Bheeshma, Duryodhana, Duhshasana, Karana and many others including Dhritarashtra, the blind king aptly described as the 'enfeebled old monarch.'

Matching Diplomats

While Shakuni and Krishna were contrasting characters, the course of the Mahabharata was determined largely by these two matching diplomats. Chanakya could have learned a lesson or two from them. Shakuni was the real mentor of Duryodhana. His pupil does not come out badly in the Mahabharata. Duroyadhan has been described as 'brave', highly skilled commander and 'a great charismatic leader'. Shakuni was not such a bad fellow after all. He is painted in darkness, because those defeated are usually at the receiving end. In the final analysis, the great war was between two leading lights, Duryodhana mentored by his uncle Shakuni and Arjuna mentored by his cousin and brother-in-law Krishna.

Krishna also does not come out clean in the great conflict. All the great commanders of the Kauravas, including Bheeshma, Dronacharya, Jayadratha, Karna and Duroyadhana were killed through deceit and treachery at the instance of our dear Lord Krishna. V S Sukhatankar, (editor of the Pune Critical Edition of the Mahabharata) has called Krishna 'a cynic who preaches the highest morality (of dharma), and stoops to practice the lowest tricks... An opportunist who is teaching a god-fearing man (Yudhishtira) to tell a lie-the only lie told in all his life. (He is a) charlatan who... advises a hesitating striker archer (Arjuna) to strike down a foe (Karna) who is defenceless and crying for mercy'.[13] Those are strong words. Krishna, however, justifies his skillful conduct of war, after the conclusion of the war, 'Listen Pandavas, the Kauravas were great warriors and you could not have defeated them in a fair combat. So I had to use deceit, treachery and magic on your behalf. We have succeeded, it is evening, now-let us go home and rest'.[14]

It was not to be. A great tragedy was awaiting the Pandava brothers and Draupadi, with all her five sons assassinated in sleep. Gandhari, the wise queen, was fully aware of Dhritrashtra's 'guilty involvement'. He himself had counted fifty-five reasons for the defeat of the Kauravas to Sanjay in his lament, 'O Sanjay! I had no hope of victory when I heard that the evil Soubala (Shakuni), the cause of the game of dice and the quarrel, though armed by magic, was killed in the battle by the Pandava Sahadeva'.[15] It was, however, too late in the day. Dhritarashtra ought to have listened to the wise advice of Gandhari and Vidura, when they told him about Shakuni's evil advice to Duroyadhana, threatening the very future of the kingdom. The war was lost by the Kauravas, when Shakuni won the game of dice for them.

War and its Aftermath

Shakuni and his son Uluka were deeply involved in the planning and conduct of the Mahabharata war. Indeed 'Shakuni's son had all his father's cunning and all of cousin Duroyadhana's grossness'.[16] Uluka had brought the message of declaration of war from Duroyadhana to the Pandavas, full of insults and invectives. The anticipated response was 'war at sunrise'. So be it! Sahadeva had also a message for his father Shakuni, 'Uluka, tell your treacherous father that he was born to destroy the race of Dhritarashtra with his clever fingers. I have a vow to renew, I will kill you with your father watching and then I shall kill him'.[17]

Sahadeva was to keep his promise on the seventeenth day, which also happened to be the last day of the war. He disposed off the son, Uluka, and pursued Shakuni riding the neck of his grey elephant. Sahadeva had a volley of invectives aimed for the ears of Shakuni, having held him solely responsible for the war. His time of reckoning had now come. The war ended with the demise of Uluka and Shakuni. Nobody mourned him except in distant Gandhara. The last word about him came from his sister Gandhari, of grey mountainous eyes, 'Gandhari, seeing Shakuni's corpse (in the Kurukshetra battle field), said that although his exploits had caused his destruction and that of his sons, he will go to heaven' (XI 24:24-27). Thus, the Kshatriyas had fought the Kurukshetra war gladly to go to heaven in a state of perpetual celebration in the abundant company of Apsaras.

Sindhu Kingdom

The Sindhu or Indus river has been the lifeline of the people living in the plains from Attock in the north and Dabral (modern Karachi) sea-port in the west since ancient times. It has been the home of the Vedic civilization, but by the time of the Mahabharata, the Sindhu kingdom was reduced to the periphery. However, the sanctity of the Sindhu river continued. It is also to be remembered that King Jayadratha of the Sindhu kingdom was one of the top maharathis of the Mahabharata war on the Kaurva side. His importance was to be realized from the fact that he married Duhshala, the only daughter of King Dhritarashtra and Queen Gandhari. He also headed the confederacy of ten kings and had the closest relations with the neighbouring kingdom of Gandhara, Kekaya and Madra. Indeed it was impossible to envisage the Kaurava confederacy confronting the Pandavas and their powerful allies without their north-western alliance with the Gandhara and Sindhu cemented by deep bonds of blood.

The sanctity of the Sindhu river has never been in doubt throughout ancient times. Devananda means the river of the gods, and the adjective applied for the Sindhu. Indeed the Sindhu kingdom and the Sindhu river are interchangeable terms. The Sindhu is referred to as the great protector in the Bheeshma Parva of the Mahabharata. It was expected to be remembered day and night by devotees. Similarly, the Anushasan Parva prescribed bathing in the Sindhu as the sure road to reach heaven after death.

Sindh-Sauvirah

Sindhu kingdom is known as Sindhu, Sindhudesh or Sindhu-Sauvirah (or Souvira, Souveera and Sauvira). The double-worded name of the kingdom was intentional, because it consisted of two provinces of the Punjab and Sindh. There were two important towns of Multan and Aror or Alor (also known as Rorik and Roruka) located respectively in the Punjab and Sindh. The Punjab part (which is presently Saraiki speaking) was known as Sauvirah, hence the Sindhu Sauvirah. The Sindhu kingdom kept expanding and shrinking throughout historic times. Jayadratha is also called the king of Sindhu, Sauvirah and Sivi[his empire extended deep into Balochistan. Sivi kingdom (modern Sibi) was a sub-kingdom of his vast empire. Prince Kartikaya (son of king Suratha of Shibi) was his close associate. He was thus the master of a vast empire that encompassed Sindh and North-west Punjab. It extended deep into Baluchistan bordering Gandhara. The name Sindhu struck its roots in the post-Mahabharata time. The Assyrians, as early as the 7th century BC, called it Sinda. The Persians Hinduish, the Greeks Indos, the Romans Sindus or Indus, the Chinese Sintus, while the Arab called it Indos. All these words are play upon the word Sindhu. It is also to be noted that the Sauvirahs were the original inhabitants of the region.

Ramayana Times

You have to get back to the earlier times of the Ramayana, to be reminded of the eternal Sindhu. Queen Kaykeyi was the princess of neighboring Kekaya kingdom. When she went into sulk, King Dashratha tried to placate her by offering parts of his empire ('the sun does not set on my empire') including Sindhu and Sauvirah to please her. It did not work then. Later on, when Rama returned from exile to claim his sovereignty over Ayodhya, he apportioned Sindhu-Sauvirah to his younger brother Bharata, who extended the empire towards the north by incorporating Gandhara into his empire. His sons founded the cities of Peshawar (Pushkalavati) and Taxila (Takshashila). Equally, Multan has been an ancient Aryan city famous for its Sun Temple.

Aror has been no less important, especially during the Buddhist times. The Buddhist classic *Divyavadana* (Tibetan version) singled out two important cities of Jambudvipa (north India). There is a famous saying, 'When Roruka (Alor) rises, Pataliputra (modern Patna) declines, when Pataliputra rises, Roruka declines'. The Arora community was supposed to have originated from Aror.

King Jayadratha was of pure Kshatriya breed (possibly belonging to Bharata / Puru lineage). Otherwise it was not possible for him to marry the pure breed Duhshala of Kuru lineage. It was hard to believe that the majority of the people of Sindhudesh were of Aryan extraction. The Rigveda was full of reference to tribal warfare and the designation of the aboriginal people to the Dasa category. The Vedic people were cattle breeders and cattle rustlers at the same time. The Vedic saga is full of tribal warfare. Not all of the original tribes were a subservient lot. The foremost among them were said to be the Painis, who were wealthy people and equal to the task while confronting the Aryan tribes. They were also traders and equally, a sea-faring community of some reputation. They must have been the ancestors of contemporary Sindhi sea-fairng traders. Eventually, the Painis must have come to terms with the invading Aryans.

Imported Brahmins

The Bharata, who ruled the north-west India with the help of the Gandharas, Sindhus, Kekayas, Madras and Bahlikas did not feel comfortable with its northern frontier. It was said to be a rough frontier subject to frequent invasions. This may have been the reason for the centre of the Indian civilization shifting from Sindhu to the Ganges. The marriage of Duhshala with Jayadratha might have taken place as a strategic decision. Probably it was a calculated decision to reverse the process. Soon after her marriage, she requested her brother Duroyadhana to send some Brahmins to tone up the Sindhu lands. Duroyadhana dispatched 30,000 Brahmins to be settled there. They were the vanguards of the Aryan civilization in Sindhudesh. They were expected to function as missionaries reforming and educating the populace. Eventually, these Brahmins became the virtual rulers of Sindh, turning exploiters and subsequently yielding ground to Muslim invaders. It led to their eventual defeat because they were viewed as exploiters by the natives.

Jayadratha of Sindhudesh

After Shakuni of Gandhara, King Jayadratha of Sindhu was the closest ally of the Kauravas. He was married to Duhshala, the only sister of Duroyadhan and her 100 brothers. He was known for his lustrous hair, and his mark of distinction was his crane banner. The Mahabharata has referred to him as the King of Mountainous Sindhu. He was also known as Sindhupati. He was a pupil of Dronacharya, along with the Pandava and Kaurava brothers. He had always wanted to score over Arjuna and went to the extent of approaching his guru Drona for his assurance. Drona replied, 'I gave the same tuition to you and Arjuna. But Arjuna practiced yoga and led a hard and disciplined life. He is the better one'.[18] His obsession with the Pandavas had no end.

When he was humiliated by Bheema, he went to the mouth of the Ganges and practiced severe penance before the three-eyed Siva. He, thus, followed the example of Arjuna who had actually preceded him. He sought the power to defeat the Pandavas in battlefield. He got the boon to defeat them only once, with the exception of Arjuna, who remained the favorite of the gods all the time. Jayadratha's father had also obtained a boon on his behalf. He was to meet his end in war only at the hands of 'the greatest of warriors, possessing the greatest of all weapons' through treachery and deceit by clever Krishna.[19] To his credit, it must be stated that he was opposed to the repeat dice game. Here he stood in the august company of great grand-uncle Bahlika, grandfather Bheeshma, Duryodhana's two younger brothers, Vikarana and Yuyutsu, uncle Vidura and Queen Gandhari who went to the extent of bemoaning having given birth to Duryodhana. How she wished she had listened to the ominous portends at his birth and had strangled him to death. The gesture on the part of Jayadratha to have broken ranks with Duryodhana, Karna and Shakuni must have been appreciated by Dhritarashtra and Gandhari and could have helped him to win Dushala's hand in her swayamvara. There is a folk tale current about Jayadratha's fondness for milk, and especially the condensed milk preparations like rice pudding, locally known as Sindhu khirni. In revenge for Jayadratha's dubious role in the killing of Abhimanyu, Arjuna had vowed to kill him the very next day. He was purported to have said, "Jayadratha is a relation, but he is an evil person. He has been brought up on khir (milk) and khirni (rice pudding), but now I'll cut him to pieces with my invincible arrows".

Courting Draupadi

After he had been selected by Duhshala in the swayamvara ceremony, he was on top of the world. He was now the poster boy for the Kauravas. He was on his way home from Hastinapur, accompanied by a bevy of kings and 600 chariots. He was passing through the forest of Kamyaka, which was the temporary residence of the Pandavas in exile. Suddenly his hawk eyes fell on Draupadi, standing outside the hermitage, combing her lustrous black hair. He saw in mirage 'an apsara, a daughter of the gods, or a divine phantom'[20] in her and in contrast to her, 'all other women are monkeys'. He called her 'the ornament of womankind'. He forced her into his chariot and promised, 'O lovely-hipped lady, be my wife, and share the kingdom of Sindhu and Sauvira with me'.[21]

He was, thus, exercising the right of force usually exercised by the Kshatriyas. Here was Dhoumia, the family priest of the Pandavas, who kept telling Jayadratha, 'observe the ancient custom of Kshatriyas. You have not defeated her husbands in a fair fight. You have no right to take her away.'[22] The Pandavas were swifter than him and caught up with Jayadratha. Draupadi was rescued, and she did not have to go through the harrowing experience of the dice-game incident being repeated again and again to her. Bheema sheared off Jayadratha's lustrous hair. He felt ashamed, with five prominent tufts on his head, like shinning hilltops. Finally, he was let off at the instance of Yudhishtira. He was considerate to him on account of his cousin-sister Duhshala and 'long-suffering Aunt Gandhari'. Jayadratha had, however, no feelings of remorse, instead he begun to plan his revenge by placating three-eyed Siva through ascetic penance. He reduced his body through prolonged hunger with his swollen veins showing. Siva granted him the boon of fending off the Pandavas, minus Arjuna, only once in the battlefield.

Abhimanyu at Bay

The time for reckoning had arrived. The Mahabharata was about to reach its crucial stage. It was the day of Abhimanyu 'with Arjuna busy with his own battle plan fending off the fearsome Trigartas at the farthest end'. Abhimanyu succeeded in entering the Chakravyuha and, thus, found the opening for the Pandava army to act. The gap was opened by him, but it was immediately blocked by the mighty Jayadratha rushing his troops and sealing the breach, with Abhimanyu trapped behind enemy lines. His reinforcement consisted of large-sized Sindhu steeds, 'well-trained fleet swift as the wind and obedient to the commands of his charioteers' and 'his car (chariot), duly equipped, looked like a weaponry edifice. His standard bearing the device of a large boar in silver'. Abhimanyu was stranded with the Pandavas watching helplessly, to fight singlehandedly the seven Kaurva maharathis to the right and the left of him.

The impressive lineup confronting him included Duroydhana, Karana, the two acharyas, Dronacharya and Kripacharya, Ashwathama, Drona's son, Lakshmana, Duroydhana's son and Kritavarman, Krishna's Vishini cousin. Jayadratha not only took vicarious pleasure in blocking the escape route for Abhimanyu, but he also strutted toward the hopeless lad, cockily boasting of his accomplishments inclusive of the boon granted by Siva to him. He also kicked Abhimanyu's head until his brain fell out. He had committed the unpardonable sin of showing disrespect to the dead body and thereby inviting revenge from Arjuna. He had indeed hit Arjuna (his father) and Krishna (his uncle) at their most sensitive spots.

Arjuna's Revenge

The puissant Arjuna targeted Jayadratha by vowing to kill him on the morrow, 'before sunset' or walk into the fire. Unfortunately Gandhari's son-in-law was a mere pawn. All this had come to pass due to the dice-game conceived by the fertile brain of Shakuni. So ran the thoughts in the mind of the great Arjuna. The dice in his view were 'in reality invincible shafts, mangling your bodies. Indeed, Jayadratha is the great stake about which we are playing today with the enemy'.

Jayadratha was frightened to death at the prospect of confronting Arjuna and at one time mulled the possibility of returning home. This was the 14th day of the war. His brother-in-law Duroyadhana had assigned six maharathis like Drona, Kripa, Karna, Ashvathama, Shalya and Kritavarman to protect him. The hedge of spears impenetrable and bumper-to-bumper had grown thick around Jayadratha. His brother-in-law had made almost perfect arrangements to protect Jayadratha, and he was looking forward to Arjuna walking into the fire after sunset. Jaydratha's crane banner continued to flutter in the air defiantly until Arjuna shot it down. It was a symbolic omen of things to come, the sun was about to go down and pretended to do so.

Arjuna called upon Pushan, god of journey, while the king of Sindhu was strolling unprotected. The sun emerged for a moment. Krishna told Arjuna, 'This is the hour', referring to Jayadratha as that 'wicked-souled wretch' and 'the heroic ruler of the Sindhu' in the same breath. Krishna once again come to the rescue of Arjuna, 'I shall employ yoga and cover the sun. Only the king of Sindhu shall see it. He will think, the sun has set and he shall relax his guard. This is when you strike when he is not paying attention, streaming like clouds against it'. Arjuna's pashupati, the gift of Siva, did the trick for him. Aimed at Jayadratha, his head decked with his black locks and adorned with ear-rings, flew past the 'orange' streaks of the sinking sun. Arjuna kept shooting a stream of arrows at it, until it fell into the lap of his father, King Vriddhahshatra engaged in religious rituals, whose own head splintered into numerous pieces on the rebound. Was Arjuna's victory to be attributed to yet another of Krishna's tricks?'. He had boasted to have spread darkness through his yogic power for the slaughter of two-in-one human beings.

7

Role Model Women

Gandhari

While Shakuni and Jayadratha have been painted in the darkest hues in the Mahabharata, thus bringing no credit to the kingdoms of Gandhara and Sindhu, Gandhari, daughter of Soubala, king of Gandhara and consort to blind king Dhritarashtra of Hastinapur, stands out as one of the most delectable characters of the land of Bharata. She was said to have the power of insight. She was beautiful, possessing legendary mountain grey eyes. She had built an early reputation for herself. The daughter of Kandahar, however, carried the burden a of curse, foretelling of her widowhood soon after her marriage. Ritually, she was married to a donkey engaged in carrying loads of dirty linen to the river site. The donkey dropped dead soon and Gandhari was absolved of the curse.

Soubala had reluctantly agreed to Bheeshma's proposal to marry her to his grandson Dhritarashtra, who was blind. The prospect of powerful alliance between Gandhara and Hastinapur was too attractive a proposition to be overlooked. The marriage took place in Hastinapur. Her brother Shakuni, and not her father Soubala, presided over the ceremony. Shakuni decided to stay back at Hastinapur for good. It proved to be a history changer. Gandhari bound her eyes with a silk scarf as the loyal and dutiful wife. It was an ascetic enterprise for her, 'Gandhari, with her eloquent figure, with her goodness of heart, her manner and her comportment made all the Kurus happy' (1.103:16-17). She remained blind-folded all these years and removed it only once, after Duryodhana was born. After all, he was her first born. She wanted to feel his thighs in order to, 'temper Duryodhana's body to invulnerability'. Thus the secret of her first born's near invulnerability was out. She finally took her blindfold off after the conclusion of the Mahabharata war. All her sons were gone. Who was to look after the widowed daughters-in-law and their young progneys?'

Determined Lady

King Dhritrashtra was blind and helpless 'most of the time'. He usually gave in when confronted by his eldest son Duroyadhana, he however looked dignified in his adversity. The sighless monarch, enfeebled and helpless as he was, had certain innate grandeur about him. In contrast, women in the Mahabharata were strong-willed and determined. The stately and majestic Gandhari had her views on all crucial matters and made no bones about it. Kunti was not in the same class but stood out from a distance. Sambha Parva pronounced Draupadi as a part of Shri (goddess Lakshmi) and Kunti, Madri and Gandhari were said to be manifestations of the goddesses Sidhi, Dhriti and Mati respectively.

Gandhari was believed to have gained extra-sensory powers through austerities. She chose to be blind voluntarily by wrapping a silk scarf around her grey eyes, but she had the third eye like that of Siva to forsee things. Dhritrashtra always turned to her for advice. She was straight forward and direct, but listened to others with respect. Like her brother Shakuni, who had decided to stay put at Hastinapur after her marriage to Dhritrashtra, she had grey mountainous eyes and was like her brother, 'both straight and beautifully shaped'. The buck stopped here. They were aligned on the opposite sides on all crucial matters. She was called his left eye, which was unfortunately overruled in the end by 'his right arm' represented by the evil-duo of Shakuni and Duroyadhana. She won in the end, but it was too late in the day.

Gandhari's Children

Gandhari earned a great name for her ascetic enterprise and was rewarded by Siva to be mother of a hundred sons. In another version, island-born granduncle Vyasa was impressed with Gandhari's skill as hostess and gave her the boon of one hundred sons. Gandhari became pregnant soon after her marriage and stayed pregnant for two years. She gave birth to one hundred sons and one daughter named Duhshala. Duroyadhana was the eldest born. His birth coincided with the weird howling and screaming of 'carrion eaters', terrible carnivores and... (nervy) jackals'.[1] The soothsayer Brahmins minced no words in describing these terrible ominous signs. Dhritarashtra's half brother Vidura said, 'It is clear that this son of yours will bring about the destruction of this lineage. There is peace in abandoning him and great disaster in nurturing him'.[2] The king did not have the heart to strangulate the new-born infant. The rest is history of tragic proportions, which proved equally disastrous for Gandhara and Sindhudesh alike.

New Generation

Sambhava Parva contains a colourful account of the birth of one hundred sons and a daughter, over and above the 100. Soon after Gandhari was 'afflicted with her expanded belly', the king employed a Vaishya maid in attendance. She also conceived at the same time and gave birth to her son, 'who was famous and wise and he was named Yuyutsu of mixed lineage'. He fought on the side of the Pandavas and survived the war. He was the only son of Dhritarashtra who survived the war. While Duroyadhana was the eldest, Yuyutsu came next in order of seniority by birth, followed by the notorious Duhshasna, with their only sister Duhshala ranking the fourth. Vikarna who ranked the 19th was the one who opposed

Duryodhana and Shakuni in their conspiracy to rope in Yudhishtira to play another dice game.

We have the authority of the narrator of the epic, Vaishampayana, in praising the character of the king's 100 sons, 'O King!... know that they were all brave and unrivalled charioteers. They were all skilled in battle, all knowledgable in the Vedas and wise in the ways of ruling. They were skilled in the science of relationships and were radiant in knowledge', They were also married to wives 'who were their equals', and the king married Duhshala to 'Jayadhratha, the king of Sindhu'.[3] Seemingly it was the heaven on earth for Gandhari and her progeny.

What went wrong there? One of the greatest tragedies of all times was in the making in the Mahabharata war. The entire burden fell on the shoulders of the daughter of Soubala, who tried to make the best of the bad bargain.

Forgiving Gandhari

The wise Vidura had forseen the tragedy and King Dhritarashtra was left repeating his maxim without acting on it, 'the great calamity that will destroy the seed of Kshatriyas has now arrived and we are powerless'.[4] Duryodhana, during his last moments, taunted Yudhishtira, 'Enjoy the barren world–it is now yours... You have a world to yourself, a (widowed) world without friends, horses, chariots, elephants, forts. Enjoy her'.[5] He could also have directed his ire at his distraught mother who never stood by him on account of his wrong doings.

The brave lady had foreseen the tragedy and momentarily thought of cursing Krishna, Yudhishtira, and his brothers for leaving her and the blind king issueless, but Vyasa dissuaded her by advising her, 'This was not the time', to blame or curse anyone. She found it hard to be dissuaded for she had been deprived of her sons, grandsons, brothers, nephews, her son-in-law and her entire male family. She found it hard to pardon Bheema, who had killed her eight sons on the last day of the war and ended killing her eldest son Duryodhana through trickery in the end. She must have been reminded of the day she had removed her eye cover briefly, to glance at the strong thighs of the infant Duryodhana. It was the mother's proud expression of her instinctive love for her new born. She had taken pity on the blind king, who was entirely bereft of any clutch in his old age.

Debt to Pay

Gandhari was preoccupied because she had other debts to clear. She was busy collecting 100 golden vessels for performing the intricate rites of the '*shradha*' for each of her hundred Kshatriya sons. She had a debt to pay. She was subsequently freed of the debt after performing the rituals she owed to her sons and grandchildren. The great burden was now off her chest. In normal circumstances, her sons would have been obligated to perform the ritual for her. Now the process had been reversed. She had also time to think of her widowed but beloved daughter, Duhshala, who had her own mourning to do. It was a pathetic sight for her. She had a horde of her daughters-in-law wailing loudly, on the Kurukshetra battlefield within her hearing distance. Gandhari had enough on her plate. She was also to mourn the death of her six brother's and her nephew Uluka. She was confronted with the mourning and wailing Draupadi, who had lost her five sons, through treachery while they were asleep. Gandhari was overheard telling Draupadi that her grief was greater than hers, but she was absolved by placating others, rather than thinking of her own grief.

Gandhari was a strong critic of the war. She was also an acute observer of the scene, watching events from close quarters. Her interventions were subtle and she was always on the side of peace. She was as much critical of her husband, as of her elder son and brother. While grieving over the death of her sons, she kept her cool. She chose to be chief spokesman of the grieving and suffering Kaurava women. She held Krishna responsible for the war and told him in no uncertain terms that she did not mourn as much the dead as the living, like her blind husband and widowed daughters-in-law, and other teeming humanity.

There was no public expression of grief by Gandhari, but there was plenty to preoccupy her in her public grief. It even made Krishna join Gandhari and Dhritarashtra in shedding a tear or two. Her misery was compounded due to her divine vision which let her go over the entire Mahabharata war day-by-day and moment-by-moment. She could re-live the slaughter of each of her sons reel by reel. She could find no rationale for the 18-day war. She attributed all this to her karma, as well as of her daughters-in-law' for sins committed in past lives. She also realized fully that it was not the actual fact. The Mahabharata was to be attributed to human folly, repeated again and again.

Rational Explanation

She also had a rational explanation for the Mahabharata war. She attributed it to the machinations of her elder son and her brother Shakuni. How she wished Shakuni to have stayed back in Gandhara and not blighted the peaceful atmosphere of Hastinapur. She showed no remorse for Shakuini's corpse lying in the battlefield. She never pardoned her eldest son. On his deathbed, her son Duryodhana, however, remembered her with much affection and wished to be born and re-born as her loving son, perhaps to be another Duryodhana in age after age.

In the end, it was left to uncle Vidura, and her step-son Yuyutsu and his faithful charioteer Sanjay (of the clairvoyant vision) to comfort the ageing king, 'Uncle Vidura would press the hand and … his forehead and Yuyutsu would massage his father's feet and legs, trying to make peace flow into that body rocked with the mind's agony'.[6] Gandhari needed no props of this kind, but she was a pillar of strength to the surviving Pandavas and Kauravas. She repaid the debt with compound interest that Gandhara, the land of her birth, owed to Bharatvarsha. Gandhari is fit enough to be adopted as a role model for the native Pathan community. It shall be an honour to them.

Daughter of Kandahar

'The daughter of Kandahar had all but forgotten her homeland in the hurly-burly of Hastinapur. So much was happening around her. Her marriage to the blind king Dhritarashtra was a boon to the couple. He saw the world through her eyes, 'I know it', Dhritarashtra stood and walked to the Ganga even though he could not see the view of the Ganga river outside. Gandhari knew that he liked to feel the sun's rays on his skin and listen to the waves of the slowing river. 'Belive me, my lady, I know it'. She had an entire brood to look after. She shared their joys and sorrows in equal measure. The happy times were a brief interlude in her long life.

Finally the Mahabharata war came upon her as a load of heavy bricks. She was neutral on the side of the just cause. When her eldest son Duryodhana sought her blessing on the eve of the war, she told him bluntly, 'yatho dharma stato jayah', (where there is Dharma, there lies victory). Each day of the war brought sorrow upon her head. 'Today how many are left?' Each child left (dead) was a new sorrow. At the finale she was reconciled to the inevitable, 'there is nothing to hope for, with nothing to fear.' It was virtually the end of the yuga. There was nothing left for her but to preside over funeral rites and perform oblation for the dead on the battlefield.

The couple, accompanied by Vidura and Kunti, moved to the foot of the Himalyas as their future abode. It was not to be. They were constantly restless. They moved further deep into the forest in high mountains and were consumed by nagging fears. It was virtually an act of sati, initiated by the male companion.

Just before the act of living sati, with a difference, Gandhari was reminded of her beloved home land, 'since we came here, the mountain breeze, the thick carpet of needles under foot, the light smell of pines, the sighing of the forest in the breeze, and the constant murmuring of the river, all have reminded me of Gandhara, and without realisation, I sighed'. The long-drawn Hastinapur interlude was a mere fullstop in her life, and it was Gandhara alone that counted in her thoughts, buried deep in her fathomless subconscious. Her companions from Gandhara days addressed her as the 'princess' and the Kaurva Queen of Bharatvarsha, was the 'Princeses of Gandhara' at the bottom of her heart. Swaha it was for her.

Ashwamedha Horse

Kalidasa was the Ashwamedha horse that turned out to be a friend, buddy and confidant of Arjuna during the entire journey of one year after the war. It proved to be the journey of discovery for Arjuna, travelling the entire Bharatvarsha. He had a running dialogue with Kalidasa, the

Ashwamedha horse, who was the master of all he surveyed with the right to unlimited entry in all directions at his free will. He was the king-horse of divine origin. He stood out from the rest of the tribe, with his black head held high with his eyes identifiable with 'the constellation of white marks required by the Vedas. He was all black upto the middle of his body, the rest of him was white with a great white tail that swished this way and that way like a royal fly swish. He was so completely what the Shastras decreed that one might have thought him painted. I (Arjuna) recognized him as the horse that had come in my dream'.[7] Was the horse born and bred in Sindhudesh too? Instinctively, Kalidasa took Arjuna in the direction of Sindhudesh, his probable homeland. Many a year ago, his elder brother Yudhisthira, on his yatra to the holy lakes, had visited the Saindhava woods to behold a number of small artificial lakes. For Arjuna, his visit to Sindhudesh was a novel experience. The Sindhus were known to be excellent horsemen and fighters. The Saindhava warriors put up a brave fight against Arjuna, with whatever soldiers that were left after the massacre of the Sindhu army during the Mahabharata war. 'They had put up a brave fight and with the inauspicious cosmic omen emerging during the battle, Arjuna collapsed and Partha fainted', creating concern among the gods in the heaven who had always favoured the Pandavas. They had an emergency conclave and 'all the (celestial) rsis, as seven rsis (celebrated in the Vedas) and Brahman rsis muttered mantras for the Partha's triumph. Arjuna rallied' (14.74: 23.24). After all, he was assumed to be the manifestation of god Nara on earth.

Father's Killer

The Saindhava warriors kept rallying again and again. Jaydratha's son Sauratha was the new ruler of Sindhu. He was believed to be as much of a womanizer as his late father. He was about to lose his blighted land. He took fright and committed suicide instead of putting up a fight with Arjuna. He died of 'sorrow and despair (soka, dukha and visada) after hearing that Arjuna, his father's killer, was coming' (14.77 27-30). In another version of the Mahabharata, Suratha has been described as the brave prince who was afflicted with grief at the death of his father, and 'the heroic father' of the infant proceeded to face Arjuna 'for the safety of all Saindhava warriors' but subsequently 'decided to give up his life breaths'.[8]

The Saindhava Kshatriya's were fighting in defence of their national sovereignty and to protect the honour of their deceased King Jayadratha, 'recalling that it was Dhananjaya (Arjuna) who had killed their King Jayadratha, then hurled their darts and javelins with great force'.[9] The remnant of the warriors fought bravely but were ultimately out-fought and ran away leaving the widowed queen Duhshala to her resources. She was left to comfort Arjuna all by herself, carrying her grandson in her arms by the side of her chariot.

Grieving Sindhudesh

While Gandhari hated the very face of her brother Shakuni, she had a soft corner for her son-in-law Jayadratha. How did she supplicate with the great rishi Vyasa to bless her with a daughter, 'Let a daughter be born to me' to be blessed with a son-in-law, for the affection felt for their sons-in-law is great..., then surrounded by sons and daughter's son, I may feel supremely blest'.[10] Gandhari grieved as much for her sons as for her son-in-law, joined by Kamboja and Yavana wives of Jayadratha, grieving over his dead body and protecting it from the wild beasts besides crows and vultures in the battlefield. Gandhari felt for her daughter, Duhshala,grieving over the death of Jayadratha by accusing Krishna of committing culpable murder, 'Why, O Krishna, did you not show the same regard for that Duhshala once more? That daughter of mine, of tender years, should be a widow... Alas, alas, behold, my daughter... is running hither and thither in search of the head of her husband'.[11]

Jayadratha was not the only causalty in his family. His pious father Vriddhakshatra had to die along with him for no fault of his. He was not participating in the war but he became its causalty by default. His son Sauratha committed suicide as mentioned earlier. His 'powerful' brothers Valahaka, Anika and Vidarana died along with him in the battlefield. So were the entire lot of twelve Sauvira princes casualties of the Mahabharata war. They were known to ride chariots drawn by chestnut horses of the famous Saindaha breed. The distinguished names of Sindhu heroes recorded are as follows: Angaraka, Bhramare, Guptaka, Kunjara, Prabhankara, Prarapa, Ravi, Satrunjaya, Srinjaya, Suprabiddha and Sura. Thus the entire ruling class of Sindhudesh disappeared on the seventeenth day of war. In Varna Parva of the epic, they are described as 'These strong-limbed and noble youth are flowers of the Sauvira chivalry'.[12] They were all to die.

Duhshala Stranded

Duhshala, frightened to death, was left all alone expecting no mercy from Arjuna leading his Ashwamedha horse into the hostile Sindhu kingdom. Her hair was dishevelled and her dull eyes said it all. The baby, her grandson, slept soundly in her lap. Arjuna had arrived on the scene and was soon confronting her. She placed her baby grandson at his feet and asked for mercy for him. He was the only surviving great-grandson of Dhritarashtra and could rightly lay claim to the throne of Hastinapur. Arjuna recalled suddenly that Duhshala was the only cousin-sister left in the world. He had no real sister of his own. He was reminded of their young days, when she rode piggy back on him. Here was a long lost 'cheerless sister' meeting equally 'cheerless brother'. The little infant was the peace-maker. He bent his head respectfully and, 'he solicits for peace'.[13]

Dushala is referred to as Arjuna's *bhagini* or sister. Confronting Arjuna, she referred to the hapless grandchild in her lap as 'the son of thy sister'. She reminded him, 'as Prikshit, killer of many enemy heroes, was born to Abhimanyu, so this grandson of mine was born to (her deceased son) Suratha', (XIV, 77, 39). Dushala made a moving appeal to Arjuna by beseeching him to 'spare the grandchild of this hapless sister', who was bowing his head in reverence, 'begging for mercy', after losing both his father and grandfather. He was, however, completely oblivious of his past and the tragedy that had struck his family.

Dushala described her deceased husband as 'that wicked Jayadratha', and she meant every word she had said. She ended her Shakespearean monologue with the ringing statement, 'Behold the child of thy sister's son'.

Arjuna was speechless for a moment and then rued the entire tragedy of the Mahabharata, calling it 'that trail of tragedy' and concluded by cursing that 'Kshatriya Dharma' for the entire holocaust. He placed Dushala at ease by assuring her that the entire tribe of the Pandavas would be at her beck and call in future in any emergencies.

The entire Mahabharata flashed before their eyes. Arjuna reminded himself that her son Sauratha and his son Abhimanyu were of the same age. Her tragedy was much greater, but she spoke words of wisdom to her cousin. She confessed to hating her elder brother Duryodhana and Karna for their follies. For Arjuna, his visit to Saindhava was a nobel experience.

Renewing Fraternity

Dushala had come to the conclusion that the dice game was the end of the world. She did not want to marry Jayadratha, after his disgraceful performance, resulting in sheared hair on the eve of his marriage to her. Her most telling words come at the fag end of her dialogue with Arjuna, 'I thought then that Kshatriyas were like a disease and it is bad karma to be born a Kshatriya'.[14] Arjuna responded by agreeing with Duhshala and further adding that his mother, Kunti, thought alike. In the meanwhile, the baby woke up and started howling. A new world was being born. He was sprouting his first teeth. There was 'milk sprouting above the rim of the lower gum'. Arjuna and Duhshala had made great friends. She invited him to stay on to take part in Sauratha's cremation ceremony, as the only male member of the family. He lit the yajna fire and snapped the bow into two pieces bending it on his knees. He, in return, invited Duhshala to join them in the performance of the Ashwamedha yajna. She politely refused. She did not want to be reminded of too many sad moments associated with Hastinapur. Arjuna kept his promise given to his cousin. After the Ashwamedha ceremony, Yudhishtira did not forget to keep his promise of installing Duhshala's grandson by anointing him to Jayadratha's throne to continue his life. The grandson of Duhshala occupied the same throne of Sindhudesh as his grandfather. Thus, after the war, Duhshala's descendants were the only ones left of Gandhari and Dhritarashtra lineage. The possibility of Duhshala being made her father's *putrika* by adoption was never raised.

Shakuni's Country

It was time to move. There were other worlds to conquer. Arjuna was, however, at the mercy of Kalidasa, who had plans of his own and he kept Arjuna guessing. Finally, Kalidasa moved in the direction of Gandhara's snow-bound mountains. Shakuni was gone and so was his eldest son Uluka. Five of Shakuni's brothers were also no more. His sixth brother, Vrishaka, was the anly one to survive. Gandhara, the brave land of skilled horsemean, was now ruled by his younger son described as 'the brave son of Shakuni' in the Mahabharata. He got the message of Arjuna's arrival on the scene. He was ready to do battle with Arjuna, and they had an exchange of arrows as greetings, followed by drawn swords.

Shakuni's wife jumped between the combatants, intervening to stop the fight. She was an ageing beauty. She had tears in her eyes, which won Arjuna to over her side. The swords were down. As an act of remarkable diplomacy, she reached across and joined her son's hand and Arjuna's plam to palm. The peace agreement was 'signed' without being drawn and minus signatures. Arjuna understood the gesture and responded suitably. Gandhara and Indraprastha had become friends and were no longer enemies. Shakuni's widow was magnanimous in confessing that the Kauravas were at fault and they had been punished deservedly. He melted once again when confronting the Gandharan Queen Mother. The Mahabharata described him as 'the puissant Vibhatsa' (another name for Arjuna). He marvelled at her radiant majesty. He ended up by saluting her. He affectionately addressed Shakuni's son as 'my brother' and reminded himself respectfully of his 'mother Gandhari', and thus peace was made in time. The response was equally affectionate and respectful. Arjuna was left wondering how she managed to spend her entire life with the evil-minded Shakuni. Duhshala and Shakuni's widow were a total contrast to their husbands. Arjuna's mind had now begun to be clear of the cobwebs. Earlier he had thought of Gandhara being chockfull of fever-spirits and Shakunis.

Peace on Earth

He was all alone with Kalidasa again. It set him thinking, 'The moment we had lived reverberated in me. I felt that they had happened many times and was still happening and that the trail we took was taken many times as though no other thing or way was possible'.[15] Shakuni's widow and Duhshala had instilled in his mind the belief, 'the earth wants peace'. Earlier also he had the doubts. He had refused to battle his relatives on the eve of the Mahabharata war. The Krishna-Arjuna debate on the subject is so enthralling, indeed, it is the essence of the Gita. This episode is known as Arjuna vishada.

> *'Arjuna has slumped into the chariot*
> *and laid down his bows and arrows.'*[16]
> *'His mind tormented by grief,*
> *and his sad eyes blurred by tears'*[17]

This ends with his clarion call

> *'... I shall not fight (he) fell silent'* [18]

The great classic is not about war but about peace. Its message about the futility of war and its advocacy of ahimsa. "The Mahabharata calls ahimsa the 'heart of dharma' and in its last book, reiterates what the snake-lizard has said 'Ahimsa is highest dharma'. Krishna charged Arjuna with running away from battle. He was one of the earliest pacifists and concientious objectors of our times. There comes a point when it is argued, 'It requires a very special type of courage to be 'cowardly' in the Arjuna manner. The point is that Arjuna, for whatever reasons, suddenly stands for ahimsa, the humanist, and Krishna, the militarist. And basically there cannot be reconciliation between these two fearfully opposed philosophies'.[19] Gandhari had accused Krishna of not preventing the war, but actually igniting it.

Arjuna had supporters in Duhshala and Shakuni's widow. He had won over Gandhara and Sindhu to his side after defeating them, he had also won over Kunti, his mother, Gandhari his aunt, Draupadi, his other wife and Uttara his widowed daughter-in-law, and all women who had lost their sons. Uttara's innocent query must have kept haunting him, 'Why do we have to keep producing babies, if they are to die in war all the time'? The Mahabharata, in essence, is no war tragedy but a triumph of the spirit of womanhood in somewhat constrained circumstances.

Let us now leave the epic era and migrate to more recent times and lesser wars.

Section - IV

Baloch Universe

8

The Progressive Highlander

THE Balochis are of Iranian descent, who settled down in Makran centuries ago. They passed through several decades of internal strife, which forced them to the Suleiman ranges and Derajat plains bordering the Indus river. They also spread wide into the Kalat state, which was hitherto dominated by the Brahuis, a tribe of probable Dravidian origin, which can trace its descent to the Indus Valley Civilization. The 'national migration' westward is celebrated in the Balochi ballads. The Rind and Lasharis bonded together. One poem said, 'Come, let us leave this barren land; let us spy out the running streams and sweet waters and distribute them among us; let us take no heed of tribe or chief'.[1]

Baloch Migration

Sohrab Khan Dodai was one of the earliest fortune hunters. He settled down near the vicinity of Dera Ismail Khan, of which he, along with his son Ismail Khan, were the rightful founders. He offered his services to the Langahs, the rulers of Multan, who allotted him a jagir, 'as a means of securing tranquility of the frontier'. Similarly, the other adventurer, Haji Khan Mirrani, was accompanied by his son Ghazi Khan. The Mirranis ruled for three centuries and their collapse resulted in anarchy for several centuries, until the rescue came with the arrival of Robert Groves Sandeman on the scene in 1866. Ironically, Sandeman followed in the footsteps of Ghazi Khan Mirrani. Sandeman has been rightly called Ghazi Khan II,whose province extended beyond Dera Ghazi Khan, to the entire Balochistan. The Langahs, the Mughals and the rulers of Sindh depended on the Baloch for maintaining peace and prosperity in the trans-Indus territories. Mir Chakar had led the great migration from Makran, and as believed, had 'aided Babur and Humayun in securing the Delhi throne, in fact, lived on in Baloch legends as the image of an ideal chief'.[2] The Baloch were, thus, active participants in determining the direction of Indian polity of the late medieval times.

The House of Mirranis

The Mirranis of Dera Ghazi Khan were rulers with a difference. They had a vision of establishing a stable Baloch state in the western banks of the Indus. Ghazi Khan Mirrani of the Dodai branch of the Baloch was initially a cattle owner, who then began to construct small inundation canals drawn from the Indus. From pastoralism, they transited to 'establish a relatively fixed agricultural base for themselves and in the process to transform the political foundations for their authority. Indeed, canal construction provided the foundations ultimately for a new form of Baloch state in the middle Indus basin, linked increasingly closely to the state system of the Indus plains'.[3] The minority Hindus were in fact suppressed earlier, but now the Mirranis encouraged them to be equal partners by developing commercial markets for them. There was a great migration of the Hindus from across the Indus and Sindh, especially from Aror. Here was a classic instance of reverse migration under progressive rulers. The agriculture there had a capitalist colouring, whereby the surplus was usually employed for state activities. The Mirranis had begun to fancy themselves as equal partners in the Pan-Indian framework of the Mughals. Ghazi Khan had attended the durbar held by Emperor Akbar at the Attock fort.

Tribal Organization

Subsequent to migration from Makran, the Baloch tribes came to settle in the Suleiman mountain ranges, spreading as an arc around Dera Ghazi Khan district and the upper ranges of Sindh. The Indus river was the farthest limit for them, but they also occupied territories beyond the Indus. A number of tribes disappeared altogether, or merged with others with the flux of time. It is possible to have a count of a dozen or so Baloch tribes. However, at least one, the Seria of Rajanpur, is of non-Balochi origin. Another of the major tribes, Khetran is closely allied to the Mazaris, and is of mixed origin. There is also a Saraiki element in its composition. This particular 'tumun' (tribe) is composed of a number of segments with difference in origin, thus casting doubts in the ethnic purity of several Baloch tribes. Their importance lay, however, in their control over the 'kalapani' (perennial hilly water channels). They alone had an independent base in agriculture in the hilly tracts and scope for commercial activity on account of surplus cropping.

Each tribe was jealous of its 'lands, and running water, wealth and cattle'. Pastoralism, agriculture, cattle raising and raiding were common to Baloch tribes. It has been truly said that cattle raising and cattle raiding were done together. There was no shortage of outlaw bands of mixed origin, which vended and raided in stolen animals. In such instances, the outlaw gangs cut across the tribal boundaries. At least one notorious cattle-lifting gang was identified during the early British days, which consisted of the Marris, Bugtis and Khetarans.

Marris, Bugtis and Legharis

The Marris and the Bugtis were located on the borders of Sindh and were no beneficiaries of the benign policies of Ghazi Khan Mirrani and Robert Sandeman. However, the Bugti Chief, Shahbaz Khan, was central to British frontier policy as a negotiator and mediator on behalf of the Raj. The Khosas were the largest landowners of all, but the hereditary enemies of Legharis, who were also in perpetual conflict with the Marris.

It was like a roller-coaster game in which all the tribes participated, formed alliances, broke them and renegotiated them with unpredictability which was simply breath-taking. The Legharis were the smartest of the lot. They had appropriated a large share of water from the inundated canals system. Their tumundar, Jamal Khan Leghari, was one of the most prominent mediators on behalf of the British rulers as a go-between Baloch chieftains. He performed this role to perfection. The Talpur Mirs of Sindh were a branch of the Legharis. They were rulers of Sindh in the late eighteenth century. Thus, there was a powerful confederacy of Legharis and Talpur Mirs. The Khosas were placed at the other extreme. They were 'hereditary 'blood enemies' of the Legharis. The Nathanis, like the Legharis, were very close to the Sikhs. They were the pioneers of canal irrigation and had large agricultural investments in the plains.

Miracle of Irrigation

The Gurchanis were responsible for the security of Harrand and Dajal frontier. They were distant from the plains, retaining their customary traditional practices intact. The Bugtis were difficult and they refused to fall in line. The Mazaris of Rajanpur, a comparatively poor tribe, benefitted little from the canal construction. So is it equally true of the Marris. The Mirranis were pioneers in constructing inundated canals in the district, and brought prosperity to the regions which had disappeared for centuries altogether. Their genes in innovation must have travelled to other Baloch tribes. Balochi interest in voluntary canal investment increased in the course of time. The importance of Indigo plantation was soon realized. The Hindu capital also began to flow in, into the region, in plenty. The Legharis, Mirranis, Nathanis, Khosas and several tribes migrated in large numbers from the hills and travelled down to the plains to find their employment in canal construction, which now became critical to the consolidation of political power under the large umbrella of the British Raj. Robert Sandeman alone was responsible for the miracle that took a mere decade to achieve.

Search for Water

In a nutshell, the potential of the tribe was to be measured by its access to water. The history of the Baloch is the search for sources of water, but the British had prejudices and wrong notions about their way of life. This comes out clearly in the first regular settlement report (1869-74) of the Dera Ghazi Khan district prepared by FWR Fryer: 'The Biloches are robust and manly, but they look upon war as their trade, despite agriculture and the arts of peace'.[4] Even though they were primarily pasture people, the rationale for their movement from Makran lay in the adoption of agriculture as the essential way of life as much as their main profession of pastoralism. The British administration had to modify their earlier assessment, as confirmed by Robert N Peherson who had made an elaborate study of the social organization of the Marri Baloch tribe: 'Pastoralism was central to the Baloch's own sense of identity and provided the framework in which many features of Baloch culture found their clearest impression',[5] David Gilmartin, one of the most perceptive observers of the scene, was to supplement this. But irrigated agriculture was also central to the dynamics of Baloch economic and political organization. 'Indeed interaction between pastoralism and agriculture has long moulded both Baloch identity and Baloch role in state building'.[6]

It is, however, to be noted that the process of 'state building' and 'Baloch identity' were associated with the very persona of a tribal chieftain. He was the pivot around whom everything was centred. The process of the consolidation of power of the tumundar (tribal chieftain) was reinforced by the British consolidation formula. The Tumundar was, thus, central to the future of the British 'forward policy', a doctrine essential to Sandeman and the British India administration.

Anarchic Situation

Robert Groves Sandeman arrived on the scene in 1866, seventeen years after the Sikhs were ousted as the rulers of the Dera jats. They attempted to consolidate power, but they were viewed as transient birds-of-passage. Anarchic situation prevailed in the Dera Ghazi Khan district. This was the state of affairs when Sandeman took over as Deputy Commissioner of Dera Ghazi Khan. The Marris and the Bugtis were constantly fighting with each other on the borders and there was no peace and order, in what was euphemistically called the State of Kalat. The Bolan Pass, which was strategically located on the road to Kandahar, was closed for traffic and trade. The Mirrani canal system was in ruins. This situation was not peculiar to the Derajat alone, because anarchy prevailed in the entire belt of the Punjab districts. Jungle occupied vast spaces and continued to occupy larger and larger areas. Even the life of the British officer was not safe beyond a few kilometers away from habitation.

The hills and their tribesmen were a closed chapter. In the words of Richard Issac Bruce, 'The country outside our own territory was a terra incognita'[7] The close-door policy was sanctified by the Sindh officials who looked after the affairs of the hills. For them, the 'closed policy' was their sacred dharma. They closed their eyes to the anarchic developments taking place behind their backs. They looked helpless, when the trade kafilas were stranded for months at Shikarpur, because of the closed Bolan Pass. They looked equally helpless when the accession of the Khan of Kalat in 1857 brought about strife and civil war. They also closed their eyes to rebellions that broke out in 1865 and 1867. They had no explanations to offer to the suffering of trade kafilas stranded at Shikarpur on the Sindh border of Balochistan.

Closed-Door Policy

It is only in troubled times and during complete anarchy that the messiahs appear on the scene. At last the messiah made its appearance in the person of Lt. Robert Sandeman. The young deputy commissioner was truly faced with a dilemma after taking charge of the Dera Ghazi Khan district. He was confronted with a) the Bugtis and Marris on the rampage, and b) the anarchy in the neighbouring state of Kalat which was on the verge of a civil war. His dilemma increased because Sindh refused to give him a helping hand. He was told that the affairs across the border in Kalat were none of his business. His appeal to the political superintendent at Jacobabad (Sindh) for redressing the issue was rebuffed. He was curtly told that 'the Khan [of Kalat] had no power over the Marri and Bugti tribes, although they were nominally his subjects, and could not be expected to control them; the Punjab officers must therefore trust their military posts to keep them in order'.[8] In other words, practice the 'closed-door policy' to perfection. It was, however, all hollow theory with no substance in it.

Challenges to Authority

Robert Sandeman was made of sterner stuff. He believed in the principle of 'the tide which, taken at the flood, was to lead to fortune.' He was confronted by Ghulam Hassain, a Bugti outlaw in 1867, who commanded a force of about 1000 Bugti and Marri tribesmen out on looting sprees and creating mayhem all around. He even dared to raid the plainsmen on the Harrand border. This was a direct challenge to the authority of the young administrator, who decided to take matters in his hands. The Marri chief was persuaded to visit him and told to settle the matter by returning the looted property. In return, he was allowed to levy salt tax on his borders and this was the commencement of Robert Sandeman's system of tribal service. It proved completely successful, and thereafter, peace on the southern Punjab border was secured'.[9]

Middleman Chieftains

This was only a temporary solution. Robert Sandeman had a larger vision in marrying peace and security with development as the lasting solution. It was necessary to involve the Balochi highlanders in the entire process. The first task was to give due recognition to the tribal chieftain, as well as give due regard to him. They were expected to be prime intermediaries between the tribesmen and the British administration. The next job was to involve the hillsmen in the process of agricultural expansion in the plains. There was thus going to be close relations between the highlanders and the plainsmen. This was done through the state by giving due right to canal lands to them. Here was an ideal situation in which highlanders, plainsmen, the tribal chieftains and British administration were equal participants. The (canal) irrigated lands were generously parceled between them. Before it happened, the canals had to be constructed. It had to involve voluntary labour to be offered by the potential beneficiaries. His rewards were rights to land and water for rich cultivation. Here was a mass participation without the introduction of democracy and its norms. There was an obvious shortage of capital. The lacuna was filled by inviting the Hindu minority as full participants. They naturally contributed the capital. The cost to the state was minimal on account of these measures. This was also a model followed by the Mirranis four centuries ago. Tribal chieftains were 'gods' to their tribesmen on account of such measures. Sandeman, by now, must have been viewed as a 'super god' presiding over a hierarchy of minor 'gods'.

Natural Humility

By the time the stewardship of Robert Sandeman came to an end he had transformed the shape of the moribund social organization of centuries in less than a decade. Time was ripe for him to turn to new pastures. Balochistan was awaiting its turn to be upturned, as it had happened in the Dera Ghazi Khan district. Now he was to operate on a grander scale and for the entire world to watch. The Mithankot conference on the state of Kalat in 1871 was a challenge to him and a trial balloon. It took him the next five years to achieve his new objective.

Robert Groves Sandeman

Robert Groves Sandeman (1835–1892) came to India to join his father's regiment, the 33rd Bengal infantry, during the times of the East India Company. He made a great impression on Sir John Lawrence, who appointed him to the Punjab commission. It was his destiny to land himself the job of the District Magistrate of the Baloch-dominated trans-Indus district. The posting there must have been viewed as 'unattractive as the trans-Indus district of the Punjab', but to Robert Sandeman, it was a godsend opportunity. He had the entire laboratory to experiment with new ideas and with no one looking over his shoulders. He spent a decade there and his appetite for challenges remained undiminished at the end of his term in 1875. The early demise of his wife and two young children, all the three of them as victims of diphtheria, unburdened him of any personal responsibilities. He went on to conquer the state of Kalat without firing a single shot. He was the founding father of British-administered Balochistan. He had everyone, including the Nawab of Kalat, his warring chieftains and disputing tribesmen, eating out of his hands.

He was the architect of the Balochistan agency and remained in the post of the agent to the Governor General in Balochistan, for another sixteen years. He loved his Baloch and undoubtedly was the architect of contemporary Dera Ghazi Khan, Balochistan and the Kalat state. He died in harness at Las Belas on 29 January 1892, after a brief illness. He spent thirty-six years in India uninterruptedly (except for brief home leaves), of which, most of the years were spent on the Baloch frontier.[10]

To his credit he changed the shape of the south-west frontier beyond recognition. John Jacob, Herbert Edwardes and John Lawrence have been called 'the Paladins of the South'. Robert Groves Sandeman was also one among them. Probably his achievement was of much greater order, but has unfortunately gone unrecognized. He had a great sense of history, besides, he was a history-maker. He had also a great sense of humility. He was aware of the fact that the 'Great Events' are composed of 'Little Moments' cumulated over time. He had the necessary patience, fortitude and openness to win over friends rather than make enemies. This comes out in the conversation he had with the Khan of Kalat after his long march at Mustang in 1876. The conversation went like this. The Khan of Kalat said, '*Pahle Sati, Piche Roti*'. Literally, it means, 'First the rod, then food'. It may also be translated as 'Hit them with rod, then pat them on their backs'. Or it could also be translated, 'Punch their heads, before you pamper'. This must have been the true version of the Nawab's dealings with his subjects. Sandeman was quick in the repartee and contradicted the Kalat Khan in no uncertain terms. He conversed in pure Urdu, '*Pehle bat, Piche lat*'. When translated literally, it meant, 'First a word, then the stick', meaning, 'Reasoning before strike'.[11]

Highlanders

This is how Sandeman set the example in dealing with the 'wild' tribes on the Dera Ghazi Khan frontier. In his early days of posting in the trans-Indus district, he romped through the territory bordering British India, unescorted by military escorts. He went from village to village and literally from door to door enquiring, soliciting and mentally absorbing the prevailing situation. His first principal in life was to listen to others patiently. This technique came naturally to him and it was not cultivated artificially. He had a great advantage in being a Scot. After all, he was also a highlander. Thus, while dealing with the Balochis of the Suleiman ranges, he was one highlander talking to another.

Sir Robert changed the shape of the north-west frontier. The nature of the dialogue changed. The emphasis was on development. Diplomacy also changed its colouring. It was no longer concerned with war and peace alone, but with development, which became the order of the day with much deliberation. Inconceivably, the instrument of this change was the tribal chief or tumundar as he was locally known and regarded. The entire tribe benefitted from the developmental progress. He did not disturb the status quo but sought to change it subtly. The political authority, tribal chiefs and the populace were equally enthusiastic participants. Political participation, democratic institutions and transforming social organization were overlooked (and perhaps left to the future), and there was total stress on economic development and progress, besides the decrease in social tension, and slow and steady introduction of capitalist forms of production.

Canal Irrigation

How did he go about achieving his objectives? His strategy was multipronged which he sought to achieve in a short time. He recognized at the outset that the Balochi were central to his strategy and must be dealt with on a priority basis. They constituted more than one-third of the population of the district. They also wielded tremendous power on the frontier, on the plains and as a backup among Baloch tumuns across the frontier. They were essentially pastoral, but only partly dependent on agriculture, based on three indigenous irrigation streams: 1. Kalapani (perennial hill irrigation streams), 2. Kurez (underground water course) and 3. Rodkohi (seasonal streams).

To them agriculture was a part-time enterprise, with pastoralism as their main source of livelihood. The trick was to make them substantially dependent on canal irrigation from the Indus river. Sir Robert sought to do what the Mirranis had done to transform the district beyond recognition. Water was central to the very existence of the Baloch. Sir Robert sought to bring a revolution by constructing a network of canals and thereby introducing his subjects to capitalist economy with one stroke. Since another one-fourth of the population consisted of the agriculturist Jats, thus, sixty per cent of them were dependent on agriculture. Here was a miracle that was awaiting. After Nawab Ghazi Khan Mirrani, Sir Robert Sandeman was another messiah to follow the footsteps of his predecessor on a grand scale. Here is an ideal instance of the close connection between pastoralism and agriculture.

Capitalist Enterprise

The Hindu minority played a crucial role in bringing about the transformation of the district. From historical times, there has been an ambivalent relation between the majority and minority communities of the region. The Hindus, mostly of Khatri and Arora communities, played the same role as Jews in Europe. They played a well-defined but limited role in social organization. They were, however, the masters of the market economy for centuries. Khatris, especially, were capable administrators. Sir Robert not only assured security for them but also made them equal partners in his scheme of transformation of agriculture. They were expected to provide capital for canal construction. They were also encouraged to upgrade themselves as proprietorial landlords. It should not be forgotten that the landed gentry was on the top in the social hierarchical structure, parallel to the process of Sanskritization in Hindu society in India. They had now a stake in the development process. They were the instruments of promoting market economy. They helped in transforming the town into regional markets. It also attracted the Shikarpuri traders to spread in the district. Once again Robert Sandeman followed the footsteps of the Mirrani Nawab by making the Hindus his equal partners. Religious tolerance became an essential credo of the development process.

Teamwork

All credit is due to Sir Robert for creating something out of nothing. It was eventually a team work. Imagine him as the head of a corporation, with his compact team which worked under his leadership but silently delivered on time. Sir Robert had his ten Paladins,of which four were Britons: R I Bruce, Ronald Wingate, Thomas Henry Thornton and H S Barnes, at least three of whom are on record chronicling the days of their association with him. The other three were tribal chieftains heading powerful Baloch tribes, Sardar Imam Baksh Khan Mazari, Sardar Jamal Khan Leghari and Shahbaz Khan Bugti. They represented the most powerful among the Baloch tribes. They acted as middlemen settling disputes as well as liaising with Sir Robert and his team.

Irrigation Policy

The three parts of the triangle (one of his major policies) consisted of his advisers of the Hindu background, two of whom were natives of Dera Ghazi Khan and one belonged to a family with the title of Diwan since the time of the Sikhs. The threesome were: Rae Hittu Ram, Diwan Ganpat Rai and Pandit Suraj Kaul. While Hittu Ram was one of the most powerful men of his days, who advised Robert Sandeman on Baloch affairs, Diwan Ganpat Rai was the adviser on Pashtun affairs. These ten men shaped the British imperial policy on the empire's south-west frontier. The political map of that part of the world was determined by the confabulations of the ten Paladins and Robert Sandeman.

Sir Robert Sandeman must have believed in the domino theory. Thus, he had a great vision of maintaining a close relationship between British imperial power, tribal organization, political loyalties and water control on the one hand, and irrigation, canal construction and sustainable agriculture on the other. The focus was on the Baloch, in his policy formulation. The consequence was political stability and enhancement of state power and formation of commercial capital. While irrigation was given prime importance in his scheme of things,, the central objective still remained the expansion of power by adoption and implementation of his 'forward policy'. He had spelt the death knell of the 'closed policy', with its wrong-headed emphasis on stability. In his scheme of things, the Baloch and his tribal chieftains were to play a crucial role. Thus, the British imperial policy was defined by the role of irrigation and construction of canal system. The district was his laboratory for the purpose.

Nawab Ghazi Khan Mirrani

Nawab Ghazi Khan Mirrani remained Robert Sandeman's inspiration. Nawab Ghazi Khan died nearly four centuries ago, but his ghost continued to haunt his worthy British successor, in a cause that needed to be celebrated. He was the first great state builder in the Derajat. His model was to experiment with small inundation canals limited to the river Indus during the flood season. He was ably assisted in this laudable cause by Raja Manak Rai, his revenue minister, after whom is named the famous Manaka canal. Mirrani was also responsible for the Haibatwaka canal. His larger objective was the consolidation of central power through stable agriculture; Mirrani provided supervision, limited capital and political leverage. Voluntary labour also played a critical role. Commercial capital from his Hindu nationals was also an essential component of his experiment. He was a liberal and no narrow-minded Baloch with communal blinkers in his eyes. Essentially, he was a visionary who must have inspired Sir Robert, who had undoubtedly a much grander vision than envisaged hitherto.

State Building

There were also other actors besides the Mirrani chieftain -- like Makhdum Rajan Shah of Sitpur who built the 70-mile long Dhundi canal in about 1740–but none of them had Sandeman's grand vision. Thanks to the bounties of the river Indus, the district never suffered from famine. Water, however, remained the lifeline. Sir Robert gave the people the necessary satisfaction. By the time he had ended his decade-old tenure as District Magistrate of Dera Ghazi Khan, he had a tally of fourteen irrigation canals to his credit. Those included Manaka, Kasturi, Dhingaria, Shoria, Nur and Dhundi. The canal system had a total length of 741 miles. These were functional for 150 days in a year. A large area benefitted from the combined well and canal system. About twenty per cent additional land benefitted from the overflowing Indus during floods. By the time Sandeman was ready to depart for Balochistan, he had transformed the face of agriculture in the trans-Indus reigion by delinking it from pastoral economy, and, instead, he turned it into a surplus economy with commercial capital bias. Thus, a parallel economy had been developed within a decade. It assured political stability. The process of state building had started in right earnest. Especially the Baloch had a stake in the system. He was also successful in promoting commercial trade by developing trade towns. He had drawn the Hindu minority into his framework. They had now a vital stake in his system. The other agricultural community of Jats had benefitted from his policies. Above all, he had expanded the frontiers of British India beyond Kalat. He also demonstrated the success of his forward policy, which had now become the fulcrum of British India.

Baloch Psychology

The Baloch has a distinguishing look, demarcating him from the rest of the people. He could be singled out in a crowd, with his curling long hair falling down his shoulders, his large turban placed awkwardly over his head and his impeccable white dress. He has been called 'a fine martial race', 'free from bigotry', 'temperate in habits' and 'likeable in his manners', but he would never compromise with his honour and counter force with force. He was in line with the Pathans in refusing to bow down or comprise with '*zor*' (force) or '*zulum*' (atrocity). Robert Sandeman had understood his psychology. He was fond of saying, 'You cannot tame a Pathan or Baluch by *zor* (force)', that is to say, merely by coercion and threats, backed up though they may be by the spasmodic force of repeated military expeditions. In the slang of the day, you may 'hammer' them as often as you may please, and you may cow him for a time, 'the man to whom blood feud was a cherished hereditary possession will be even with you when an opportunity arises'.[12] He has long memories and he never forgives and forgets. He equally remembers the favours done and is notorious for his sense of loyalty. His instincts, habits and manners are formed by nature. He is like a free bird and hates to be imprisoned. Unlike the Pathans, he is totally subservient to his chieftain. He is a man of the collective and thus easy to handle in any situation.

Religious Tolerance

Above all, he is to be distinguished for his greatest virtue-- religious tolerance. He is unlike the Pathan, who is vulnerable to the influence of the illiterate village moulvi, as his guide and religious mentor. The Baloch leader, Akbar Mustikhan, has put it well: 'Baloch has less of God in his creed and less of devil in his character, unlike the Pathans'. The other prominent Baloch leader, Ghaus Baksh Bizenjo, has reinforced the same argument forcefully, 'Maulvi representation is limited to the Pushto-speaking area. We, Baloch, are very different from the Pathans in this. I am yet to meet a Baloch pir. We can never be fanatical about religion'.

Religion, to the Baloch, is marginal to his existence. He is most amenable to merge his identity, when placed in a different environment. His movement to the plains in pursuit of canal irrigation transformed his outlook in life as reflected in the following popular saying about those Baloch who, having migrated to the plains, had permanently turned Jats and for which there is a British proverb, 'While those who stayed have remained Balochees'.[13] These characteristics of mobility and change are also to his advantage.

Hindu Minority

The subordination of the Hindu is prominently indicated in respect to social restrictions with regard to dresses and other practices, like taboos in respect of the means of transportation. The minority had practically no role in political decision-making. The fear of persecution was always there. It hung like a Damocle's sword over their head, because they never hoped to be integrated, except on the margins. They were, however, indispensable in day-to-day life of the Baloch. At one time the Prime Minister of Kalat was a hereditary Hindu. This exception did not prove the rule. The Baloch could not do without his Hindu surrogate. Such an intolerable situation could not have escaped the attention of any perceptive observer. To some extent, the Hindu was discriminated against not because of his religion, but because he was outside the Baloch parameter. As one perceptive British official put it: 'Amongst the Baloch, the treatment of Hindu traders and their families, through who all monetary transactions are carried out, was to a point of honour'.[14] The Hindu minority was indispensable like the protected animals in the zoo. He carried the burden of commerce and trade on his shoulders. He also maintained accounts and functioned as an administrative assistant to the tribal chief. He lived on the periphery, but he was equally indispensable. Here was a dialectical relation that was strained on occasions, but otherwise functioned as business as usual.

Tumundar as an Institution

The institution of 'tumundar' (tribal chieftain) is peculiar to the Baloch tribes. Robert Sandeman found virtue in institutionalizing this authority to deal with the tribes. The tumundar had the necessary authority to deal with the tribes, also prestige and standing, so the British found it convenient to deal with tribal affairs through their various offices. The existing institution was reinforced in the process. The British had also dealt with princely states in a similar manner. The tumundar was viewed in par with princely rulers for practical purposes. They had their own laws and traditions, administrative machinery and channels of delivering justice. The British imperial India found it convenient to upgrade the tumundar to the same level.

This convenient arrangement was gradually institutionalized by Robert Sandeman. It was a welcome relief to all concerned. The tribals were left to the entire mercy of the tribal chief. Thus, social reform was next to impossible in this scheme of things. It had implications which need to be discussed elsewhere. So long as it lasted, the arrangement was a welcome relief for the imperial power and tribal chiefs. Especially, it was welcomed by the tumundar because he had the full backing of the imperial power in dealing with his subjects and other rival chieftains. The tribal chieftains could now rest in peace and tranquility under the vast umbrella of the Raj. Tumundars must have been most beholden to Robert Sandeman,they responded to his gesture in the fullest measure possible.

So far,the role of the tumundars was confined to that of 'assertive military leader' who were expected to protect Baloch cattle grazing grounds from intruders, as well as give protection to the tribes from cattle thieves. The role of the tumundar had been transformed after he became the sole conscious-keeper on behalf of the tribe in dealing with intra-tribal disputes. Now the central authority vested in the Raj. Increasingly, the Raj became supreme authority by default. It, however, assured peace and stability for long. The authority of the tumundar was reinforced and the authority of traditional institutions like *jirga* was reduced to nominal. The tumundar was provided with guns, money and horses to reinforce his authority. He had now time to think about developmental measures. He was tempted by the Raj with lands that could be used for canal irrigation, provided he got his tribe involved in voluntary labour for canal construction. It was a quid pro quo which benefitted everyone. The peace that had eluded the Baloch for centuries looked like returning to them.

The Sandeman System

This was triumph of the Sandeman system. He had the toughness of the Scot in him, but he was not dour like his compatriots. He had the knack of winning friends. The sudden death of his wife and his two young kids put the steel in him. He was against violating norms and traditions and treated them as sacrosanct. Those who dealt with him knew before, where he stood. It was possible to read his mind. He respected loyalty above all other virtues. He provided money, guns and houses to his loyalist chieftains. He employed a number of prominent tumundars as his moderators. They were required to soften blows, before he confronted his adversaries. Prominent among his intermediaries were Sir Imam Baksh Khan, Nawab Jamal Khan Leghari and Sir Bahram Khan. They were his conscience at the gathering of collective *jirgas* of tribal chieftains. In return, they were suitably rewarded. The very fact the tumuns (tribes) headed by them were the richest needed no proof. Robert Sandeman was, however, allergic to employing munshis and babus, who he considered the most unreliable and untrustworthy go-betweens.

He was kindhearted and friendly, a fact that has been recognized by his worst enemies. He knew everybody of importance during his time. We have the authority of Sir Frederick Roberts to testify this fact; 'He was acquainted with every leading man [of the leading tribes] and there was not a village, however out of the way, which he had not visited'.[15] We have already mentioned his *padayatra* through the wilderness of the tribal belt of Dera Ghazi Khan hilly tracts, with no personal armed escort, in his early years of sojourn in the district. Thomas Henry Thoronton was his close associate for many years and he was eminently successful in unlocking the secrets of his success: 'Sir Robert Sandman was no such rustic and his native Scot shrewdness early taught him that if we expect a frontier tribesman to exert himself on our behalf, we must make worth his while to do so'.[16] In other words, to put it less sophisticatedly, everybody has his price and he expected to be rewarded in return. Better still, Sir Robert turned around the formula by transforming the relationship into partnership. Now this theoretical proposition remained to be translated into reality, the task which Sir Robert wasted no time in performing.

Swords into Shears

The development of agriculture was a key to Sandeman's success. He found in several tumundars a potentially progressive outlook and qualities of liberal-minded leadership. Agriculture was not terra incognita for the Baloch. Pastoralism and agriculture were his common heritage. The Baloch also had considerable experience in *kalapani* irrigation. Now he was ready to expose himself to an entirely new world. His tumundar was also ready to give him a helping hand, but he was called upon to play an entirely different role. He had, however, to be tempted with large chunks of land (in the plains) with potential for canal irrigation at practically no cost to him or his tribesman.

In return, the tribals were required to offer voluntary labour to clear jungle growth and dig canal channels to water newly-acquired lands. The Baloch beneficiary of such largesse, had a stake in the stability of the land. The clan of guerrilla warriors had been turned into agriculturalist with entrepreneurial skills and high stake in the British Indian empire. The Baloch had, thus, 'crossed the frontier'. This must have been a revolutionary change for him and his environment. Here was an experiment carried out by constructing a network of canals irrigating the southern Punjab tip.

Leghari and Hindu Traders

The benefit of the development largesse is best seen in the person of Sir Jamal Khan Leghari. The Legharis were known to be friends of Sikh rulers and the British administration. Jamal Khan functioned as an intermediary of Sir Robert. He and his tribe had the advantage of access to both–hill torrents for water-grazing lands and canal water for irrigation in the plains. He and his tribesmen were beneficiaries of stable agricultural income and had access to generous credit provided by the Raj, as well as additional income accruing through surpluses generated by commercial agriculture. In his person, Jamal Khan owned approximately 114,000 acres of which 12,000 acres were irrigated by canal water. In addition, he had about 2,500 acres irrigated by radhukis in his hill territory. He died in 1881 and is remembered as the foremost native capitalist of Dera Ghazi Khan. Here is a concrete instance of British awareness of the importance of agriculture and (irrigation) in designing relationship with tribal chiefs.

There was a tremendous transformation in the psychology of the Baloch. The other beneficiary was the Hindu trader who was earlier given less than his due. He earned not only respectability, but accumulated capital by promoting regional markets. He also turned to land ownership because he owned capital in plenty. The Hindu got upgraded by being a landlord and landowner. The Hindu also benefitted by associating himself with the Raj by joining the administrative hierarchy. The lower-level jobs were staffed by the Hindus, who also came into day-to-day contact with the British administrative machinery directly. Thus, there was a hierarchy of stakeholders of the Raj besides the British themselves.

Sandemanite Policy

The role of irrigation in British rule has paid powerful dividends. It has drawn the Baloch, the Jat and the Hindu minority within the British administrative framework effortlessly. This has been done by assuring the stability of traditional institutions and the further promise of reinforcing them. The hands-off policy of the British administration paid handsome dividends to the establishment. The tribal social order remained solid as ever. It has been protected from the process of modernization. The Baloch was carefully kept protected from the legal framework of British India. His customary law was given due preference. The tribal chieftain retained his powers, which was further reinforced by his accumulation of land and wealth. His position was effected marginally by the levying of water taxes and applicational property rights. There was, however, a subtle change in the situation, which had escaped the attention of all. The British authority-- in the person of the deputy commissioner and the extra-assistant commissioners-- had the stamp of real rulers, with the tumundar playing a second fiddle to them. It has been said that the extra-assistant commissioner had replaced the tumundar in settling disputes among tribesmen. Such was the subtle power of the Raj in taking over by the clever technique of the creeping-in process.

Thus, there were both advantages and disadvantages of the Sandemanite policy. There is no dispute over the truth that it stirred a hornet's nest, and there was no knowing where it would all end. Sandeman had achieved more than what lay within the power of any of his contemporaries. His intentions were honourable and he has to be looked upon in the same manner. In retrospect, the Sandemanite transformation was no more than a cosmetic change. Not much changed for the Baloch in the following one hundred years (till the 1990s). He still remains mired in tradition, which is that of the jackboots preventing any progress. The key lies in his traditional social organization to be transformed beyond recognition, and brought on par with other modernized societies.

Forward Policy

Sandeman was the foster parent of the British 'forward policy', but there were several others who laid claim to its fatherhood. The doctrine of forward policy could be explained at its barest in tactical terms. It was essentially Sandeman's idea to have an activist policy toward the Baloch tribes. Occupying the Suleiman hill perimeter of the Dera Ghazi Khan district, he began to design a system that spanned the entire territory by crossing it. The idea was to violate the *lakshman rekha* and thus bring the Baloch within the British orbit. This was the least costly way of expanding the area of political influence without firing a single shot. How was such finesse to be achieved?

It involved constant dialogue with the tribal chieftains and by using them as intermediaries for opening a dialogue with the tribesmen by proxy. It was to be done by resolving intra-tribal disputes and benefitting them monetarily by employing them for rendering 'paid service' to protect the frontier and keep the mountain passes open, without interruption. By no means was it Sandeman's original idea, but he was following the footsteps of Sir John Jacob of Sindh fame. The essential idea was to expand the reach of the empire and extend it beyond the district to the state of Kalat and toward Afghanistan, to counter the expansionist policy of the Russian Czar, who had put the fear of God in the minds of British India.

When Sandeman began to design his forward policy to counter the Russian reach, his first task was to imbibe knowledge of the tribes in order to understand them. He began by extending his hand of friendship and benign patronage to tribal chieftains. It has been called a policy of 'ethnic subversion of the Baloch' by reaching out to him across the frontier and to do little things to benefit him. As David Gilmartin has put it pithily: 'The frontier was thus defined, in British eyes, not by intrinsic differences, of those without and within, but by the reach of Britain's power of association, understanding and incorporation'.[17] Robert Sandeman could provide a lesson or two to Dale Carnegie in the art of wining friends. The framework was cleverly built around the myth erected around the person of Robert Sandeman. Partly the myth was self-created and substantially it was created by those around him. Myths spread very fast by word-of-mouth. His name began to be taken in awe among the tribals and plainsmen alike. This particular myth was perpetuated after he ventured across the frontier and visited the tribal chiefs without being escorted except by his tribal hosts.

Historic Antecedents

The debate about the 'close border policy' and 'forward border policy' is interminable, and, it had permeated the British India administration at its highest echelons at the viceregal level. You had the Lawrencites and Lyttonites' sabre-rattling against each other. Lord Lytton was Sandeman's favourite Viceroy, who was opposed by the other Viceroy, Lord Lawrence of 'close border' fame.

The debate centred around the entire 950 miles of Punjab and Sindh frontiers. Of this 800 miles constituted the border of the Punjab, of which the 200-miles stretch covered the entire Dera Ghazi Khan district border. Historically, the three portions of British India were subjected to different treatment, which in several instances, were antithetical to each other. The part of Punjab which constituted more than half the length of the entire boundary also included the present-day North-West Frontier Province. It covered some 600 miles, 'a stretch of mountains and often inaccessible territory which no one, Mughal, Afghan or Sikh had ever ruled. They had claimed sovereignty but none had ever attempted to administer it; but all efforts to administer the territory had failed because the Pathan, the king of this unconquerable land, had somehow managed through raids and plunder, to preserve throughout the ages its parochial independence and culture'.[18] Thus, the fate of the Punjab was left to its resources and God.

John Jacob and Sandeman

The earliest experiment in dealing with the frontier inhabitants took place in Sindh on the Baloch border. Brigadier General John Jacob of Sind/Sindh formulated the upper Sindh policy in the late 1840s and 1850s by creating a frontier tribal service called 'Baloch guides' to police the entire tribal belt in Sindh. This was a limited experiment, but it yielded positive results. John Jacob took care of future disputes by banning possession of land on both the sides. Limited communications were opened but there was a line of demarcation between 'moral frontier', as it was picturesquely described as between 'roving cattle keepers of the hills' and 'civilization'. John Jacob, like many other contemporary administrators, was inspired by the utilitarian values of John Mills and Jeremy Bentham. Here was a laboratory in British India for experimentation with the ideals of transformational political economy. The unlocking had been done by John Jacob on the Baloch frontier, the gaps were filled by his apt pupil Robert Sandeman. The essential objective of both of them was the legitimization of imperial power.

The arrival of Robert Sandeman as Deputy Commissioner of Dera Ghazi Khan, in 1866, heralded the second phase of the Baloch revolution. He followed John Jacob in several respects, but he also broke away from his predecessor by tempting the tribals to move to the plains as full participants in canal irrigation projects. Sandeman had, thus, sought to break the barriers between the hillmen and plainsmen. At the same time both of them respected traditional values and customary laws even after the tribals migrated to the plains. Subsequently, the Dera Ghazi Khan model of development was emulated in other parts of the Punjab with varying results. Both Jacob and Sandeman brought about peace and stability, as well as development to the region.. Thereby the empire proposed and the British power got legitimized.

Balochistan vs Khyber Model

The classic example of the 'closed policy' is the 'Khyber System', as contrasted with the Jacob-Sandeman 'Balochistan system', and is the primary instance of the British forward policy. These two contrasting systems have been debated endlessly, but both of them are poles apart in the means employed and ends achieved. The Baloch system believed in intervention, development and stability. The Pathans were at a disadvantage, when compared with their neighbouring Baloch. That the Pathans were statusquoist by nature and so opted for the closed frontier system instinctively, is a myth perpetuated for long and needs to be exploded. The Baloch system has been adopted in the laboratory experiment conducted in Pathan-dominatd Gomal and Tochi territories of Balochistan, successfully, exploding the myth that Pathans do not want change and are statusquoists. The Baloch system was applied in this instance with positive results, disapproving the cherished belief of Pathans being 'no-change conservatives', and centuries-old die-hards. Admittedly, there is no tumundar as an intermediary, who could have connected the Raj with the general populace. The institution of *jirga* is, however, equally strong among the Pathans, which can be exploited by relating it to their innately healthy instinct.

The Khyber system awaited its own Sandeman. The truth of the matter was Robert Sandeman's partiality towards the Baloch, who gave name and fame to him. The Baloch remained his first love. The Pathans never stirred him to total commitment. Let Thomas Henry Thornton, who happened to be a close associate of Robert Sandeman, have the last word: 'The management of men is always a difficult and delicate task, especially of such wild spirit as those of the semi-savage, but fine manly and warlike races who inhabit our borderland…no such difficulties exist which cannot be overcome but by a firm, fair, conciliatory and unbiased policy, carried out with tact, courage and perseverance'.[19] The paragraph quoted above has a distinct overbearing smell of British imperial arrogance, but the underlying instinct is in the right place. Thornton corrected himself fast when he rued his earlier remarks: 'We seemed to have looked upon them as a nationality of irredeemable, with whom we have the less to do the better'.[20]

Disputing with Sindh Officials

The Khan of Kalat was the nominal head of the confederacy, which included the frontier hill regions of the district. The Baloch flowed in and out of the national border between Dera Ghazi Khan and Balochistan. In the meanwhile, Robert Sandeman had begun to spread his wings by establishing working relations with his Baloch tribes. While Col Phydre had specific assignment relating to Baloch tribes and the Khan of Kalat, Robert Sandeman had no defined jurisdiction in this matter. Hence, he was bound to come into conflict with Col Phydre, Superintendent of the Upper Sindh frontier. Col Phydre and his supervising boss, Col Sir S William Morewerther, Commissioner (Sindh) (then a part of the Bombay Presidency) were also bound to come into conflict with the Punjab officer because of the same reason.

Col Phydre insisted in recognizing the Khan of Kalat as the head of the confederacy, who could settle between the quarreling tribal chiefs who had little regard for him. But Col Phydre also recognized that the Khan was a nominal and not effective head of the confederacy. The colonel was to remind all and sundry of the 1854 treaty he had with the Khan. Hence, he considered himself as the sole authority of the British suzerainty. Col Phydre and his boss Sir William Morewerther were for strengthening the authority of the Kalat ruler, rather than weakening him. Here was one 'blind man' leading another 'blind man' in the person of the Khan of Kalat. The Sind commissioner was oblivious of the realities, when he went to record bombastically, 'the fact is Baluchistan is going through a phase which must inevitably occur when, in the progress of good government, feudal institutions come into conflict with the central power'.[21] The Sindh officers were flying in thin air and running away from realities by providing unrealistic bureaucratic solutions.

In contrast, Robert Sandeman continued to deal directly with tribal chiefs and employ intermediaries, messengers and secret agents for the purpose. He also made frequent trips to the tribal belt. It was believed that there was not a single hamlet that he had not visited. He settled disputes and laid the law for them to their mutual satisfaction. Within five years of his stewardship of the Dera Ghazi Khan district, he began to pressurize his superior Punjab officers to allow him to intervene in disputes between the Khan and his Sardars. His suggestion was forwarded to the Viceroy, Lord Mayo, who recommended the holding of a conference of Sindh and Punjab officers at the highest level. The result was the scheduling of the conference in the beginning of 1871 at Mithankot in the district. At last, Robert Sandeman had arrived on the scene with a bang and henceforth, his forward policy was to be the order of the day.

Mithankot Conference, 1871

'Lord Mayo fully understood the gravity of the situation, and directed Sir Henry Durrand (of Durrand Line fame), then Lt. Governor of Punjab, to take up the issue with Sir William Morewerther (of Sind cadre) for a reconsideration of our policy'.[22] The real combatants were Robert Sandeman and Col Phydre. Unfortunately, Henry Durrand suddenly passed away. It was now decided to hold the conference on February 3, 1871. While Sindh was represented by its Commissioner, Sir William Morewerther, and Col Phydre, Superintendent of the Frontier, Upper Sindh, the Punjab was represented by its newly-appointed Lt. Governor, Henry Davis, two provincial secretaries, the commissioner of the Derajat Division, and Captain Robert Sandeman.

While Sandeman was the key player, his opinions in the matter were hardly considered. The Sindh school of thought prevailed because the conference had decided that, in future, 'the political matters of the British Government with the British tribes in the frontier shall be handled by the Government of Sind in its entirety. So far as the tribals were concerned, Robert Sandeman, of Punjab cadre was to report to his inveterate enemy Col Phydre.The suzerainty of the Khan of Kalat over his tribal chieftains was confirmed. All dealings with the tribal chiefs were to be conducted via his good offices.' Obviously, the participants must have put blinkers over their eyes by asking for the impossible. Such a blinkered approach would have generated civil war conditions in the Kalat state, because no self-respecting chieftain would have reconciled himself to such a situation. The conferee must have been living in an imaginary world. It skirted the basic issue of strained relations between the Khan of Kalat and his disloyal chieftains. No wonder, there was a 'national uprising against oppression' in Kalat in 1872.

The Fallout

Robert Sandeman was one of the few who could speak with authority on the subject. He also commandeered a host of tribal chieftains, who were ready to follow him and his bidding. He was, however, all too junior to be listened to with much respect in the administrative hierarchy. Col Phydre was jealous of his wisdom, virtues, popularity and success, and he manouvred successfully his boss, Sir William Morewerther, who had to retire in disgrace in 1876. Sir Henry Durrand, had he lived, could have given a helping hand to Robert Sandeman, who, in turn, was in no hurry. He decided to bid his time. He was mentally preparing himself to wait until eternity. His time was to come after an agonizing wait of five years. 1876 was his year of glory and he had many more years of celebrations in the cause of the Baloch, which was both his weakness as well as a strong point.

9

Balochistan's Hindu Connection

THE very mention of Balochistan stirs the passions of a Baloch and makes him totally emotive. It reminds him of his glorious tradition going back to several centuries. The concept of Balochistan as a nation stirs the deepest recesses of his mind. It consists of three parts. The Khan of Kalat, however, lays notional claim to the entire territories of Balochistan, extending to Iran from the west, to Afghanistan in the north, on the east toward the North-West Frontier Province, and in the South towards the Punjab, also laying claim to the territories extending to the river Indus. The Khan of Kalat is a Brahui himself and largely rules territories populated by the Brahuis, the Balochi and miscellaneous races, largely concentrated in Makran.

Makran is virtually another country, with a large coastline of 750 miles. Col B E Holdich described it as the land of 'myrrh and spikenard' and asserts that 'the euphoria of the sandy wastes and the mangroves of the swamps are still as much as Arrian (the Greek historian) describes them'.[1] Makran

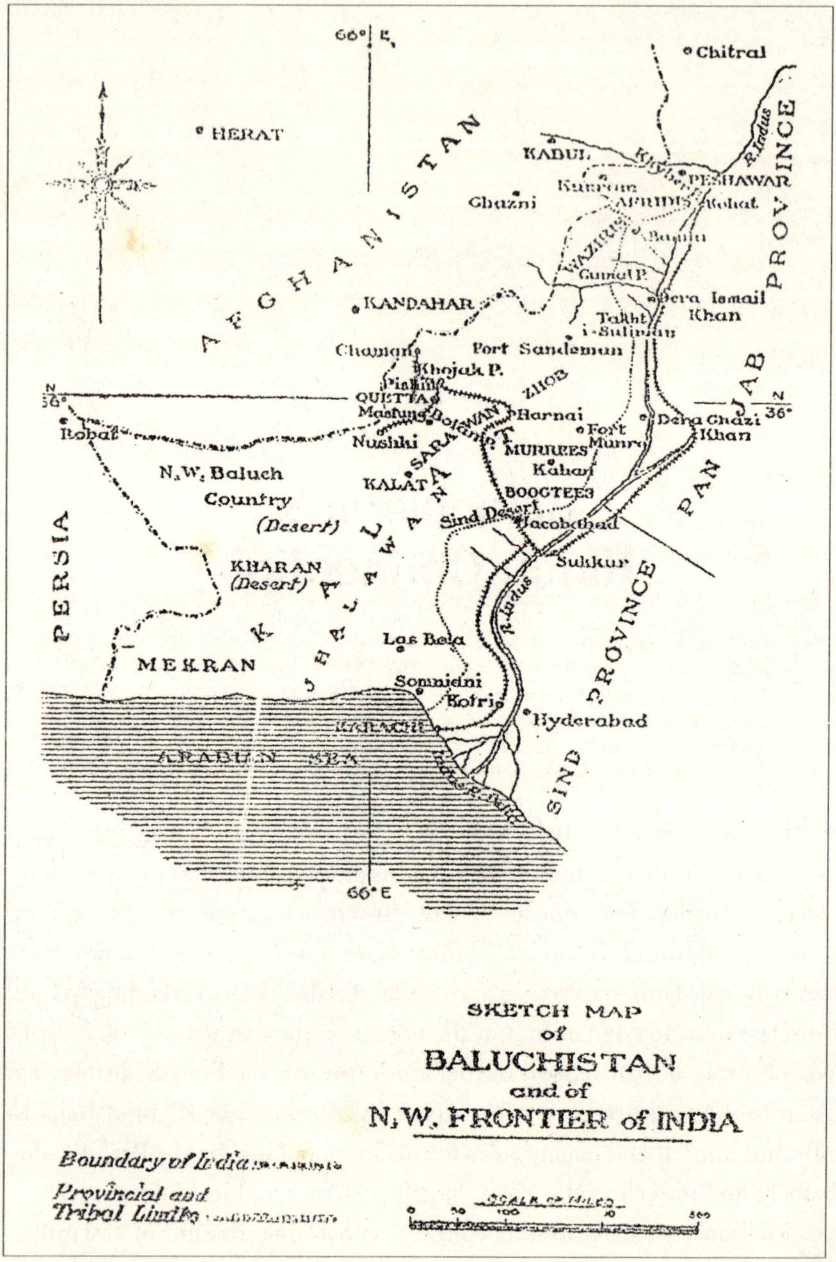

Source: Thonoton, Thomas Henry. Colonel Sir Robert Sandeman, Kohn Murray, London, 1879

is largely populated by Gitchkis (of Sikh/Rajput origin), Baledis (of Arab extraction) and Nausherwanis (of Persian/Baloch origin). Similarly, Las Bela, bordering Sind are Sindhi and not Balochi speaking.

What is actually called Balochistan, with its capital headquartered at Quetta, is an agency for Balochistan created as a new British protectorate responsible directly to the Government of India. It was carved out of the Khanate of Kalat in 1877 at the direct initiative of Sir Robert Sandeman, who was appointed as the first agent of Balochistan to the Governor-General of India. Afghan districts of Pishin, Sibi, Chattel and Share Amidadded were added to it after the Afghan war. The British Balochistan is the most fertile portion of all. It is largely Pathan dominated, with few Baloch establishments.

To Hell and Back

The vast spaces of Balochistan have been described unfavourably by numerous travelers since the times of Arrian.

The Makran region was now in the kitty of the vast Caliphate empire. His messenger reporting about the Makran region to Caliph Umar wrote in poetic verse:

'O Commander of the faithful!
It's a land where the plains are stony;
Where water is scanty;
Where the fruits are unsavory;
Where men are known for treachery;
Where plenty is unknown;
Where virtue is held of little account;
And where evil is dominant;
And a lesser army is useless there;
The land beyond it is even worse.'

This is the most evocative description of the unetched condition of the Makran region during medieval times. Things have not improved much during the subsequent years.

Sir Charles Napier has compared the land to hell incarnate, which 'must have been the place where, after the creation of the world, the spare rubbish was shot down'. The *Gazeteer of Balochistan* in the words of its chronicler adds to the gloomy picture, when describing the physical environment of Makran. 'I should say, take one of those big brown stones one sees all over Balochistan which, looking as if they had just come out of a fire, very aptly represent Makran, and, just dot a few speks of green on it and the picture is complete. The people are a wretched lot, very dirty, very greedy, and very uninteresting'.[2]

Balochistan is truly a land of rugged and bare mountains, waterless courses, dry and brown valleys and stark plateaus. Apparently there can be no relief to the eye as far as one can see. Wheresoever a little grass grows, there are camels, goats and sheep to be found. Rainfall is scanty. There are plenty of mangroves to be found in the western belt. There are no permanent rivers to be followed in the entire region.

The landscape has, however, the majesty usually associated with the Sahara of African continent. It is also the land of romance associated with the folktale of Shirin and Farhad. Above all, it is in the very psyche of the Baloch. How does it matter, if the British ruler and the Bengali Babu find it difficult to adjust to the environment? Here is an amusing tale of 'Bengalee Baboos' employed by the Sindh-Paschim Railway, running away from the scene in Balochistan at the first danger signal, after submitting a petition to the Chief Engineer: 'Honored Sir–The petition of the undersigned Bengalee Baboos humbly showed that cholera having broken out in the railway works to remain here is instantaneous death. What can a Baboo give in exchange of his soul? We leave here today by the six O'clock train in anticipation of sanction

Yours Obedient humble servants,

Signed (about twenty-nine)'[3]

Contrast it with Sir Robert Groves Sandeman, who lived and died for the cause of the Baloch for twenty-six years of his professional career. When on the deathbed, 'It was stated by the next Lady Sandeman that he was uttering the words, "Baloch people" to the last'.[4]

Fertile Balochistan

It would be wrong to assume that Balochistan is no more than a waterless and neglected desert land. The fertile valley of Panjgur was watered by a number of streams, and cotton, date and grapes were also cultivated there. The Southern part of Balochistan, now constituting the Dera Ghazi Khan district of the Punjab, thrives on vast cultivated lands; thanks to a network of canals linked to the river Indus. Things have improved considerably as we move towards northeastern part of Balochistan,with considerable concentration of the Pathan community.

It is blessed with a chain of streams flowing from the mountains, beside kerezee, the underground water channel peculiar to this part of the country. This channel usually runs for two to three miles constituting an effective network of irrigation channels watering fields and orchards. There are shafts in the irrigation channels at an interval of about 100 feet for drawing out water. In fact, some of the finest fruits are grown in this part of the countury. Mustang is famous for its grapes and melons. Quetta has earned a great name for its peaches and apricots. Apozai is famous for its pine forest and woods of Chilgoza, another appetizing variety of dry fruits. The name of Apozai has been changed to that of Fort Sandeman, as a tribute to Robert Sandeman.

Reformation Zeal

The desolation to which Balochistan had been subjected was largely man-made. It is the genius of one single individual who reversed the process. Sandeman, posted to Dera Ghazi Khan from 1866 to 1875, transformed the situation through the mechanism of introducing canal irrigation. The Mirrani tradition was revived effortlessly. Things appeared beyond redemption when he took over the Balochistan regency. The Khanate of Kalat was on the verge of a civil war. The mountain passes were once again opened to flourishing trade between India, Iran and Afghanistan. The roads were made communicable. A network of railway lines was introduced for the first time. Agriculture, including fruit culture, was revived extensively. Peace returned through the mechanism of arbitration between quarreling tribes. The authority of the tribal chieftain was restored. Balochistan was now a thriving province of British India. All this was achieved in the short span of fifteen years. Several Afghan districts were incorporated within Balochistan regency.

At last the Baloch, the Brahui, the Pathan and other communities had learnt the art of living together and practiced it by example under a benign administration. This was made possible, because Robert Sandeman had decided to expand his vision beyond the limits of the Dera Ghazi Khan district. He was determined to adopt the Baloch and his causes. Nay, he must have been born a Baloch in his previous birth. Kalat literally means 'fort' or 'stronghold'. Robert Sandeman had turned Balochistan into a Kalat. How did all this come to pass is a saga that needs to be recapitulated at length.

Post-Mithankot Developments

Sandeman lost the battle at Mithankot conference in 1871, but won the war decisively over his Khanate policy. Kalat was his next target and he began to work on his strategy and lost no time on it. He recognized from the outset that the Baloch was completely alienated, and in order to win him over to his side, he began to work assiduously by winning over the tribal chiefs to his side. He had the grand vision of winning over the top bureaucracy of British India, the Khan of Kalat, the tribal chiefs and the Baloch populace in general. 1877 was the year of his triumph and he was appointed to the highest post of agent to the Governor-General in Balochistan. (Hereinafter referred to as AGG). Balochistan agency was virtually his creation, but he had to work hard to achieve his ultimate objective.

He had a score to settle with the Sindh administration, who disputed with him over the status of the Khan of Kalat vis-à-vis his tribal chiefs of Brahui extraction. Sandeman was clear in his mind that the Khan was no more than the head of the Confederacy of Chiefs, who was reputed to work through consensus in a federal system. He was expected to honour the 'Unwritten Constitution' of his predecessor and abide by the tribal conventions of his predecessors, and, additionally, respect the tribal convention and norms in dealing with the tribal chiefs. Justice was not only to be done to the tribal chiefs, but they were expected to perceive it in the right spirit. It was also practical politics. The tribal chiefs were too powerful to be ignored. There was also a lurking danger of civil war. Hostilities broke out at regular intervals in defiance of the nominal Kalat ruler. Sandeman was bold enough to work in defiance of the Mithankot resolution; as it had recognized the Khan of Kalat as the supreme ruler by totally overreaching the rights and privileges of the tribal chiefs.

Turning the Tide

Having brought peace and prosperity to the Dera Ghazi Khan district, he was ready to perform yet another bigger task. He was an officer and a mere lieutenant in the ranks of the Punjab army. Moreover, Kalat did not fall in his jurisdiction. However, he had the temerity to persuade higher authorities to assign him the new challenge bordering beyond his province. He advocated the 'friendly negotiation' policy to achieve his hidden agenda regarding Kalat. He even offered to go on a mission to Kalat to settle the dispute between the Khan of Kalat and his rebellious chieftains. He was rebuffed time and again by the Sindh authorities, but he had the hearty backing of the Punjab government and the Calcutta authorities in this endeavour. He successfully attempted 'possibly the most daring of his exploits...to persuade the Marri chiefs after a particularly successful raid to return their plunder and make submission with he remaining alone as a hostage in Marri country till [the tibals] [he] had returned from Sind'.[5]

He sent such persuasive plaints that the Viceroy of India was truly impressed and allowed his mission to proceed ahead in defiance of whatever came in his way. The Sindh authorities were mesmerized, but not at all impressed by his capabilities to defy and, yet win hands down. Thereafter, he simply ignored the Sindh authorities, devised his own rules and regulations to meet resistance. He had achieved his goal of reconciling the differences among recalcitrant parties without overlooking his main objective of expanding the frontiers of the British Indian empire (through general consent of his subjects). The message travelled all over Balochistan and beyond. The mission to Kalat was also a grand show in the style of an impressive Indian marriage.

Mission to Kalat

The firman of the Governor General in the council of 21 October 1875 was to direct Captain Sandeman, to 'go via the Mari hills to Kalat, where he was to ascertain and report how the Khan of Kalat and the Brahui Sirdars could be reconciled; and how the Bolan Pass and the Cheitali route could be kept open to traffic'. Sir W Morewerther of Sindh was his boss for this particular mission, from the political aspect, but he was largely ignored as future development showed. Captain Sandeman proceeded on this mission on the 23 November 1875 and was accompanied by Captain H Wylie, one of his closest advisors in Balochistan affairs. He was also accompanied on this mission by Munshi Hittu Ram, Superintendant of the deputy commissioner's office, and Ganpat Rai, clerk of the deputy commissioner's English office, Dera Ghazi Khan.

The Hindus from the Dera Ghazi Khan district were to rise very high and play a very important role in the coming future of Balochistan for the next seventeen years. Consequently, they were also with him at the time of his death in 1892. In fact, they were his constant companions and virtual eyes and ears and listening posts for him.

Captain Sandeman travelled in style. He was accompanied by a vast conclave of 750 horsemen and 330 footmen, besides several Baloch sardars of Dera Ghazi Khan and the hilly region.

Dera Ghazi Khan Tumundars	**Hill Sardars**
Imam Baksh Khan Mazari	Mehrulla Khan Mari
Jamal Khan Leghari	Ghulam Murtaza Khan Bugti
Ghulam Hyder Khan Gurchani	Bloch Khan Khetran
Miran Khan Dreshak	Kadir Baksh Khetnan
Ghulam Hyder Khan Lund	...
Sikand Khan Khosa	
Mazar Khan Lund	

The Mazari, Leghari, Gurchanu, Dreshak, Lund, Khosa, Marri, Bugti and Khetran tribes constituted the cream of the Baloch tribes and their Sardars constituted Sandeman's informal Jirga. Captain Wylie, Hittu Ram and Ganpat Rai constituted his 'inner council'. It was a delegation which must have impressed the Khan of Kalat and his dissident Brahui chieftains.

Long March to Kalat

Sir William Morewerther was all long under the impression that Robert Sandeman was to confine his role to settling of Marri and Bugti affairs and do no more. On the contrary, Sandeman's mission had automatically expanded to envelop the entire Kalat. The fact of the matter was that the Khan of Kalat and his warring lieutenants were sick of constant quarreling and, therefore, they were subconsciously exploring a via media out of this imbroglio. The entire Balochistan was 'torn by dissension and civil war' since the current Kalat ruler resumed office in 1852. In 1862 he had been disposed, and by 1865 and 1867 the Sardars had risen in revolt in the entire state. Things continued to be unsettled during the next decade. All the combatants were ready to go on long leave from fighting among themselves. Sandeman's 1875 mission took advantage of the opportunity. It also became a public demonstration because he was accompanied by eleven prominent Baloch tribal chieftains, and a grand army of 750 horsemen and 330 footmen.

The entire kafila was welcomed by the Khan of Kalat and his warring tribal chieftains with open arms. Notwithstanding the peremptory conduct of the Sindh commissioner, Sandeman marched and pushed towards the Bolan Pass, on his way to Mustaug and Kalat. He offered services to the warring parties as an honest broker. Peace returned to the area in no time. The resultant situation was welcomed all around and both the Punjab government and the Government of India viewed this mission as successful. A word of enthusiastic shabash followed from his sponsors. The Viceroy was totally impressed by Sandeman's policy of 'friendly negotiation', which had succeeded beyond expectations. This also demonstrated the success of his 'forward policy' yet again.

While Sandeman was successful in offering his services for mediation;

his role was highly appreciated in Lahore and Calcutta. Sir Morewerther was unaware of the developments taking place behind his back, and, telegraphically, demanded of Calcutta to put Sandeman on trial for gross insubordination for his conduct, which was 'indiscreet, unbecoming, and contrary to orders and that he had consequently recalled him, and trusted he would be instructed to return at once for venturing in matters with which he had no concern'.[6] It had taken Robert Sandeman years to cross swords with the Sindh authorities, and, finally, to corner them after a decade. He had now his revenge. The 'daring young officer' charged with gross insubordination had turned the table. The Government of India in its wisdom had decided to divest the Sindh authorities of all responsibilities relating to the State of Kalat and transferred its responsibilities to the Commissioner of Derajat under whom Robert Sandeman then functioned.

Thus, Sandeman became the wholesale boss of the Kalat show for all practical purposes. However, this particular job was still incomplete, he was still awaiting the call from Kalat. The Government of India was in entire agreement with him, that the assignment he had undertaken of settling disputes within the state of Kalat needed to be cemented further by another visit. He was sent back after a few months.

Forward Policy Celebrated

The result was the famous Mustang agreement with the Khan of Kalat in June 1876. The signing of the agreement coincided with the settling of the disputes between the Khan and his tribal chieftains, by referring them to the jirgas or the councils of the Sardars and the Khan's vakils for a final settlement.

The Mustang agreement had laid down rights and duties of the Khan and the Sardars, between them and regarding disputes between the Sardars themselves. It also laid down the rule of the British Government as the final authority. In essence, Robert Sandeman became the super boss as the final court of appeal. The Mustang agreement thus sanctified the advent of the British Indian Government as the masters of Balochistan. It came to pass without firing a single shot. Logically, it created a state within state of the agency of Balochistan, headquartered at Quetta. Robert Sandeman was appointed as the first Governor-General's agent in Balochistan. The agreement reduced the Khan of Khan to a subordinate status. Makran was also created as a state within state with a Nazim to run it under the thumb of the political agent (Kalat State), who, in turn, reported to Quetta directly. The chain of command was clear. The British government had put a seal of approval over Sandeman's 'patented forward policy'. It was adopted as the frontier policy on principle of filling up empty spaces and leaving no vacuum for potential enemies.

Lord Lytton, the Viceroy of India, became Sandeman's foremost advocate and, indeed, put a seal of approval on the forward policy in a famous dispatch addressed to the Secretary of State for India, in which inter alia he stated 'of one thing we feel certain. It is to be conducive to British interests, as we have no doubt it is, to influence the tribes and people who lie beyond our borders; we must be in contact with them. It is by the every day acts of earnest, upright English gentlemen that lasting influence must be obtained, not by sporadic demonstrations, nor any sudden or temporary influence purchased by money or presents. If at length in binding more closely the people of Kalat to us by making them feel the benefit of piece and the power for good exercised by the British government, we shall have added an additional bulwark to our empire. An important part of the empire will no longer be harassed by mistrustful, wild and dangerous neighbours, and our officers will have chiefs and populations to deal with who welcome their councils and receive as their best friends'.[7]

Kitchen Cabinet

Sir Sandeman was on top of the world and the master of all he surveyed. His series of successes were entirely due to his management skills and his kitchen cabinet which was composed of his British, Hindu and Baloch associates. The office set up of the AGG in Balochistan was headed by his first Assistant, Richard Isaac Bruce, who had worked with him as Assistant Commissioner, Rajanpur (Dera Ghazi Khan district), thus with considerable experience of dealing with the Baloch affairs as one of his closest associates. In turn, he was assisted by Col L S Reynolds as his second assistant and

Captain H Wylie as his third assistant. Khan Bahadur Haq-Nawaz Khan gave a local flavour to his kitchen cabinet. One of the members of the kitchen cabinet was Suraj Kaul, a Kashmiri Pandit, who was also with him in his Las Bela sojourn and the aborted Makran mission.

The other two, Rai Bahadur Hittu Ram and Diwan Ganpat Rai, were natives of the district and were associated with him during his Dera Ghazi Khan sojourn, which had actually educated him in the Baloch affairs and prepared him for a larger role in Balochistan. Diwan Ganpat Rai had joined him in 1874 and accompanied him to Marri as his native assistant. He was Sandeman's advisor in Pathan affairs, as Hittu Ram was largely his adviser in the Baloch affairs. Rai Hittu Ram was his closest adviser, towering over the rest of the team. In the words of Lieutenant Col Richer, Hittu Ram was 'an eye-witness and a principal actor' in all his major actions. He was also 'the most trusted of all Sandeman's officers'. Sir West Ridgeway called him 'the best of the best lot'. He was a genius by any existing standards, and a many-splendoured human being. There was an argument going around during the times of Sandeman in Balochistan about, 'And it may be worthwhile to note that among those numerous wiseacres who love to discover that every prominent man's work is really done by someone else, some held that all Bruce's work was done by Hittu Ram. Thus, if both had been right, we should have led to the conclusion that it was Hittu Ram who acquired and organized Balochistan. Both, of course, as is usual in such cases, were entirely and ludicrously wrong, but the fact that such a notion was at all possible shows how prominent was Hittu's share in the administration and how deep the impression made by his administration, by his ability and force of character on those who came in contact with him'.[8]

Hittu Ram

The bio-data of Hittu Ram makes an exciting story. It is a rags-to-riches story. Born in 1843 at Shikarpur (Dera Ghazi Khan) in a small shopkeeper's family, he had learned Multani Lhanda, Urdu and some Persian in his younger days. He started his professional career as assistant clerk in the deputy commissioner's office at the age of sixteen. He had a charismatic personality and began to rise very early in ranks. He made several jumps to the posts of patwari (1862), judicial clerk (1866), second-Grade Reader (1870), and first-grade reader (1872) followed by another jump to the regular post of superintendent, deputy commissioner's vernacular office, the very next year. Robert Sandeman had taken over as the deputy commissioner of the Dera Ghazi Khan district in 1866. Hittu Ram could have hardly escaped his sharp and roving eyes. In fact, Hittu was his eyes and ears as regards the Baloch affairs. Sandeman took him along during his investigations of the Kalat imbroglio. In the meanwhile Hittu Ram published in 1875 his history of the Dera Ghazi Khan district in Urdu with the title of Gul Bahar, making him an authority on Dera Ghazi Khan and Baloch affairs. The fact that Hittu Ram had five jumps in posts in the decade under Robert Sandeman speaks for itself. After Sandeman moved to Quetta as the first AGG in 1877, he took Hittu Ram and Diwan Ganpat Rai along with him. Hittu Ram was further promoted to the post of first native assistant to the AGG during the same year. Thus, Hittu Ram spent another fifteen years working under his boss. Those years were the most exciting for both of them, coping with the problems of Las Bela, Makran, Kalat and the Dera Ghazi hilly region. He was promoted to the post of extra assistant commissioner, a position considered very high for Indian aspirants in those years.

Even after the death of Robert Sandeman in 1892, Hittu Ram performed the duties of the political adviser to HH the Khan of Kalat; he was further escalated to the post of assistant political agent subsequently. He even acted as an AGG briefly during Robert Sandeman's absence from his august post. Amidst the diverse assignments which became his lot for well over three decades, Hittu Ram also found time for academic diversions. Besides the histories of Dera Ghazi Khan and Balochistan, both in Urdu, he also had an unpublished manuscript in Balochi language and literature to his credit. Here was a man of high-caliber sagacity, intellectual integrity, restless energy and utter devotion to the Balochi cause in this god-forsaken part of the subcontinent. All those qualities found complete fruition in his varied and rich life extending over sixty-seven years. He retired in 1896 with full honours on health grounds, living the life of a country gentleman, and passing away quietly in 1910.

Big Brother

A random sampling would indicate the yeoman services Hittu Ram rendered to Robert Sandeman and his associates like Richard Isaac Bruce and to the cause of British empire in general and the Baloch cause in particular. Above all, he loved his Baloch and adopted his cause as his primary obligation. He accompanied Robert Sandeman on his first visit to Kalat in 1875 and he was there at his deatbed when Sandeman breathed his last in Las Bela. The last person beside the new Lady Sandeman, to exchange notes with him, was Hittu Ram, who was also requested to convey his last 'salaam' to his associates and tribal chieftains. His importance can be gauged from the fact that very frequently he presided over the jirgas at tribal chieftains' meets and settled disputes in the name of the AGG. He was there to investigate the Marri raid during 1880, and was assigned on deputation with the Afghan boundary commission the very next year, and in the same year he sat over the jirga for settlement of the Marri-Bugti disturbances.

In 1888, Hittu Ram was assigned the duty of the Kalat settlement work, as well as sent on special duty to the Bolan Pass; besides he was assigned on special duty with Sandeman during the same year. He also accompanied Sandeman on his Makran deputation during 1885 to settle intra-tribal disputes. He was also with him during Sandeman's second trip to Makran in 1892, which was aborted due to the sudden demise of Sandeman during his halt at Las Bela. Hittu Ram was Robert Sandeman's shadow that would not go away.

Robert Sandeman and his deputy Richard Isaac Bruce 'constantly employed Rai Bahadur Hittu Ram ..., with most valuable results, ... he was an official of high rank ..., and with a wonderful character for impartiality'.[9] All credit is due to Robert Sandeman, who was searching for a person of Indian origin to match his own extraordinary abilities, which, no person other than Hittu Ram had. They worked together and restored peace in large spaces of Kalat, where only chaos prevailed for centuries together. They were together for fifteen years in the service of Balochistan contributing towards the work of pacification, consolidation and organisation. Robert Sandeman never had enough of Hittu Ram, his loyal deputy as testified to by Lt. Col C. Archer: 'whenever a specially difficult piece of administrative of political work was to be done, especially important jirga to be guided to a sound decision, some miracle of the production of supplies and transport in the midst of barren wastes to be performed, Hittu Ram was almost invariably the agent employed, particularly if the matter concerned the Brahui or Baloch part of the province'.[10] Hittu Ram could converse both in Brahui and Balochi languages with ease and make the dialogue flow freely, and yet made certain that his authority remained unquestioned and the lakshman rekha was not crossed, yet the impression went around that he was the friendliest person on earth, who was expected to deal fairly, honestly and with sympathy.

Sandeman-Hittu Duo

Under the terms of the treaty of 1876, AGG had become the supreme arbiter of disputes between the Khan and his Sardars. The Khan was given due formal honours, but the actual power had slipped away from his hands. While Sandeman was now the final court of appeal, the real decision-making authority vested with his deputies of whom Hittu Ram stood out: 'But in the essential question of the nomination of Sardars, the summoning of jirgas for the settlement of inter-tribal disputes, and the general preservation of peace in the country, the agent of the Governor-General is recognized all over Balochistan as having taken the place of the Khan, and his mandate naturally commands a great deal of respect and obedience than did ever to that of 'his Highness'. These are the actual words abstracted from the Balochistan Report of 1886.

In actual fact, Hittu Ram ran the show in the name of Robert Sandeman. He presided over the *jirgas*. He negotiated with the Khan and Sardars in the name of the AGG. He placated them. He cajoled them and finally he enforced his decisions with iron hand. He was here, there and everywhere. An example or two would do underlining his indispensability.

The waywardness of the Khan and other rulers as well as Sardars is indicated by a shooting incident that took place in 1893, whereby the Khan, after a heated argument with his Wazir, attempted to kill him in open darbar. He actually shot him dead, as well as his son aged 19-20 years old, and his father (a bed-ridden and helpless cripple of 94 years). The matter came to the attention of the AGG, who decided to send Hittu Ram to Kalat 'with the rank of Honorary Political Agent, and salary of one thousand rupees, and ninety rupees travelling allowance'.

There is a sequel to this story. Hittu Ram became a victim of intrigues and jealousies in the office of the AGG soon after the passing away of Robert Sandeman in 1892. There were shrill demands for his recall, but to the credit of J.W. Brown, Secretary, Foreign Department, Government of India, the newly-appointed AGG was snubbed in the following ringing words:

'The Government of Balochistan made objection to (Hittu Ram) owing to his being a Hindu. I will explain that the employment of Hindu (for the disbursement of Rs 55,000 only) is probably in consonance with the old tradition of Balochistan (The Khan of Kalat) himself wished to appoint a Hindu as his Wazir'.[11]

The bureaucracy that had taken over the agency persisted in its nefarious game of bringing down Hittu Ram a notch or two from his high pedestal. J A Crawford had succeeded Robert Sandeman as an officiating AGG and he had the gumption to write to headquarters asking for the recall of Hittu Ram. 'The Political Agent in Kalat informs me that the importance of the position and work assigned to the Rai Bahadur had of late much decreased, and also that His Highness had on several occasions complained of the heavy cost to his state of the pay and allowances of Hittu Ram's appointment'.

Thanking the Associates

The resentment against the Sandeman-Hittu Ram duo surfaced during Robert Sandeman's life. Sandeman felt very much had gratified at the performance of Rai Bahadur Hittu Ram and Diwan Ganpat Rai for the services rendered by them, and, consequently, Sandeman lost no opportunity in awarding them suitably. He recommended the grant of jagir on the Indus river bank in their home district of Dera Ghazi Khan. Accordingly, he recommended the grant of a jagir of 300 acres to Hittu Ram, and thereby an endless correspondence ensued, the essence of which is contained in this communication from Robert Sandeman to the foreign department, Government of India, inter alia stating the following: 'Request for the grant of a jagir of 300 acres of land rent free for life to the Deputy

Commissioner of Dera Ghazi Khan who deserved (Hittu Ram) to enter into an agreement in the event of land being acquired to him on the river bank, to the effect that if the land were [was] washed away by the water he would have no claim to compensation. The land would have a very much greater value in his eyes if he could obtain it in the particular place which he has set his heart, and to attach to such a grant, if given as the banks of the Indus, the conditions mentioned by Mr Thoburn [Deputy Commissioner] would appear to render the grant a mere farce for the Indus which is constantly changing its course'.[12] Terrence C Cain has rightly pointed out, 'It looks as though the Indian Political Secretary who had read the file there meant to sabotage the scheme'. That Hittu Ram ultimately got his jagir and enjoyed the benefits of retirement as a country gentleman turned out to be a story with a happy ending.

Last Message

Sir Robert rated Hittu Ram the highest among his closest associates. Even at his deathbed he sent for Hittu Ram several times and, in fact, the state matters were uppermost in his mind, 'My mind is not easy', he said, 'at not being able to see about these things myself. I beg you to see that they are properly attended to'.[13] Sir Robert passed away on 29 January 1892. His last words were, 'Where are the people? I cannot speak without the people' and he quoted once or twice from the Holy Bible, 'If the trumpet give[s] forth an uncertain sound, who shall prepare for battle?'[14] After Sademan's sudden death, his closest associate Hittu Ram was reduced to zero. Hittu Ram lingered on for a few more years but the zest had gone out of his life. There was no life beyond Sir Robert. The atmosphere had suddenly vitiated and Hittu Ram had unpleasant experiences handling the Kalat situation. He continued at his job for another four years but he had no heart and mind in his work. Finally, he retired due to failing eyesight and survived for another fourteen years, living his days at his native place of Rajanpur. Pygmies had taken over from a giant and men like Hittu Ram and Ganpat Rai had nowhere to hide.

Lt Col C Archer, who wrote the preface to Hittu Ram's book, replaced Sandeman in Balochistan is fulsome in praise of Hittu Ram. He had exhausted the entire adjectives in the vocabulary to describe the man behind the man. It seems to be a correct measure of the man. The praise includes 'his intellectual and moral qualities', 'a great leadership', 'a wonder character for impartiality', 'unassuming, kind and hospitable', 'strong bend towards religious study and enquiry', 'the spirit of military hero', 'force of personality', a man of strong sagacity and a 'country gentleman'. Here was a person coming from a humble background rising to the highest position and helping in the process to acquire the large territory of Balochistan, almost in a fit of absentmindedness, deserves our total admiration. Lt Col Archer again has the last words: 'He was barely five feet in height and thin even out of proportion, so that, with his large head, thin body, and spindle legs he presented at first sight almost grotesque appearance resembling not a little some benevolent gnome of a German fairy tale. It was impossible to be in company with him for many minutes without feeling the force of personality in this little wisp of a man, as he sat deeply sunk in the arm chair or bolt upright with his small legs twisted under or in front of him; without recognizing the strong sagacity expressed by his face, with its wide open forehead, strongly marked nose, and small piercing eyes under heavy eyebrows. And the impression made was deepened by his one great physical endowment, his voice-deep powerful, and with a clang in it as of metal'.[15]

Diwan Ganpat Rai

Diwan Ganpat Rai was also a resident of Dera Ghazi Khan. He belonged to a distinguished and respectable family drawing his lineage to the Mughal times. He was another close associate of Robert Sandeman, who was completely overshadowed by the personality of Hittu Ram. He was a quiet worker, who made his mark in an unobtrusive fashion. He was a specialist like Hittu Ram, who retired as Extra Assistant Commissioner. His last assignment was as Wazir of Las Bela. Udho Dass Diwan, the Nazim of Makran, was his younger brother. He was awarded with the CIE (Commander of Indian Empire) honour. He was awarded a Jagir in Dera Ghazi Khan, the honour which again he shared with Hittu Ram. The careers of both ran parallel, except that he handled the Pathan affairs, for which he was honoured with a medal. The concerns of both ran parallel except for the fact, while Hittu was the public face, Ganpat Rai was the private face of Robert Sandeman. Both of them served Robert Sandeman loyally when they were stationed at Dera Ghazi Khan and Quetta. Both of them joined him on important missions whether it concerned the Kalat imbroglio, disturbances in Makran or the Marri-Bugti troubles.

Both of them were also in the dog house after the death of Robert Sandeman. While Hittu Ram was disgraced at the end of his long career in his Kalat posting as the Wazir, Ganpat Rai was also confronted with the same situation in his last posting as Wazir in Las Bela. Both of them were charged with the 'fault' of being Hindus and running the show, for all practical purpose, for themselves. Hittu Ram was an Arora by caste and Ganpat Rai was a Khatri by birth, but they appeared to be twin brothers to the outside world. One of the greatest virtues of Ganpat Rai was that he felt at home by working behind the scenes. He was thus the other alter ego of Robert Sandeman, to be contrasted with the flamboyant Hittu Ram, whose booming voice could drown the voice of the entire audience facing him. Both of them fitted in the scheme of things, perfectly performing different roles. If one were to employ the musical analogy, three-some would have formed a trio-string orchestra with Robert Sandeman as the conductor, Ganpat Rai playing the melodious and soft piano, and Hittu being in-charge of the high-strung violin.

The agency of Balochistan was Pathan dominated, as contrasted with Kalat state and Makran territories. Ganpat Rai's strong point was his specialization in Pathan affairs. The very fact that Quetta is a Pathan country and several districts of Afghanistan had been incorporated into the agency, it was essential to have expertise in dealing with both Baloch and Pathan affairs. Ganpat Rai was indispensable to Sandeman for his expertise in Pathan affair. He was his deputy during the Afghan War (1878-80) and helped him greatly in opening the Gomal Pass route to Kandahar. Ganpat Rai was awarded the Afghan-war medal in recognition of his services. He also accompanied Sandeman on a highly successful mission to Kandahar. He also performed a number of secret political missions for his mentor. He was with Sandeman on his Zhob tour (1888-80) and the Sherani expedition (1889-90). Here were demonstrations of the 'forward policy' in action. The Russian bear had to be kept out of Afghanistan at all cost by gradually incorporating Afghan districts into the agency. Here Ganpat Rai proved to be very handy.

Award of a Jagir

It was in recognition of his services that Robert Sandeman recommended the award of a jagir of 1000 acres to Ganpat Rai in his home district. This came to be passed in 1889, but he was refused the privilege on that occasion. Sandeman re-opened the question in 1892. His enthusiasm for Hittu Ram and Ganpat Rai never waned. He, once again, recommended the award of a jagir to Ganpat Rai and made a strong case to this effect, in his communication of 2 January 1892 to the foreign department. He recalled Ganpat Rai's numerous services which are 'essentially political and involved "hardships" and "danger to life" and indeed his "health suffered consequent on his exposure to exceptional severities"'. He also reminded the foreign department of his illustrious family background. His ancestors were also honoured by the Mughals, who awarded the title of 'Khwaja' to his ancestor Buhra Mal. Earlier the title of 'Diwan' was conferred on his grandfather, Diwan Sukhram Das, by the Sikh government.

The bureaucrats in the foreign department were equal to him in this task. The low-ranking deputy secretary mocked at the suave but determined Robert Sandeman in his communication dated 20 March 1892. 'There is enough on the file to show that Ganpat Rai's services have been already suitably awarded by "rapid promotions". In his reply the astounded AGG protested over the use of the word "ordinary" in the context of Ganpat Rai whose services in his views had been "quite exceptional"'. The unintended humour and puns must have passed over the head of Robert Sandeman, who persisted with his demand in rewarding Ganpat Rai. Finally the jagir was offered, but the quantum was reduced from 1000 to 500 acres. The bureaucrats were irreconcilable and put a reservation clause which read as follows. '... and that it must not be supposed that service in Baluchistan even meritorious and approved service, carries with it a right to such an award'. The communication of the foreign department is dated 20 April 1892.

Diwan Ganpat was in the Balochistan service for many more years, but he, like Hittu Ram, was marginalized, so much so that he had no control over events in Makran, leading to the recall of his younger brother, Diwan Udho Dass, as Nazim of Makran, following the civil disturbances there. Simultaneously, he was himself in trouble in his capacity as Wazir of Las Belas at the same time. In both the instances, the Hindu factor played a crucial role, as it came to pass for Hittu Ram in his last posting as Wazir of Makran state. In all the instances, the vacuum was created after their mentor Robert Sandeman passed away in 1892.

Makran Re-Visited

Makran, bordering Persia, is generally known as Kech-Makran to distinguish it from the Persian Makran. Together, those constitute the Makran. Kach or Kacch is a term applied to the most alluvial soil in or near the beds of streams. The word Makram is said to be a corruption of the Persian phrase 'maki khoan' (fish eaters), identifiable with the 'chyaghagi' of Arrican Greek. Lord Curzon considered the name to be Dravidian and believes that it appears as Makara in the Brihat Samhita in a list of tribes contiguous to India in the west.

The indigeneous races of Rind, Hot and Malik ruled after the Arabs. The Balochi, who were originally from Persia, settled in Makran for centuries and subsequently migrated to Balochistan and the west bank of the Indus river. They followed the Baledis (of Arabian stock), who were in turn ousted by the Gitchkis of mixed Rajput/Sikh stock. The Gitchkis came under the sovereignty of the Khan of Kalat in the middle of the 19th century. Makran came to the British notice in 1862, for the construction of the Indo-European telegraph line. In 1879, the western boundaries were settled with Persia.

Internally the matters had gone from bad to worse owing to the endless defiance of the Khan of Kalat by his rebellious chieftains. He was in constant conflict with the Gitchkis, Nausherwanis and other races, until the settlement was effected by Sir Robert Sandeman during his 1883–84 trip to Makran. This also proved futile. At least, in Makran, his policy of 'negotiated peace' had proved a failure. Makran had proved to be in a state of civil war. The tribes fought with each other, they quarreled within the tribe, and they continued to fight with the Khan of Kalat individually and collectively.

Racial Disequilibrium

Hills and valleys alternate in this dry, barren and waterless wasteland with a base population of three persons per square mile. It has a coastline of 750 miles with a few good harbours. According to Plutarch, only one quarter of Alexander's army survived the return journey home from here. There are no perennial streams. However, there are well-watered valleys of Panjgur, Kej and Mashkhel. The Panjgur valley is believed to be the jewel in the crown. In the eyes of the Baloch, the Panjgur valley is 'an earthly paradise'. It is also the most troublesome spot in Makran, populated by the quarrelsome Gitchkis and Nausherwanis. The Gitckhis have drawn their power since the middle of the 18th century from the arrangement with the Khan of Kalat, whereby, 'he allowed the Gilchis [Gitchkis] to retain a considerable portion of their power, and established system of government, under which the administration was carried out jointly by a Naib representing the Khan of Kalat and the local Gitchkis chief, between whom the revenues were divided'.[16]

Herein lay the roots of future trouble. The third element in the situation, again a troublesome lot, was the Nausherwanis, a Baloch tribe of Persian extraction, for whom the British had no kind words. They were the masters of 'the droves of camels, sheep and goats', and have been described as 'inveterate freebooters'. They have also been singled out as a 'race of strong-willed, bold, adventurous and able men, bitter opponents of despotism, and stern upholders of rude justice, which animates the administration of tribal bodies, but according to western ideas, are inveterate freebooters'.[17]

State of Civil War

For twenty years before Sandeman's mission to Kalat in 1876, Makran, along with the entire Kalat state, was in a state of anarchy. While Sandeman had succeeded in bringing prosperity to the Dera Ghazi Khan district, and restored peace in the state of Kalat, Makran continued to be in a state of turmoil during his rule of Balochistan (1877–92) and erupted from time to time, because of firm belief among the Makranis that no justice could be expected from the domineering Brahui confederacy that ruled the state of

Kalat. Peace was only momentary and brief pause and interregnum amidst prolonged periods of unrest and civil war.

The contradiction was inherent in the situation. After all, Makran rightfully belonged to the Gitchkis who were its original inhabitants as well as rulers. Unfortunately, they also quarreled among themselves. From time to time they were joined by the Nausherwanis, to put up a joint front against the Kalat ruler, whom they refused to recognize as the legitimate ruler of Makran. Sandeman hoped to resolve temporarily the dispute between the rulers and the Gitchkis and Nausherwanis under his powers of direct intervention. Trouble, however, erupted again in 1882 when during a raid of Panjgur, the Gitchkis chief was slain. There was also trouble because Sandeman had overruled the selections of the next chief of Gitchkis. This was an excuse for Sandeman to take over the administration of Makran, and accordingly, a formal agreement was executed with the Khan, whereby the AGG was granted full powers to resolve disputes in western Balochistan and enforce normalcy in the name of the Khan of Kalat.

Restoring Order

There were only cosmetic changes but nothing really changed in Makran to cheer Sir Robert or the Makranis. Two senior British officers, including Mr Crawford, the acting political agent, were deputed to investigate matters in 1889. Things had not improved and, in fact, the principal Gitchkis chief prayed for the introduction of direct British administration. Sir Robert was himself exasperated by the existing situation. While congratulating Lord Curzon on his taking over as Secretary of State for India in his letter dated 22 November 1891, Sandeman claimed that he had 'not only established peace in the province, but also great prosperity', but he rued the hostile attitude of the Government of India headquartered at distant Calcutta; 'I think that my policy of peace and goodwill is far better than the policy of pure coercion'.[18] The hurdles in his faith, however, did not dissuade him to travel his lonely path.

His troubles were mounting. In 1891 Major Muir, political agent, was wounded by the Kalat's Naib Chief at Kej. This was clearly a dangerous signal. He decided upon his personal visit to Makran during 1891–92.

He was desirous of personal intervention with the Makran chiefs and his political agent on the spot. He had decided to keep track of events by confronting them, but, in order to observe protocol, his officers posted to Makran were expected to function in the name of the Khan. His career came to a sudden end with his premature death. If he had any regrets, he must have had about the deteriorating state of affairs in Makran. In another letter dated 12 January 1892 to Lord Curzon, he opined, 'By acting as a paramount power, we can retain both sides as friends, and still prevent civil war and their doing injury to each other and to ourselves. We can make both sides most useful'.[19] Playing both sides did not work as the events unfolded following his death. Makran was a cauldron that continued to burn before and after his death.

Nazim Udho Dass

Diwan Udho Dass, younger brother of Diwan Ganpat Rai, who was posted as Wazir in Las Bela, was in the high ranks of extra assistant commissioner and had served as native assistant in Makran for several years. He was posted as Nazim of Makran by virtue of his delegation to the Khan of Kalat. He was, thus, the king of all he surveyed. H S Barnes, the AGG, had a good word for him, and went on record that 'he (had) done exceedingly well in a difficult and lonely appointment far away from any support and deserves encouragement'.[20] This communication dated 17 May 1897 was followed by two other communications recommending his salary of Rs 500 per mensem, but advising his withdrawal of additional request for the award of the title of Rai Sahib to him because after all, 'I think one reward at a time is enough'. Udho Dass went on performing his duties with 'quite earnestness' for which he was mentioned. He was no 'Chota Sandeman', but he attempted to combine efficient administration with development. It took just two years of his rule as Nazim to get into serious trouble.

Mehrab Khan, the brother of Gitchkis sardar Shah Umar, revolted, because earlier Robert Sandeman had refused to approve his nomination to chieftainship, notwithstanding the recommendation to this effect by his father. On a different occasion, he was refused the possession of the fort he very much desired. Mehrab Khan was short-tempered and hence he was determined to spread trouble by raising the banner of revolt against the Raj. Mehrab Khan imprisoned the Nazim at Turbat Fort, after taking its possession forcibly on 8 January 1898. Diwan Udho Dass managed to escape and was provided shelter by the Naib of Kej, who himself had revolted earlier. The drama began to unfold with varied response to the crisis situation.

Enveloping Revolt

The hands of the agent, H.S. Barnes were more than full. The Rind tribe had also risen in revolt. Baloch Khan, the notorious Nausherwanis freebooter, abused the Nazim publicly by complaining of lack of good governance. The letter from Mehrab Khan to the native Assistant, Gwadar of 8 January 1898, makes a very interesting reading. It was issued in the name of Allah to the faithful Momins:

'Nasser Min Allah wa futeh harch wa basher ul Momin'

It means 'When comes the assistance from God, the victory comes, soon after, and it is a good tidings for the faithful'. It was pronounced as a revolt by the suffering populace and accordingly, 'on the night attack on him we captured him...we spared his life...and it was owing to the oppression of the Diwan he had brought the casatrophe upon himself'.[21]

Another letter was also issued by the rebelling Sardars: 'When the country came into hands of the "Sarkar", Diwan Udho Dass followed the advice of... 'and excepting committing tyranny and oppression day and night had no other work to do...and through the time of our grandfathers we had never given one-tenth of the produce'.[22] The cat was now out of the bag. The Nazim enforced the law of the land by collecting taxes.

Plethora of Charges

With the passage of time, charges began to fly right and left. The British officials had direct responsibility in this matter for a variety of reasons including, a) 'for treating Mehrab Khan indifferently; b) Levying of revenue taxes (an unusual practice in Makran); c) the vitiated communal atmosphere, besides d) general resentment against the colonial rule. Udho Dass was an easy target. The Khan of Kalat charged that the Nazim's household 'was constituted entirely of Hindus and relations of the Nazim'. On close enquiry, Lt. Barnes found the charge baseless. By March 1898, a Charge d 'Affaires had taken over from Barnes, who pompously asserted in his communication of 16 March 1998: 'The Nazim is apparently much to [be] blame[d] for the late disturbances. It is proposed to remove him eventually, but not at once'.[23] It was true to the extent that the Nazim was physically present in Makran and he was totally oblivious of the conspiracy: Someone had to be a fall guy, and who else but the Nazim ?

Some sanity was introduced into the proceedings after Col Henry Wylie (an old associate of his elder brother, Diwan Ganpat Rai) as the officiating AGG by May 1898. In his communication of 25 May 1898, a clear four months after the crisis erupted, he laid partial blame on Diwan Udho Dass, attributing the revolt to 'the undoubted enthusiasm of the Nazim' ('The Taxwallah') who must have been 'out of touch with the people' and thus 'losing their sympathy', but in his view Udho Dass was not 'a bad or corrupt officer'.[24] He was an upright officer and undoubtedly this was one of the greatest crime. Col Wylie went into the depth of the matter and had a plethora of reasons attributed for the unrest, some of it due to Diwan Udho Dass.

Substantive Reason

Col Wylie has listed a variety of causes which led to the rebellion and those were largely beyond the province of Diwan Udho Dass. The major reason lay in overlooking the claim of Mehrab Khan to chieftainship. He also referred to the unrest prevailing in north-west India, especially in Pathan lands, which spread fast and was catching on like wildfire in Balochistan. He also referred to the murder of an Englishman in Persia bordering Iran, the story of which had spread like wildfire in Makran. The result was an air of defiance, because 'our troops were heavily, and not always successfully, engaged with the Pathan tribesmen, tended to excite men's minds, and led to a belief that we were seen to be drawn into sea'. It is not surprising that many of them should have taken the opportunity to rise against the Khan of Kalat's authority, and attack our survey camps'. The matter did not end here, because the whole of Makran turned against the Raj. The

Nazim told Col Wylie that 'he had been informed by the Gitchkis in Kej that the British and Persian governments had ceased to exist, and a Balochi millennium was to hand, when everybody would be able to plunder and quarrel to heart's content'.[25]

Col Wylie ended his long-winded epistle, dated 17 May 1898, by paying a left-handed tribute to Diwan Udho Dass. '[His] zeal and ability have been frequently brought to your notice by officers visiting Makran. I can only add my testimony to the truth of their remarks. He has a very difficult role to perform, and the way it is carried out is beyond all praises'.[26] The policies that Sir Robert Sandeman had designed were bursting at the seams because the small and puny men had replaced him and, more particularly, his trusted lieutenants had been sidelined.

Hindu Phobia

In the entire literature relating to Sir Robert Sandeman's saga, never had the words 'Hindu' and 'Muslim' appeared. Suddenly, during post-Sandeman times, it became fashionable to ostracize the 'Hindu', and especially the '*banniah*' in him. The entire literature about the Makran episode is a blame game in which the minority community is pilloried.

H S Barnes, the spokesman of the Raj, calls the Nazim a 'Hindu though very capable', as though, thinking of the Hindu in the context of Makran was unimaginable. Naib Musa Khan was well-intentioned, but added insult to the injury by calling the Nazim a 'banniah' (bania) and not a strong man, more probably, on account of his Hindu background and aptitudes, and, possibly, on account of his genes. The Khan of Kalat had no compunction in blaming the Nazim's entire household being 'constituted entirely of Hindus'.[27] The charge proved to be totally false upon independent investigation.

Col Wylie, the officiating AGG, crossed all limits, when he talked of Diwan Udho Dass, as he had the misfortune to be 'a Hindu'. He compounded his folly by his reference to the case of his elder brother, Diwan Ganpat Rai, who was awarded C I E honour, and as well as a distinguishing medal for his services during the Afghan War. He happened to be the Wazir of Las Bela state about the same time; 'It is a doubtful policy to place a

Hindu over a Mohammedan population, and we have seen the experiment fail before in Balochistan, where indeed only to quote the example of Las Belas, in which state a very good and able official quite failed as Wazir and where he has been successfully followed by a Musalman'.[28]

Diwan Udho Dass was a small fry but he was to pay a big price for the entire Makran being on fire during his brief tutelage. Surely, he must have suffered from numerous lacunae in his character to deserve such ignominy. Or, it was written in his stars or the policies inherent in the framework designed by Robert Sandeman, with the tribal chieftain as the fulcrum around whom the entire polity evolved and had failed. The policy was based on the assumption that 'the Baloch was loyal to his chief as a highland clansman to McLvor. Consequently, government can deal safely with a Baloch Tumundar as with any other united monarch'. Here was the Scot Highlander talking to the Baloch Highlanders on the same plane.

The Nazim paid a heavy price for believing in the rule of law and implementing it in real life without discriminating between the poor and rich. Earlier, the poor paid taxes and the rich and powerful escaped due to right connections. Previously, the Khan of Kalat shared the revenue with the Makran Sardars and now they were faced with the incongruity of paying taxes, which was strictly enforced by the Diwan, the 'banniah', who was, in reality no bania, but a distinguished Khatri with the lineage that could be traced to the Mughal days.

Varied Responses

The British responses to the troubles were confused, varied and somewhat contradictory. The baloney days of Sir Robert were no more. They were now confronted with the harsh realities of Makran. It was the major crisis confronting the north-western frontier. For a change, it was not the Pathan who was revolting. The initial response of Barnes the Agent, came twelve days after the rebellion broke out. Apparently, it was self-congratulatory: 'As to the causes, I am inclined to think that of rather the matter of congratulation that the Government of Khan's Nazim should have lasted so long without trouble',[29] thereby absolving the Nazim and turning to other causes for the trouble.

He, however, began to shift his position gradually. If Barnes had one opinion (on 20 January 1898), his communication of 28 January 1898, to the Foreign Department said, 'It is likely that the Nazim may have identified himself with one of the many rival parties in Makran'.[30] Evidently, Udho Dass had forgotten the 'Gayatri Mantra' of Sir Robert in befriending' one and all, and having no enemies. That Sir Robert forgot his own maxim in dealing with Mehrab Khan, who had been overlooked by him and his advisors. It was he who was the root cause of the current Makran trouble.

The truth of the matter was that if anyone had to be charged with responsibility, it had to be no other than Robert Sandeman, the actual 'Bheeshma Pitamah' of Balochistan. Naib Musa Khan of Rekizen, 'a very shrewd and old gentleman', told the political agent of Kalat on 25 February, in great confidence, '...the real reason he explained in very simple words'. He said. 'Baluch Khan was angry about Bit Fort [denied to him]. You have brought a strong government [to the country] which levies revenues from all alike, whereas formerly only poor paid. Mehrab Khan is young and hot-headed. The Nazim is a banniah, and thus country requires a strong man to govern it'.[31]

Rule of Law

There was no law of the land in Balochistan, but only ad hoc laws and regulations which were employed arbitrarily and at sweet will, as the occasion demanded. There were the Frontier Crimes Regulations, the Tribal Customary Law and the Muslim Shariat Law. Above all, the will of the tumundar prevailed in the end. The total anarchy was undoubtedly perpetuated by Robert Sandeman and his minions. The Customary Law Manuel published in 1932, followed by the establishment of judicial courts in Quetta in 1935 brought about some semblance of order. The basic requirement of the rule of law was, however, missing from the Book of Sandeman.

Thus, the changes brought about by him in the structure of the state of Kalat were no more than cosmetic. The Udho Dass' of the world could do no more than they did under the circumstances. Such persons deserve our sympathy. Col Wylie considered Diwan Udho Dass a gentleman, 'who was sincere, honest, committed and development-oriented during his brief tenure as Nazim'. It was testified to by Col Wylie, when he happened to visit the village of Sardar Shahbaz Khan: 'We saw at his village some really respectable buildings and some kerezes [water channels] newly opened, while the people seem contented and of a better class than usually found in Makran'.

Section - V

Social Identity

10
Khatri Caste

IT strains one's imagination to visualize the Indus Valley Civilization being born in a far-flung desert bordering Balochistan, watered by the ancient Sindhu. Similarly the Vedic civilization was nurtured in a semi-desert on the banks of the favourite river of the Rigvedic lore. Equally, the hilly tract of Potohar Plateau located next to the Indus basin (near modern Islamabad and the ancient Taxila) was the home of the Vedas and ancient classics like Mahabharata, which was a Kshatriya lore and most probably 'penned' by them. Imagine the ancient Rishis being inspired by the insipid landscape.

It is the same *karambhumi* where the Kshatriya community originated, and, in turn, most probably gave birth to the present-day Khatri and Arora communities that spread their wings from the Potohar region in the north-west, and to Multan in the southwest, Lahore, the epicenter of the community. The Arora takes off where the Khatri leaves. They belong to the Saraiki-speaking Sindh, headquartered at Aror, the ancient capital of

Sindh, spreading to southwest Punjab, which is also Saraiki speaking. The Arora and the Saraiki are coterminous with each other.

The third element is the Sarasvat Brahmin. The Sarasvat are the Brahmin of the Indus basin. The Khatri and Arora are the raison d'etre for the very existence of the Sarasvat Brahmin. The Sarasvat are officially designated *purohits* (priests) of both the Khatri and Arora communities. They are so liberal as to be the *purohit* of the entire Hindu *samaj*, including the Dalit. They are, however, primarily the priest of the Khatri and secondarily of other communities. In fact, true to the principle of hierarchical organization, the status of respective Sarasvat *gotra* (sub-castes) is measurable by the status of the Khatri *gotra* to which it administers. Whether it is the Indus Valley and Rigvedic civilizations, or great Indian classics, or Khatri, Arora or Sarasvat communities, the uniting factor remains the Indus River.

Kshatriya Cult

The term Kshatriya evolved over a long period of time. It tells a great deal about the sociology of the Indian civilization. Rigveda is the first to mention it. The name occurs fifty times in the great Indian classic. It connotes both dominion and might. The variants of the term include ksatra, ksataram, su-ksatrasa, su-kstra and su-kstran. All these variants are a play on the term Kshatriya and establish the fact of its rawness in initial stages of development of the Kshatriya varna. Rigveda, however, makes no mention of varna in the entire classic. The term Kshatriya is imprecisely used, because it is employed both in singular and plural. It is actually for the first time in Atharvada that the term denotes both dominion and Kshatriya varna jointly.

The Yajurveda sanctifies the term Kshatriya, meaning the Kshatriya varna specifically. The four-category caste divisions must have got sanctified by the time of the Yajurveda. The term continued to denote dominion or power in addition. The latter meaning signified the acceptance of the distinct features of the Kshatriya varna. The term, with its new meaning, continued to be promoted by the Brahmin, and hence it got sanctified as the varna. Consequently the virgin term Kshatra, employed by the Rigveda, got dropped.

Followed the 'Tattiriya Brahmana' which associated the three higher varnas with the respective Vedas.The Brahmins were linked with the Sama, the Kshatriya with the Yajur and the Vaishya with the Rigveda. This division is a matter of much speculation, but, at least, it goes to establish that the three varnas were viewed on par until the Brahmins had not gained superamacy. The Brahmin were still awaiting the call of Parasuram to vanquish the Kshatriya definitely. The Vedic gods of the Kshatriya have been identified as follows: Indira, Mrita, Parjanya, Rudra, Varuna and Yama.

Defining Power

The term *rajanya* is also used for Kshatriya, to denote a class that had begun to wield power and enjoy it. The varna divisions must have sharpened to the extent of specialization. They must have become symbols of power and authority by the time of Panini, who defines *rajanya* as the descendants of the king. The consolidation of the Kshatriya class had been sanctified by the Brahmin, and the Kshatriya were pronounced as the protectors of the Brahmin as well as of dharma, besides being the lords of the world. Obviously, there must have been an understanding, in the sense of 'you pat my back and I shall pat yours'. Faith and power had come to a mutual understanding. In fact, the Brahmin had gained much more in the bargain.

There are, however, still graces attached to the varna organization. It was flexible and not rigid. It was still possible to migrate to the higher varna. The great and renowned Vishwamitra, the Kshatriya, who contributed several Vedic hymns achieved the distinction of migrating to the higher class. Krishna was a Yadav, who authored the great Gita, and was indeed a Brahmin of Brahmins without migrating to the higher varna. These are, however, exceptions which necessarily do not prove the rule. There was no proof to establish that there was a separate fighting class, or there were identifiable military or non-military classes. There was also constant migrations across the north-western borders, necessitating absorption of foreign elements. There must have been smart mechanisms to meet with such eventualities. At least, some of them must have been absorbed as *rajanya* or Kshatriya. The Brahmin must have come handy to issue suitable certification.

Stabilizing the Kshatriya

The Vedic society was an evolving system, democratic by instinct and egalitarian in nature in the initial stages. There was a constant transfusion of blood. There were opportunities galore for the enterprising. There was no streamlined and regular fighting force, necessarily recruited from a restricted class. The Atharvaveda is very categorical in claiming the *vis* (common people) as constituting the main fighting force. The term 'balan' was used for fighting forces. Since there was a constant movement, extending over centuries from across the north-western border, some of the migrant must have joined the fighting forces. In course of time, some of them must have got upgraded by pushing their way into the Kshatriya varna. The Brahmin must have been very pliant in the distant past, as they have been in recent times, for instance, in respect of Shivaji, a Maratha chieftain upgraded to the status of Kshatriya.

With the passage of time and transition into the Sutra period, things began to get rigid. It is only then that the Kshatriya began to be identified as *rajanya* and the fighting force, which in addition were sworn to protecting the Brahman and dharma. The pact between the Brahmin and the Kshatriya was obviously at the cost of the other three varnas – the Vaishya, Shudra and the Untouchables in which the clever Brahmin managed to have the upper hand.

It is the learned Panini, who put the stamp of approval on the root of the word Kshatra by linking it to the Kshatriya. In Panini's scheme of things, rajaneya, ksatra and kshatriya got linked and Kshatriya came to denote the Kshatriya class. The great transition took place from the times of the Rigveda, and through the 'Brahman' and Sutra periods. As the varna system began to get more specific, it also rigid.

Stabilizing the Varnas

Rajanya means descendants of the king employing power, dominion and authority. The original Sanskrit term Kshatra means 'country', thereby implying authority and power. Even the Persian terms Kshatrapa, derived from the same root as pa means 'to protect' so clearly the Buddhist word Khattiya means the same as Kshatriya. It refers 'to the members of the Aryan nobility'. The Pali-English dictionary is more specific when it described khattiya as 'a member of one of the clan recognized as of Aryan descent'. The Buddhist stress on royalty is obvious due to the Buddha's own descent from the Kshatriya royalty of Aryan descent.

There are both negative and positive elements in the resultant situation. There was a time when the Kshatriya and Brahmin intermarried on equal terms. This was no longer true in later times. Matters got stultified in the process of getting stabilized. It was no longer possible to cross the boundaries by the time of Panini. Accordingly, Panini mentions four varnass as the Brahmin, Kshatriya, It (or the Vaishya) and the Sudra. The three top varnas were given the designation of Arya (also known as *dvijas*, or twice born). The divisions had a racial connotation. By implication, the Untouchables were the native Dravadians and leftovers of the Indus Valley Civilization.

The Vishnu Purana narrates the story of Bharadwaja, the son of Brihsapati, who had four grandsons, of whom two became Brahmins, while the other two became Kshatriya, with all the four belonging to the Bharadwaja gotra. Sadly those happy times are no more. All this was done in the name of purity of the Aryan race and for maintaining the integrity of the varna system. It was, indeed, a meaningless exercise, as it is sought to be proved in the succeeding pages. Unfortunately, it is a myth that has been perpetuated generation after generation.

Doubtful Exaggerations

The Indian religious-mythology-historical text suffers from its fondness for analogies, which confuse rather than clarify. There is also a considerable element of exaggeration in such formulations. Here are flights of imagination, fanciful to the extreme. Vasishta Dharma-Shastra, for instance, asserts that 'the Brahmin was his mouth, the Kshatriya formed his arms, the Vaishya his thighs, the Sudra was born from his feet'. Obviously the reference is to one of the Hindu trinity.

Unfortunately, even the Buddhists have fallen victim to the tyranny of the Sutra formulations. They have also divided the society into four varnas, sometimes called varunas, (or Vana), Khattiya, Brahman, Vessa and Sudha. The veneration in which the varna is held in India among all communities including the Buddhist, Muslim and Christian is inexplicable in national term, or except as the byproduct of an inherited psyche, or, in other words, varna must be in the Indian genes. It is a myth that cannot be wished away, and needs to be viewed in historical terms. It shall not be a matter of surprise if it is discovered on further research, that the Indus Valley Civilization was as much susceptible to the varna as past and contemporary Indians are.

The fact of the matter is that in the Sutra period, the Kshatriya as a fighting or warring class is a violation of the Vedic injunctions. The contemporary reality is supportive of the Vedic worldview in this regard. The original Kshatriya families of Vedic period came from two different backgrounds. The first and original group must have belonged to the conquering tribes of the Aryan vintage. In normal circumstances, they must have constituted the high-level varnas. The second category belonged to the indigenous people, most probably of Dravidian stock, of those who were the leftovers of the vanquished people, in other words, the residue of the Indus Valley Civilization. There could not have been any stratified divisions at this stage, with the migrations taking place from one class of varna to another. The flexible inflow and outflow must have been stratified by the Sutra age.

Racial Assumptions

The German Indologist Fick says, 'Kshatriya corresponds to the Vedic *rajanya* and is applied to the successors of the conquering families under whose leadership the Aryan stocks had secured their new settlements in the Gangetic lands, and, also, to the overlords of the indigenous people who had been able to maintain their independence in war against the foreign invaders. The Kshatriyas then were by no means of one and the same race. They represented the political power and embodied the idea of a community which stood above the family, above the caste, the idea of State. We have no right to speak of the Kshatriya 'caste' in the modern sense of the term. The Kshatriyas formed a ruling class and were not necessarily warriors, any more than the army was necessarily recruited only from Kshatriyas'.[1]

This is all a matter of speculation and deduction from the minimal sources at the disposal of historians and archaeologists. All this has come to pass because of the oral tradition of history in India. Whether the Aryans migrated from foreign lands is also a matter of debate, equally based on questionable hypothesis. Whether the Vedic civilization was a transition from the Indus Valley Civilization is a question equally debatable. However, several eminent historians like M S Vats, R P Chandra, B N Datta and V.P. Kane have argued for a relationship between the two, in contradiction to the view of several eminent historians of Marxist orientation. Similarly, whether the modern Khatri are worthy successors to the ancient Kshatriya still continues to be debated. The modern Khatri does not have the slightest inkling of the lineage of their own worthy predecessors. These are questions that still remain to be answered in the future.

Kshatriyas into Khatris

The three great Kshatriya lines of ruling families consisting of Solar, Lunar and Yadav dynasties have been well documented for more than fifty generations. Subsequently, the lines have got blurred. The war of the Mahabharata was a great dividing line. The Yadavs moved to Gujarat and walked out of history due to a series of internecine wars. The Solar line terminated during the Mahabharata and so did the Lunar line, subsequently. The Parasuram story has also to be properly interpreted. It was a struggle for power between Brahmins and Kshatriyas, ending in the victory of Brahmins and the complete decimation of the Kshatriya.

There is a veneer of exaggeration in the Parasuram myth, but it was otherwise a graphic account of the war to end all wars through complete decimation, to the extent that Parasuram, the incarnation of Vishnu and defender of Brahminic orthodoxy, decimated even the infants-to-be-born in the wombs of Kshatriya women. The beleaguered and hopeless women took shelter with the Sarasvat Brahmins of Thaneshwar, situated on the banks of the now-defunct Sarasvati river. They took pity on them and gave them shelter by proclaiming them as their daughters. That explains the intimate connection between the two communities.

To this day, the Sarasvat Brahmins are *purohits* to the Khatri gotras. They are the unusual Brahmin community who readily eat otherwise 'forbidden food' at the hands of their Khatri *jajmans*. There is a delightful twist to this tale, 'because Parasuram, in his wrath, bade them to eat kacha bhojan (non-fried but cooked food) from their hands for testing of the relationship and only when they did so did he spare the women. So their children were called Khatri instead of Chattris'.[2] Similarly, the Arora ancestors saved their lives by declaring themselves as 'sur' (others), but, logically, they got separated from the mainstream Khatris.

Literary Prowess

Sir Denzil Ibbetson and Sir Edward Maclagan were remarkable British Indian civil servants who produced a definitive study on the Khatris of the Punjab (and Saraiki homeland) in their census reports of 1883 and 1892 which remain a classic contribution to scholarship to this day. They have found the closest resemblance between Kshatriya and Khatri, to the extent of asserting that the Khatri of modern India are worthy successors to the Kshatriya of ancient times. It should not be forgotten that the Potohar Plateau was the original homeland of the Khatri community. So was the Potohar said to be the homeland of the Kshatriya. This is the land of Taxila, much before Taxila came into existence. Here were the Vedas and the Mahabharata composed. These classics were subsequently upgraded to suit the convenience of the Brahmin community by incorporations. Hence there are grounds to believe that these classics are tour de forte testifying to the literary métier of the ancient Kshatriya. The Potohar Plateau borders the Swat Valley and is not far away from Peshawar.

Dr G A Grierson has argued that there was a long-drawn-out struggle for supremacy between the Brahmins and the Kshatriyas. While Kurukshetra was the home of Brahmianic orthodoxy, especially the Potohar Plateau, Multan and the Gandhara were the head-quarters of unorthodoxy and liberal thought. In fact, the Swat Valley, which is next door to Potohar (on the other side of the Indus River), was also the headquarters of unorthodox Buddhism and indeed the powerhouse of unorthodox philosophy and worldview. To get back to the mainstream argument, it should also not be forgotten that the ancient Khshatriya had demonstrated powers both with the pen and the sword, as well as shown their effectiveness in running the affairs of the state.

Icnoclastic Thought

Initially the ancient Kshatriya were not only imbued with the spirit of war, they had a sense of history, a literary framework of mind, as well liberal and unorthodox worldview, besides carrying out a ding-dong battle with the Brahmins. While the Madhyadesa was the centre of orthodoxy, headquartered at Kurukshetra, the north was the home of unorthodox and learned Kshatriya. Multan, for instance, was the see-saw battleground between the unorthodox Sun worshippers of Vedic inclinations and the Vaishnavites, followers of orthodox Brahminism influenced by the Puranic beliefs. The Kshatriya must have had a different sense of history and was exposed to new ideas, on account of his geographical location on the borders.

Accordingly, the Kshatriya played a great part in the early days of Indian history in contributing to the literature, whose reading is essential for correct understanding of those times. We have seen the results of their literary forte in the epics and the Puranas, overloaded as they are presently with Brahminic accretions. The general trend of the ancient Kshatriya was monotheistic and ethical. It was not anti Brahminical but 'anti-Brahmanist', and opposed to the orthodox Brahmins of the old Upanishad school of thought, which was mainly taught by the Brahmins of Madhyadesa. The Sankhya-Yoga and Bhagavata systems are in their origins connected with a number of Kshatriya names.[3]

The truth of the matter is that north-west India has been iconoclastic by the very circumstances of its very location. This tradition must have been transmitted to the Indian by his Kshatriya ancestors, via the Khatri successor who had emerged on the scene about the beginning of the Christian era. Swat is also the home of revolt from the Buddhist orthodoxy. Sikhism is a part of its latest heritage. This part of the world has been Vedantic, both at conscious and unconscious levels. It has categorically rejected the Upanishadic exposition in favour of the pristine Vedic thought.

Vedantic Sikhism

Sikkhism reproduced in essence the Vedantic philosophy of monotheism and ethics. No wonder, all the ten gurus including Guru Nanak and Guru

Gobind Singh were Khatris of Bedi and Sodhi sub-castes. Two of the other gurus were of Trehan and Bhalla sub-castes. The Guru Granth Sahib is based strictly on the *ragas*, as if in a tribute to the Samaveda. In essence, Sikhism is the personification of the thought of the ancient Kshatriya, in a language communicable to the common man. Its appeal lies beyond its traditional clientele. It was readily adopted by the Jats of the Shudra varna, who had hitherto remained outside the pale of the Brahminic orthodoxy. No wonder, 'The position of the Bedi, the Sodhi and other quasi-sacred sections of the Khatris, as the teachers and leaders of the Jats and other tribes, is essentially that which they occupied at the time of Mahabharata, and it would be of great interest to investigate whether the modern Khatri teaching is based on any literary work or tradition descending from the old Kshatriya literature'.[4]

The Vedanta may have its roots beyond the Kshatriya parameter, considering it was a long road from the Vedanta to Kshatriya beliefs and to the Khatri cult, ending in the philosophy of Sikhism as expounded by Baba Nanak and other nine gurus. Its roots possibly lie in the Indus Valley Civilization, which were transmitted onwards via the Vedas. Lot more research needs to be done before establishing the chain. Who knows, if one may stumble upon new discoveries? There is an underlying chain that opens the vistas well beyond the local version of the Vedanta. It is, however, too early to come to any conclusion. The first thing is to discover the underlying unity between the Kshatriya, Khatri and Sikhism.

The Origin of the Khatri

The Pancha-Dravidas, or five classes of southern Brahmins, must be the purest Brahmins, as compared to the Pancha-Gaudas, or five classes of northern Brahmins, who are considered 'more corrupted, broken and scattered', but certainly, Kshatriya were equally 'corrupted, broken and scattered', and more so than the Brahmins. The Kshatriya were in the direct line of attack of a series of invaders from across the frontier. The Kshatriya had either to vacate power or compromise with the invaders. There was a long list of invaders who included Greeks, Persians, Parthians, Bactrians, Indo-Scythian, Shakas, Huns, Tatars, Mongols and the Arabs who, except for the Arabs, chose to be absorbed into the Kshatriya varna to claim legitimacy. Then came the Buddhists who questioned the very legitimacy of the varna system itself. The Kshatriyas were made completely dysfunctional after the advent of Islam.

The Rajputs, who claim descent from the ancient Solar and Lunar gotras, were certainly late entrants to the Kshatriya fold. They had no connection with the Kshatriya of north-west India, the original claimants of the proud legacy. The Rajputs must have achieved the elevation, thanks to the manipulation of the clever Brahmin. Rightly, Todd does not accept the claim of the Rajput being pure Kshatriya. He views them as a mixed lot of converted Buddhists, Huns and Takshaks, who attached themselves to 'the pure Kshatriya families'. It was thus a matter of convenience suiting all concerned. In other words, Rajput families were born of 'the debris' of Kshatriya dynasties. While the rishis might have created the four Agnikul Kshatriyas, Prahar, Solanki, Panwera, Chauhan, who in turn gave birth to Chhatris or Rajput houses, all of this finds no mention in the Kshatriya tradition, as recorded in the post-Vedic literature.

Comparison and Contrast

There is more circumstantial evidence to establish the case for identity roots between the Kshatriya and the Khatri, than between the Kshatriya and the Rajput. North-western India centred around Potohar was the birth place of both of them. The Sarasvat Brahmin has been designated as the purohit to the Kshatriya and Khatri alike. This convention has prevailed over several millennia for the Kshatriya (read Khatri), since the Vedic times. H A Rose, in his census report, refers to territorial groups, with the place of proximity or honour given to the Lichhandi or Khatri of the Upland, meaning north-west Punjab. The other groups are centred around Multan and Peshawar. All these places are to be found in the larger Punjab and are intimately associated with the Vedic civilization. It was also the homeland of the ancient Kshatriya, as it is the land of the Vedas and Mahabharata. This, however, does not conclude the argument about the respective Kshatriya and Khatri identities.

The debate must go on. Unfortunately, the chronology of both

Kshatriyas and Khatris is a matter of pure conjecture. For instance, it is not known whether the Xathroi mentioned by the Greek historians, is the same as the Kshatriya. Incidentally, the Greek accounts were the first to document Indian history. Here are a few mention of the origin of the Khatri. The legend of Raja Risalu is related to Raja Risalu of the Chopra sub-caste, who ruled between 400 to 500 A D. Again, the exact dates are not available. This much is, however, certain that the Khatri gotras had become familiar by that time. It also goes to establish that the *baraghar* (twelve houses or sub-castes) of the Khatri community had come into existence by the time. Again, and there is the danger of fiction taking over where the facts are scarce and dubious.

Conflicting Views

The Khatri claim to be Rajputs and, hence, their descent from the Kshatriya is also dubious. In reality, the Khatri do not have the remotest connection with the 36 clans of Rajputs. It is an accepted fact that the Sarasvat Brahmins of the Vedic vintage were their official purohits, and, in turn, they have an hierarchy of jajmans who continue to be associated with them from one generation to another, and 'traditionally, the Khatrie were linked with other communities by *jajmani* or patron-client relationship. Mutual dependence for routine and ceremonial events made the different communities work like a well-knit social system. They maintain a *jajmani* relationship with the barber (Raja), Mirasi, Dom, tailors, washerwomen, water-carriers and some others. These communities participate in social and religious gatherings'.[5] The Khatri are also closely linked to the Arora, who not only claim to be Khatris but also are pretender claimants to the Kshatriya heritage. The fact, however,remains that it is not possible even to establish at this stage whether the Khatris were the direct descendant of the Kshatriya.

The existing evidence is confusing and purely speculative. There has been a running battle among social anthropologists who are equally divided for and against the propositions. H H Risley believes that Khatris are actually descended from Vaisya, allegedly because of their association with the Sarasvat Brahmin. There is an element of truth in it, because today, the Khatri constitute the finest class of moneylenders and bankers, known for their sharpness in money matters throughout north-west India. The Pathan and Baloch tribals are prone to trade their assets, rather than the lonesome local Khatri and this fact is religiously believed throughout the tribal belt. There is also another thesis which brings both of them together. It is believed that Brahmin and Kshatriyas have joined together to create the new caste of Khatris. This may be probable in the context of the Parashuram myth, and, for the Kshatriya women having been given protection by the Sarasvats.

Khatri Nomenclature

The Kshatriya are designated as *Rajanya* (belonging to royalty). They are considered the warrior class among the four-level varnas of social organizations. There are doubts galore about the Khatri having self-assumed this heritage. It shall be interesting to analyse the literal meaning of Khatri gotra terms. The literal meanings, in several instances, seem to indicate their professions in the past. The highest ranking gotras or subcastes are Khanna, Mehra and Kapur. They are termed *daighar* (literally two and a half houses). The term Khanna is derived from khan (mine), and, in other words, they are assumed to be sappers. The term Mehra is derived from Mihir, the sun and similarly Kapur gotra is related to the moon. In mythology, there have been famous struggles between Solar, Lunar and Agnikula dynasties. In any case, the Sun symbol is highly regarded in Hindu mythology.

There are eight gotras that may be counted on the tip of the fingers. Their literal meaning implies a military association. Here is the list. Kakkar/Seth was originally Karkar, which implies power and strength. Mahendru gotra is drawn from the Sanskrit word Mahendra, meaning 'the lord of the earth' or chief. Similarly, Sahni is the corruption of the Sanskrit word Sainani, the head of the army or commander-in-chief. Suri, also spelled Sheri and Suri, means a brave soldier. Vij is borrowed from Vijaya or victory, implying successful qualities of leadership. While Uppal gotra stands for fearless warrior, and the word is drawn from Sanskrit, Patti/Pattipati, means an officer heading military formation. Last, but not the least, Tandon is an abbreviation of Martand meaning the Sun, but it is said to mean the warrior. Here is a smell of war in the air, wherever the Khatris are found. There is also an equal emphasis on the quality of leadership, no doubt a special attribute of the military class.

Military Connotations

There are also many other sub-castes where names imply military functions. It is indeed true of almost the entire spectrum of the Khatri gotras. Bohra (currently spelt as Vohra) means column in military formation. Dhawan/Dhavan is said to be a messenger or communications expert. If the Chhabras are sappers, Chadhas (of Potohar) are the cavalry, who must have been a part of the army of Porus, confronting Alexander the Great. Supporting them could be the Bhallas wielding spears, Kochars in full armour, and leading them must have been Dhawans with expertise in archery. It is not hard to imagine military formations of yore consisting entirely of the Khatris. Not to be left behind are Astors, the weapon experts, Khagges and Talwars wielding their swords, fully backed by the Aggechal, the explosive experts.

Even the Khatri toddler must have blabbered in military jargon. 'What a fall my countrymen' because present-day Khatris have expertise only in wielding pens, or writing of the wahis (book-keeping records) in Lahanda, in the village stores spread over north-west India and Afghanistan. Since a warrior by definition has to be the ruling class, there were several gotras of the Khatri clan who were concerned with the administration by definition. Puri gotra, for instance, meant town administrators. Chopras have been known as revenue officials since the Mughal times. It should also not be forgotten that Raja Todar Mal, Khatri by caste, was Akbar's revenue minister. He must have favoured the Chopra subcaste with the job of revenue officials. Marwah of the Sarin group claim Central Asian origin from the famous town of Merv. Bhandaris have been blessed by the holy saint Baba Farid, '*tumhare bhandara bhare rahe*' (your buns shall remain full), and therefore they were called Bhandaris. The Khatri gotras are a gold-mine to be discovered by social anthropologists to unwind the hidden link between Khatris and Khashtriyas.

Organizational Khatri

The Khatri society is an amorphous and complex social organization, and its 'hierarchical set up with particular reference to what is called societal stratification. *Dhai, char, bara* and *bawan* and stress on the exogamous marital relationship demand scrutiny and closer attention'.[6] The stress on the exogamous marital relations may have its justification in medical sciences, but its rigid character is astonishing. The group or section into which the Khatri are divided are like a close corporation into which entry by others is prohibited.

Khatris are divided into three main groups: 1) Bari, 2) Bhanjahi and 3) Sarin. The Bari consist of twelve sections and hence the name bari on top of the table, and is further divided into several sub-groups called dhams: 1) Dhaighar, 2) Charghar, 3) Chhighar, 4) Baraghara or Bara zati. The Dhaighar (two-and-a-half) are found depending on the interpretation. While *charghar*, *chhighar* and *baraghar* consist of four,six and a twelve sections. The second group is divided into two sub-sections which are called Bunjahi, or fifty-two in number. While Sub-Group I consists of Khokrian gotra or sub-castes, Sub-group II is called Bunjahi Khas or Kalan. The Group III consists of the Sarin section, which came into being in very controversial circumstances, during the time of Ala-ud-Din Khilji. It got stratified into the groups called Bari Bunjahi, Sarin and Khokrain. The broad division into groups is hereby presented in a tabular form:

Group I	-	Bari
Group II	-	Bunjahi
Sub-group I	-	Khukrain
Sub-group II	-	Bunjahi Khas or Kalan
Group III	-	Sarin

Ala-ud-Din Khilji Incident

Ala-ud-Din Khilji attempted to impose widow-remarriage upon the Khatris. There was a practical reason to do so. Many Khatri soldiers had died during the Deccan campaigns. His Khatri Diwan, Udharaman put forward the proposal to suggest widow-marriage as the solution, after consulting the

Khatri Pradhans, Lalu and Jagatthar, of the panchayats. This raised a storm of protest. The slogan 'Fie, down with Lallu, Jagdhar' travelled across the ranks of the Khatris throughout the length and breadth of the country, forcing Khatris together on a common platform.

The first to offer resistance were Dhaighars, Khanna, Mehra and Kapur clans, who were in the top of the Khatri social hierarchy. The entire Bari, consisting of twelve sub-castes, came out publicly in their support. They were followed by the Bunjahi consisting of 52 caste, sub-castes inclusive of the Khokhran clan, who were already marked due to their active participation in another rebellion. The western Khatris mobilized to send a delegation consisting of fifty-two to present their case at court. Subsequently, they came to be known as the Bunjahi. This also became the basis of social hierarchy among the Khatri as they represented Groups I and II.

There was another Khatri group who were hesitant to join the protest. They were afraid to be branded as rebels. They chose to remain the silent spectators. They were mostly concentrated in Delhi and Sirhind, much nearer to the court, contrasted with the western Khatri headquartered at Lahore and Multan. As many as 377 sections of the Khatri clan deputed 56 delegates representing four of Dhaighar and fifty-two others who came to be known as Punjahi-Kalan Khas (senior Bunjahi). The remaining 321 sections who boycotted the protesting delegation came to be known as Ansars or supporters of the establishment. The silent section came to be known as the Sher-i-Ain, the followers of the Muslim Shari'a. Subsequently, the name was changed to Sarin and they constituted Group III as indicated above. Whether the social hierarchy got stratified due to the edict of Al-ud-Din is debatable. There must be also other reasons for the consideration. There was, however, one major fallout of the historical incident. It resulted in a reduced presence of the Khatri in medieval armed forces.

Bari Khatri

Today the Bari group is made up of two exogamous sections, and its name is derived from Barah, '12' sections.

1. Khanna
2. Mehra/Malhotra
3. Kapur — Senior
4. Kakkar/Seth
5. Chopra
6. Talwar
7. Sahgal
8. Dhawan/Dhavan
9. Weedhavan/Wadhawan — Junior
10. Tandon
11. Bohra/Vohra
12. Maindhara/Mahendra

They are further divided into several sub-groups (dhamas):

1. Dhaighar (two-and-a-half sections,
2. Charghar (four sections)
3. Chhaighar (six sections)
4. Barghar or Bara-zati (twelve sections)

The above-mentioned twelve sections constitute the top of the Khatri social hierarchy, with the first three sections constituting the cream. Unfortunately it also granted lower status for women. Their status is entirely dependent upon who can marry whom. Generally speaking, the Khatri avoid marrying into four sections, viz., those of the father, mother, father's mother and mother's mother. It creates special problems for the Dhaighar of the highest pedestal consisting of Khanna, Mehra, Kapur and Kakkar. They are forced to confine their bride-hunting among two-and-a-half sections, instead from the hierarchy of the four in which they are placed. They may take brides from sub-castes at the lower scales of hierarchy of Khatri social organization, but the male of the species are denied similar privilege. The entire social organization is based on the complex structure of who can marry whom. The Dhaighar, for instance, cannot give their daughters in marriage to anyone but a Dhaighar without losing status, and being downgraded to the Baraghar In essence, the system is chauvinistic, howsoever it may be justified in biological terms and in defence of exogamous marriages.

There are also territorial divisions of Baraghar which cut across the status of sub-sections to some extent. In this category the place of honour is be given to the Uchhandis or 'Khatri of the uplands' (north-west), located around Potohar Plateau on account of its intimate association with the Vedas and the Mahabharata. They are, undoubtedly, of the highest status among the Khatri clan. Next come the 'Lahorien' who are equally considered the crème de crème in the community, followed by the 'Multani',who are equally respected, because they come from the ancient town of Multan. The last, but not the least, come the 'Bharochi' from the ancient town of Bhera or Shahpur. The category of 'Sacred Khatris' consisting of the Bedis and the Sodhi is a class apart and is discussed separately.

Bunjahi Khatri

There is a mention of the Bunjahi in the *Ain-i-Akbari*: 'The Kshatriya (now called Khatris) form fine races, the Suraj-bansi and Chandrabansi. There are more than 300 tribes of those Kshatriyas, of whom 52 (Bawanjis) are pre-eminently distinguished, 62 (Baraghar) are of considerable importance.... Some of their descendants, abandoning the profession of arms, have taken over occupations and their class is known to the world by this name'. (Blochman's tr., III, 112).

This group comprises 52 sections by convention, as it is evident from the name, Bawanjahi/Bunjahi. In actual fact the number of groups vary and is actually in excess of the conventional number. They are divided into four sections. Sub-group I is the best known. It is called the Khokhran. It consisted of eight sections originally, and hence it is known as Ath-zatia or Ath-ghar sub-group. Sub-group II is known as Bunjahi khas or Kalan. It is also called Asli-Pukha (or 'real') or Bari Bunjahi comprising 12 sections. Sub-group III is Bara or Elder Bunjahi with 40 sections. It is addressed collectively as Dhaman or Dharaman. Sub-group IV is known as Chhota or Younger Bunjahi with over 100 sections. It is also called Ansar or Sair or Bunjahi Khurd'.

Some of the prominent sub-castes among the Bunjahi Khatri include Bahl, Bhandari, Handa, Katial, Khullar, Lamba, Makan, Nanda, Pasricha, Puri, Sikha, Soni, Thapar and Vij. A glance at the Delhi telephone dictionary shall establish their prominent identity. Khokhran also have a separate identity from the other sub-groups of Bunjahis. They are, as a rule, endogamous and hence constitute a separate identity. Their association with the Potohar Plateau also keeps them apart from the rest.

Khokhran Khatris

The Khokhran are the Bunjahi Khatri with a distinctive Kshatriya past. They trace their origin to the Khorasan province spread over Iran and Central Asia, the locale of historical cities like Nishapur, Merv, Bokhara and Samarkand. There is no doubt that they belonged to the warrior class. Porus or Purushotthama of the Porus or Puru Janpada (kingdom) was headquartered at the ancient town of Bhera, the town closely allied with the Khokhran Khatri. He was believed to be a Sabharwal Khokhran. He was defeated by Alexander in 326 B.C., thus underlying the fact that the migration from Khokhran preceded the invasion. The Purus are also mentioned in the Rigveda 7.96.2., which has located them on the banks of the Sarasvati.

How the Sarasvati River, Bhera, the banks of Jhelum, Khorasan province and the Puru Janpada got linked up is a matter for further study. It is only the testimonial of oral tradition which attributed the origins of the Khokhran back to Khorasan. It is not improbable, considering the fact that Buddhism had spread its wings to Central Asia and the Hindu dynasties were rulers of Afghanistan as late as the 11th century. The last Hindu Shahi kings were located in the same part of the world.

The Khokhran were originally an offshoot of the Bunjahis. They have continued to maintain their separate identity due to a variety of reasons. History has favoured them and enabled them to maintain their separate identity. They have resisted persistent pressures. They have belonged to a compact geographical area. They are, as a rule, endogamous and thus in reality form a separate sub-identity. Again in their case also, marriage rules have been the determining factor. They also observe both Hindu and Sikh practices.

Khokhran Divisions

Originally this group constituted of eight sections and was known as Alhzatra or Ath-ghar. In another classification, the number has been raised to ten, the two clans which have been included are Chandok/Chandhok and Ghai. Of the eight original, six clans belong to the Chandrabansi gotra. They have been divided into four Dalmas or Thalmas. Since three of the Thalmas are of the Chandrabansi gotra and form three exogamous divisions, intermarriages are banned within the Thalma due to the same Brahmanical gotra. Marriage remain the deciding factor in determining the identity of Khatri sub-castes, with the entire superstructure resting on one single assumption. Indeed, the history of the Khatri clan is for maintaining the purity of blood and the subordination of women to tyrannical rituals. There is also a smell of racialism about it, indeed a historical compulsion for the Hindu, ingrained in his very genes.

Original Divisions (8 Classes)[7]

Serial No.	Thalma/Clan	Gotra
1.	Anand	Chandrabansi
2.	Bhasin	-do-
3.	Chadha	Virbans
4.	Sahni	Surajbansi
5.	Suri	-do-
6.	Seth	-do-
7.	Koli/Kohli	-do-
8.	Sabharwal	-do-

Additional List

Serial No.	Thalma/Clan	Gotra
5.	Chandok/Chandhok	Suryabansi
6.	Ghai	-do-

In respect of the nine clans, Kuldevtas are Durga Mata, Bhadrakali, Bhagwati and Vaishno Devi, all these goddesses being the manifestations of the female Siva cult. In yet another version, all these clans are of Suryavanshi gotra as opposed to the Rose version indicated above. Shri Manmohan Singh, the Prime Minister of India, is a Kohli Khokhran from the Potohar Plateau.

Sarin Clan

There has never been a Martin Luther and champion of reformation among the Khatris. The proposal for the re-marriage of widows by Al-ud-Din Khilji was not a part of any reformist movement. It was made on account of the reasons of the state. The Sarin got identified as a separate group due to the compulsions of state politics. The Khatris were equally divided down the middle. It brought the western-zone Khatris face to face with those of the east. They were simply frightened of the royal displeasure. In fact, the Sarin are an amphorous group. It is also true that the traumatic impact of Ala-ud-Din may have been exaggerated. There is little historical evidence regarding the truth of the incidence.

The Sarin comprise a large number of twenty grades, each consisting of 6 sections, even though the actual number amounted to 123. They are divided into two sub-groups consisting of Bara, or elder section, and Chhota or junior Sarin. They are also divided into four classes in qualitative progression. The more prominent sub-castes are enumerated below; Bahl, Bhalla, Bhandari, Handa, Katial, Khosla, Khular, Kumar, Kundra, Lamba, Madhok, Makan, Malhan, Nanda, Sachar, Pasricha, Pusu, Sinha, Soni, Thapar, Trehan and Vij. It may be of interest to note that Bhalla and Khosla are placed on the highest pedestal and Bahl, Khular, Kumar and Puri are placed in the second category.

11

Sikh, Muslim, Arora and the Sarasvats

Sikh Khatris

There are four gotras of Khatris considered 'Sacred Castes'. Ten Sikh gurus belonged to the Khatri-sub-castes. Guru Nanak was a Bedi and the second guru, Angad was a Trehan. The third guru, Amar Das was a Bhalla and his descendants are called Bawa-Bhalla. Guru Arjan Dev, Guru Gobind Singh (the tenth guru) and several other gurus were Sodhis. The Kiratpur Bir (the Sacred Book, *Granth Sahib*), is in the custody of the descendants of Guru Arjan Dev at Anandpur Sahib. The four gotras to which the Sikh gurus belonged are from the class of 'Sacred Khatris', while their actual status in the Khatri hierarchy has remained unchanged. They are, however, regarded highly among the Sikhs. The descendants of Guru Nanak are called the Nanakputra or 'Children of Nanak'.[1] In the uncertain times of medieval Punjab, they used to escort caravans to safety and were duly compensated. Their sacred descent assured safety for the caravans.

The Sacred Khatris are placed in the Khatri hierarchy as indicated in the following table:[2]

Gotra	Hierarchical Position
- Dhaman-Burjahi or Chhota Sarin	Bedi/Vedi
- Chhota Sarin	Sodhi
- Bara Sarin	Trihan
- Bara Sarin	Bhalla

Hindu Connection

In another classification, Bedis are classified as Bunjuhi. The Sodhis remain Sarin, but they intermarry with Bedis. Perhaps this is the only known exception to the caste rules and regulations. The origin of the Bedi is traced to Kalpat Rai, who had gone to study the Vedas at Banaras and hence the name Vedi or Bedi. The Holy Book of the Sikhs contains the finest exposition of the Vedanta for the common man. Guru Govind Singh's *Bichitra Natak* traces his descent and that of Guru Nanak to Lord Rama's sons Lava and Kush. Indeed, Sikhism was born in defence of Hinduism. The relations got somewhat strained due to political competition between the Arya Samaj and Tat Khalsa (true khalsa) for the past several decades. Incongruous as it may seem, the Arya Samaj is equally, a vocal supporter of its own version of the Vedanta.

The Khatri stamp seems to be strong in the Sikh tradition. It should be interesting to note that the Chibbar gotra has been traditionally associated with the Sikh religion. Even today, there are many Hindu Khatri households, where the reverential reading from the Granth Sahib is a daily ritual, along with the recitation of the Gita and the Ramayana. The Khatris are the most devoted followers of Sikhism. They and other Hindu sub-castes have the practice of dedicating one of their sons to being converted to Sikhism. Indeed, they practice Hinduism and Sikhism simultaneously. There was a time when no distinction was made between Mona (clean-shaven) and keshdhari (bearded Sikhs). It is no longer true. Even though the sub-castes, to which the Gurus belonged, are low down in the Khatri hierarchy, the gurus introduced hierarchical reforms to break down caste and class barriers. Even then, their descendants continue to stick to their

Khatri antecedents. Indeed, the caste barriers are too deep in the Indian psyche to be challenged partially.

Khatri Muslim

Muslim Khatri are predominantly to be found in the Punjab and Gujarat, Khatris who converted to Islam are known as Punjabi Sheikh. They have maintained their Khatri identity. They mostly belonged to Multan and Jhang and come from the Kapur gotra. Kashmiri Brahmin converts are also known as Punjabi Sheikh. Sheikh Mohd. Iqbal belonged to the same category. They are concentrated in Lahore City. The 'Sheikh' is an Arabic word meaning, 'elder of a tribe, Lord, revered old man, or Islamic scholar'. This nomenclature must have reminded the converts of their Kshatriya heritage of *Rajanya* and their post-Kshatriya ancestry. The story is told of the late Fazle-Hasun, Member, Viceroy's Executive Council, who used to invite Brahmin priests for suggesting suitable marriage dates for his family members. He was a Saigal Khatri. Muslim Khatris are traders par excellence, especially the Parachas who need to be singled out. They also trade beyond the frontiers of India like their Hindu Khatri counterparts, reaching as far as Central Asia. They are converted Khatri marrying only among themselves. Punjabi Sheikhs, both Punjabi and Kashmiri, are mostly non-agriculturist and urban, with their main profession confined to commerce, trade and public service.

Thanks to Raja Todar Mal, Revenue Minister of Emperor Akbar, the Khatris have been appointed Quanungo (revenue officers) since the Mughal times. So many of them got converted and hence they are known as Quanungo Sheikh, hereditary registrars of landed property. Since it is a hereditary office, the position has been passed from one generation to another. It is a crucial position in respect of property rights; hence the social position of the Quanungo Sheikh was enhanced beyond proportion.

The conversion took place among a wide spectrum of Khatri sub-castes including Duggal, Jerath, Kapur, Mahindra, Puri, Saigal, Seth, Talwar, Vohra and Wadhawan. Prominent contemporary distinguished Punjabi Sheikhs include Najam Sethi, former Editor-in-Chief, The *Daily Times* and

Friday Times (Lahore), the industrialist Mian Rafiq Saigol, Wassim Sajjad (Quanungo Sheikh), politician, Aftab Ahmad Vohra, Amin Saigol, Sheikh Maula Baksh and Mian Mohd. Mansha. While the Punjabi sheikhs are largely absent from politics, they are represented in large number among the intellectual class, the arts and professions.

Gujrati Khatris

In Gujarat, the Khatris are Muslim converts concentrated in the district of Kutch. They speak Kutchi and use the Gujarati script. They still follow several Hindu practices. They were the Saivites whose ancestors were the Hindus of Lohana and Bhatia sub-castes from Sindh. They are known by the name of Khoja, a corrupt form of the Turkish word 'Khwajah', meaning the Lord. They were converted during the times of Ahmad Shah due to some dispute with the Brahmin purohits. They are divided into two groups. They are a small but compact group who migrated from Sindh about the middle of the 16th century and adopted Islam.

They are also found in Diu and Daman, Maharashtra, and Tamil Nadu. They go about their business quietly and are largely confined within their community. The Khojas are divided into two sub-groups: (1) Anashari and (2) Ismaili or Aghakhani, on the basis of their beliefs in Islam. They are greatly influences by the Shia and Islamic beliefs. The Agha Khan's influence is uppermost among them. One positive effect of their association with the Aga Khan group is their rapid advancement in education. They are essentially traders by profession.

In Tamil Nadu, the Khojas are known as Nizarians, Nizari and Imami Ismailis, or the followers of the Aga Khan. The majority of the Khojas are leading businessmen and are also among the professions. In Maharashtra, the Khoja are called Khoja Shia Anashari and Firkai-Jajoria and are spread over the western coast of Maharashtra. The Khojas of Gujarat have also a Multani connection. The Khoja continue to maintain their separate identity. They have a traditional community council or Jamat to settle disputes and lay down guidelines. They are also present in Karachi. Yusuf A. Patel, a Kutchi Khatri, has published a two-volume study of Muslim Khatris in Gujarati from Karachi in 1976.

Punjabi Khoja Community

There is a biting saying about Punjabi Khojas attributed to Guru Nanak:

Atth thag te atth thatheav,
Atth sunare te atth lohar,
Atth chaka battri,
Hikk kamla jeha Khattri.
Khatrio to bhana banaca Khoja,
Jeo vala nu ganda baraga,
Khoja so sohre da Sahna.
Khoja shebd lapeto a mohra.
Sui vangun sanjre, nikle vang talwar.
Ek bhakkeo uro Jaffro, Nanka
rakakh rakhh lee Kirtar'

The English translation is as follows:
'Eight robbers and eight brass- workers,
Eight goldsmiths and eight blacksmiths,
Eight times four make thirty- two,
Equals one fool of a Khatri.
Khatris broken up make a Khoja,
Like stinking oinment on the hair.
A Khoja is a father-in-law in a hundred,
A Khoja is poison with honey.
Enters like a needle, comes out like a sword.
From this Kho of (i.e. the word Khoja),
Oh Nanak may God save us'.[3]

Arora Community

There is a popular saying that 'the Khatri are Kshatriya of Multan and Lahore and the Arora are Kshatriya of Aror', in Sind located near modern Rori and Sukkur. Aror is a headquarters of the Aror community. It is located eight kilometers east of Rori. It used to be located on the banks of River Indus, which changed its course, it is believed after a massive earthquake, that took place in 962 A D. It also used to be the ancient capital of Sindh.

It was the capital of Raja Dhir of the last Hindu kingdom of Sindh. The present course of the river lies to the west of Aror. The capital was moved from Aror by the Arabs in 711 A D. It was also close to Mahenjodaro, the headquarters of the Indus Valley civilization. The trading town of Shikarpur, the family house of the Jethmalanis, also does not lie too far away from Aror. From Aror to the Derajat and Multan is called the land of the Arora. It also happens to be the Saraiki homeland. Indeed, the Saraiki homeland is coterminous with the Arora homeland.

There is also a theory which assumes that Ror (Arorkot), Aror, Arora are derivatives of one another. Some believe that the Arora are the most untouched proto-Indo-Europeans. After all, the majority schools of thought of historians, advocate, that the Aryans are actually indo-Europeans who entered India from the north. The Arora, or Rora as he is often called, is an excellent trader, who competes with the Khatri in south-west Punjab, Afghanistan and Central Asia. At the same time, he does not tire to declare himself to be a Khatri. His domination is complete in Saraiki-dominated Sind, Bahawalpur, Multan and the Derajat. He overwhelms the Khatri in terms of sheer numbers, but he equally hankers after the social prestige that is attached to the name of Khatri, even though the Khatri shows reluctance in accepting him in his ranks.

Four Versions

There are four versions of the origin of the Arora. We have also referred to his possible Indo-Iranian origins. The Arratas (Archemoans) are mentioned in the Mahabharata, living in the westerly neighbourhood of the Punjab (Badhhas), they migrated via Afghanistan (Archuna) to Sindh and settled at Aror. They are now traced to the times of the Indus Valley Civilization. They are singled out as one of the communities which never moved out of Saraiki Sindh and southern Punjab, even after the Indus Valley Civilization collapsed. They are, thus, assumed to be the pristine and the original Aryan group. According to another version mentioned in the Bhavishya Purana, it refers to the myth of Parashuram, who had driven them from their homeland, like the other Khatris, to settle at Aror, after being driven in the direction of Multan.

There are also two versions of the Parashuram myth. One thing is, however, certain–that the Arora, along with the Khatri, had been the victim of the internecine warfare between the Brahmin and Khashtriya. This is one version. Yet, in another version, the Arora were dispersed by Parashuram, but they denied their Khatri origins by calling themselves 'aur'. That explains the origin of Arora. Incidentally, Parashuram chose to destroy the Kshatriya with the slogan of 'Na nag'.

The Khatri identity of the Arora is sought to be established by referring to the Jagat section, Chapter 15 of *Bhavishya Purana*: "Those born in 'Nag' and Brahm Jati, living in Arovat community are the Kshatriyas'. In yet another version, they were cursed by a faqir (mendicant) and they had to flee from Aror from its three gates in the direction of north, south and west, when the three groups of Uttradhi, Dakhna and Dohra (or Gujarati) were distinguished.

Khatri-Arora Connection

The Parashuram legend established the close relations between the Khatri and the Arora. There is also a link provided by the Sarasvat Brahmins, who are considered 'the Brahmin of the Punjab' (Saraiki homeland). They are divided into seven sub-groups. The highest two sub-groups are designated as the Brahmins of the Khatri. The lower-down sub-groups have been designated as the Brahmin of the Arora community. The Brahmin gotras who are listed as the Brahmin of the Arora community include the following: "Kalia, Kapuria, Bagga, Malie, and Bhaturie. The list of Brahmin varies from place to place. In Bahawalpur, the number of Brahmin gotra for Aroras numbered 12 (Bara Jat). The fact, however, remains that the listing identified Arora separately from the Khatri gotras, and, further, they are placed lower down in the scale of values, implying thereby that the Khatri have a separate identity and are placed above Arora in a scale of hierarchy. In other words, the Khatri and his Brahmin purohit, both are ranked above his Arora counterpart."

George Campbell is of the view that they, Khatri and Arora, are ethnologically the same and indeed they are admixed with each other. In some instances, the Khatri marry Arora girls, but the reverse is not true.

While the Khatri are most reluctant to place the Arora on par with them, Arora is vociferous in claiming to be a Khatri. There is also a belief that about Samvat 200, the Khatri of the Arora brand fell out and separated. Sir George Campbell in his *Ethnology of India* calls the Arora as 'a large subordinate class' of Khatris, "somewhat lower, but of equal mercantile, equal energy, called Rors or Aroras. The proper Khatris of higher grade will deny all connection with them, or alternatively admit that they have some sort of bastard kindred with Khatris; but I think there can be no doubt that they are ethnologically the same, and they are certainly mixed up with Khatris in their avocation. I shall treat them while kindred as genetically Khatris".[4]

It may be of interest to note that the All-India Khatri Conference has accepted Arora, Sood and Bhatia the allied groups, with whom the sharing of roti (food) and beti (daughter) is accepted in respect of marriages. Similarly the sharing of roti (but not beti) is permitted in case of Sarasvat Brahmins, in recognition of the fact that they have remained the alter ego of the Khatri since the Vedic times.

Arora Divisions

There was said to be a conference of the Arora panchayat, presided by Gosain Sidh Bhoj in 143 A D, to debate basic issues of concern to the community. There was a proposal for reformation, but no unanimity for it. Those who were in favour of introducing reform were designated as Dakshin (of southwards), those who wished to stick to old traditions were called Uittar (or northwards), and those who wished to remain neutral were termed as Paschim (of westwards). Most probably, the divisions were between the trans-Indus, Multani and Gujarati Aroras indicating the direction towards which they resided. In fact, it was a clear-cut geographical definition.

'That is how the three sections of the Arora community were born: Uttaradis, Dikhanas and Dahras'. The western Arora called Dahras belonged to Gujarat and they were numerically insignificant. The Aroras of Punjab (and Saraiki homeland) have four divisions, namely, Uttaradhi, Dakhna, Dhara (Gujarat) and Sindhi. All names ending in 'Ja' and 'ani' are usually

Sindhi and Gujarati Arora. All the Arora groups have a common gotra, Kashyap. Usually Uttaradhi are divided into Bahri and Bunjahi on the pattern of the Khatri. The Arora are divided into sub-castes on the principle of paternity, maternity, and local place names. Intercaste and widow marriages are common among them, unlike the Khatri who are particular in strictly adhering to conservative caste connections. The Arora are also said to practice Chadar ceremony on the pattern of the Jat; the deceased husband's brother has the first claim to marrying his widow.

Bari Group

The Arora emulate the Khatri all along the line. Among them there are Uttaradhi, Bari, Banjabi divisions; those are strictly practiced. The elite Bari group among the Uttaradhi consist of the 12 sections:

Sub-Group – I

1. Ghumai
2. Nirula
3. Monga
4. Bazaz
5. Sikri

Sub-Group – II

6. Manchanda
7. Pasricha

Sub-Group – III

8. Kantor
9. Mamak Tahle
10. Gurware
11. Wadhwa
12. Sethi

They are the elit of the elitist among the Arora. There is also a Banjeh group (52 sections), lower down the line.

Almost parallel to the Bari Khatri, 1 to 7 sub-groups marry, but will only take wives from subgroups 8-12, but would not reciprocate like the Dhaighar among Khatris, and equally 1-5 sub-groups are loth to give daughters to other sub-group members. Similarly,there are a plethora of Arora gotras as in case of the Khatri. There are some gotras which are common to Khatris and Aroras. Sethi/Seth, for instance, is common among them.

Somehow the Arora community is renowned for producing medical practitioners called Unani Hakims. Some of them claim to possess certain powers for particular diseases. Nangias are one such community that has produced renowned Hakims. The Duas lay claim to have curative power of curing spasm in the back or loins by a mere touch. The pain called chuk may be cured by Duas again, by reciting the following chant: '*Dui Seth hari, phulan bari, dole dari, khannechil (waist) karindi sari.*[5] Seemingly the powers were granted by local pirs or pious ancestors. The Dhingras are also said to possess such curative powers.

Animal World

'Fox', 'hencock', 'bullock' and 'shepherd' are common names among the Anglo-Saxon community. In fact, the Arora community scores over the rest. Several of the Arora gotras are named after animals. It reads like the encyclopedic world of the entire animal life common to the Saraiki homeland. Here goes the list:[6]

Sub-Caste gotra	**Animal**
- Chutani	Bat
- Gaba/Gauba	Calf
- Ghera	Deer
- Giddar	Jackal
- Ghora	Horse
- Hans	Goose
- Kukar/Kakkar	Cock
- Kukreja	Cockrell
- Lumar	Fox
- Machar	Mosquito
- Makkar	Locust
- Manda	Ram
- Nagia	Snake
- Nang-pal	'Snake-Charmar'
- Sipra	Serpent

Even though the Arora are strict vegetarian by convention, it does not necessary show their love of animal. The nomenclature must be the totems; to speak the language of sociology and social anthropology.

Plant Life

There are other Arora gotra named after plant life. The Arora seem to exhaust the entire world of botanical and zoological sciences. Obviously there was no other purpose than the totemic beliefs. Here is the list of plant life in the Arora context:

Sub-caste/gotra		Plant life
- Chawla	-	Rice
- Gera	-	Ochre
- Ghia	-	Clarified butter
- Jandwani	-	Jand tree (desert specific)
- Kasturia	-	Kasturi, musk
- Katphal	-	Wood or timber
- Mehndirata	-	Henna
- Mungi	-	(a kind of) plant
- Dabraj	-	(a kind of) plant
- Sawi-kuti	-	Green herb
- Sela	-	Pipal tree
- Taneja	-	(a kind of grass)

If the apical ancestor of a clan is nonhuman, it is called a totem. The clans of particular totems shun certain things. The Gera sub-caste is said to avoid the use of the colour ochre and the Kasturi shun the use of musk, but it must have been difficult for the Gheia community to avoid the use of ghee (clarified butter), which is ocher. There are several other groups with names ending with 'ja' and 'ni', and they are invariably Aroras. Several Lohana sub-castes of lower Sindh also have names ending in 'ni'. Here is a sample list of Arora names ending with two suffixes:

	'Ja' ending
Ahuja	Pahuja
Aneja	Satija
Baweja	Satuja
Jadeja	Tuteja
	'Ni' ending
Ajani	Jethamalani

Numerous distinguished contemporary personalities in commerce, manufacturing, professions, the arts and the intellectual life have the Arora stamp.

Kirar at Bay

The Arora has a striking resemblance to the Jew as a targeted minority. They are indispensable because of their money lending profession, as well as for being bankers and shopkeepers. They are persecuted and envied at the same time. They are marked out from the rest of the community. They also happen to be in a hopeless minority. They are racially different and follow a different religion. They have been among the conquered race and subjugated over the millennium. Usually, there would be a single Arora family present in the entire village. Khatris are subjected to the same persecution. They are usually prohibited from wearing a turban. A skull cap would do for them. They would not even be allowed to ride a horse. A donkey would do for them. There are no written instructions, but those are unwritten but effective laws. They eat different food. There are usually vegetarians. They are the victims of spiteful jokes, puns, sayings and proverbs. They suffer from the disease of 'prejudiced majoritism', however, with Christ-like patience.

It shall be instructive to record sayings, proverbs and jokes to illustrate the social prejudices. The frequent charge hurled at them is of cowardice: 'The thieves were four and we eighty-four, the thieves came in and we ran away. Damn the thieves'. And again, 'To meet a Rathi (peasant) with a hoe makes a company of nine Kirars feel alone.' The British scholars and administrators, with knowledge of local condition, also damned the Kirar 'of inferior physique', 'a cowardly, secretive, acquisitive race, very necessary and useful it may be in their places, but possessed of a few manly qualities, and both despised and envied by the great Muslaman tribes of Bannu (in North-Western Frontier Province)'.[7] The term Kirar is applied uniformly to both, Khatri and Arora traders, but it is most specifically intended for the Arora counterpart, who numerically outnumber the Khatri trader in the countryside.

The Kirar is not entirely resourceless on the principle of 'the pen is always mightier than the sword'. There are several other proverbs which underline the innate authority and power of our beleaguered Kirar, as, for instance, 'Vex not the Jat in his jungle, or the Kirar in his shop or the boatsman at has ferry, for if you do they will break your hand'. But the old time suspicions return the pitch, 'You can't make a friend of a Kirar than a satti [companion] of a prostitute'. The fear factor of the innate powers of the Kirar haunts those who deal with him, 'Trust not a crow, a dog or Kirar, even when asleep'.[8] His customers are mighty afraid of him at heart, because their inability to understand accounts or financial deals. The Kirar is a master of these arts. His accounts books are maintained in an incomprehensible Lahnda/Multani script, which he alone comprehends. Lahnda is all consonants and hardly any vowels, with multiple interpretations. Only God and the Kirar can interpret the ancient Saraiki script, with its possible roots in Mesopotamia and the Indus Valley Civilization.

Sarasvat – Kshatriya Alliance

The Sarasvat Brahmins are the Brahmin of the Khatri. Both of them are of Aryan stock and belong to Panchanad, the ancient name for the Punjab (and Saraiki homeland) west of the Indus. The origins of the Prakrit language is owed to them, promoted by them through abundant poetry and drama, as well as by developing its grammar. It is the most advanced among the Indian dialects. The Sarasvat are intimately connected with the now defunct Sarasvati River. They belong to the Panch Gaud branch of the Brahmins. Their origin is owed to the sage Sarasvat, and they are believed to have originated from him; he is believed to have lived on the banks of the Sarasvati River near Thaneshwar in modern Haryana, the locale of the Mahabharata lying in its vicinity. They are now all over the country. They are spread over Sindh, Gujarat, Konkan coast and Karnataka. They, however, remain the Brahmins of the Punjab (and Saraiki homeland), who played a significant role in developing the Vedic lore.

Here emerges the Parasuram lore once more. Fleeing from the general massacre, a pregnant Kshatriya woman managed to escape his hawk eyes and took refuge with a Sarasvat woman, who readily gave protection to her. When the child was born, the Sarasvat protector virtually brought him up as her progeny, by investing him with the *janeo* (sacred thread) and teaching him the Vedas and training him in the Kshatriya martial arts. When the Kshatriyas lad married, he gave his 18 sons the names of the rishis, who came to be the Kshatriya gotras. Probably, the story refers by implication to intermarriages between the Sarasvat Brahmins and Kshatriyas. It is even believed that the Khatri community carries Sarasvat blood in its vein. To this day, there is a practice of purohit and jajman eating together. The Parasuram lore is a myth underlying the close relations between the two communities and their continuing association. It also tells us about the bloody rivalry between the Brahmins and Kshatriya.

There are two other variant versions of the Parashuram episode to be located in the Mahabharata. Parshurama, the axe-wielding Brahmin, was said to be a direct descendent of Bhrigu, one of the sons born of Brahma the creator. His father, named Jamadagni, had been killed by the Kshatriyas. He had decided to avenge his death by the mass murder of the Kshatriya community. He allegedly eliminated the entire Khshatriya male population from the earth. In Sambhava Parva, there is a graphic description of the gruesome mass murder in the words of Bheeshma, talking to his step-mother: 'Then (Parshaurama) again took up his bow to conquer the world. Using his wonderful weapons, the great souled descendant of Bhargava used his arrows to exterminate Kshatriyas from the world twenty-one times. The Kshatriya women everywhere had offsprings through (Sarasvat) Brahmins who were self-controlled.[9] The Vedas had very cleverly pronounced that the progeny, born of such liaison between male Brahmins and female Kshatriyas, belonged 'to the one who accepted the hand', in other words, 'That is, the person who married the mother, not the one who begot the son'[10]. Logically, 'With dharma (and not sex) on the mind, (the Kshatriya women) united with the Brahmins. The world has, thus, seen the resurgence of the Kshatriyas'[11]. In other words, the generations of Kshatriya to come not only had Kshatriya blood running in their veins, they were qualified to be as much Brahmins through the unintended miracle of cross-breeding.

Another version of the Parashurama episode is to be found in the Vamshavatarana Parva of the Mahabharata. Vaishampayana, the original narrator of the great epic, goes over the episode more elaborately, while talking to King Janamejaya, the illustrious greatgrandson of Arjuna: 'In ancient times, after destroying the Kshatriyas on earth twenty times, Jamadagni's son... began to practice austerities'[12] but with no thought of any expiation. Now, 'the world was thus bereft of Kshatriyas by one of the Bhrigu lineage'. What was to be done? The Sarasvat Brahmins came to the rescue of the beleaguered Kshatriya women. A practical solution was found, 'Kshatriya women used to come to Brahmins to fill their wombs. O tiger among men! Brahmins who were rigid in observance of their vows had intercourse with them during their productive periods, not out of lust, not when they were not in season. O King! thus, thousands of Kshatriya women conceived and gave birth to many Kshatriyas of great power, boys as well as girls, so that the Kshatriya race might thrive. Thus the Kshatriyas race originated from Kshatriya women through the ascetic (Sarasvat) Brahmins.'[13]

Role Model Devayani

These are myths which contain a grain of truth. No doubt, there was a destructive struggle between Brahmins and Kshatriyas for political supremacy in ancient times before the Mahabharata war. The locale of struggle must have been the land of the Sapta Sindhu. It had resulted in restoring the supremacy of Brahmins in governance once again. The Sarasvat Brahmin were in the frontline in restoring communal harmony and order as the balancing factor. It also goes to prove once again that we are all children of mixed blood and products of accidental miscegenation. It, equally, goes to prove that the purity of race is a pure and simple myth. The recent advances in DNA studies are the last and final nail in the coffin of race.

On the one hand, we have Parashurama of the distinguished Bhargava lineage, the axe-wielding avatara of Vishnu, who exterminated the Kshatriya race and created five lakes of blood as proof of Brahminic superiority and supremacy, and, on the other hand, we have Devayani, again of the Bhrigu lineage, who set an example by proposing to Yayati of the distinguished Bahata-Puru lineage, and forcefully doing so in no uncertain terms. She laid the foundations of the Kshatriya – Brahmin liaison by arguing at purely an intellectual plane, and, to her credit, by actual practice.

Universal Purohits

The Sarasvat Brahmans cater to all sections of the community, from the Dhaighar Khatri to the lowly Dalits, who were placed at the bottom of the ladder. In Gujarat, the Sarasvat are referred to as Husaini Brahmins, as they used to receive annual dakshina from the local Shia community. Among their clients were Memons and Khojas, who had converted from the Lohana community of Sindh. They are believed to have given succor to the besieged Imam Hussain during the Karbla battle with Yazid. The famous Lohana community had once belonged to Lahore and fled to Sindh, giving rise to the assumption that L K Advani and the Khoja, M A Jinnah are brothers under the skin. So is Azim Premji a Khoja.

There are five sub-groups of Sarasvat Brahmins in an hierarchical order. The status of the sub-group is in direct proportion to the category served by it. Shuklas are said to be 'the Brahmin of the Brahmins'; they are purohits to the Dhaighar Khatris. Sub-group II are Brahmin of Khatri of the Burjahi, Khokrin and Sarin. The next category are the Brahmins of Arora, and so on and so forth as detailed below:

'Sub-group I - Brahmins of Brahmin' called Shukla
Sub-group II - Brahmins of the Khatri
Sub-group III - Brahmins of the Arora
Sub-group IV - Brahmins of Jats
Sub-group V - Brahmins of Inferior castes, e.g. the Chamars.

Further, each of the sub-group is divided into grades on the analogy of the caste system. thus:

1. Panchzati
2. Bari
3. Bunjahi
4. Inferior Jats

The Shukla Brahmin comprise the following gotras, and along with it are listed the purohit gotras of the Khatris, to establish the truth of the high-class Brahman serving the high-class Khatris. It also proves that the Jajman determine the status of the purohit. It is, however, not true the other way around.

Panchzati (Shukla Clan)

Gotra	Client Khatri Gotra
Gallia	X
Malla (Mahle)	Vohra
Kapuria	Kapur
Bhaturia	Mahendru

Alternative List

Gotra	Client Khatri Gotra
Jetli/Jaitli/Jaitley	Khanna, Tandon
Jhingran	Seth, Kakkar, Baijal
Mahle	Vohra
Kumria	Seth
Trikha	Talwar

Panchzadi or 'five sections' are called 'Pachhada' or 'western'. The alternative listing is generally accepted to be constituted of four (plus one) sections of Dhaighar of the Bari group. The strict adherence to Dhaighar shall lead to the following listing of the Shukla Brahmin clan. Jhingran, Jaitley, Kapuria and Kumria. Thus in reality the four constitute 'the Brahmin of the Brahmins' along with their four high-calibre Khatri gotras. The reference to 'Pachhada' is meaningful, because the word is purely of Saraiki connotation. It goes to prove the intimate Indus connection of both Khatri and Sarasvat Brahmans. Together the two communities represent the north-west India. They are also close to each other for another reason. Sarasvat accept both *kachcha* and *pakka* food from the Khatri, a rare occurrence among the Brahmin community.

Further down the line, the Sarasvat Brahmin of the Arora is divided on parallel lines of Panch-zati and Bari groups. Here is an illustrative list of clients' sub-castes of Arora with the parallel listing of Brahmin purohits.

Brahmin Purohit	**Arora Client Gotra**
Nangu	Gulati, Mongia, Sachdeva
Lapiya	Chawla, Kharbanda, Khattar
Tanksals	Dua, Nagpal
Mattar	Kurana, Satija
Gaindhar	Chatkar
Joshi	Nahra

Among other high-caste Sarasvat are to be included the following gotras: Bali, Bhardwaj, Chhiber, Datta, Dube, Mohanna, Pathak, Shouri, Tewari and Vaidya. Parallel to this is the illustrative list of low-caste Sarasvat Brahmins : Bhanot, Kirar, Kapila, Pande, Punj, Sandhu and Tejpal. It is as if it was written in their destiny to service lower castes down the rigid Hindu hierarchy.

Konkan Brahmin

The Sarasvat Brahmins were brought to Goa, the Konkan coast and Uttar and Dakshin Kannad districts by force of circumstances. They must have migrated via Sindh, Gujarat, Maharashtra and finally to the Konkan coast for reasons still suspect. It is a long distance to travel from the Punjab, all the way to the western coast. There is again a Parashuram connection. It is believed that the Sarasvat Brahmins were brought all the way to Konkan to be comfortable in the new welcoming environment.

The important Sarasvat Brahmin lineage includes Desai, Prabhu, Kamat, Pai, Tambe, Pinge and Naik. The major concentration of Saraswat is to be found in Karnataka. They have similar surnames as the Goanese, but include additional surnames like Balliga and Sheth. While the counterparts in the north are conservative, the Kannad Sarasvat is one of the most advanced communities in India. They are divided into two groups: 1) Gaud Sarasvat, and 2) Saraswat. The two divisions 'show differentiation in occupational, social and religious matters'. Among the Saraswat Kannad are many in public service including contemporaries like K V Kamath, Nandan Nilekani, Girish Karnad and Shyam Benegal.

Maharashtrian Counterparts

Sarasvat Brahmins of Karnataka are in direct competition with their Maharashtrian counterparts. Gaud Brahmins concentrated in and around Poona, and are eminently distinguished for their superior intellect and intelligence. Dharmanand Kosambi and his equally-distinguished son, Damodar Dharmanand Kosambi are the most distinguished among them. Dharmanand (1876-1947) was a Buddhist scholar of Goan extraction. His son, Damodar, was a polyglot, renowned mathematician, public statesman, statistician, Indologist and Marxist historian, all qualities combined in one person. Dr R G Bhandarkar was a fellow Sarasvat. The Bhandarkar Oriental Research Institute, a pioneer institution that nurtured the definitive edition of the Mahabharata, is a tribute to the intellectual competence of the Sarasvat Brahmins. Even Shobha De', the Jackie Collins of India, was born as Shobha Rajadhyaksha to a Sarasvat Brahmin family of Maharashtra. Thus, the Sarasvat Brahmins of Karnataka, Goa and Maharashtra have a proud Saraiki and Punjabi connection in thier consciousness.

The Sarasvat Brahmins have also spread their tentacles all over the remaining India. Several Sarasvat families of western India had emigrated from Bengal. They, in turn, had originally migrated from the Sapta Sindhu homeland. Two former Prime Ministers of India, Morarjibhai Desai and Atal Bihar Vajpayee (Shukla), are also Sarasvat Brahmins.

Section - VI

Linguistic Bonds

12

Saraiki and its Dialects

RUTH Benedict defines 'patterns of culture' as a set of qualities like aesthetic, values and common personality that make up Saraiki society (culture) and it is claimed to be the proud inheritor of the Indus Valley Civilization. Saraiki is an ancient Indo-Aryan language. There is an increasing tendency to demarcate the Saraiki identity by disowning its western Punjabi and Lahnda heritage. There is an increased Saraiki consciousness in the air in claiming, 'Saraikis (too) have their unique culture i.e. psyche, food habits, folk dances, music, poetry, idioms, dresses and way of living'. Paradoxically enough, Saraiki culture is young in getting recognition, but it is old in historical terms. It has continued to be extremely pluralistic in its essence.

Saraiki homeland is both a lacquered culture and a cultural template. In the words of Shivaram Karanth, (who talked in the context of India), which is equally true of Saraiki *wasaib**, 'It is impossible to say surely what is nature and what is alien, what is borrowed out of love and what has been imposed by force.'

Saraiki homeland is situated at the south-west corner of peninsular India. From the Ionians, to the advent of Islam, it has grugdingly welcomed the intruders, had a dialogue with them and gradually learned to absorb them in the mainstream, but it has also managed to retain its distinct identity. It is thus old and young at the same time. Saraiki wasaib survives and it must be beholden to the Saraiki language for being the continuum. The language has provided the Saraiki wasaib its sustenance. Saraiki language has its roots deeply embedded in Indian culture and civilization, which has, in essence, acted as the banyan tree. It is definitely a many-splendoured language on account of its pluralistic content.

Lahnda Language

The Traditional name for Saraiki is Lahnda, which is a contemporary Indo-Aryan language belonging to the Indo-European language stream. It is completely distinct from Punjabi, it is spoken by more people, with which

---

* There is a plethora of terms employed for purpose of Saraiki national identity; Maa *boli, maa dharti, sanjan, vakhrap, moonjh* and *wasaib*. These terms are interrelated and are like musical piece reaching its crescendo in the finale. Moonjh is a collective symbol of *maa boli, maa dharti* and *wasaib*. *Sanjan* is considered symbol of 'national identity' rooted in *maa boli* (mother tongue) instead of religion, thus providing the Saraikis with a secular identity stamp. *Vakhrap provides* a sense of 'intimate identity' similar to that of *Sanjan*. Wasaib is the most debated concept special to the emerging Saraiki consciousness. It provides a link between 'language, land, culture' and remains the linchpin embodying *maa boli* and *maa dharti*. It is also viewed as the ultimate, 'being the blend of language (including literature), geography, history and culture' of the Saraiki-speaking people.

There is also an increasing acceptance of lotus flower as the symbol of Saraiki consciousness. Remember its association with the divine birth of Buddha. It is called *Neelphul* in Saraiki, Neel meaning blue and Phul meaning flower, equally translated as lotus flower or water lily, 'metaphorically based on the Siraiki word neengir; a virgin, an unmarried woman or girl or a spinster'. *Neelphul* and *Neengir* both stand for purity. In Sanskrit, Lotus in generally known as Padma, Blue lotus as Utpal and lotus that grows at night is know as Kumuda. Thus the Hindu and Buddhist symbol of sacred lotus has come to be adopted as the symbol of Saraiki nationalism, deeply rooted in Sufism.

it is often confused. Sir George Grierson (1851–1941), the distinguished author of Linguistic Survey of India (1919), called it western Punjabi or Lahnda, and it struck a chord among British administrators of his times. He, however, preferred the term Lahnda. He called it the language of western Punjab, and he has elaborated the position of Lahnda vis-à-vis Punjabi, as follows: 'It may be briefly stated that the whole Panjab is a meeting ground of two entirely distinct languages–viz. The Dardic parent of Lahnda which expanded from the Indus Valley Civilization eastwards, and the old Midland language, the parent of modern western Hindi, which expanded from the Jamuna Valley westwards. In the Panjab they overlapped. In the eastern Punjab, the wave of old Lahnda had nearly exhausted and old western Hindi had gained mastery, the resulting language being Punjabi. In the western Punjab, the old western Hindi wave had nearly exhausted itself, and the old Lahnda had gained the mastery, the resulting language being modern Lahnda. The latter language is, therefore, in the main, of Dardic origin, but bears traces of the old western Hindi. Such traces are much more numerous and of much greater importance in Punjabi. Lahnda may be described as a Dardic language injected by western Hindi, while Punjabi is a form of western Hindi infected by Dardic'.[1]

The term Lahnda was used in 1889 for the first time on record. It was employed initially by the C.M.S. missionary, Rev. William St. Clair Tisdail in his book *A Simplified Grammar and Reading Book of the Punjabi Language (London)* to describe the mixed literary language used in the seventeenth century Sikh account of the life of Guru Nanak. Later, writers have preferred the feminine 'Lahndi'. Much earlier, in 1813, it was called the 'Wuch' language by the great William Carey, a Serampore missionary, who embarked on the ambitious task of preparing grammar of all major Indian languages singlehandedly.[2] Grierson had actually called it southern Lahnda in 1919. There was, thus, a century of effort to discover the identity of the language. Earlier, the terms Lahnda and Lahndi were used interchangeably. There is another peculiarity about spelling the word. The sign 'h' in 'Lahnda' or 'Lahndi' is not to be pronounced, except for total stress. In fact the correct pronunciation is 'Lendi' or 'Landa'. There is now a clear line of demarcation between the words 'Lahnda' and 'Lahndi'. Lahnda is actually a geographical term, meaning 'towards west or towards the direction where the sun sets'. In other words, Lahnda indicates direction and Lahndi indeed means the language of Lahnda area (west). Thus, Lahndi is the preferred term over Lahnda in our future discussion.

Lahndi is an ancient language but it has taken 'a while to be accepted for its separate identity. It has been overshadowed by Punjabi for centuries on account of political domination of Punjabi-speaking elite in influencing events. Lahndi is, unlike Punjabi, a Dardic language, much in common with other Dardic languages like Kashmiri, Kohistani and Shinai. Dardic languages are borderland languages located in the northern periphery. Lahndi is surrounded by languages of the Dardic type on three sides, east, north and west. Admittedly, this influence has extended beyond into Punjabi and Saraiki Sindh. Lahndi is, however, much closer to Sindhi than Punjabi, but in reality, it is correct to say that the relation is triangular. To quote S S Kohli, 'Lahndi and Sindhi are sister languages which have a near relation with Punjabi'.[3]

Melting Pot

Geographical boundaries are hard to define due to political sensitivities and ideological delimitations. There are also no physical features of consequence to demarcate geographical boundaries. Not even rivers of the dimension of Indus act as impediments. Lahndi is spoken on both banks of the mighty river with slight variations. Lahore, the heartthrob of Punjabi culture, is in fact the nodal point joining southern, western and northern Lahndi dialects. U A Smirnov makes a weighty point when he asserts, 'Punjabi is gradual and in the western subdialectic of the latter, e.g., in Lahauri, we can detect peculiarities typical of Lahndi'.[4] This has led to several British administrators/scholars interpreting the terms variantly. George Grierson called the language 'Lahnda', besides naming it western Punjabi. E. O'Brien called it Multani language, a name associated with the heartland of the Lahndi language and culture. It, however, delimits it within the confines of Multan and its environment. Lahndi is spoken much beyond the Multani dialect and its confines.

Similarly, R F Burton delimits it further by associating the language with a racial community. It is a misnomer to call the language Jatki. Jats, as a community, are not confined to western Punjab, because they are scattered all over northern India. It would be true to call Punjabi a Jatki rather than Lahndi. A Juke offers a compromise by calling the language both Jatki and western Punjabi. The language came to be termed Jatki in places like Dera Ghazi Khan, to distinguish it from the language of the Balochi. The conventional boundaries are hard to decipher, because not only Punjabi, Sindhi and Lahndi have differed boundaries, but also due to a plethora of sub-dialects extending from Peshawar on one side and Aror in southern Sindh on the other. The sub-dialects are thus the melting points of the language.

Geographical Boundaries

There is a geographical environment and language network enveloping Lahndi from four directions. The two environments are coterminous on occasions, but not so all the time. There is, however, a broad network that defines the delimitations of Lahndi. While Pashto and Balochi languages are to be found in the west, it has Punjabi on its eastern borders. Rajasthani is to be found in the south, with its south-west occupied by Sindhi. While Pashto and Balochi are Iranian languages, the rest of the languages are of the Indo-Aryan language stream, which are spread like an arc around Lahndi as their sustaining prop. While Kashmiri and Kohistani are located in the north-western region, Shinai shines exactly in the northern direction. The following table provides a synoptic view of the situation.

Language	Origin	Direction
Punjabi	Indo-Aryan (western Hindi)	East
Pashto	Iranian	West
Balochi	Iranian	West
Rajasthani	Indo-Aryan (western Hindi)	South
Sindhi	Indo-Aryan	South-West
Shinai	Dardic	North
Kashmiri	Dardic	North-West
Kohistani	Dardic	North-West

The Lahndi language is spoken over a vast geographical area lying approximately between 70° and 74° east longitude and 28° and 34° north latitude. More people are estimated to speak Lahndi or so-called western Punjabi than the Punjabi language itself. It is spoken from the foothills of the Pir Panjal to the bazaars of Peshawar in the north and travels all along the Indus, with its epicentre at Multan, and after crossing Bahawalpur, it ends its journey in the south. It reaches the ancient town of Lahore in central Punjab and overwhelms itself from three sides. From Attock to Multan, and Peshawar to Pakpattan, Lahndi language rules the roost, or, in other words, 'Commencing somewhat south of the point where the Sutlej merges into Indus River, the western boundary of the Lahndi tracts run northwards along the right bank and mountainous regions of the Indus to reach its destination somewhat north of Peshawar. The eastern boundary begins south of the town of Bahawalpur, passes northwards through the towns of Sahiwal, Gujranwala and Jhelum and terminates somewhat north of the city of Muzaffarabad'.[5] The boundary in the south-west direction extends even beyond Bahawalpur, to Aror, the ancient capital of Sindh bordering Sukkur. Political boundaries may not coincide, but it is difficult to erect cultural barricades.

Colonial Character

Lahndi is placed in a paradoxical situation. It is one of the oldest Indo-Aryan languages, with its roots going back to the Indus Valley Civilization. It has been lost in its identity. It is still in search of space to which it can lay claim as its own. The predicament lies in its colonial or subordinate character. It has continued to be treated shabbily, so much so that there is a strong lobby which views it no more than a mere dialect of Punjabi. The British colonial power found it convenient to confine it within a subordinate status by naming the language as western Punjabi. Grierson is undoubtedly the chronicler of modern Lahnda language, but then he has also confined it within the nomenclature of western Punjabi.

A case may be made in the context of its colonial character. With the advent of Islam, its Persian/Arabic character came into prominence, suppressing its links with fraternal Sanskrit and its variant Prakrit. In essence, Lahndi is essentially a Prakrit language. There has also been a superimposition of Persian/Arabic vocabulary over it. Lahnda has remained static in its content, more so because Punjabi has also continued to dominate it. The Lahnda consciousness has been at its lowest. Consequently, it has failed to develop a body of literature to distinguish it. It has continued to be a folk language. It is the people's language par excellence, but lacking in cultural values.

The reason lies in its subordinate status. In contrast, Punjabi language has liberated itself by continuing to receive nourishment from its fountainhead in western Hindi. It also reformed itself by being a part of the Bhakti movement. Sikh gurus created new forms of literature. They invented a new script to suit its contemporary requirement. Paradoxically enough, the initial thrust to reform was inspired by its Lahndi connection. On the contrary, Lahndi language and literature continued to be suppressed, with occasional spurts as seen in Sufi literature and thought. Lahndi has to travel a long way in great spirits to make up for centuries of neglect. Undoubtedly, credit is due to several pioneering British linguists, who have helped unwind the system more than a 150 years ago, which it is hoped keeps unwinding itself. Lahndi is due for renewal and reconstruction. Its original and traditional vocabulary and its way of life and indeed its code has remained intact. Only the priorities need to be determined for a transformation into a vibrant, modern language.

Lahndi into Saraiki

Grierson was the strongest advocate of Lahnda because the expression was 'short and adoptable'. He was following the tradition of Lahnda script which was in vogue for centuries together. The language was confined to oral tradition, except for maintaining account books, written in Lahnda. The language had thus come to be accepted as the instrument for maintaining accounts, or oral language of the masses. It resulted in local adoption of varying names like western Punjabi, Jatki, Hindki, Multani and Hindko. The Hindki is spoken in Dera Ghazi Khan and it has affinity with Sindhi Saraiki, due to its vicinity and migrant character of the population in upper Sindh. Hindko is identified with 'Hindus' to some extent, especially in

Peshawar, but it is largely the language of non-Pathans in the North-West Frontier Province and north-east Punjab in the Jhelum-Chenab river basin. There has been, however, a turn-around about employing the term Lahnda or Lahndi for naming the language. There is also a general consensus, presently to substitute it with the term Saraiki; it is also spelled as 'Seraiki', 'Siraiki' and 'Saraki'. The general consensus about the term and also in its transliteration format is welcome, to the extent it brings about cultural unification among the disperate regions, where Saraiki and its sub-dialects are spoken. It is also a welcome sign of self-assertion.

Variety of Names

Grierson was again a pioneer in identifying the main dialects and, to some extent, its sub-dialects to provide a panaromic view of the Saraiki language. He had given the language a unity of command, which it was hitherto lacking. For Grierson, Saraiki had three main dialects. 1. Southern, or 'Standard', 2. 'North-Eastern', and 3. 'North-Western'. Each of these has several sub-dialects. According to him, the place of prominence is to be given to the Standard dialect, which is further divided into three sub-dialects: 1. 'the 'Standard Proper', 2. 'Multani', and 3. 'Thali'. It is surprising that Grierson gives prime importance to the Standard Proper and not to Multani, knowing well that Multan is the traditional headquarters and the heartthrob of Saraiki culture and language. The Standard Proper is spoken in Shahpur and adjacent districts. It also goes by several local names. It is called 'Jatki' in Jhang and Lyallpur. 'Punjabi' is another sub-dialect spoken by immigrants from Punjab who cultivate agricultural lands. 'Jangli' is another sub-dialect spoken in the region. It is also the spoken language of the nomad tribes. There are several other sub-dialects to be counted. 1. 'Kachhi', 2. 'Kachni', 3. 'Thalichhri', 4. 'Bardi Boli', 5. 'Jalalardi Boli'.

Notwithstanding Grierson, Multani sub-dialect constitutes the core of Saraiki cultural nationalism and not the Standard Proper spoken in Shahpur, which is not even considered Saraiki by several purist Saraiki advocates. It is spoken in Multan and adjacent districts including the Bahawalpur states. It is locally called 'Hindki' in Dera Ghazi Khan and 'Hindki', 'Hindi' and 'Jatki' in Muzaffargarh. The other local names in Dera Ghazi Khan are those of 'Hindi', 'Jatki', or 'Derawal'. The Balochi call it 'Jagdahli', meaning the language of the Jats. It is also called 'Derawali' in Dera Ismail Khan district. The Hindki variety of Multani is also spoken in upper Sindh. It is known as 'Siraiki' or 'up-country' Sindhi. Precisely, it is called 'Siraiki Hindki' to distinguish it from the Siraiki form of Sindhi. It is a language of the immigrants including the Baloch. Multani differs from the Standard Proper for its pronunciation, especially due to its tendency to employ double consonants of the Sindhi language. The third sub-dialect of the Standard Saraiki is called 'Thali'. That literally means 'desert' and, in fact, it is a vast sandy desert tract which extends from the Salt Range in the north down to Muzaffargarh district in the south. It is formed by the confluence of the Indus, Chenab and Jhelum rivers. It includes parts of several Standard Proper-speaking districts and Multani-speaking Muzaffargarh. It is also spoken in Dera Ismail Khan and parts of Mianwali district on the other side of the Indus. It has several other sub-dialects including 'Hindko' and 'Mulki' in its baggage, besides 'Derawali' spoken in Dera Ismail Khan which is quite distinct. Thali is largely uninhabitable, because it is not only sandy but is also marshy. It is the backwaters in the right sense of the term.

There is also a fourth sub-category consisting of minor sub-dialects like 'Khetrani', 'Jaffini' and 'Kandahari'. Khetrani is spoken by the Khetran tribe living in the Suleiman Range. It is a freak language, very much influenced by the Hindki of Dera Ghazi Khan, and, to a considerable extent by Balochi, the dominant language of Balochistan. Kandahari is spoken by the Hindu traders settled in Kandahar in Afghanistan. It is very much influenced by the Derawali sub-dialect. Khatri and Arora traders settled in Kandahar must have spread the language.

North-Eastern and North-Western Dialects

The North-Western dialect[6] constitutes the second category of the Standard dialect. The salt range is its identity, having Thali in its south. Christopher Shackle refuses to recognize the group of languages to be the genuine Saraiki dialect.Shackle sarcastically terms the group 'north-western Lahnda', referring to them as both clumsy and misleading. There is a group of four sub-dialects spoken in the compact space of the Campbellpur district, in which Attock town is located: 1. 'Sohai', 2. 'Dhonni', 3. 'Ghebi' and 4. 'Awankari'. These sub-dialects are spoken on the left bank of the Indus. Grierson also links 'Hindko' with the north-western group, which is spoken in Hazara and across the Indus in Peshawar and Kohat.

It is called Hindko, because it is assumed to be the language of the Hindus, most of whom lived in urban areas. Peshawari Hindko is considered a sophisticated sub-dialect, so much so 'Peshawar Hindko' has been cultivated as a vehicle of literature to a greater degree than the other northern dialects considered so far, and it is beginning to be known as a North-West Frontier Province Hindko.[7] Professor Shackle further asserts that it is best to treat Peshawar Hindko as forming a separate group of its own, at the same taxonomic level as the group we have termed 'Hindko Proper'.[8] It is also spoken in Kohat and Hazara with hardly any literary pretensions. The north-western dialect hangs in the middle, by partly agreeing with southern Saraiki, and partly with north-eastern Saraiki. This dialect is no match for what Grierson terms as the Standard dialect. It is merely a secondary dialect, with special local features. It is the spoken language of the Salt Range.

The north-eastern dialect of Saraiki is spoken in parts of the salt range, but it is essentially the language of the Potohar tract. It is known as Potohari. Its significance lies in its ancient roots. It is the land of the famous Taxila University. Panini, the grammarian, was a resident of the same area. Rawalpindi district and parts of the Jhelum district are its locale. Potohari and Multani are the most significant sub-dialects with much cultural significance. The north-eastern dialect encompasses space as far as Poonch, Muzaffarabad, Uri and the foothills of the Pir Panjal. Its variants are usually associated with tribes and locales. The sub-dialect spoken in the Murree Hills is called 'Pahari'. It is 'Poonchi' in Poonch.

North-eastern and north-western dialects have deep fraternal association. The Salt Range links both the dialects, with the north-western Saraiki standing in the middle, both ends occupied by the north-eastern Saraiki. North-eastern dialect, however, differs substantially from the southern or Standard dialect of Saraiki. There are wide differences in terms of vocabulary and grammar. These parts of the country have been subjected to repeated incursions from foreign lands. At the same time, the essence of the original dialect has been retained. North-eastern dialect is also distinguished by its high degree of nasalization. There is a special stress on 'nearly every final vowel'. Nasalization is a feature common to the whole range of Saraiki dialects.

Divergent Views

Thanks to the pioneering work done by George Grierson, Christopher Shackle and U A Simirnov, the Saraiki/Lahndi identity has been established in the world of scholarship. Eminent linguists like S K Chatterji have placed Saraiki on par with other modern Indian languages. They are conscious of its peculiarities, especially the paucity of recorded literature due to its oral tradition. It has remained a folk language for long. The colonial situation, both internal and external, have been a major handicap in its development. Its genuine strength lies in the fact that it has retained its original vocabulary intact. The additions are on the margin and have remained on its periphery. It is an ancient language and its past awaits to be discovered, for its present to be read. The language has continued to be deep-rooted in history and closely linked with ancient culture. Its folklore is rich and its Sufi tradition is very deep.

The debate about its geographical boundary and its core and periphery content is welcome. Here Professor Shackle parts company with George Grierson who has a larger vision of the pan-Saraiki homeland, extending from Peshawar and Rawalpindi to Multan and Bahawalpur, extending beyond to Sukkur, in the land of Sindhi 'Siro' ('Up-river north', or 'Siraiki', 'the language of the north'). He has suggested six geographical divisions, which are in consonance with the contemporary political movement for Saraiki homeland. But here Professor Shackle does injustice to history by delimiting the Saraiki space to suit the momentary political convenience. Geographical divisions suggested by him are as follows:

Name of Division	Areas covered
(1) Central	Multan, D.G. Khan (North), Muzaffargarh, Bahawalpur (Central and Southern)

(2) Southern	Rahim Yar Khan and Dera Ghazi Khan (south)
(3) Jhangi	Jhang and adjacent districts
(4) Shahpuri	Shahpur, parts of Jhang and Lyallpur
(5) Sindhi Siraiki	Northern Sindh,
(6) Northern (Thali)	Mianwali and Dera Ismail Khan

Sindhi Saraiki is the language of the immigrants. Shahpuri is exclusive to Rawalpindi, Peshawar and Sargodha. Sibi and Kacchi belong to distant Balochistan. Sindhi Saraiki scores over other dialects, because it is used bilingually with Sindhi. It is a language of 'considerable literary importance'. It is also known as 'Saraiki Hindki'. It is renowned for its deep Sufi roots. It is possible to include the names of Sachal Sarmast and Shah Abdul Latif in the Sindhi Siraiki roll of honour. Similarly, Bahawalpur Saraiki has been a vehicle for literary contributions. It is possible to include the name of well-known poet Khwaja Ghulam Fareed in the Bahawalpuri roll of honour.

False Delimitations

Appendix I contains the classification of dialects of Saraiki, which are also divided in two categories: 1. Core dialects and 2. Subsidiary dialects; along with a detailed chart of a plethora of sub-dialects. Since it is a situation in flux, the chart should be considered illustrative. It should, however, help to understand and not confuse the situation. There is no general agreement among the linguists about either the core or subsidiary dialects and their sub-dialects. The chart is neutral to the extent that it gives equal importance to all dialects and sub-dialects. While Jatki is spoken widely in its variant sub-dialects, Multani dialect remains the queen bee. It may be considered the core dialect, which has widely influenced other dialects and sub-dialects, because, 'It is spoken over a greater area than that of each other's dialect, the number of its speakers being also bigger, it serves as a veranacular in the region which is culturally and economically most developed throughout the Lahndi tract. Multani has influence on all other dialects, gradually turning into the prop dialect. There can [be] no doubt that with the creation of broad foundations for literature, the contralising role of Multani will still become greater'.[9] There is also greater Saraiki consciousness in Multani-speaking territories than elsewhere.

Besides Multani, Hindko is another dialect with much potential. Especially the Peshawar Hindko is to be singled out for the purpose. It has a considerable degree of sophistication as in the case of Multani, the 'Mother Dialect'. Peshawar Hindko is delimited by the fact of being citybound. Hindko, in its variant forms, is spoken in several other neighbouring districts of North-West Frontier Province and the Punjab, but it lacks any degree of Saraiki consciousness as in the Multan region. Peshawar dialect and its sub-dialects are merely a local phenomenon. Grierson, however, considers delimiting 'Hindko' to mean 'the language of the Hindu', and similarly he understood 'Hindko' to be a synonym of 'Hindus'. Grierson further downgrades it by calling it 'as a mongrel product of city life' and views it as having a subordinate status vis-à-vis Pashto. Multani does continue to maintain its premium position.

Southern Versus Northern Dialects

Grierson makes a distinction between southern and northern dialects. Southern dialects are clustered around Multani and extend as far as the southern borders of the salt range. These are dialects and sub-dialects of the plains. The northern dialects are divided (by him) in two parts: 1. North-western, and north-eastern. Both of these sub-categories are located in the salt range area and towards the north of it. These sub-dialects, especially of the Hindko variety, also cross the right bank of the Indus and beyond Peshawar, Bannu, Kohat and Dera Ismail Khan district. Prominent among these are Potohari and Peshawar Hindko. The other sub-dialects include a variety of Hindko and numerous other sub-dialects including Awankari, Ghebi, Dhanni, Suhai and Chachi. Every ten miles or so of travel results in a change in the sub-dialects. Even defining their identity is problematic and to categorize those may turn out to be a meaningless exercise, except to bring some order in a confusing situation. There are marked differences between southern and northern groups. There are substantial differences in respect of the vocabulary as well. Above all, 'it is impossible to sharply delimit the dialects of both groups, since they are variants of the same language. Frequent forms, on the whole more typical of one group of dialects, are used in the other'.[10]

There is no agreement on the broad contours of the Saraiki language itself. Historically, Saraiki has suffered from a sense of delimitation. That it has no character of its own. It has essentially remained a communicative language. In recent years, with increasing stress on consciousness of the Saraiki identity, attempts have been made to introduce a variant of Arabic script as the authentic Saraiki script. There has been no attempt to modify and adopt the Lahnda script, it is rather imperfect for purpose of literary pursuits. It should, however, not be forgotten that the Gurmukhi script is the improved version of the Lahnda script. It has been used for centuries by the Sikh gurus as the vehicle of promoting Sikh faith. It is also widely used by the Sikhs and Hindus who subscribe to the Guru Granth Sahib.

Siro Saraiki

Sindhi and Saraiki are said to be closely allied languages. Two languages have been called 'a kind of half and half language, half Lahnda and half Sindhi'. It is spoken by immigrants from western Punjab, the original homeland of Saraiki language. In fact, southern Saraiki has been so much impacted, that it has adopted Sindhi's double consonants effortlessly. Sindhi has even features common to other Dardic languages like Kashmiri. It also has a notional affinity with Saraiki, which is again a Dardic language. Sindhi has much empathy towards Dardic languages. It is also to be accepted that Sindhi is equally kindred to Punjabi and Saraiki. It does not have too much empathy for the neighbouring Rajasthani, because the desert is an overwhelming barrier. It is also a geographical and mental barrier. Rajasthani is also kept at a distance, because of its direct link to the central group of Indo-Aryan languages.

It should be made clear at the outset that Siro Saraiki is not Sindhi, but the language of the immigrants from Saraiki-speaking western Punjab. There was a large-scale migration during the 16th-19th centuries, most of who settled on the right bank of the Indus. The migrants spread themselves all over Sindh gradually. The Baloch also participated in the process. They, however, decided to adopt Siro Saraiki as their mother tongue like other migrants. It should also be made clear at this stage that Siro Saraiki is not

Sindhi, but a dialect of Saraiki allied to Hindki, spoken in Dera Ghazi Khan. So here is an instance of Saraiki or Lahndi planted on the soil of Sindh.

Hindki Connection

Dera Ghazi Khan borders on Sind on the right side of the river Indus. This part of Sindh is known as upper Sindh, contrasted with lower Sindh reaching out to Karachi at its farthest end. The justification for Saraiki Hindki is easily explained. There is considerable traffic between Dera Ghazi Khan, Bahawalpur and Balochistan on one side, and the Siro on the other. This process has been continuing for at least three centuries now. Consequently, Hindki of Dera Ghazi has come to be adopted in the Siro effortlessly. There are also historical reasons for the connection with the Punjab district of Dera Ghazi Khan.

The Kalhera kings of Sindh have also been rulers of Dera Ghazi Khan district for centuries together. There is a considerable traffic between the Siro country and Dera Ghazi Khan due to the continuity of historical relations. The descendents of the Kalhera kings are residents of Dera Ghazi Khan district. In Dera Ghazi Khan, the word 'Siriki' came to be recognized as a common appellation for natives of Sindh. Since the Siro is the language of the immigrant, it is the most pure Saraiki mixed with Sindhi as the secondary player. The Siro is also the homeland of the Arora community, who are now spread all over the western Punjab, exceeding in number than the Khatri community in the Punjab. The upper Sindh frontier or Siro is the homeland of the Saraikis, who, much to the credit of the native Sindhis, have learnt to live with them peacefully. It is also to be remembered that the speakers of Saraiki Sindhi, or more accurately, the Siro are mainly immigrants from western Punjab, who have gradually transformed the landscape. There are several local names for the Saraiki Sindhi. 'Jatki', 'Multani', 'Punjabki', 'Punjabi', 'Jaghdali' (of Baloch origin), 'Ubheki' (i.e. language of the north and rivers), as well as Siraiki.

Geographical Delimitations

Sindh is usually demarcated into three divisions: 1. The Lar, or lower Sindh, 2. Vichalo (central Sindh) and 3. The Siro, or upper Sindh. It is called upper

Sindh because it is situated to the north of Vichalo. Most of it is situated on the right bank of the Indus river, adjacent to Dera Ghazi Khan on the right bank, and Bahawalpur state on the left bank. Dr Ernest Trumpp is considered to be one of the greatest authorities on Sindhi language; he calls Siro Saraiki as 'the purest form of language', and, in support of this argument, Grierson is tempted to quote a proverb about 'the learned man of the Lar (or lower Sindhi) (being no more than) an ox in the Siro'.[11] Again and again it needs to be stressed that the spoken Siro is not Sindhi, but a form of Hindki spoken in the neighbouring Dera Ghazi Khan. The word means Siro the upper Sind, 'or that part of the province which lies north of Schwan on the Indus. From this is derived the word Siriaki, an inhabitant of the Siro and Siriki, the language spoken in the Siro'.[12] In other words, while the Siro is about the geographical connotation, Siriki is the language spoken, and Siraiko are the residents of the Siro. Siro, Siriki and Sirdiko rhyme excellently. To this rich vocabulary are to be added two more enrichingening terms: 'Siraiki' and 'Sindhi Siraiki'. While Sraikia is considered as 'the language of the north', Sindhi Saraiki stands for the language of the immigrants and, of course, Siro is understood to mean 'up-river', north. The play upon the word is endless. The word 'Sir' is the fountainhead. It means head (from which it is derived), which literally means 'the extremity of anything'. Saraiki, which is owed to the pure Sindhi Siro, is not a Sindhi language. It is another version of Lahndi, spoken chiefly by the migrant jats and the Baloch. It is amusing to realize that Siro Saraiki is of Sindh, but it is not a Sindhi language, largely spoken by residents of non-Sindhi origin, who continue to speak their native tongue on 'foreign soil'.

Appendix I

Classification of Dialects of Saraiki Language*

Part - I Core Dialect

Dialect	Sub-Dialect	Where Spoken
Multani		Spoken in Multan, Muzaffargah, Dera Ghazi Khan, Bahawalpur and Rahim Yar Khan districts
	Derawal[1]	Dera Ghazi Khan
	Khetrani[2]	Beyond borders of D G Khan and beyond the Suleiman range in Murree Hills.
	Jaffiri	Beyond borders of D G Khan and beyond the Suleiman range in Murree Hills.
	Kandhari[3]	Kandahar state (Afghanistan)
	Bahawalpuri[4]	Bahawalpur and Rahim Yar Khan districts
Thali[5]		Jhang, Lyallpur, Shahpur, Sargodha, Mianwali, Gujrat, Gujranwala and Thaal region. Also in Dera Ismail Khan and Bannu districts of NWFP
	Jangali	Jangal Bar Tract
	Jatki[6]	Jhang, Lyallpur and Montgomery districts
Jhangi		Jhang district
	Kacchri	Named for the alluvial plain of Kacchi, SE of Jhang Town
	Thalchri	Western region
	Chinawari	Right bank of Chenab River
	Niswani[7]	North Jhang
	Punjabi[8]	East Montgomery district
Saro-Saraiki[9]		Northern Sind

Part - II
Subsidiary Dialects

Dialect	Sub-Dialect	Where Spoken
Hindko[10]		Cambellpur, Peshawar, Kohat, Abbotabad and Hazara districts
	Peshawar Hindko	Peshawar Town and G T Road villages east of Peshawar in the direction of Nowshera, bordering Campbellpur district
	Chachhi	North Cambellpur and Southern Hazara
	Kagani	Kagani Valley
	Attock-Haripur Hindko	Haripur (Abbotabad district)

	Kohati	Kohat City
Potohari		Spoken in Rawalpindi, parts of Jhelum district and neighbouring region
	Dhundi-Kairali	East Hazara
	Pahari	Murree Hills
	Poonchi	Poonch district
	Tinouli	SW Hazara
Miscellaneous[11]	Avankari	Talagang tehsil
	Ghebi[12]	Pindi Gheb tehsil
	Dhanni	Estern Part of Jhelum district
	Sohai[13]	East Fatehganj tehsil
	Chacchi[14]	Northern Attock and Southern Hazara
	Tinoli[15]	Hazara

Note:-

1. Also known as Hindi, Hindki, Jatki, Derawal and Jagdahli. Baloch call it Jagdahli.
2. Spoken by the Khetran tribe
3. Spoken by local Afghan Hindus and Sikhs.
4. Also known as Riyasti.
5. Named after Thal, a desert region bordered by the Indus river to the west and Jhelum and Chenab rivers to the east. It is called Mulki in Mianwali. It is also known as Jatki, Hindko, Hindki and Derawali. The last refers to the vicinity of Dera Ismail Khan (west of the Indus river)
6. Spoken by Jats.
7. Spoken by Niswana tribe.
8. Spoken by migrants from Punjabi - speaking region.
9. Also known as Siro, Siraiki, 'Up-country Sindhi'. Language of Punjabi and Baloch migrants.
10. Also known as the language of Hindus as contrasted with Pushtu. It is the most sophisticated of Hindko sub-dialects, with a corpus of respectable literature to its credit. It is also a spoken language of the villages along the G T Road, known as Khalsavi (Tappa Khalsa). Its literal meaning: 'Language of the Indus'.
11. C Shackle has proposed to set up a group called Hindko Prper comprising dialects of Cambellpur district comprised of Avankari, Ghebi, Chacchi and Kohati. Grierson gave them the name of north-west Lahnda. These sub-dialects are closely allied and merge into each other separately either at the Salt Range, hill or river barrier.
12. The Avankari and Ghebi sub-dialects are closely related to each other.
13. Related to Dhanni group
14. Related to Ghebi.
15. Spoken by Tinomal group of tribes.

* This is a tentative classification based on the writings of several authorities including the following:

1. Grierson, G A Comp. and ed.	Lingustic Survey of India, V. 8. Pt. l. Low Price Publications, Delhi, 1919.
2. Schackle, C	Hindko in Kohat and Peshawar. BOAS, 43, pt. 3, 482-510.
3. Marica, Colin P	The Indo-Aryan Languages. Cambrisge, 1990

13

Unity and Diversity

Indo-Aryan Language

Many Punjabi scholars find it difficult to stomach the fact that Saraiki or Lahndi (or more correctly, Laihandi) is a language different from Punjabi. It is argued further that this fact can be based on linguistic analysis. Saraiki is different from Punjabi for the simple reason that it is a Dardic language possessing several characteristics that ally it with Kashmiri, thus establishing their Indus connection. Similarly it can be argued that Punjabi is a stepchild of Saraiki. The reality is different. Saraiki, Punjabi and Sindhi are sister languages allied to each other. Saraiki and Sindhi are twins, forming together the 'Aryan vocabulary'. Sindhi has equally impacted Saraiki spoken in upper Sindh, as well Saraiki spoken in neighboring south-western Punjab. They are like Hindi, Rajasthani, Gujarati, Marathi, Oriya, Bengali and Assamese Indo-Aryan languages and, in turn, along with the mother tongue Sanskrit, a branch of Indo-European family. They have common roots in history.

For the sake of convenience, they have passed through three stages of development: Old Indo-Aryan (OIA), Middle Indo-Aryan (MIA) and New Indo-Aryan (NIA). The history of Saraiki language and its development must be viewed in this very context.

The earliest form of OIA originated in the 'Vedic'–the language in which the Vedas were composed–on the Saraiki soil. This was followed by literature that was composed in Sanskrit, which ceased to be a language of common communication by the sixth century BC. It, however, continued to be the language of scholarly discourse up to the 11th and 12th centuries. It was essentially the spoken and scholarly language of the Saraiki territories. It would not be wrong to assume that Sanskrit language was born and bred on the banks of Sindhu or Indus river. Sanskrit was thus the Saraiki gift to the Indian civilization. Old Indo-Aryan was followed by the second phase, or the MIA phase, which is conveniently divided into three consecutive sub-phases: 1. Pali, 2. Prakrit, and 3. Apabhransha. The birth of Pali coincided with the rise of Buddhism. It was a language of the people and an expression of revolt against the stylized Sanskrit; and Presumably it was the spoken language 'in the north-west parts of India from about 500 BC to the beginning of the Christian era'. It was again a Saraiki connection that ran deep with Pali as the language of the masses and school of expression. At one time, Buddhism was the dominant faith of the Saraiki landmass (and Sindh). The adoption of Pali and acceptance of Buddhism were inductive of social revolution that swept across the north-westen India. It also brought the entire Indus landmass from Gandhara to Kaekaya and to Sindhu together as one cultural and social framework. In other words, it heralded the rejection of Vedic tradition that had its original roots in the Saraiki landmass

The second phase has a common label of Prakrit for a bunch of languages that replaced Pali with local emphasis. The final phase is labeled *Apabhransha,* which literally means scattering or breaking up into pieces. It is in this phase that modern languages like Saraiki, Punjabi, Sindhi and the rest were born while the period of Prakrit extend from the Christian era to around AD 500, the Apabhransha developed around the 11th century AD, coinciding with the advent of Islam into India.

The Birth of Apabhranshas

Saraiki language is a major constituent of Apabhranshas, which however, did not evolve at the same time. It has the elements of Sanskrit, Pali and Prakrit in its basic structure. It was also impacted by other Apabhranshas and foreign elements because local influences indeed demarcated Saraiki from other Apabhranshas. There was considerable give-and-take with other Apabhranshas, especially in the neighbourhood like Sindhi and Punjabi. It was also impacted by other Dardic languages like Kashmiri, Kohistani and Shinai. Sanskrit continues to be the mother language of all Pali, Prakrit and Apabhranshas. Since Sanskrit was born on the Saraiki soil, it has a special connection with Saraiki in respect of its basic structure. Equally, Saraiki has been greatly impacted by foreign influences due to its strategic location. It has withstood all foreign intrusions and has succeeded in retaining its basic original structure. Similarly, it has elements of Pali and Prakrit, which need to be brought out through scholarly research,employing multi-disciplinary tools.

There are also considerable variations, when Sanskrit and Pali are juxtaposed with Apabhransha like in Saraiki. There are variations which are common to them, when contrasted with Sanskrit and to some extent with Pali. Sanskrit is different in terms of its structure from Apabhransha in several respects. Sanskrit and Pali have verbal forms which are synthetic. It has plenty of compound words and Sanskrit is very playful about them. Sanskrit has three genders, singular, dual and plural. Pali has simplified vowels, but the language is still very synthetic. It has also three genders. When we come to the Prakrits, those are less synthetic than Vedic Sanskrit and Pali. There is a striking transformation when we come to Apabhransha. While it is next to impossible to date the exact birth of Saraiki, it is possibly the eleventh century, which is also the probable date of birth of its sister language Punjabi, which like other Apabhranshas, was more analytical rather than synthetic, when compared to Sanskrit and Pali.

Synthetic vs Analytic

There is a interesting progression from Vedic language to Sanskrit and to Pali, followed by Prakrit, with Apabhranshas holding fort at the end in this prefect evolutionary order. Sanskrit was a highly synthetic language employing suffixes and prefixes and perhaps the most economical language in existence. Pali comes a notch below. It is still synthetic, but vowels are simple. While Vedic language is of the Rigvedic people, Pali was its popular expression and the language of Buddhism. Prakrits are less synthetic than Vedic, Sanskrit and even Pali. Most of the nouns and adjective end in O and hence Prakrits are called 'O ending languages'. Apabhranshas, variantly estimated to number from three to thirty are more analytical than even the Prakrits. They are also 'O ending languages'. The Saraiki Apabhransha is predominately a synthetic language, considering the fact its rich vocabulary consists predominately of words which have found their way from Sanskrit. Loan words form a minor proportion of its vocabulary and while those have been assimilated, but it was 'no-no' to foreign sounds. Thus loan words have a distinct Saraiki resonance about them.

Prakrit into Saraiki

Sanskrit is the great-grandparent of practically the majority of Indian languages, so is Pali but the direct lineage of Saraiki and other Apabhranshas remains to be traced to their direct parentry, namely Prakrits. There is no agreement about the actual number of Prakrits. There were possibly five Prakrits, the existence of which are recognized but which was the parent of Saraiki is still shrouded in mystery. The five major Prakrit are: 'Shaurseni', 'Mahavashtri', 'Magdhi', 'Ardhamagdhi' and 'Paisachi'. Shaurseni was spoken in north-west India and was possibly the ancestor of Saraiki and Punjabi. There is no proper evidence to support such a claim. Grierson is also of the firm opinion that there is no hard evidence to establish the particular form of Apabhranshas spoken in the Saraiki area. He, however, surmises, as based on deduction from Greek sources, possibly some form of Paisachi Prakrit was spoken by the people of western Punjab. This information is deduced by him on the basis of Greek writings about India. The transition from Paisachi Prakrit to the associate Apabhranshas is a missing link. The number of Apabhranshas varies as widely from three to thirty. Which one is associated with which one is a mystery wrapped in enigma.

This much is, however, known that the people of the ancient Gandhara and Kaekaya who presumably spoke Vrachadha-Paisachi-Prakrit were 'fond of saying a word twice over in order to indicate repetition or continuance..., but in Gandhara there are two famous rock-inscriptions of the Indian Emperor Ashoka (Circa BC 250) at Shahbazgarhi and at Mansehra which are couched in what was the then official language of the country. This was a dialect form of Pali, distinguished by several phonetic peculiarities that are still absorbable in the Dardic languages and in Lahndi and Sindhi.[1] Compounding is a rather common way of forming words in Saraiki. It is also very rhythmatic. Usually two words are joined by a hyphen to form compound words, e.g.

> *'mar-kat', beating (literally 'blow-blow'),*
> *'mar-kuttai' beating (literally 'blow-beating-up'),*
> *'daru-dirmal 'treatment' (literally 'treatment medicine'),*
> *'mal-sabab' 'things', 'goods' (literally 'things-things')*[2]

Saraiki Vocabulary

The Saraiki vocabulary, accumulated over several millennia, makes a revealing reading. The Saraiki linguistic experts have been able to identify four variant influences over historical times:

(1) **Tatsamas or Semi-Tatsamas:** Such words of Indo-Aryan Sanskrit origin which have kept their identity intact, are indeed the 'virgin' vocabulary untouched through the centuries. Semi-Tatsamas are words which have become some what chiseled as impacted by local conditions. The Tatsamas vocabulary still form the core of contemporary Saraiki.

(2) **Deshis (indigenous):** Such words as have been traced to a Sanskrit or Prakrit root, but whose origin is yet to be established.

(3) **Tadbhavas (Middle Indo-Aryan Prakrit):** It has a profusion of Sanskrit which have undergone changes in Prakrit and have thus been localized, and

(4) **Contemporary influences:** The most prominent are the influence inspired by Arabic and Persian vocabulary indicating the predominance of Islamic influences.

In the early '30s H Bahrim made a statistical study of the Avankari vocabulary which yielded the following interesting results:

Indo-Aryan [Tadbhavas] vocabulary	60 per cent
Foreign loans	20 per cent
Deshi word	15 per cent
Words of obscure origin	4 per cent
Tan or stam words	1 per cent[3]

The results in respect of Saraiki vocabulary are likely to be same as both Saraiki and Avankari share the same vocabulary. Thus, the core vocabulary of Saraiki substitantially retains its Indo-Aryan soul.

Kirakki Alphabet

Lahnda alphabet, also known as Multani script, has been employed for centuries by 'non-Brahman and non-official people' for 'temporal and commercial purpose'. It is a script with possible roots in Mesopotamia and the Indus Valley Civilization. It is thus an inheritor of ancient civilization. Lahndi-speaking Sikhs frequently use the Gurmukhi alphabet to write texts in the Lahndi language. Popularly, it is known as Kirakki-the characters used in writing accounts. There is a certain play upon the word in the Saraiki language. Probably its route is to be traced to 'kira', meaning insect or snake, reptile or snail, which has given birth to the term 'Kirar', meaning Hindu shopkeeper, which has further generated the term 'kirrakha', connected with Hindu (Kirrakhi) breakfast time. 'Kirakhi' also means 'writing dahna', that is the language with double meaning. Lahnda, by its very nature, possesses double meaning. It has inadequate store of consonants and several alphabets that are missing from its vocabulary. The following saying aptly explains the situation:

'Kirakhi di ukhat, dilh dola hikh'

(In Kirakki writing, a lump of earth and earthen pot are the same)

The characters of the Lahnda alphabet, along with its transcription in English and Arabic/Persian characters, has been indicated in Appendix I for comparison. Saraiki people have never adopted it. It has no written characters of its own. It has no literature to its credit. It has only a stock of folk poetry transmitted orally from generation to generation. The Lahnda alphabet is good enough for writing accounts, and is indeed the language of the shopkeeper hiding rather than explaining things. The written word is to be found in Urdu and to some extent, in Gurmukhi characters. It is also known as 'clipped alphabet' for obvious reasons. Unfortunately, 'It is a very incomplete alphabet, vowel signs being hardly ever used except while using initials. It is, in fact, generally legible to none except for the original writer'. It has, however, historical connections with several Indo-Aryan scripts including the Mahajani characters of Marwar, the Tikri of the Punjab hills, and the Sharda alphabet employed in Kashmir. In most cases vowels are not employed and even if they are, one and the same character correlates with several vowels simultaneously. For instance, the vowels 'a', 'e' and 'u' are denoted in one and the same way respectively. Similar is the case with consonants. The results are hilarious and certainly not made for easy reading. It is also liable to secrecy, resulting in misguiding others.

Sikh Connection

The Sikh holy scripture *Janam Sakhi* contains an account of the life and times of the Sikh gurus and is written in Lahndi mixed with Punjabi, underlying the significance of Saraiki to the Sikh religion. Obviously there was a conscious attempt to associate both Saraiki and Punjabi speaking people with Sikhism from its very initial stages. In fact, Janam Sakhi is a script which is half Lahndi and half Punjabi. Thus, the Sikh gurus had sent a clear message of unity between Lahndi and Punjabi people. This momentum is carried forward in the *Adi Granth*, the holy book of the Sikhs. Three groups of texts from the *Adi Granth* are to be found in the original 'Old Saraiki' or 'Old Multani'. The foremost work is attributed to Baba Farid (1175-1265), the founder of the great Chishti dynasty of Pakpattan. Four short hymns and 130 shlokas are attributed to him. Those are the earliest examples of literature in Saraiki.

The second group consists of two short hymns of Guru Nanak (1469-1539) in which the Saraiki element is very distinct. Guru Nanak is believed to have visited Multan and those verses are indicative of his association with the local people. There is another set of shlokas of Guru Arjan (1563-1606) in three parts, consisting of several pairs of 20 stanzas, a salok and 69 shlokas, respectively. Guru Arjan Dev attributed each shloka as dakhna and each set as shloka dakhni. Dakhna and dakhni clearly imply the south-western part of the country. Several commentators believe that Guru Arjan Dev refers to 'the language of the south', more specifically a mixture of 'Lahndi' and Sindhi. Too much should not be read in this Saraiki connection of the *Adi Granth*, which has a pan-Indian vision, and, to the extent, it has incorporated the Lahndi writings, it has established the Saraiki identity as a part of the larger Pan-Indian identity. Much deeper Saraiki connection is indicated at several other levels. Lahndi alphabet is the very superstructure of Gurmukhi script. The word 'gurumukh' means the sacred words emanating from the mukh (literally mouth or lips) of the Sikh gurus.

Brahmi Inspiration

Both Lahndi and Gurmukhi have a Brahmi connection. Brahmi script is the original Aryan script. The most distinctive feature of Brahmi is its curves, alternating with linear straight strokes, both of these are to be found in Gurmukhi and Lahnda scripts, more particularly in Gurmukhi, wherein a conscious effort has been made to enhance its aesthetics. Brahmi was continually influenced by several foreign scripts, Kharosthi being one of them. Brahmi script was further refined by 'five curves' and embellished with flourishes, with a small headline over each letter. This stage was known as Kuntil, meaning curved and it was further refined to the Siddhamatrika, which was very popular in north India. With the rise of Prakrits, several scripts including Devnagari, an off-shoot of Nagri, Ardhanagari (West) and Sharda (Kashmir) were born. It is possible to develop relationship between Lahnda and Gurmukhi on the one hand, and Devnagari, Ardhanagari, Siddhamatrika, Sharda and Brahmi on the other. There are several scholars who ascribe Gurmukhi to Lahnda, and to Takri, a branch of Sharda used in Chamba and Kangra. There is a chain that links all these script into a unity.

Besides similarity with Lahnda script, Gurmukhi has similarity with Gujarati, Nagari, Sharda and Takni. The similarity of these scripts with

Gurmukhi is most striking. Among these scripts, Lahnda and Takri scripts are native, because those were commonly used for accoundting rather than religious purpose. At the very closest, Punjabi provided the link between several other languages and their scripts, as reflected in the *Adi Grantha*; 'The prevailing idiom of the AG (*Adi Grantha*) varies between the western Hindi-based religious lingua franca of the Sant preachers of later medieval north India, usually referred to as 'Santbhasa' or 'Sadhukari', and various types of Punjabi proper. Among the latter at least three broad varieties can probably be distinguished as 'Eastern', the closest to western Hindi; 'Central', corresponding to modern Majhi; and 'Western', corresponding in part to what the LSI [Linguistic Survey of India] loosely termed 'Punjabi merging into Lahnda....'[4]

Gurmukhi Script

The Encyclopaedia of Sikhism is coy in giving credit to Guru Angad for inventing Gurmukhi script by merely 'attributing' it to him, and also hesitates in giving credit to the Lahndi script for its inventiveness: 'The letters no doubt existed before the times of Guru Angad (even of Guru Nanak) as they had their origin in the Brahmi, but the origin of the script is attributed to Guru Angad. He not only modified and rearranged certain letters but also shaped them into a script. He gave new shape and new order to the alphabet and made it precise and accurate. He fixed one letter for each of the Punjabi phenomena. Use of vowel-symbols was made obligatory, the letters meant for conjuncts were not adopted and only those letters were retained which produced sounds of the then spoken language'.[5] The obvious reference is to the lacuna in Lahndi script, which were sought to be filled by the resourcefulness of Guru Angad.

Grierson has no hesitation in assuming that while Lahnda is the mother script, Gurmukhi is its much improved version of the next generation: 'The Gurmukhi alphabet is an improved and polished form of Lahnda, and to have been invented by Angad (1538-1552 AD), for the purpose of recording the scriptures of the Sikh religion. It is said that he found that Sikh hymns written in Lahnda were liable to be misread, and he accordingly improved it by borrowing signs (especially vowel signs) from the Nagari alphabet and by polishing up the forms of the existing Lahnda consonants'.[6] How much would matters have improved, if the Gurmukhi script had been adopted by the Saraikis, considering that the Gurmukhi script was only a modified but improved version of Lahnda, especially it had filled the gaps both in respect of Lahnda vowels and consonants. Gurmukhi has further advantage of its aesthetics, in shaping the alphabet as an artist would do it. After all, one must remember that Gurmukhi is merely an improved version of Lahnda. It did not work out for practical reasons, because both Sindhi and Saraiki chose Arabic/ Persian version of the alphabets. This brought about a cultural divide among different communities, which still remains to be bridged.

Guru Angad—The Artiste

Guru Angad, the second guru of the Sikhs, lived in the shadow of Guru Nanak and occupied the gaddi very briefly, but he left a mark on the cultural and literary scene of India. He had deep roots in the traditions of India, but he was also aware of local situations. Guru Angad, like Guru Nanak and other Sikh gurus had a pan-Indian vision. Brahmi script was his original inspiration. Brahmi (from few century BCE to 5th C E) at one time had wide acceptability on account of its simple curves, alternating with straight strokes in Punjab, Gandhara and Sindh. The Brahmi script improved further during the Gupta period (4th and 5th century C E). It developed fine curves and embellished flourishes with a headline over each letter, and this became further ornamental and came to be known as Kuntil, meaning curved. Gurumukhi characters have striking similarities with other languages including Saraiki, Gujarati, Nagari, Sharda and Tikri. Their pan-Indian character is established by the fact that the characters are either exactly the same or essentially alike. There was an artiste in him. He had his eye on Lahnda and at the same time, he viewed Punjabi and Lahnda in the larger context of the Indian linguistic tradition, with Brahmi script as the fountainhead. On the one side, it was Lahnda representing the local situation, and on the other, was Brahmi to be placed in the larger framework. Guru Angad went about reconciling both. Basically, he was working on an improved version of Lahnda. Angad re-arranged and modified the Lahnda alphabets. He sought to fill up the gaps, especially vowels that were given their due place. He brought about the stylistic discipline by employing curves and writing in straight lines. He, thus, reconstructed the 'old Lahnda' or 'Old Multani' script. It was no longer confined to the account books of the baniya. Punjabi was crucified in the melting pot and was qualitatively transformed as contrasted with old Lahnda, which chose to be static. Punjabi was qualitatively a different language, and it lasted because it also turned out to be a scriptural language.

This dialogue between two languages did not add to Saraiki. After all, Punjabi was altogether a different language. The communication gap became ungulfable between the two sister languages, due to circumstances. Punjabi is now written in Gurmukhi and Arabic/Persian scripts. So is Saraiki, employing the Arabic/Persian script with suitable modifications. The communication channels are no longer open between the two sister languages on account of differing scripts.

Vocabulary

Prakrits gave birth to Apabhransha languages and Saraiki has not outgrown that stage. Prakrit literally means 'vitiated' and which is indeed an appropriate description of Saraiki in its present stage. It has got bottled up for a variety of reasons. E O Briens calls it a 'rough language' 'having somewhat the charm of wild flower in a hedge, whose untamed luxuriance pleases more than the regular splendour of the parterre. Even in early Prakrit times, the dialect of the Indus Valley earned for itself the contemptuous epithet of 'apabhransha' or vitiated. There is a wheaten flavour and a reek of cottage smoke about Multani which is infinitely more natural and capitavating than anything which the hidebound language of the eastern parts of India can show us'.[7] The judgement may appear too harsh but it contains a backhanded tribute to Multani, the most sophisticated of the Saraiki sub-dialect.

Saraiki is still an innocent folk language. It has a large corpus of oral literature, mostly rural based, consisting of stories, songs, proverbs, romances, satires and other forms of folk poetry. Folk poetry is the strongest point of Saraiki language. No wonder, the elite have an attitude of 'affectionate contempt' towards it. Most of the literature has a religious basis. The best comes out in Sufi literature with Islamic overtones, but Sikh literature is to be found in Punjabi and not Saraiki. While Bhakti movement has impacted the Saraiki homeland among the Hindu community, it has produced no worthwhile literature in Saraiki. The best work produced by the classical Muslim Punjabi literary tradition is about Heer and it has attained world-class status in literary values.

The Saraiki homeland is a cattle-based economy and maximum number of words are to be found for the cattle including cows, buffaloes and camel. It is indeed a wasteful employance of the vocabulary and is a clear indication of the language lacking in sophistication. As the languages grow, those become economical to the extreme. Saraiki is yet to learn the lesson. The generic names for cow, for instance, are not to be found in Saraiki. There are special names for the animal in every stage of 'fecundity, harness, age, colour and temper'. There are even separate names for cowdung for each stage of freshness. In respect of camels, for instance, great value is given to the number of teeth they possessed and they are named separately.

Cow Vocabulary[8]

Ga	-	cow after five years
Vachchi	-	calf while suckling his mother up to about a year old
Vahrki/ Vehrki	-	a heifer from one to 2½ year old
Vehir	-	a heifer from 2½ to 5 year old
Gavi	-	a collection of many cows
Gava	-	connected with cows
Dharao	-	heifer about 3-year old fit to bear young for the first time
Pehun	-	cow after its first calf
Su	-	delivered of a calf
Khattar	-	a cow that refused to give milk
Lamm	-	young sua bearing a calf
Dufen/Duin	-	After its second calf
Trithal/trijin/triin	-	having its third calf

Kanj/phanc/
pharar/pharari - barren
Gabbhan - in calf-pregnant (only for animals)
Hala/holi - cow/bullock having horns
Sandhan - a cow that has not been ill
Purdhin - a cow in calf again soon after calving
Dhaggi - a poor cow

Saraiki is also rich in kinship vocabulary. There are separate expressions of father of father-in-law, brother of father-in-law, father of brother-in-law, brother of mother-in-law, son of father's brother and daughter of father's brother. The kinship of the extraordinary type was usual in tribal and feudal communities of Saraiki homeland.

Grammar

While Sindhi, Punjabi and Saraiki have been called sister languages, there are marked difference between Saraiki and Punjabi in their fundamental characters. While Punjabi came under increasing influence of western Hindi, thereby resulting in some growing peculiarities to it, Saraiki was subjected to such influences but it retained its pristine original character. There are also several other differences that demarcate Saraiki from Punjabi. Punjabi is an analytical language as contrasted with Saraiki, which has retained its original synthetic character. It should be remembered in this connection that this characteristic of Saraiki is again a gift from Sanskrit and Pali, which are both distinguished for their synthetic characters. Saraiki is also well-known for its double consonants; especially it is true of the Lahndi. It has been correctly said that Punjab is the meeting point of two entirely different languages, which are increasingly charting different paths.

A. Jokes, the compiler of the largest Lahnda dictionary, should know when he asserts, 'Western Punjabi or Jatki' is 'quite a different language' from that spoken in the Easten Punjab'. In his Lahndi dictionary, he was able to assert on the basis of actual count of every page, 'containing an average of 36 words, only about two that coincided with Punjabi ones'.[9] Another distinctive feature of Saraiki lies in the vowel sounds being frequently analytical. Equally, consonants are often pronounced after a short vowel with emphasis on the doubling of letters. Saraiki rejoices in cerebral and nasal letters, which is most pronounced in Derawali sub-dialect of Saraiki. What is distinguishing about Saraiki is that it has retained its ancient Sanskrit connection by retaining the old Sanskrit verbs. Saraiki is a laboratory for studying Indian languages.

Appendix II

Lahnda Alphabet

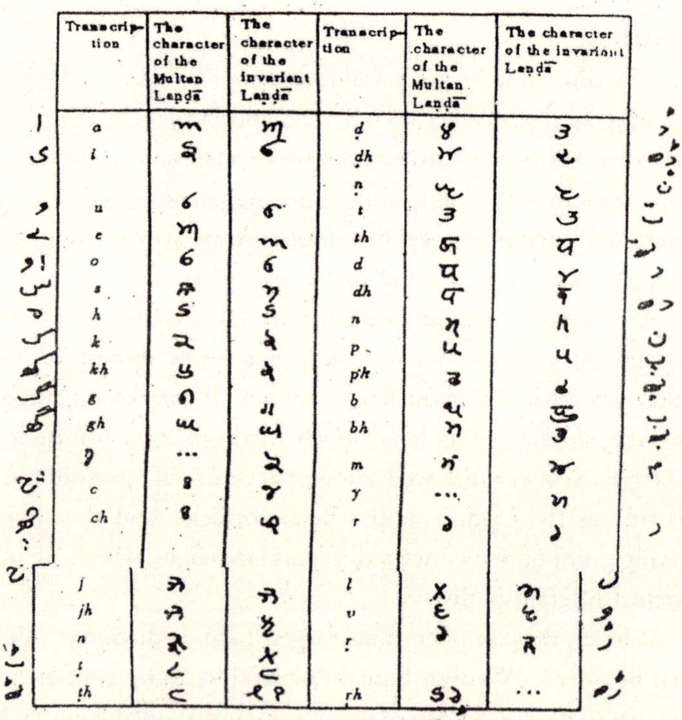

Grierson[1], 311

Section - VII

Literature and Liberal Tradition

14

Baba Farid to Shah Husain

IT is virtually impossible to draw a line of demarcation between Saraiki and Punjabi literature. It also makes sense to treat Saraiki, Punjabi, and Sindhi literature at par. The best of the literature was produced during medieval times. It has a Sufi stamp with basic secular content. There is a popular Sufi saying about 'neither being a Muslim, nor a Hindu, but being both'. There is also a saying about being 'half Sunni' and 'half Shia'. Especially Saraiki and Punjabi literature are placed in the same predicament. While Punjabi and Saraiki linguistics have their separate identity, the literature is identically the same, except for the Bhakti literature of Sikh faith, with exclusive Punjabi stamp on it due to historical reasons. Admittedly, there is much more of Saraiki content than Punjabi in it, because Saraiki language is more amendable to popular literary exposition.

Prominent Literary Figures

The truth of the matter is also established by looking at the background of eminent literary figures appearing in this distinguished gallery. It is possible to count eleven of them for the present study. The list is headed by Baba Farid (1175-1265), and Khwaja Ghulam Farid (1845-1901) is to be counted as the last of the series. Their time spans seven centuries in all. It is interesting to note that ten of eleven eminent literary figures belong to the Saraiki homeland, and can rightly be claimed to be Saraikis by birth. In other words, ten of these illustrious figures were born in the vicinity of Multan, Jhang and Bahawalpur, which also happen to be the heartland of Saraiki-speaking folks. Two of them were located in Sindh and at least one of them had a Sindhi-Seraiki connection. Consequently, the underlying ethos is Saraiki, with large Punjabi and Sindhi flavour. It is also Saraiki which is indeed the link language between Sindhi and Punjabi, Punjabi and Saraiki are in fact twin sisters, which seek to discover their identity in unity and not the diversity. At the same time, the pre-eminence of Saraiki has to be recognized. It has been long in coming.

Baba Farid (1175-1265), more popularly known as Farid-ud-Din Shakaragunj, was undoubtedly the pioneer in laying the foundations of Saraiki literature, hitherto confined to oral tradition and narration of folk tales. He was born at Kothiwal, a village about ten miles from Multan. He assumed the status of a Sufi saint and his khanqah is located at Ajodhan (Pakpattan). His verse has merited inclusion in the Guru Granth Sahib. He was followed by Farid Sani (1450-1554), a spiritual descendant of Jang-i-Shakar, who was influenced by Kabir and pantheism was adopted by the Sufis under his influence. There is still unresolved dispute about the identity of two pioneers, who are often confused to be one and the same person. The next in the roll of honour is Damodar, a Gulati Arora, belonging to Chuchak village in Jhang. He was a contemporary of Heer and recorded the Heer legend, based on the actual happenings. Baba Farid, Farid Sani and Damodar were the pioneers of Saraiki literature.

Shah Husain and Company

The next phase of Saraiki literature is associated with the name of Shah

Husain (1539-1593), the founder of Saraiki poetry in real sense of the term. He belonged to Chiniot in Jhang and was a convert from Hinduism. He has been called a Vedantic Sufi poet. He is also known as 'Madho Lal Husain' for his attachment to a Hindu young man. Half of his verses are in the female voice and discusses gender relations. Shah Husain stands apart in his singular majesty. He was followed by Sultan Bahu (1629-1691) who too came from the Jhang district (village Awan). He was a Qadri pantheist, renowned spiritual teacher and scholar of Sufism, but in fact lived in a royal style.

The Saraiki literature came into its own during the eighteenth century. It became the people's language. Those were disturbed times on the eve of the collapse of the Mughal empire. Bulleh Shah (1680-1757-58), born at Uch Gilanian (Bahawalpur Sate), was a Syed belonging to the liberal Sufi sect of Qadris. He is considered the greatest Saraiki poet who speaks the language of the people, and, in a reciprocal gesture they recited his verses endlessly. He was an iconoclast. His contemporary happened to be Shah Latif (1689/90-1752), the greatest of the Sindhi poets, who is revered in the entire Sindh. He wrote in 'Lar kind of Sindhi'. He was a Sufi scholar, saint and 'jogi'. His work *Shah Jo Risalo*, patterned on Heer, is his greatest contribution to Sindhi literature. The third of their contemporary was Ali Haider (1690-1751) who belonged to Kachian village (Multan). His was an orthodox interpretation of Sufism. He was a great master of the language and called God 'Ranjha, the lover'.

Warris Shah (1722-1798) lived near Pakpattan, the town which is associated with Baba Farid. His name is associated with his seminal work *Heer Ranjha*, with its locale in Jhang district. Apparently a love story, it is a Sufi treatise with yoga colouring, and undoubtedly a secular work, whose verses permeate folk literature narrated even today. There is nothing comparable to Heer Ranjha in Saraiki literature. Sachal Sarmast (1739-1829) was a contemporary of Warris Shah, whose poetry made almost similar impact in Sindh. He was a free thinker and employed Hindi and Sanskrit words in his poetry extensively. Khwaja Ghulam Farid (1845-1901), born at Chachran (Bahawalpur), was the last in the series of Saraiki literary figures. He was a Chishti Nizam mystic. What unites the entire lot is their Sufi background with deep roots in Hindu traditions of yoga and Vedanta.

Saraiki Templates

These ten literary figures, exclusive of the Sindhi Shah Latif, constitute the entire corpus of Saraiki literature. There is no fiction, drama, essays and criticism beyond. The emphasis again is on folk literature. The Quissa poetry constitutes the entire foundation of Saraiki literature, which apparently does not speak highly of it. The Quissa poetry of Heer Ranjha, Sassi Punhu, Mirza Sahiban, Laila Majnu and Sohni Mahiwal are practically the entire repertoire of Saraiki literature. Sufis remain in the frontline, the Sufi theme in Saraiki literature is a dominant theme, it is an expression of liberal thought of folk traditions. Whether it is Babur, Nadir Shah or Ahmed Shah Abdali, the Saraiki poets were in the frontline in resisting them.The invaders were branded 'Quandharian' (from the direction of Kandahar) and looked upon with contempt. Sufi literature was of the liberal type, mostly of the Chishti and Qadri brand, who kept their channels of communication open with the Hindu community. Sufis were the pioneers of Hindu-Muslim dialogue. They were in regular touch with the pioneers of the Bhakti tradition. They used to have regular dialogue with the 'Jogis' who roamed about freely. Kabir had the greatest influence upon some of them. His pantheist ideas fascinated them. Sufis also joined hands with them. Shah Latif, for instance, spent several years in their company.

Pristine Roots

Sufi literature also made extensive use of Sanskrit/Prakrit vocabulary and, in this process, they were searching for their pristine roots. The Vedantic thought definitely underlay their foundation, even while they drew inspiration from Islam, they were also groping to come to terms with the Hindu philosophy. Here they were helped in the cause by Sikh gurus, who were doing the same thing at the same time. The very fact that the sacred book of the Sikhs incorporated the poetry of Baba Farid is sufficient proof of the seriousness of the dialogue process. For that reason, Guru Nanak is called '*Nanak Shah Faqir Hindu ka Guru and Musalman ka Pir*'. Here

Saraiki, Punjabi and Sindhi literature are to be found in the same ranks. However, it is a matter of regret that the Hindu Bhakti movement in Punjab and Saraiki homeland did not employ native languages as a vehicle of expression of Bhakti thought. Kewalarama (1644) wrote in Brajbhasha and hence, his poetry fell flat. It could not make any local impact, whatsoever.

The intensity of feelings and not restraint is the distinguishing feature of Saraiki literature. This intensity is reflected at best in advocating the divine cloaked as erotic love. Suffering is the distinguishing theme. Separation, patterned on the Radha-Krishna theme and unfulfilled love ending in tragedy, provides the main motivation for the literature. By implication, the contemporary situations are viewed in the larger context and thus made universal. Poetry is usually required to be sung and for that reason, extensive use is made of traditional ragas. It is essentially an anti-establishment literature.The Mulah and the Kazi are usually shut out. Foreign invaders are not welcomed. They are defied. It is essentially a poetry of revolt. It ought to be judged by international standards of criticism. It is a matter of regret that the English-speaking scholarship in India and abroad has overlooked the potential asset.

Baba Farid (1175-1265)

Khwaja Abu Ishaq was the founder of the Chishti Silsilah (order or school of thought), named after his native place. The Chishti Silsilah is considered to be the oldest among Sufi schools of thought. The Chishti order was founded in India by Khwaja Moin-ud-Din Chishti of Ajmer. The famous saint, Khwaja Bakhtiyar Kaki of Delhi was his disciple. One of his important disciples and Khalifa named Sheikh Farid, Gang-i-Shakar was responsible for the establishment of the Chishti Silsilah in Punjab. His original name was Farid Masud. His most famous disciple was Hazrat Nizamuddin Aulia of Delhi. He was born at Kotiwal near Multan. He established his khanqah at Ajodhan, now known as Pakpattan. The early Chishtis 'recreated Sufi experience of divine reality in the indigenous language'. Baba Farid and Amir Khusraw were the role models. They shunned royalty and rejected wealth. They were liberal in their outlook and were indeed leaders of the masses, cutting across the differences between Hindu and Muslim. The major influence of Indian Sufis remain in their contribution to poetic literature in varied languages, including Persian, Urdu, Hindi, Bengali, Saraiki, Punjabi and Sindhi.

Much is owed to Sheikh Farid-ud-Din Masud Ganj-i-Shakar (1175-1265), popularly known as Baba Farid of Pakpattan. He is one of the foremost medieval mystics who founded the Sufi cult in north India. He was also the founder of the Chishti Silsilah in the Punjab. Moin-ud-Din Chishti was so much impressed with him that he told his murshid Bakhtiyar Kaki, Baba Bakhtiyar, 'You have caught a noble falcon which will not build his nest except on the holy tree of heaven. Farid is a lamp that will illuminate the silsilah of the derveshes'.[1] Baba Farid achieved his high status by performing arduous practices like Chillah-i-makus, by reciting the namaz, tying his feet to a peg, after remaining suspended by hanging himself upside down in the well. This practice is almost like practicing yoga. In one of his shlokas he says:

> *'Farid, my dry body hath become a skeleton; Ravens peck at the hollows of my hands and feet, up till now God hath not come to my aid, Behold His servant's misfortune.'*

It is believed that he performed penance for six months.He thus sings in praise of God whom he addresses as his beloved:

> *'O ravens, you have searched my skeleton and eaten all my flesh*
> *But touch not these eyes, as I hope to behold my beloved.'*

Love Theme

In the true Indian tradition, he employs the female voice in his verses. He talks of love as the most significant relationship between human beings and god. After all, mysticism is a message of love. He viewed god in his dynamic context. His god is a God of Love. Baba Farid offered love in times of much strife and suffering. His message of love was universal, 'His greatness was the greatness of a loving heart; his miracles were the miracles of a deeply sympathetic soul. He could read a man's inner heart by a glance at his face and spoke the words that brought consolation to a tortured heart'.[2] How does one resolve the dilemma of chasing between worldly goods and love for God is the question posed in the following shloka:

> *'Farid, what am I to do my love, for the streets are muddy, and the house of [my beloved (God)] is far away. If I set out my cloak will be soaked, but if stay my love would be severed'.*

If love is one side of the coin, the other is *viraha* (separation), a favourite theme of Indian poetry. Baba Farid is no exception to the rule. He sings of love and separation at the same time. Here is the dialogue that he has with the pitch-dark Koel:

> *'Koel why are your wings so black?'*

The Koel replies:

> *'It is the fire of separation which has burnt my wings.'*

Mass Language

Baba Farid talks of love, separation and God with a purpose. It is not to be viewed in isolation. That would be doing injustice to him. He had a wider purpose in mind. It was not merely for personal salvation. He talked of love as the universal theme, in which Hindus and Muslims, especially the downtrodden were addressed. He wanted to carry his message to the mass in a language that they could comprehend easily. He envisaged establishing a new social order: 'True to these ideals, Baba Farid strove day and night to create that atmosphere of love and good-will which was, and is even today, the greatest desideratum of human society. A healthy social order, free from dissensions, conflicts, discriminations, hatred and jealously—were things he longed for. In love, faith, tolerance and sympathy, which even included the enemy, he found the supreme talisman of human happiness. 'Do not give me scissors', he told a visitor who had presented a pair of scissors: 'Give me a needle. I sow. I do not cut'.[3] Here is another Mohandas Karamchand Gandhi of the thirteenth century. He was almost a contemporary of Ramanuja (1017-1137), Madhava (1139-1217) and

Nambarka (12-14th centuries), all stalwarts of Bhakti movement who sang of love and God, like Baba Farid. They may not have known each other, but they talked the same language.

Vedantic Connection

Baba Farid sings of duality of separation and love and of living and death in his poetry. There is,however, a difference which should not be overlooked. He portrays life and death in the same spiritual context. It is also to be noted that Baba Farid reaches Vedantic heights without being aware of it. Death is the constant refrain as it is evident in the two shlokas. Baba Farid died at the ripe age of ninety, but death was his constant companion.

> *'Farid see what has occurred. The beard has gone grey.*
> *The end is nearer, the past is left far behind'.*
>
> *'Farid you have grown old your body has begun to totter,*
> *Even if you live for hundred years,*
> *Yet you have to perish and return to death'*

Baba Farid was a multi-splendoured personality; as well as a pioneer in several fields. He is the father-figure of Saraiki and Punjabi people. He was responsible for the establishment of Chishti mystic order in Punjab. He wrote compositions in chaste Saraiki, as the foremost literature of Saraiki and Punjabi. Guru Arjan Dev was so much impressed by his writings that his writing, both shlokas and dohas, find place in the Adi Granth. He is the only Muslim mystic, who was so honoured. His poetic works are written in simple language. He was a people's poet. His words are extensively quoted and his maxims are frequently traded among the common people, who find their lives reflected in his writings.

His mysticism is satisfying for the common people, because they seem to find spiritual solutions to their day-to-day problems, which Carlyle calls 'the divine significance of life'. He stayed at Ajodhan (modern Pakpattan), which was strategically placed as the principal ferry across the Sutlej, and the meeting place of the ancient western road from Dera Ghazi Khan and

Dera Ismail Khan across the Indus. Today, the major Chishti khanqahs are located mainly in the Multani-speaking areas of Saraiki language. His message gets across through his poetry to the Saraiki people with facility. He is indeed above all the people's poet of the Saraikis.

Unusual Qualities

If one were to sum up Baba Farid's poetic contributions in a few words, those shall be 1. simplicity, 2. people's poetry, 3. female orientation, 4. social relevance, 5. universality, and 6. linguistic jugglery. The Farid-Bani corpus is very parsimonious. It comprises a 130 verses of which many are to be found in the *Adi Granth*. There are 83 couplets derived from various sources which are attributed to Baba Farid. Their authenticity is, however, doubted. The entire corpus is not a large one, compared to the large impact made by his poetry. Those are indeed signature poetry of all times. Their simplicity is astounding but is equally complex. Saraiki poetry is no different from folk verse. Herein lies its complexity in its simplicity, because the poet in Baba Farid resorts 'to skillful device through which (he) makes himself his own subject. In this way, the monograph-like words turn into a powerful dialogue, because the other person who Farid addresses is often no other than the common given human condition'.[4]

Najim Husain puts the same idea differently. For him the 'austerity of rythm (which) is supported by a strikingly plain vocabulary', or what he calls 'the deliberate ordinariness of his words'.[5] 'The austerity of rhythm' is combined with 'inner confidence' which brings out 'changing shades of feelings' representing 'the inner emotional strength'. There is a clear indication of the deliberateness joined with apparent simplicity.

People's Language

Simplicity is the signature sign of Sufi poets like Baba Farid of the Saraiki background. Baba Farid has been truly dedicated as the people's poet. His ecstasy lifts one to the exalted state of mind. It is truly a secular experience of the spiritual kind. The sweetness of language and the simplicity of expression are to be marveled. Its simplicity in complexity reaches 'the greatest heights of ecstasy, humility, meditation and asceticism'[6] by experiencing it in life and living it. Female voices also make their appearance in Baba Farid's poetry. Thus his shlokas have a bearing on gender relations. He uses the female voices in his verses. God is addressed in female in his poetry, but there are no erotic poetry in his compositions. His ideal woman is a *sohagan* (married woman), who cherishes the bliss of union with her husband. In any case, women are not much visible in the world of Farid, who was himself a much-married person.

Baba Farid's poetry at its best has been called 'the shared social experience of the community'. His poetry is entirely based on dialogue between the narrator and the audience. The social experience, as expressed in poetry, is based on consensus. It is thus a powerful vehicle for communication with the people and an ideal instrument of social reform. The *Adi Granth* pays the greatest tribute to Baba Farid by honouring him by making him a Sant kavi. The Bhakti movement was preceded by Baba Farid. It emerged in the scene by the 14th century, Baba Farid precedes it by a century and he was thus posthumously honoured by anticipating the Bhakti-Sant tradition in the Punjab. This only establishes the fact of community shared by Bhakti and Sufi movements alike. Baba Farid was a great social reformer. Languages play a major role 'in this reproduction of human experience'. Baba Farid played a major role in turning the Sufi experience around in Punjab. He transformed a moribund language like Saraiki by turning it around beyond recognition. He did the same to the Punjabi language.

Dohra Poetry

Doha in Hindi is called *Dahra* in Punjabi. It was the most convenient instrument, being the couplet and in the shortest 2-line verse form; it is the most economical, and for its parsimonious character it undoubtedly makes the most powerful impact. It is simple and complex at the same time. It is easy to grasp by the audience, and disciplines the poet by challenging him to say the most in the shortest space possible. Baba Farid made a very skillful use of the doha. The sant kavis from Kabir onwards used doha as a powerful medium of expression in their poetry. The dohas were recited by common people in their homes and public places. It has also become a powerful medium in the Punjabi literary tradition popularized by the

Sikh gurus. Najim Husain should have the last word on the subject, 'The inner confidence is always present in the Dohas whether the poet strains to resolve a conflict or record an intensely powerful experience. Farid's verses, as is often taken for granted, are not finished pieces turned out of the didactic aloofness of a seasoned teacher. They often are, within their diminutive compass, scenes of involvement, decision and representation'[7] It is not difficult to predict that Baba Farid's status shall grow with the passage of time. He is nowhere to be found in the category of world-class poets. He needs to be discovered. Indeed, he is a master of Indian ethos rooted in the ancient tradition, besides his undoubted mastery of Islamic heritage. He was able to achieve so much as a literary giant, when literature was not his major preoccupation.

Farid Sani (1450-1594)

Farid Sani was a spiritual descendent of Ganj-i-Shakar. Not much is known about his poetic competence except the *Farid Baani* which is attributed to him. He is also confused with Baba Farid and his poetic works, both shlokas and dohas, are attributed to him amidst endless controversies. He was a great admirer of Kabir. Some of his writings match word-by-word with Kabir's poetic words and ideas. Equally, there is so much confusion about what is attributed to Kabir. Both he and Shah Husain had accepted the influence of the Bhakti cult in the 16th century and integrated the same in their respective writings. Farid Sani was a contemporary of Hindi poets Raskhan and Rahim, known to be confirmed Pathan Vaishnavas. He employed the people's language and tried to build bridges between the Hindus and the Muslims through his poetic works, full of Vedantic pantheism. Like in Hindu tradition, he advocated God to be the redeemer of the soul, and also advocated the practice of wifely devotion, latitudinarianism and the practice of humility, besides his firm belief in the doctrine of grace.

There is so much common with the Sant poetry in the *Farid Baani*, that it obtains instant approval from Christopher Shackle, whose remarks apply equally to Baba Farid and Farid Sani: 'It is, after all, for the distinctive literary expression of regional variety that the vernacular literature is chiefly interesting, since even their most substantial classics tend to have achieved their status through successful reformulation in regional terms of ideas and values central to the high Indo-Muslim tradition, rather than through the introduction of significant thoughts. Thus, to note their achievement as decorative rather than innovative is, however, in no way to belittle their intrinsic literary interest, which provides so attractive a contrast to the extraordinary relative homogeneity to the metropolitan Perso-Urdu tradition'.[8] It may not be a high-calibre literature, but it is innovative to the extent it talks in a different language and addresses an entirely new audience. They talk of religion of the secular kind. There is also a serious attempt to build bridges by introducing the indigenous philosophical thought without inhibition. The so-called 'metropolitan Persiano-Urdu tradition' is given a deep burial. In the process, much respectability is given to the local dialects. The new forms of Prakrits like Punjabi, Sindhi, and Saraiki are given a new lease of life.

Kabir the Inspirer

Kabir inspired Farid Sani and was his murshid (guru) without formal recognition. He was actually a descendant of Baba Farid. The Chishti heritage rightly belonged to him. He was also conscious of his Indian heritage. He looked at Kabir as his role model. Pantheism in Indian thought inspired him which he practiced in his real life. Kabir was a bridge between Muslim Sufis and the Hindu Bhakti. Farid Sani decided to follow him by bringing the Sufis and the Bhakti movement on the same platform. Farid Saini was the pioneer to introduce Bhakti cult to the Sufi movement in India. He was so impressed by Kabir that he also emulated his poetic style. It would be no exaggeration to assert that Farid was a true Vedantist. To be more precise, his poetry betrays the influence of Vaishnav Vedantism. His latitudinarianism had much practical uses. The idea was to bring the Hindus on the Sufi platform, incorporate their philosophical essential thoughts into the Sufi mainstream ideas, by speaking to them in their own language. Baba Farid was pioneer in this direction. His example was followed by Farid Sani, who can rightly claim to be the first Multani poet. His vocabulary is comprehensible to the contemporary audience.

Poetic Verse

Farid Sani's poetry is totally inspired by Kabir, not only in philosophical thought but also in 'stealing' ideas and words line-by-line. His poetry is thus a backhanded tribute to Kabir. Indeed he has introduced Kabir to the Saraiki audience without their knowing about it. Very cleverly he has introduced the same audience to Vedantic pantheism through the backdoor. He has inspired the entire generation of poets with Sufi orientation to Hindu beliefs and thought. The Saraiki tradition has been localized and to a large extent made secular. Farid Sani was not great a poet like his predecessor Baba Farid and those who followed him like Shah Husain and Bulleh Shah, but he has left his mark on the Sufi cult by turning it native. Farid Sani took the idea from him and described God as husband and himself as one of his countless wives. 'God, the Husband has many wives and all are possessed of many good qualities. How can I have his vision?' Similarly, the theme of love and separation is taken up in a big way, thereby placing a seal of approval on the Bhakti concept of directly commuting with him, having a dialogue with him and making God the centre of the earth in his personal life. 'Anxiety is my bedstead, strung with sorrow, and, the bedding and the quilt are of yeaning for my Lord (*viraha*)'. Viraha or separation becomes the theme song of life and an erotic element is introduced by the poet at this stage:

'I have not slept with my Spouse (God) tonight, and my limbs ache; Go and ask the deserted ones how they pass their nights awake'. Extremity in love seems to be the meeting ground between Bhakti and Sufi cults: 'I would burn my body like a furnace, and feed the fire by my bones; Yes, I shall walk on my head if the legs tire, only if I were to meet my Beloved. Here there is a striking difference between Baba Farid and Farid Sani. While Baba Farid sings of the hovering death as his major theme, love and separation are the major preoccupation of Farid Sani, influenced by Kabir, his mentor.

Numerous verses of Farid Sani confirm striking familiarity with Kabir not only in ideas but also in words. The truth of the matter may be established in the following famous doha of Kabir:

> *'Mati kahe kumhar se tun kion rondhe mohi;*
> *Ik din aisa aega main rondhun gi tohi'. (The clay addresses the potter, "Why does thou tread me over? One day, when thou will be dead, I will tread over thee in the same way'.*

The same verse has been copied by Farid Sani in the following manner:

> *'Farid khak na ninde khaku Jad na koi,*
> *Jinandia paira talai moia upari hoi'*

('Do not speak ill of dust, O Farid, for there is nothing to equal the dust. In life it is beneath thy feet and after death, it is upon thee'.)

Kabir did not care about external symbols. Farid Sani is equal to him in copying him:

> *'O Farid, if, thou wanted to go on Haj to Mecca,*
> *the Holy Mecca is in thy heart'.*

Here are ample examples of copying with compliment.

Baba Farid vs Farid Sani

There is a hot controversy that continues to rage with regard to the verses of Baba Farid. His authorship is doubted regarding shlokas and dohras attributed to him. There are several distinguished scholars believing Farid Sani to be the original author. The confusion gets multiplied, because there is no extant biographical work in existence. There is nothing more than legends to go by for our record. Eminent scholars doubting the authorship of Baba Farid constitute a powerful lobby. Those ranked against his authorship include M A Macauliffe, Dr Lajwanti Ramakrishna, Dr Gopal Singh and Professor K A Nizami. The arguments put forward by Macauliffe are not tenable. He substituted Farid Thani in place of 'Farid Sani' or Farid the second in his multi-volumed history of the Sikh religion, forgetting the fact conveniently that Farid has been described as the first Punjabi/Saraiki poet in the Adi Granth. Dr Lajwanti confines her argument by quoting a single couplet. Professor Khaliq Ahmad Nizami is on much more solid ground as a meticulous biographer of Baba Farid, when he argues, 'the picture of Sheikh Farid that emerges from these *shlokas* is more akin to the Sheikh Farid of the fabricated malfast'.[9] There are others who present a counter argument by quoting a reliable source like *Siyarul Auliya*, which says that 'Faridud-din Ganj-i-Shakar' wrote verses in Multani.[10]

It has been rightly pointed out that poetry is a true barometer of the poet's being. It reflects his personality. Every word is weighed by any respectable poet. His poetic work contains his life experiences and his total sagacity and wisdom. The words employed by him are true reflection of his hesitations, struggles and mature judgment which he expresses, to be communicable to the entire community. Baba Farid has all the '*riyasat* (penitances/to his credit striving'), which truly got reflected in his writings. No signatures are available, but it makes sense to read between the lines; 'These verses, as we will see below, are characterized by a unity of experience and language. Such unity is realized through years of sustained reflection that bends one's experiences of the external world as well as of inner being with one's thought and words. In other words, the words of such poetry cannot be separated from the person behind them who happens to be the locus of the experiences'.[11]

Shah Husain (1538-1600)

Shah Husain is ranked the highest among the earlier poets along with Baba Farid, Bulleh Shah and Warris Shah. His grandfather was a Dhodha by caste and weaver by profession, who converted to Islam. He was responsible for introducing new imagery to poetry. He was born in Lahore and the grateful residents of the city remember him to this day by celebrating the Basant-Panchami day in his honour. He was a precocious child who memorized the Quran at an early age. He was a restless soul who was led to Sufi mysticism through his interest in spirituality. He was given to bouts of exhuberance from his early days in public. He would wear trinkets at his ankles and dance in ecstacy to the tune of music:

> *I being a alang (ascetic).*
> *Am proud of Malang only?*[12]

He remained a Malang all of his life. A sect called Malmati is named after him. He was usually found in the company of a Hindu saint called Madho Lal. He came to be popularly known as Madholal Husain. He spent most of his time in the company of dancing girls and prostitutes. He drank and danced. He was usually found to be high after taking bhang. He was a nonconformist. He was essentially a spiritual being who sought to concentrate his full attention on God by violating conventional norms. He called himself 'the fakir of God'. Love and separation were the main themes of his poetry. He authored 160 *kafis*, besides shlokas and other compositions set to music, the practice introduced by Sikh gurus. Ranjha and Heer were his vehicles for the love of God: 'Ranjha has become a Jogi And I am his Jogin'. If one word was to sums up Shah Husain's life, It shall be 'masty' (ecstacy). He spent days and nights in masti and his indulgence was his response to the material world as his protecting veneer.

He used the terminology of weaver for the expression of his mysticism. Following the example of Farid Sani, Kabir, who was also a weaver by profession, was his role model. Husain says:

> *'Naan Husaina te Jat/Jullaha.*
> *Gaalian dendian taanian wallian.*
> *(My name is Husaina and my profession is weaving. All the weaver girls call me names).*

He viewed God through the imagery of weaving of tana (warp) and bana (woof). His obsession with pantheism is inspired by Kabir and after Farid Sani he emulates Kabir in many of his verses. Indeed, each and every verse of his is imbued with pantheism. He says:

> *'Ape ek anek kahavai, sahib hai bahu rangi'*
> *(The one: has appeared in many forms and colours. He is of innumerable colours)*
> *'Asan andar bahar lal hai'.*
> *(We have God inside us as well outside'.*

His pantheism shines through his entire poetic output. Like Farid Sani, Shah Husain not only steals Kabir's philosophy of life, but he is also obliged to him in literal terms:

> Shah Husain: *Tainu Sahu nal ghunghat keha*
> (Thou shouldst remove the veil from thy face and see the Beloved, thy Husband)
> Kabir: *Ghunghat ke pat khol tohe pia milenge*
> (Remove the veil, thou will see the lover)
> Shah Husain: *Mat pita bhai sat banita, nali no boi janda.*
> (Mother, father, brother, sons or wife, nobody would accompany thee to God).
> Kabir: *Mata pita lok sut banita, aut ne chale sanga*
> (Mother, father, sons, wife or the others, none accompanies the man to God).

Shah Husain was a man of apparent contradictions. He led a permissive life but he was a master of disciplined poetry, which was socially relevant and philosophically correct. He raised the banner of revolt against religious bigotry. The times were also right.

Above Bigotry

Shah Husain lived in the liberal times. Emperor Akbar was the ruler in Agra. His court was full of advisors with liberal outlook towards life. Sikh gurus had opened a dialogue with the other communities. Bhakti movement was at its highest. Even Punjab had been impacted by the Vaishnava Bhakti movement. Nath Jogis roamed the streets of towns and villages of the Punjab. Sufi saints joined the Jogis in experiencing their rituals and practices. Mullahs and Kazis were on the defensive. Their absolute supremacy was being questioned. Shah Husain was in the centre of this debate: 'Declaring the superiority of the path of life to that of the Shari'a, he says, that seeker who adopts the path of love need not perform the religious obligation. The fire of love once let in the heart exalts the seeker automatically to God. Love unites the lover, with the

Beloved. 'In the communication between the lover and the God' says Shah Husain, 'no mediator, he meant Muhammed, the Prophet, is required to mediate'. The lover of God abandons not only the obligaticns of God as enforced by the Shari'a, but he forgets even the stages of the mystic path... Snubbing away the Mullahs he refuses to listen any more to them aft-repeated arguments, which he declares unconvincing. It is thus his firm belief only to enjoy the vision of God, who adopt the faith of love'.[13] Shah Husain, Bulleh Shah and Warris Shah held the fortress firmly. No mullahs and kazis dared to cross their paths. They had to bide for time. Poetry had become the convenient vehicle for attempts at the synthesis of Hindu philosophy, Muslim beliefs and Sikh practices.

Hindu mythology was the fashion of the day. Shah Husain venerated Rama and Krishna through his verses. He says:

> *'Ao kude ram nam dhiao'*
> (Come on maidens, let us join together
> and talk of our beloved Rama)'.

While Rama is believed to be of fair colour and Krishna is dark-complexioned, but both faces and colours in contrast are celebrated:

> *'Sanwal Madha ya'.*
> (The dark complexioned is my bosom friend)

The images of Vrindavan and Krishna with his gopis are flashed in his *kafis*. Even the words have the Brajbhasha coloring:

> *'Main Bairagee' and*
> *'Main Brindaban ki bairagan'*
> (I am a devotee and I have come from Vrindavan.)

Shah Husain's God is not merely addressed as Allah but has also Hindu names like Rama, Krishna, Hari and Sanwal [Sanwala (dark)].

Vedantic Pantheism

He was aiming higher by claiming to be a perfect Vedantist and an open advocate of pantheism. He goes the whole hog by advocating the cause of pantheism with no full stops or reservations. His God appears in many shapes and forms, and it is to be found inside the man and outside. His God does not stand apart from his own creation and he is very much part of it. He says:

> *Ap ek anek kahavai, Sahib has bahu rangi*
> (The God has appeared in many forms and colours. He is of innumerable colours).
> *Aran andar bahar lai hai*
> (We have God inside and as well as outside).
> The weaver in him emerged and he used work vocabulary to express his metaphysical thought:
> *Tane pete ikbo sutar, dutia bhiuo na jana*
> (Whether warp or woof, it is the same cotton thread').

Love and separation are two sides of the coin. The intensity of love has no proper measuring rod. Here he employs the simile of Heer and Ranjha to reinforce his argument. To Shah Husain, Heer is the symbol of intense love. She is the mystic in search of her lover, the God. He calls himself 'Heer'. There is a depiction of wifely love borrowed from Sikh scriptures. Ranjha is the eternal beloved and Heer the eternal lover. Separation is the hallmark of this love.

> *friends, Please do not call me 'Heer'*
> *Address me as 'Ranjha',*
> *I have merged myself in Him.*
> *I have become one with my Lord.*

He reaches the most sublime poetic statement in the following verse, when Heer (or he) claims to be the beloved instead of being a lover, expressing the unrequited love as its most sublime. Shah Husain says:

Mahi mahi kukadi main ape Ranjhan hai
Ranjhan, Ranjhan mainu sab ko akho.
Heer no akho koi.
Main ape hoi ape

Mystic Poetry

Those were the best of times. It was lucky to be alive during the seventeenth century. It was the age of liberalism in India. Mysticism reigned supreme. The Sufi and Bhakt saints were in regular dialogue with each other. Literature became the most sublime instrument of mystic expression. Punjabi/Saraiki mysticism found its finest spokesman in Shah Husain. He was more at home than the venerable Baba, because he was less subtle and more communicable than him. He was the master of expression taken from day-to-day life. His poetry is full of life. It sings and is definitely lyrical. While Baba Farid stands apart as an objective observer, Shah Husain touches the tenderest chord of the heart. He speaks to you person-to-person. Like his characters Heer and Ranjha, he sheds tears, supplicates and argues gently with you. The fire of separation equally burns the observers of the scene. Shah Husain must have been a master of psychology of emotions.

While the poet in him is in full command of the situation, it effects the observer, nay hurts him deeply to the core. He is a master of his words, similies, metaphors and terminologies. Evidently the poet in him has been deeply effected by his acquaintance with the Bhagvata cult. The Krishna of Vrindavan with his horde of gopis expressing sentiment of *viraha* (separation) and *prem* (love) in playful acting with Krishna which had a deep influence on Shah Husain. He must have been in constant dialogue with Vaishnav Vedantic Bhakti saints and poets who had invaded the entire Indus basin. Kabir was another powerful influence in the entire region. The very fact he towers above the rest of the tribe of poets who followed him speak for his universal character. His poetry is timeless because it confronts us with the basic questions of life that trouble us the most.

15

Bulleh-Warris to Sarmast

SAIN Bulleh is a poet of mystic school of thought. There are critics who have rated him with Jalal-ud-Din Rumi and Shams Tabriz. He lived through disturbed times. His poetry is of the people and they have remembered his verse by memorizing it. He is essentially a poet of the oral tradition. For more than a century, his verse was not on record. Yet he lived through the memories of the ordinary people. His verse continues to reverberate in the fields, in the zenanas and redlight districts and in the streets of villages and towns of the Punjab. The Sufis also took to heart his kalam. His real name is Abd Allah or Abdullah. He is affectionately called Sain Bulleh Shah, Bullah Shah, Bulleh Shah and Bullah. By whatever name he is called, he is the most beloved poet of all, owned by one and all. He has also been called 'the love-intoxicated iconoclast', 'The Sheikh of both the worlds', 'The Man of God', and 'the Knower of Spiritual Grace'. His signature was Bullah or Bulleh. In one of his Kafis, he says:

'Bulleh Shah da watan Kasur
Jithe lami lami khajoor'.
(Bulleh Shah resides at Kasur (near Lahore),
which is known for its fine long-texured dates).

He was actually born at Uch Gilanian village in the state of Bahawalpur. He was thus a Saraiki by birth, a fact which is reflected in his verses. His family moved to Malikwal in Sahiwal district when he was still young. Finally his family shifted to a village fifteen miles from Kasur. His murshid (guru) was Inayat Shah, the true successor of the famous Mian Mir of Lahore. Bulleh called him 'the beloved thug of Lahore'. He has addressed Shah Inayat in his poetry as khasim (husband), shohar, sain, dilbar, sajan and yaar. His murshid was a low-caste Arrayan (horticulturist by caste), even then he was the focus of attention of Bulleh Shah, whom he equated with God. He was also known as Shah Inayat Qadri Shattari

Poetry as Magic

Bulleh Shah has been called a magician. His poetry has been termed 'ecstatic verse'. He weaves magic by his simple and uncomplicated poetry. He was said to compose poetry in a trance and recited in ecstasy. He was greatly inspired by the scum of the earth. He composed poetry, recited it in public and danced to its rhythm. *Kafi* was the main form of his poetic verse. The first printed edition of his work appeared in 1880. Before that it was communicated orally from one generation to another. Indeed his poetry gives the distinct impression of common speech or conversation. The apparent simplicity and apparent naiveté of his style foxes you. That is why the Urduwallahs termed this genre of popular writing as 'an undistinguishable variety of popular balladry'. Nothing is far from the truth. This tradition is very special to the Saraiki homeland. Baba Farid was its mentor. There is considerable element of complexity in this apparent simplicity. Bulleh Shah was a multi-splendoured personality. His poetry also contained a message. He was also a social reformer. He lived in the prolonged period of political instability and disintegration. This was also the time when the Sufi and Bhakti movements found a meeting ground in the land of the Five Rivers. This was also the age of poetry, music and dance–the times of the highest refinement of Indian cultural values in all walks of life.

The genius of Bulleh Shah is primarily owed to his Saraiki heritage and blending of traditions of three mainstreams — the Saraiki folk tradition, and the Sufi and Bhakti movements. His facility in employing 'the native images and forms of local poetry', with its Saraiki roots traced as far back as the Indus Valley Civilization, with what Christopher Shackle describes as the 'resources of the classical tradition' that had no parallel. The official tradition is traced to the Persian Sufi poetry with predominantly Islamic elements. It is primarily spiritual in its content. The third element is again drawn from the classical literary tradition of north India. It is the Hindu element substantially drawn from the Sant Kavis of the Bhakti movement. This amalgam has structured the genius of Bulleh Shah. Credit is also due to the person of Bulleh Shah himself: 'Bulleh Shah, a man of great erudition ... composed in sophistical material form, created complex rhyme schemes as no other practioner of Punjabi verse has done before and since his times. Yet he succeeds in getting across a rough oral effect, as if the poems he composed were a spontaneous everyday expression'.[1] Thus the fourth element in the situation was the personality of Bulleh Shah himself:

'I Know Not What I am'

His range of writings was wide. Underlying his facile poetic verse was the deeper philosophical thought. He was the master of combining simplicity with depth. He wrote about Sufism, Bhakti movement, religion, Vedanta, his murshid, Krishna, Heer and Ranjha in the background of his running dialogue with God. Here is an instant of a kafi, simple in expression and set to music, yet with multiple meanings underlying it with a definitive world view:

'Balla! Ki Janan main kaun'
'I know not who am I!'

Neither a Momin (believer) and not a mosque-goer,
Nor a practicing Kafir.
Neither cleansed nor dirtified,
Neither am I Moses nor Pharaoh

Ballah neither I know who am I!

Neither a saint nor a sinner,
Neither celebrating nor mourning.
Neither of earth nor of heavens,
Neither of fire nor of wind.
Bullah I know not who am I?

Neither have I reached the inner depths of faith,
Neither am I born of Adam and Eve,
Neither have I identity,
Neither am I among the rank of those who pray,
Nor those among the apostate.

Ballah I know not who am I
I was the beginning, I shall be the end.
Nor do I recognize the others than the one
Who would be wiser than I?
Who put my murshid eying me.
Ballah I know not who am I?

Inayat Shah

The Qadris of the Land of Five Rivers were renowned for their interest in the Hindu philosophy and thought. Prince Dara Shikoh was a Qadri mystic. So was Shah Inayat Qadri Shattari, the murshid and guru of Bulleh Shah, who in turn was his khalifa. Bulleh simply venerated his guru and placed him on the highest pedestal.

'Guru calls Himself Allah, and Himself becomes, the prophet and Ali ... He lives in the heart of everyone.' Inayat Shah, who was a true successor of the famous saintly Mian Mir of Lahore, was a low-caste Arrayan belonging to the gardener community. Bulleh's adoption of the guru raised a storm of protest in his high-caste Sayid family, and this agony got expressed in one of his famous kafis:

'Balhe mon samjhavan aiyan, bhainan te bharjayan.

'Man le Balliya sada kahna, chad de pala Raiyan.
Al Bani Ali noon toon kyon lika laiyan'.
(To coax Balhe descended his sisters and sisters-in-law.
'Listen to us
And give up mixing with the low-caste Arrayan,
You are a scion of Ali, and the Prophet,
Why do you shame your fair name?')

Bulleh Shah was defiant as ususual. He simply adored his murshid. He attributed to his Guru whatever happened, he deemed it was orderd by him. He pined for him. For him there was,

'Neither God in Kashi
Nor in Mecca.'

His murshid was all in all for him:

'Tere Ishq nachaya kar thayya thayya.'
(It is your love which set me to rhythmic dancing)

Very little is on record about Inayat Shah and his khalifa, Bulleh Shah. There is very little known about his training or his close relation with his guru, beyond what is hinted in the corpus of his poetic works. Inayat definitely had a profound effect on Bulleh Shah in respect of his spirituality. He is also on record to have adopted Rumi as his role model, who also simply adored his percepter Shams. Bulleh Shah considered his murshid as an embodiment of God. He was being modest in deifying his murshid, because he outgrew him substantially. He had a large vision of being a social critic and reformer.

Religious Apostate

There was no doubt that Bulleh Shah was an apostate. He totally rejected the conventional religion. He had no hesitation in proclaiming it from the house top. He proclaimed repeatedly that he was neither a Hindu nor a Muslim, neither a Sunni nor a Shia, and neither a Arab or a Turk. He was tired and sick of reading the Vedas and the Koran. He did not discover his God hiding behind the Holy Word. Neither did he discover his God in the Hindu holy places, nor was he found in Mecca. God is neither in holy places nor in religious centres. He also rejects the very ritual of visiting temples, mosques and gurdwaras as an exercise in futility, and indeed he had no hesitation by scoffing at the practice:

'Lumpens live in the Hindu temples,
And sharks in the Sikh shrines.
Musclemen live in the Muslim mosques.'

He said, you shall 'Pour not on prayers, forget the fasts', mullahs and kazis his targets, he is not afraid of being called an apostate. 'Wipe off the kalma from the sight'. He was also conscious of his predicament, because 'they [mullahs and kazis] have tied my hands tight'.

'They will call you a kaffir,
You should say – yes, yes.'

He says, 'to hell with prayers', but there is still graces left about him, because 'Bulleh loves the Muslims, And salutes the Hindu God'. Here is a gesture offering temporary truce:

'Bulleh tends the path of love.
It is an endless road'
'My Mecca is in my Ranjha'.
Love conquers all and for him:
Crying Ranjha day and night
I've become Ranjha himself.

Bulleh discovers his God in Ranjha, an ideal of conventional love. Ranjha is also viewed as a Jogi and his spouse is seen in symbolic gesture of Saraiki poetic tradition.

Mysticism Redefined

There is a famous verse attributed to Bulleh Shah of the younger days. It says:

'Shariat sadi dai hai, Tareqat sadi mai hai'
(Shari'a is our nursemaid, and the path of Sufism is our mother.)

He was an iconoclast and social confrontationist, whose conception of love involved categories of conflict and defiance. It was a matter of time before he moved away from tradition. He was already talking of 'Mecca is there where lives my love' and spoke the language of Kabir when he sang,

'He has the Koran in his hand,
And in the same the holy thread'

He was already talking of famous apostates like Shamas Tabrez and Mansoor for raising the slogan, 'I am God' and thereby being executed as retribution. Earlier Sufis found it difficult to view Sufism minus the essential component of the Shari'a. There were simmering of revolt which began to show in early Islam. Qalandars were the first to reject the role of the Shari'a in spirituality. In other words, while Shari'a was considered subjective, spirituality was viewed objectively, much beyond the narrow confines of religion. Bulleh Shah began to play with words and ideas indicating his dissent:

> *'Bulleh Shah, the beloved is found within you, and humanity is ignorant of the truth.'*

Indeed, his other verse is very much pointed and direct:

> *'Mecca is there where lives my love.'*

Kabir was the most decisive in painting the inherent gulf between the religious establishments and spirituality. For him, his God was within him. The great Sufi poets like Shah Husain, Bulleh Shah and Warris Shah were very much under the influence of Kabir. Though Baba Farid preceded Kabir, but he must have anticipated his philosophy and thinking. Bulleh Shah was totally devoted to him because he filled in the gaps in his thinking. His God no longer required the services of the Messanger of God. His God was directly approachable. He found it convenient. His God was like his next-door neighbour. Numerous verses are devoted to God. While Bulleh Shah was his 'mehbooba' (beloved). God was depicted by him as his mehboob (lover). Other nomenclatures coined by him for God include the following: sajan, sayan, mahi, sain, show or shahar, Ranjha or Ranjhan. The intimate and friendly titles include 'well-wisher', 'master', 'husband' and Ranjha. His place of worship is no longer Mecca, but lies in Takhat Hazara, the home village of Ranjha, which is actually within you. Bulleh Shah, the Sufi ,was only a short step away from adopting the Vedanta.

Vedanta Influences

It did not take too long for the Sufis to realize that the Shari'a did not answer their requirements. This was especially true of the Qadris and Chishtis. While Baba Farid was a Chishti, Bulleh Shah belonged to the Qadri cult. They had come to realize that it was essential to assimilate the indigenous culture into their spiritual framework, paving the way for 'the development of supra or cross-religious spirituality'. In order to widen the network, compromise was necessary. It was found essential to marry Islamic terminology with Vaishnav imagery. The Sufis found it convenient to identify with the Vedanta. The ideas like the identification of the murshid with God, monotheism, yoga practices, the concept of wifely devotion and transmigration of soul were adopted to expand the audience for the purpose of discourse. Thus, Sufism bent to score points.

Bulleh Shah was to be found in the frontline. Prof Lajwanti Ramakrishna thought Bulleh Shah to be a firm believer in the 'Advaita'. He accepted the Vaishnava idea of the Grace of God. He adopted the doctrine of Lila or sport also:

> *'Oh Jama sada pahen ke*
> *Aye tamashe ap'*
> *(God himself has appeared in the guise of the individuals to sport).*

Here Bulleh Shah played a secondary fiddle to Kabir, who must have inspired him to the renunciation of the Holy Books, whether the Koran or the Vedas, pilgrimage to holy places like Mecca and Benaras, the places of worship like mosques, temples and gurdwaras. In brief, formal religion was under relentless attack from Kabir and Bulleh Shah. Bulleh Shah was the Viceroy of the Punjab region. Baba Farid, Shah Husain and Bulleh Shah were closer to the Sant tradition of the Bhakti movement. Unabashedly he sought union with the divine on the lines of the Nirguna bhaktas. Bulleh Shah, however, was ahead of the times. His mysticism was the assertion of the spiritual against the formality of religion:

> *'Wipe off the Kalma from the sight*
> *Bulleh has found his lover within'*

Bulleh indicated that it was possible to establish a direct link with God. He was now in danger of being branded an heretic and apostate:

> *'I fail to distinguish between the faithful and infidels ever since I entered into unity. I have burnt my veil, clothes and hut in the fire of polytheism.'*

God Personified

Now that God has manifested Himself through man, Bulleh asserts his right to immortality:

'Bullah Shah we will never die,
It is someone else who has gone to the grave'

He also makes a definite statement on the same theme.

'I was in the beginning,
I was in the end
Who can be wiser than me'

The events begin to fall into their places. God adopts his *lila* in no time by appearing in the form of an ordinary mortal.

'God comes in the form of man
And comes to awaken the world.'

Whether He appears in the form of Krishna or Ranjha is immaterial to the end game. Krishna is a cowherd and so is Ranjha. Krishna plays the flute melodiously and so does Ranjha. Krishna has his Radha and so has Ranjha his Heer. At times, Radha merges her identity into Krishna, so does Heer into Ranjha:

'Remembering Ranjha' day and night
I've become Ranjha myself.
Call me Dhadhi Ranjha,
(No more I be addressed as Heer
I am in Ranjha and Ranjha is in me)

Bulleh Shah mam tad birlai;
Jad di Murli Kanha vajai;
Bauri hoe ke tain valdhai;
(When Lord Krishna sounded the flute and I heard its medlody, sayeth Bulleh Shah, I cried in agony and since then I am wailing in pain of separation. Bulleh, the Gopi, turned mad and ran towards Lord Krishna. The Gopi asks where else she should go?)

The folk hero Ranjha is raised to the pedestal of Lord Krishna and Krishna, in turn, becomes the universal folk hero, with the highest level of his acceptability in the Land of the Five Rivers, cutting across the communal divide.

Pan-Indian Vision

The 18th and early 19th centuries have been described as the age of 'indescribable confusion and anarchy'. At the same time, in those times was attained 'the highest refinement of Indian culture'. The three stawlwarts, namely Shah Hussain, Warris Shah and Bulleh Shah stood out as the major poets of Saraiki/Punjabi vintage. Bulleh Shah stands out among them as the greatest poet of liberal Sufi tradition and can lay rightful claim to leadership. He is also a major poet in his own right and deserves to be counted among the major pan-Indian literateurs whose poetry was orally communicated and was formally written only half a century later. His restless soul experimented with a variety of poetic styles like *dohas, athvaras, baramah, gandhari,* and *si-hanafis.*

From day one, he sang his poetry, accompanied by his sarangi , from the public platform.He was intimately associated with popular culture but he transcended the local by making his poetry universal. Here was a fearless critic of orthodoxy and ritualism, he actually mocked at them. He transcended the the boundaries of formal religion, his faith was the religion of love. He stressed the dignity of man. The greatness of Bulleh Shah lies in his choosing his mother tongue as the medium of expression. He blended the folk and classical traditions seamlessly. His genre of poetry combined several cultural strands–folk, Hindu and Muslim.

Ranjha as Role Model

It would, however, be wrong to assume that Bulleh Shah rejected religion outright. His concept of love included divine beauty, as in the folk traditions of the Indus region. Ranjha as a folk hero is the darling of the literati and has been adopted by both Warris Shah and Bulleh Shah. Ranjha is visualised as a 'jogi' and 'Ranjha has come as a jogi' has become Bulleh Shah's theme song. He takes immense delight in describing the 'Yogi' or Jogi or sadhu as *nur-elahi* or divine light. In one of his extremely delightful couplets, he proclaims, 'I shall set out with the Jogi/putting Tilak on my head.' Bulleh

Shah has thus established his credentials as one of the best ambassador of Hindu-Muslim understanding in medeival India.

What makes Bulleh Shah shine among his contemporaries is his concept of love, which is highly social. His poetry has a message of implied subtlety, making him a 'poet of social confrontation',involving dialectical categories of conflict, defiance and cooperation. He is the poor man's Karl Marx, talking of social conflict and its resolution in the late 17th century. There is, thus, more to Bulleh Shah and his poetry than the melodious and throatful singing of Nusrat Fatheh Ali Khan.

Damodar Das (1468-1568)

Heer Ranjha is one of the four popular romances of the Punjab/Saraiki homeland. The other three are Mirza Sahiban, Sassi Punnun and Sahni Mahiwal. Those are popularly known as Quissa poetry. They are the only text of Saraiki literature, which is simply adored by the sophisticate classes and the common folk alike. The Land of the Five Rivers is largely a village bound mass, with the traditional bards singing Heer in the village assemblies of young and old alike, listening attentively to it day after day. The story is based on the traditional folk tales of Heer and her tragic lover Ranjha. The Warris Heer is preceded by nearly a hundred poetic versions since the sixteenth century. The Heer by Warris Shah was completed in 1766 or 1767. It is considered one of the great classics of Indian literature. Other Heers preceding Warris Shah's classic are from Damodar Das, Mukbal and Ahmed Guffar among numerous local versions. The Heer Damodar is the Saraiki language poem on this famous love-legend. He was a contemporary of Heer and Ranjha and had witnessed the tragic story happening before his very eyes. Damodar Heer must have been the inspiration for his successor poets, including Warris Shah. There are several conjectures about the chronology of Damodar Das. The date may be deduced from the fact that Heer died in 1459, during the regime of Bahal Lodi (1450-80). According to another version Heer-Ranjha met in 1477 for the first time. According to Richard Temple, Damodar Das was a Patwari who completed his poem in Samvat 1692. In another version he is believed to have lived during the regime of Akbar and Jahangir. His published version became available for the first time in 1927. Damodar Heer has a degree of intimacy with the characters that is rare in contemporary literature. He has also displayed a high degree of objectivity in his character portrayls. He left a deep influence on Bulleh Shah and Warris Shah and, in turn, was impacted by Shah Husain. Damodar was a contemporary of Shah Husain whose pervasive influence is distinctly seen in his famous verse, which looks like the faithful copy of Shah Husain not only in thought but also in words:

'Ulte Heer, Heerai vich Ranjha, hall non janeh koi,
Ranjha Ranjh hinkon akha, mah ape Ranjhan hoi'.
(Turn around Heer, Heer is in Ranjha, no one knows the condition,
Talk of Ranjha alone, I have turned Ranjha.)

Heer Damodar

Damodar was a resident of Jhang, most probably in the time of Akbar. He was a Gulati Arora. He was obliged to Chuchak, the chief of the Sial, and father of Heer for helping him to open a shop in Jhang. He was thus a close confidant of the Heer family. He has mentioned in his Quissa, that he had seen the plight of Heer. He thus claims to be an eye-witness to the events happening before his very eyes, He thus claims to be acquainted with all the characters portrayed in the Heer Damodar:

'Akhin Ditha Quissa kila mam
bit nal ga nan koi
Asan munhan alaya oho, jo kuch nazar pawai'.
(Whatever I have said I had seen it with my own eyes, What I saw
I narrated. I have no claim of a poet.)

In another verse he claimed to have seen Ranjha and Heer departing together and accompanied them for some distance. His claims to 'eyewitness' accounts may be taken with a pinch of salt. Those are probably secondhand accounts. This was his way of telling stories with the prevailing fashion of the day. His language is the Saraiki dialect of Jhang and neighbouring districts. Damodar was acquainted with Vedantic thought, Yoga and Sufi practices. He talks about Islamic belief with some authority and he expounds the

Yoga belief in exchanges between Ranjha and his guru Balaknath. Above all, he expounds Vedantic thought through the union of Ranjha and Heer by merging into one personality. His sensitivity to the natural phenomenon is obvious in the following verse:

'The trees, bushes and birds also lament,
the friends dote on her,
The leaves of the trees also lament,
and the foliage and grass also wail,
O people, the old and young women weep along with seven types of domestic animals[2]

Damodar Das was not only a pioneer, but also a lamp post shedding light for those who followed him. His meter was also original, altogether departing from which is typical and popularly known as *Var*. The power of his expression is best seen in the last four lines of a stanza, a fitting tribute to the love-tragedy with multiple interpretations:

'Sun Kazi ik araz asadi, eh ekath kahani,
Loh, kalam, nah arsh nah korsi nah nazaren aweh pani,
Zamin, zamana, chand nah suraj, joti jot samani
Sahib vi sohna, suntu kazi, main Ranjhe vasat vekani'.

(O, Qazi, listen to my tale as never before, Neither tablets, nor the marker, neither the heaven, not the seat of power, neither the seas nor the earth, neither space nor time, neither the sun nor the moon is its theme. By the creator, Ranjha owns the rosy soul of Heer.)

Warris Shah (1710-1799)

Heer of Warris Shah is a long narrative of about a hundred thousand words. It is based on the traditional folk tale of Heer and her lover Ranjha. It is speculated that the folk tale had a happy ending, but Warris Shah made a tragedy out of it to give it the legendry status it enjoys. It has also a deeper meaning underlying the relentless quest of man for God. Warris Shah makes his intention clear in the invocation to God, Prophet Muhammed, his parents, Dharti Mata (Mother Earth), Khwaja Khizar the saint and Guru

Gorakhnath. His intentions are made more specific in another version of the innovation by Chattar Singh Jeevan Singh, wherein he speaks in the language of love:

'Awal hamad khuda du vird kirye,
Ishq kit su jag da moal mian
Pehlan aap hi Rabb ne ishq kita,
(First of all let us acknowledge God (who is self-evident);
Who has made love the worthy of the world, mian,
It was God Himself that first loved,
And the Prophet (Muhammad (SO) IS His beloved' [3]

There is a haunting quality about Warris Shah's Heer unmatched in both Saraiki and Punjabi literature. Love, separation, tragedy and soul-searching are considered inseparable in Sufi literature. Life has been uncertain and strife the order of the day in the history of the Land of Five Rivers for centuries altogether. There is no hope in living, but there is in life beyond. Tragedy is the order of the day, which is reflected in literature reaching its prime in Heer. The poetry of Warris Shah is a true reflection of Saraiki/ Punjabi society during the 18th century. Here are a few verses that reflect the tragedy inherent in marriage celebrations of Heer:

Doli charh di mari Heer chikha,
Menu lee challe babla lee challe,
Menu rakh lee babla Heer ache
Doli ghat Kahar ni le challe we,
Mera Akhka kadi nan manda see,
Oh same bable kithe gae challe we'.

Sufiana Content

Heer of Warris Shah is shear poetry, but it is not merely admired for its literary value and content. It has a spiritual content of the secular kind. It appeals to Hindu, Muslim, Sikh and to other communities alike for a variety of reasons including its Sufiana content, musical elements, and its ryhthm and lyrical qualities. There is a great deal of interplay of words, with the same word having multiple meanings resulting in multi-splendoured interpretations. In the ultimate analysis it is about the relentless quest of man for God. Warris Shah has a considerable gift of the gab, which shows in his verbosity and sophistication. In the final analysis, Heer is one man's Odyessy in search of God. It is his search for God that takes the form of a collective communal vision. It is not to be forgotten that after his education at Kasur under Pir Mukhadum, he shifted his residence to Malkhai, a mere twelve mile away from Pakpattan, the abode of Baba Farid. This must have been an inspiration for Warris Shah. To his credit it must be said that Heer was his heroine, the woman who was prepared to fight for her rights in the medieval Punjab with its caste-ridden social structure. He was thus ahead of his times. Similarly, Ranjha is a progressive male ahead of his times.

In a manner of speaking, Ranjha reflects the personality of Warris Shah. There are striking similarities between the two of them. Heer is believed to be a true portrayl of his own unsublimited love for a girl named Bhag Bhanu. Ranjha, like Warris Shah, had a roadmap which he was unable to reach. Thus Ranjha represented the entire ethos of Sufiana cult as viewed by Warris Shah. Warris also must have viewed shades of Krishna in him. His Sufiana philosophy is in line with Shah Husain and Bulleh Shah, and it has considerable Bhakti and Yoga content. Baba Gorakhnath, the founder of 'Kanpatha' sect of 'jogis' looms larger than life in Heer. He talks of *dharti mata* in the innvocation. Thus Ranjha reflects the personality of Warris Shah in the following respects:

- He is critical of religious fundamentalism;
- He resorted to the practice of seeking alms for his maintainance;
- He played musical instruments himself;
- He was inspired by the Jogi cult, and
- He was a devotee of Khwaja Moin-ud-Din Chishti and Baba Farid.

Finally Warris Shah epitomized the day-to-day struggles of human beings as their spokesman.

Heer and Ranjha

Heer is depicled as an extremely beautiful woman. She is a faultless beauty representing paradise on earth in future. She is a rebel, personifying the plight of women of Saraiki homeland, in distress. Her husband is painted in the darkest colours, in contrast with Ranjha, her lover to whom are attributed all kinds of meritorious virtues. She is the prisoner of her feudal and entirely oppressive social environment. She is born to the chief of the Sials, described variously as Jats and Panwar Rajputs, so dominant that the history of the Jhang district is described as the history of the Sials. She is forcibly married into the family of Kheras of Rangpur. She continues to be mesmerized by Ranjha in the manner he plays his wanjli (flute) melodiously. Here is a woman who continues to be enslaved due to circumstances beyond her control. Heer has all the making of tragedy.

Dheedo is his first name and Ranjha is his surname. His father Manju is also the chieftain of the village Takht Hazara on the banks of the Chenab. Takht Hazara has now become as famous as Heer and Ranjha, as a place of pilgrimage for lovers from all over the land of Five Rivers. So has Tila Jogan (the mount of Jogis) located in the vicinity of Bhera town. It is here that Ranjha put on the garb of Jogi while reciting the mantra of 'Alakh Niranjan'. His head was shaven, his ears were pierced for the Jogi rings and his entire body was smeared with ashes. Ranjha was a transformed person, but his heart was in uniting with Heer. Here an attempt has been made to upgrade the romance to a spiritual level. At times, Ranjha has been compared to Krishna playing his flute and Radha personifying Heer in her constant search which is endless in itself. At another plane, Heer-Ranjha romance is shown as the human soul hankering after its elusive God. The separation and love elements are viewed as duality in constant search to reach the ultimate spiritual heights. There is so much of Vedanta thought that spills over constantly in the descriptions. Ultimately, Ranjha and Heer merge into each other, thus diffusing the line of demarcation. Sufis and Bhaktas thus come to terms with each other by propounding a joint thesis comprehensible to the man on the street. Thus Heer may be considered the Bible, the Gita, and the Upanishad of the common man, with the stream of liberal Islamic thought running smoothly underneath.

Come to think of it, Warris Shah employs 'vulgar' Lahnda Saraiki spoken in Jhang and adjacent districts–the language spoken in God-forsaken Nilabar and Sandalpar–expressing the profoundest statements on love, separation, tragedy and spirituality expressed at its supreme. There is also considerable amount of sophistication shown by Warris Shah in describing the agitated state of mind of Heer, when drawing parallels with the traditional Bara Mah (the twelve months), by relating her moode with changing months and corresponding musical ragas and raginis. He seems to exaggerate by idealizing the situation. His sense of humour is misplaced. He could be accused of being vulgar. At times he has been compared to Tom Jones. These exaggerations are pardonable for being localisms. Essentially, he is in a class of his own, who has succeeded in transforming the local into the universal. And turning the 'language of the street' into respectability by bringing them on the same platform.

Shah Abdul Latif (1689-1752)

Shah Abdul Latif of Bhit in Sindh has been prounced the voice of Sindh. His poetry is considered co-terminus with Sindhi literature. Due to his Sufi background, he is called a god-intoxicated soul, or simply 'Shah' or 'Monarch' of all he surveys. Considerd the greatest of Sindhi poets, Latif was born in 1680, in a Syed family. His father Shah Habibullah predicted that his son 'Latif' would be a 'Kutb' or Pole Star of his times. The renowned German literateur, Dr. Ernest Trumpp, was the first to bring out an English edition of the classic *Risalo* during 1866 and he was followed by Dr H T Sorley, who was to write about the life and times of Shah and translated some of his writings into English in 1940. Thus, Trumpp and Sorley were solely responsible for introducing the world to his writings. His poetry has also been called 'Desert Melodies'. Sorely is one of several critics who has laid too much stress on the rusticity of Shah. He has also confined him in a narrow framework by proclaiming him as the Poet of Islam. On the contrary, L H Ajwani has viewed him 'as a typical Indian rishi' and his headquarters Bhit as 'a medieval ashram or forest, sanctuary'. Shah was a people's poet and 'the bard of Sindh' who meditated on Man, Nature and God.[4] Shah was a commanding personality, tall, handsome, rich in imagery and lyricism, who viewed God as 'Rana', 'Meher', 'Punneh', 'Tamachi', and 'Maru', thus transforming God as a part of his heritage of Sindhayat.

Shah was believed to be an Umi, an unlettered person. It is highly unlikely that his extensive acquaintance with the Koran or Jalaluddin Rumi's Masanvi, or, for that matter, his acquaintance with the thirty Surs of Indian classical music is based on mere oral tradition. He has quoted extensively from Rumi, whose writings have constituted 'a major source of inspiration' for him. He was very much alert to the outpourings of Bhakti movement literature in north India. He was also well versed in the folklore and legends of Sindh. He had spent years in the company of the Jogis. Each one of the chapters of the *Risalo* bears testimony to his scholarship. Admittedly, he was no peer to Rumi, Jami or Hafiz, but he must have utilized their thoughts to his advantage.

'Alif' to 'Be'

There are numerous fables concocted around this "Man of God". One of them relates to the young Latif who refused to preceed beyond the first letter of the alphabet, Alif, to the next letter, 'Be', because nothing existed beyond it, representing 'One' or 'Unity. He has indirectly confirmed the suspicion in a verse often quoted:

'Read one letter, Alif, the only one,
The rest you can all forget.
Let thy spirit have a cleansing
No other study for you next.'

He confirmed the sentiment in another verse:

'Turn thou pages endless
One word, only, will you probe.'[5]

The Sufi and Bhakts are fond of rejecting all formal knowledge, so has Shah Latif: 'Here is insistence upon Alif, Unity, One thing, One Word, the substratum of all things, and the vision of that one Thing. Here is declaration of the supreme duty of knowing that one word which was in the beginning and which was with God and which was God'. The concept of 'God Intoxication' confronting 'book-learning' is really unfortunate. Even Shah Latif argued for 'God Intoxication', of not going beyond 'Alif'.

His *Risalo* is a compendium of knowledge that was available to him in the circumstances of contemporary Sindh. The *Risalo* is as much about 'God Intoxication' as about book knowledge. His entire corpus of poetry is also an affirmation of his divine love. In *Sur Asa* he sings of

I springs from 'I', 'I' befits 'I',
With the blessing of this 'I', became the real 'I'".

While he was an accomplished mystic and a Sufi of the highest order, he was equally an exponent of 'Sindhyat' or the Greater Sindko, for which he has been called the 'Sage of Mehran' (Sindh/ Sindhu river). His Sindhayat encompassed the entire Indus basin from Kashmir to the Runn of Kutch where, in mythical times, the River Indus is believed to have joined the sea. He travelled extensively to places as far away as Kashmir, to Dwarka in Gujarat, and also to Multan, Jaisalmer, Barmer, Makran, Hinglay (Las Belas). That is why he has been called 'a nationalist and patriotic poet'. His *Risalo* sings of the Seven Queens of Sindh, all of them being the heroines of Sindhi folklore. Most of them had been born, bred and nourished, and equally came to sad ends in tragic circumstances, living on the banks of the Mehran or its subsidiaries like the Chenab. The *Risalo* is thus an epic not only of the Sindhis, it is also an heritage of the Saraiki-speaking people, living on both banks of the mighty river.

Islamic Beliefs

There is another legend attributed to Shah Latif. When asked whether he was a Sunni or Shia, he said neither, he was in-between. When further queried, 'There is nothing in between', quickly came the retort, 'I am nothing'. He was definitely a Sufi, but he had no preceptor to guide him. No one was sure whether he belonged to the Qadri or the Chishti order. He had, however, a firm root in the Islamic faith. In the *Risalo* are to be found the verses of the Koran in more than one hundred places. But then, he was a Muslim with a difference. He had spent entire three years wearing the garb of Hindu Jogis. He violated the Islamic injunction against dance-music or Samaa. Two Hindu musicians were his constant companions. He passed away, listening to dance music.

Above all, Shah Latif was an accomplished Sufi who observed its norms strictly. He followed principles of Sufism like renunciation, self-imposed poverty, humility, self-denial, and asserted his right to maintain a direct channel with God. He was a true Muslim, but who equally was the murshid of Sindhayat. He had a pan-Indian rather than pan-Islamic vision. Finally he viewed Islam through the pan-Indian perspective. His Sindhayat flowed beyond the frontiers of the geographical Sindh. The leading Sindhi Sufis like Shah Abdul Latif were anxious to bridge the gap between two major communities, and accordingly, they 'mainly propagated the idea of Ibn Arabi's Wahdat-al-Wujoud which seemed to bridge the gap between Islamic and Hindu mysticism.'[6]

The Hindu Connection

Shah Latif has been called the inheritor of the Rishis. He has also been called a 'Puran Jogi', the foremost inheritor of the ancient tradition, as well as 'inheritor of a precious heritage–the heritage left by the Rishis who chanted the mantras of Vedas and Upanishads on the banks of the Sindhu'. Even today, the banks of River Indus are dotted with the *Sufi khanqahs*, reminding one of the ashrams of yore. Bhit, the place of his residence, meant a 'sand dune'. It has been called a medieval ashram or forest sanctuary. He felt delighted to take solitary walks in the sand dunes in an apparent imitation of the ancient rishi taking a walk around his ashram.

Shah Latif spent three years in the company of Hindu Jogis and Sanyasis. He visited the pilgrimage centre of Hinglay in Las Bela state in Balochistan, and donned the ochre-colored clothes of a Sanyasi. He sang in praise of Hinglas on Ganja Hill and the goddess Amba Devi, the presiding deity of Hinglas, affectionately called Nani (grandmother) by its Muslim mujawir (priests):

> *Those who get acquainted with Ganja Hill;*
> *Become Jogis, forsaking all books and scriptures.'*

He was equally fascinated by Jogis residing in its foothills;

> *'Where not a bird's foot is perceptible, there flickers a flame,*
> *Who will light fire except wondering hermits.'*

He also visited other places like the Thar Desert, the Fort of Girnar (mentioned in '*Sur Sarath*') and Barmer. He also saw Puran, the old bed of the River Sindh. He travelled to Dwarka, which was no doubt on the top of his itinerary in Gujarat:

'The naked one (Jogi) went to Hingley;

The Saivites were sanctified by a visit to Dwarka.

His initiation into yoga, Bhakti and Vedanta, the traditional Hindu philosophies, during the years of wandering with the Jogis came to an abrupt end, when the Jogis told him: 'Your God is within you'.

Thus, he reached his destination of marrying Sufi mysticism with the Bhakti cult, in perfect union. He felt humble and denied such sangam in his person. He also felt incomplete: 'Alas, I have not been able to learn yoga that befts Jogis, who enshrine within them the mystery of all mysteries'.

Love of Nature

Desert is a desert and apparently it has a life of its own. Shah Latif, however, discovered it differently. Bhit, the place of his residence, inspired him immensely to feelings of deep love:

'There was a wail in the desert in the note of koel,

This distraction and tumult were verily of love.'

The immensity of the desert and its silent spaces were disturbed by the long wail of a bird,reminding him of separation, love and human bond. Marui, the desert girl, makes him pine for his beloved:

'As crane pine for the rock,
And oysters for the ocean,
Even so do I thirst every moment,
For my beloved and sweet home.'

The koel and crane are the messengers of love in Indian poetry. Shah Latif follows the same tradition faithfully. There is really no line of demarcation between physical love, pure love (for God), his love of music, love of nature and his love for the entire humanity. Sufis' love of music is notorious. Shah Latif was no exception. He invented a new variety of tambura, the drone instrument 'to blend classical and folk melodies into a unity'. He also invented *wai* or *kafi*, which is melodious in tone and as lofty and melodious as the Persian ghazal. His poetry is meant to be sung. He has been called the 'Hafiz of Sind' and his *Risalo* has been placed on par with the *Diwan-e-Hafiz* by several critics. In *Sur Sarath*, he sings of the 'Song of Spirit'. The shrill of music simply enthralled him:

> *'It is not the harp that sings,*
> *it is the very mystery of the soul that sings'.*

He was equally fascinated by the horn-pipe blown by Jogis

> *'Such an instrument is neither in Sind or in Hind,*
> *Those who have heard it,*
> *Aver it is sweeter than the sweetest harmony,*
> *They have been transported to the realm of ecstacy.'*

The love of nature and music, as well as other multiple loves overwhelmed him and he cried out in ecstacy 'Those whose self is filled with love, an eternal thirst', for them 'Love hath no limit, it knows its own end'.

Risalo and Women

The Risalo has been called the poetry of fulfillment. It is also called the poetry of gracious benediction. Some have wrongly termed it the poetry of Islam. Equally, it has been described as the rusticity of Shah Latif. It should not be forgotten that there are special qualities of his poetry, unique to him alone. He is deeply steeped in the traditional ragas and raginis. He is also in constant communion with God, as if in a dialogue with him in a state of yogic trance. His heroes and heroines are steeped in Indian traditions. He deserves to be named as the murshid of Sindhayat due to his constant championship of Sindh. He is also an advocate of Greater Sindh, beyond the physical borders of Sindh. The Sage of Mehran is an accomplished Sufi with yogic vision.

His women characters are women with a difference. They have been called the Seven Queens of Sindh as well as the heroines of Sindhi folklore. 1) Marvi, 2) Munal, 3) Sassi, 4) Noori, 5) Sohni, 6) Heer and 7) Laila. His classic *Shah-Jo-Risalo* or *Risalo* is built around these characters. His male characters in contrast, like Punhoon, Umar, Mehar, Bano and Dyach, are pale shadows. His women are in centrol of the situation. They are much greater for being the tragic characters. They are brave souls prepared to gamble in vindication of their love. They are defiant characters who preferred to take risks to achieve their purpose. They are all alone in the task ahead of them. In reality, these women are incarnation of the human soul, readying to merge with God. Essentially, they are idealized characters, somewhat exaggerated in the real sense.

The *Risalo* is the Bible to the Muslims and Hindus of Sindh alike. To the Hindus, it is a particularly nostalgic statement. It is the classic of the Sindhi people. It has multiple dimensions. It affirms Shah Latif's Islamic affidavit by underlying his familiarity with the Koran and the Hadis. It has been compared to the Masanvi of Rumi in the Persian language. It is credited with the responsibility of familiarizing the folklore and legends of Sindh. It is equally a common heritage shared with the Saraiki people across the border. It is viewed as the Sufi and Bhakti treasure trove of literature. It is equally a compendium of oral tradition and the Sindhiyat heritage. Above all, it is to be commended for its pan-Indian vision. It is one of the finest tribute to womanhood. It may have possibly taken inspiration from the Sacred Books of the Sikhs.

Sufism is the predominant philosophy of the *surs* or cantos in the Risalo. It consists of 30 *surs* of *ragas* and *raginis* like 'Kalyan', 'Yeman Kalyan', 'Asa', 'Sarang' and 'Ramkali', with each chapter devoted to an individual raga. There is a singular Islamic dirge, referring to the wails of Bibi Fatima, the Prophet's daughter, for the death of her beloved son, Husain, in the Kerbala's battlefield, in the *Risalo*. The remaining *surs* are devoted to local folklore heroines like Suhini and Sassi, living within the circumference of the Indus basin. The *Risalo* is the best tribute to unity in diversity peculiar to the Indian subcontinent, as evidenced in Ramkali, 'Here the poet has described the Jogis in terms taken from the Quran, thus transforming them into perfect Muslim saints of the highest ranks. In fact, the Sindhi mystical poets often equate the Jogis and their sub-groups with Sufi saints...'[7]

The *Risalo* must be credited with more. The descriptions of nature are singular to Sindh. How the rainy season transforms the landscape is best described in the following, lively and plulsating verse:

> *'Man, deer and buffaloes do look*
> *for rain, ducks hope for clouds'*
> *afar as though in supplication*

sound the rain quail's chant,
at sea, each morn the oysters beg
that skies the rain may grant,
Give lots of rain! With joy rampant
The herdsmen thou become.' [8]

Sachal Sarmast (1739-1829)

His full name is Abdul Wahab Sadal Sarmast. He lived to the ripe age of ninety. He was popularly known as Sachal Sarmast or Sarmad. Sachal is the diminutive of 'truth', and Sarmast means 'intoxicated' and 'God intoxicated'. Sachal was his pen name. Sarmast also means 'mystic', 'everlasting', 'perenial', 'eternal' and 'intoxicated'. Sachal Sarmast stood for all the values his name has literally represented. He was born in Daraza village in Khairpur district of Upper Sindh and remained in his village all his life. Sachal, unlike his mentor Shah Latif, was a learned scholar. He had a cosmopolitan worldview. He was, however, modesty incarnate. He loved to be loved as a dervish.

'The universe itself is governed by Dervishes,
God Himself seeks the will of Dervishes'.

He was the foremost exponent of values of humanity, love, secularism and human fraternity. Yet he was not beyond depreciating himself as evidenced in one of his Sindhi- Saraiki poems.

'We shall take the lover to our abode and flay him there',
We shall cut his flesh into pieces and roast them on rods in fire;
Then his fragments shall be absorbed in our heart and soul;
Our eternal lover is Sachu, we shall go in search of him'. [9]

He has been called the 'Shair-e-haft zaban' (poet of seven languages). He wrote poetry in Sindhi, Saraiki, Punjabi, Urdu, Persian, Arabic and Balochi. His was a religion of love, which he celebrated through his poetic output:

"Tis not in religion I believe in,
'Tis love I believe in'

He is more specific in other verses about his unbounding commitment to love and be loved.

'I live ever in love.

....

Love is neither with the kafir nor the faithful'

Sachal was an eternal lover and he sings with joy;

'The lover blooms like a lovely lotus.

For he is like an ever thirsty lotus.'

His state of ecstatic love has a definitive divine coloring.

'Divine love or unity: Beauty and majesty,

Kindness and cruelty: Two sides of the coin.'

Joie de Vivre

There is an unmistakable elan in Sarmast's poetry, in what the French are fond of calling the joie de vivre. He has also been given the honorific title of 'the Attar of Sind'. He sings with abandon:

'Sometimes, I have shouted in ecstasy, sometimes indulged'.

He loves to whirl like a dervish. He is a devotee of music and beauty:

'I dance, I dance, I dance, to my disgrace,

Everybody proceeds to say, he is madness in himself.'

Music was his inspiration and sarangi and tabla were his accompanying instruments. He had the authority of his preceptor to assert, 'Only intoxicated souls realize God'. His role model was Husain ibn Mansur al-Hallaj, who was executed in Baghdad in 905 AD for blaspheny. He was also inspird by the Sindhi Sufi martyr Shah Inayat Shahid of Jhuk, who was executed in 1718 for his open dissent. His role models confirmed him in his belief that God makes them suffer those whom he loves most:

'As Mansoor did this in dark age,

So I proclaim Divine Kinship,

I am the King, I am the King, I am that King (God).'

He has been called 'Hafiz and Khayyam rolled into one'. He sings expansively: comprehending the entire universe within his ambit:

'He is Abu Hanifa and He is Hanuman,

He is the Koran and He is the Vedas,

He is this. He is that.

He is Moses and he is Pharaoh.'

Secular Credentials

His chief disciple was Nanak Yusuf, with impeccable secular credentials. He named himself after Guru Nanak, after his visit to the Golden Temple in Amritsar. Sarmast never discriminated between the Hindus and the Muslims, 'Sachedino', the truthful, was his pseudonym. 'I believe not in the outer religion'. He further emphasized, he was 'neither a Muslim, nor a Hindu'. Here he begins to question religious beliefs and dogma about who is a villain and who is not.

"If Ram Rahim be truly same
What constitutes Ravana's frame?
On Krishna's being why did you seek
On Kansa's vengenance to wreck?'

The two maligned and notorious characters of Indian mythology, Ravana and Kansa, find Sarmast coming to their rescue by questioning the very credentials of God the Almighty.

The doubting Thomas' do not stop here but raise further skeptical querries in one of his most renowned verse, quoted frequently.

'Sometimes Ram, Sita,
Sometimes Lakshman and sometimes Daherar (Ravan)
I have made myself.
Sometimes I have shouted in ecstacy,
Sometimes in distress.'

Two of his great Sufi saint predecessors were executed for committing blaspherny. Sarmast was fortunate to escape the executioner's sword due to his immense popularity and the tolerant environment of Sindh. Like Hafiz, Sachal also castigated mullahs and maulanas, who had with glee laid claim to be true representatives of an intolerant and fundamentalist religion with double standards of conduct:

'Din and Kufr are a snare for the heart'

Accordingly there is another of his unsolicited advice:

'Now is the time when you should discard duality,
Banish religion from your mind in right earnest;
Hindus and Muslims.

Unite in the bond of love,
Before it is too late and the sun sets in the west.'

Blasphemy

There is always the danger of turning polemical in verse, but the situation is saved by daringly mocking at the establishment:

'O Mulla! If you were to taste this wine.'

Here Sachal Sarmast is in danger of reaching the limits of blasphemy.

'Why talk of Ka'aba and Qibla, these are but false consolation
Men of God visit the tavern,
Pilgrimages are the result of imperfect thinking,
My preceptor (Satguru) says;
Only intoxicated souls realize God'.

Sachal crosses the frontiers of blasphemy, but escapes 'punishmen due to sheer luck'. His popularity was a passport to safe conduct for him. 'I drink wine in the public square.' He had the compunction to equate Islam with Kufr:

'My face is Islam, my hair is kufr (blasphemy).

Logically, the sacred places of Islam like Mecca came for critical reference:

Why go to Mecca!
Circumambulate your own self!

Vedantic Rishi

He has been called the mystic poet of *Wahdat-al-Wujoud*, asserting that Allah is the only one who really exists, and as in Vedanta, the universe is nothing but *maya* or illusion. Sarmast is often acknowledged as the greatest mystical poet of Islam. His pen name in Persian poetry was Akbar (open) and he was known as Sarmast for his writings in general. His mystic philosophy is to be summed up in the Persian nomenclature, bama fist, 'Everything is He'.

His Islamic philosophy of *Wahdat-al-Wujoud* (unity of existence) is synonymous with *Hamah Ost* (All from One), and furthermore, it is a passport to spirituality, crossing all narrow religious borders:

Sachal regarded love as the path to spirituality.

Sufis and Bhakts must have come to an understanding. Vedanta, thus, falls in line as an expression of that unity.

All is illusion. The world is a make- belief,

The universe is but a moment

The Vedantic concept of Oneness finds an echo in Sufi beliefs and thereby a solemn pact is drawn between Hinduism and Islam.

Islam and the Hindu faith.

......

Each declares

Thou art one!

And Thou hath no equal'.

This is followed by a personal statement in affirmation:

'I was born ... of none,

I have neither father nor mother,

I am an infinite, I am everywhere,

And it is by mistake that men have called me Sachal'

The above-mentioned verse is a literal translation of the famous assertion by Lord Krishna in the Gita, which has reverberated over the entire globe million times over, ironically enough, delivered on the battlefield of Kurukshetra in the Mahabharata.

Jogi Incarnation

While Shah Latif spent three years in the company of Jogis, Sachal Sarmast spent no time with them, but he was very closely in touch with them. The poetry of Sachal was recited by travelling *mollaa* (Sufi fakirs) from one corner of Sindh to another. They were the exact reflection of the Jogis. They were normally dressed in saffron clothes and hanging *cholas* (shirt), head uncovered, holding *kisto* (begging bowl) in one hand, and balancing an *ektara,* a single-stringed musical instrument in the other, with *chaeryuun* (bells) on their legs, they moved from one place to the other, being on the run all the time. They were hailed as miyaans.

Sachal was, in fact, closely associated with Jogi Vishwanath, who lived in the Hindukush mountains. He took pride in proclaiming himself a Jogi:

I am a Jogi and will remain a Jogi, a mighty Jogi

I am neither a Mulla nor a Brahmin, nor do I recite

the verses of the Quran,

Neither do I recite Pothis and Pauris, nor the discourse of the Gita.

He wondered as a Jogi, smeared with ash, wearing knotted hair, carrying with him nothing but a pipe for smoking ganja. He was also fascinated with the long musical horn which always accompanied him in his bagage. He took delight in imagining himself to be a Jogi. He himself acknowledges his debt of gratitude to Jogis:

He had a Jogic hair and his body all smeared with ash,

He unravelled the entire mystery to Sachu

Annemarie Schimmel has no doubts about his talent and paid him the highest tribute possible. 'He expressed the all-embracing unity of (the Ultimate) Being, in verses so open and outspoken that his poetry in Sindhi, Siraiki, Urdu, and Persian can easily compare with the most enthusiastic verses of earlier Turkish and Persian mystics. Therefore, his compatriots compared him to one of the greatest mystical poets of Islam, whose work was interpreted as a message of suffering and inspiration, and they called him 'the Attar of Sind'.[10] He felt humble by denying such sangam in his person. He also felt incomplete:

'Alas, I have not been able to learn yoga [from] Jogis, who enshrine within them the mystery of all mysteries.'

Section - VIII

Native Sufism

16

Sufis, Sants & Liberal Tradition

SHEIKH Farid-ud-Din Masud Ganj-i-Shakar (1175-1265), popularly known as Baba Farid Shakarganj, was one of the founding fathers of the Chishti Silsilah (school of thought). He belonged to a distinguished pedigree. While Shaikh Nizam-ud-Din Auliya was his khalifa, Khwaja Qutb-ud-Din Bakhtiyar Kaki of Delhi was his murshid, who in turn was the khalifa to Khwaja Moin-ud-Din Chishti of Ajmer. Four of them were responsible for the spread of the Chishti Silsilah in India.

Of the four great Silsilah, the Chishti school's appeal lay in its humane character, more particularly symbolized by the personality of Baba Farid. He chose to withdraw to a lonely location called Ajodhan (modern name: Pakpattan) on the banks of the River Sutlej near Multan, where he had his religious training earlier. Baba Farid was a much travelled person. He had visited Baghdad, Damascus, Samarkhand, Bukhara and Nishapur, all of them being great religious, cultural and educational centres of his time, before settling in India. Khwaja Moin-ud-Din Chishti had arrived in India by the close of the 12th century and followed in quick succession by other Chishti founding fathers including Baba Farid.

Sheikh Baha-ud-Din Zakariya was the founding father of the Suhrawardi Silsilah and through his enterprise, Multan was acknowledged a top-ranking centre of learning and of spiritual life in the thirteenth century. Between Ajodhan and Multan as rival centres of Sufi movement in north-west India, the 13th century truly turned out to be the age of ferment in Saraiki homeland. Above all, Baba Farid stands out in history as unique. Prof. Khaliq Ahmad Nizami rightly points out, '…it was through the efforts of Baba Farid that the organization struck roots in the soil and spread far and wide. His piety, devotion and spiritual excellence attracted seekers after truth from distant parts of India as well from lands beyond. Very rightly does Irami calls him the ruler of the realm of spiritual discipline (Shah-i-Mulk-i-Suluk)'[1]

Spritual Being

Baba Farid was entirely a different kind of person. He was benign, considerate and a loving person with the largeness of heart. His favourite expression to everyone was 'Give me your dard (pain)', or 'May God give you dard'. It is not to be taken literally, as he explained the same expression by saying, I 'meant an eye full of tears and a heart full of devotion'. He was an all-embracing personality who applied the strictest of spiritual discipline in his personal life. He was a role model in observing the strictest discipline of poverty. He was an ascetic of the highest order. His ascetism is almost legendary. He chose to leave Delhi and decided to live all his life at lonely Ajodhan. He wanted to stay away from all seats of power. This way, he was able to exercise what amounted to the 'autonomy of his spiritual life'. This way, he had a life devoted entirely to the moral and cultural upliftment of society. For him, his religion was the practice of spirituality away from the bonds of prescribed religion. This was also the secret of his success. His audience was not confined to 'the believers of the Faith', but cut across all religions and creeds. He was secular and liberal at the same time.

He was equally talented in many respects. He was the first Saraiki poet. In fact, he laid the foundations of Saraiki literature. He was equally the founding father of Punjabi literature. He has the unique distinction of Farid-bani being incorporated in the *Guru Granth Sahib*. He was also the pioneer of khanqah life of India, where food was served free for one and all. Above all, he attempted to free women of purdah by bringing them on stage: 'For the first time, Punjabi Sufi poetry not only elevated the status of women, it also accorded her a power of transcendence. Woman, now, was defined as 'someone who had her own mind and took her own decisions'.[2] His greatest contribution lay in opening the channels of communication with Hindu religious thinkers. Jogis used to visit him frequently. He used to hold regular discussions with them on spiritual matters. Presumably, the discussions must have taken place in the indigenous language, thus laying the foundation for his poetry, communicated to the world in spoken and folk language of the people.

Mother Tongue as Medium

Increasingly, it is being recognized that Baba Farid stands all alone as the founding father of modern Indian languages like Saraiki, Punjabi and Urdu. It is a great pleasure to read him. He is parsimonious in expression, right on-the-spot, pinpointed in his words and thought. He is a purist, simple and chaste in his unalloyed use of Saraiki vocabulary, to the vigorous exclusion of Arabic and Persian vocabulary. It is the chaste Saraiki for him, spoken in the bazaars, street corners and homes. Baba Farid must have sharpened his vocabulary by conversing with his visitors in Saraiki. He has not only employed few Persian and Arabic words, he has avoided following the Hindi-loaded 'Apabhransha' tradition of employing love, romance and heroism in his compositions.

He is a master craftsman in total command of the situation. Dohras are his convenient instrument in his poetic craftsmanship. Dohras of the Hindi poetic tradition owe it to Baba Farid's inventive genius. Hamid Husain[3] has made a close study of Dohras of Baba Farid incorporated in the *Adi Granth* His findings are of much relevance. Of the actual count of 2,000 words, more than 1,800 words are in pristine Saraiki. Baba Farid has paid an unintended tribute to his adopted mother tongue by affirming its integrity in the Farid-baani. Thus, he has left a model for others to emulate.

It is to the credit of the great saint that he was the first to compose in contemporary Indo-Aryan languages, and provided guidelines and encouragement for others to follow, especially in respect of languages like Punjabi and Sindhi in the neighbourhood of Saraiki. No wonder, Saraiki, Sindhi and Punjabi are known as sister languages. He has also been called the father of 'Sindh Sagar' poetry for the same reason. Historically, the Punjab province has been an amalgam, albeit relectuantly, of the Saraiki and Punjabi people throughout the centuries. It is also a matter of investigation whether Urdu was or not the fallout of Baba Farid's experimentation in reconstructing the new language. In other words, Urdu is also attributed to have emerged out of the sangam of several languages including Baba Farid's Saraiki language, considering that Deccan Urdu is the byproduct attributable to the Sindhi Chishtis, who migrated to Bijapur and settled there.

Convertions to Islam

There remains the disconcerting and contentious issue of conversion of Hindus to Islam. There are all kinds of possibilities. Convertions could be voluntary, involuntary, forced, reluctant, for personal benefit and under perceived threat. Those could also be the result of intolerable discrimination and persecution. The fact remains that the largest number of conversions took place on account of preachings by the Chishti saints. Baba Farid was responsible for the largest number of convertions, especially of entire tribes. The Sial tribe of Heer fame is one of the most powerful tribes claiming Rajput lineage, converted by Baba Farid. The modern history of Jhang district is the history of the Sials. At least eleven tribes claim to have been converted by Baba Farid personally. Those included powerful tribes like the Khokhran, Dhudhiyan and Tabiyan. The other tribes who were converted include Kharrals, Tiwanas, Ghebes and Punwars, presumably they were all Rajput tribes. These tribes, indeed, constituted the power elite of modern Punjab.

There are diverse reasons attributed for the conversions. Husaini Brahmins found in Baba Farid their ideological messiah. He was their patron saint, whom Yusuf Husain Khan has effusively described as their 'divinity tutélaire'.[4] Prof. Muhammad Habib is categorical in asserting that 'converting non-Muslims was no part of the mission of the Chishti Silsilah'.[5] He reinforces his argument by pointing out that the early mystic records mention nothing about conversions. Schimmel is prepared to yield the ground but somewhat reluctantly by conceding, 'One particular aspect of Moin-ud-Din Chishti's teaching was that he did not insist upon formal conversion of a non-Muslim before the novice had 'tasted' the truth. Such generosity made the order very attractive for Hindus ...'[6] Farishta, however, provides another side of the story of forcible convertions by the invading rulers: 'Farishta ... says that the tribe of Khokhars was converted to Islam by Sultan Shihab-ud-Din of Ghaur. Probably a part of the tribe was converted to Islam by him. Baba Farid, too, would have converted a part of the tribe, because even now the tribe is divided between the two religions'.[7]

The Arc of Mysticism

The waters of the Indus River and its tributaries like Chenab, Ravi and Sutlej seem to flow with the Sufi movement. The Sufi khanqahs dot all the banks of these rivers. The Zindapir shrine near Sukkur in Sindh is at which both the Hindus and Muslims worship. It is a tribute to the river god, who, to the Muslims is a living saint, Shaikh Tahir, born in 952 C E, and, for the Hindus, he is the god Jhulelal or Uderalal, who never died. For the Hindus and Muslims in Sindh, Zindapir is none other than the sacred Sindhu river. Panchpirs (five pirs) of Heer are Khwaja Khizr, the lord of all the waters, Baba Farid Shakarganj, Lal Bahadur Qalander, Sheikh Baha-ud-Din Zakariya and Makhdum Jaharinyan Jalal Bukhari, who all bless Ranjha, the maverick 'Jogi'. Panchpirs are the icons of the Sufi movement in the Saraiki heartland and beyond in the Sindh Sagar circumference. Lal Shahbaz Qalandar, who used to be called Raja Bhartari by the Hindus, is identified with the Hindu gods. His shrine at Schwan in Sindh is an important Siva worship landmark. Panchpirs is an instance of Hindus and Muslims coming to terms with each other in the best of Sufiana tradition.

The Sindh Sagar Sufism is to be viewed as an arc, with Bhit of Shah Abdul Latif located in lower Sindh, constituting its western extremity and Lahore constituting its eastern extremity, with Multan with its satellite holy places of Pakpattan and Uch located right in its centre. Of the four major

Sufi schools of thought, three, namely, Suharwardiya, Qadria and Chishti were located in Multan and in its vicinity. Data Ganj Baksh (Ali-al-Hujuris) is, however, considered the father of Sufism in India. He lived in Lahore. Jhang was by no means a holy place, but it was associated with some of the famous Sufi poets like Damodar Arora, Sultan Bahu, Shah Husain and Warris Shah. There is thus the closest relation between liberal Sufism and the Saraiki homeland. Lahore, however, sitting on the periphery of Saraiki homeland was actually in the centre of the the development of Sufiana. West wind constantly blew in the direction of the east, and equally in the opposite direction.

Lahore, the Cultural Heartland

After all, Lahore and not Multan, was the cultural centre and pulsating heartland of the Punjab. There was, in fact, a one-way traffic in the direction of the east. Bulleh Shah was born near Uch, but he moved to Lahore to be very near to his murshid Inayat Shah. Warris Shah was born in the vicinity of Pakpattan, but studied at Kasur, next to Lahore. Mian Mir was born in Sindh but he ended as the patron saint of Lahore. The great iconoclastic Sufi poet Shah Husain was again the resident of Lahore, whom the city honours every year by celebrating the spring festival to commemorate him.

Mian Mir, born in 1549, stands out from the rest, "as a last word one could say that Miyan Mir recalls Farid in many ways. He carried forward his legacy of strict poverty, distance from politics and rulers and emphasis on raising the edifice of spiritual culture on autonomous grounds.... At the same time, however, his emphasis on realizing the spirit rather than the form of the Shari'a... indicate his independent stance towards the Shari'a–a hallmark of the Sufis of unitarian tradition. But he was probably the 'last great master in the tradition in the Punjab'".[8] Mian Mir was celebrated by Dara Shikoh (1615-59) in his book on him. He had met Jahangir and Shah Jahan and conversed with them. He was, however, so humble that he refused to call his followers *murids* preferring to be addressed by them as yar, an endearing term for a 'friend'. He was to lay the foundation of the Golden Temple in Amritsar, at the invitation of Guru Arjan Dev. He was to Lahore, what Baba Farid was to Ajodhan and Sheikh *Baha-u'd-din*

Zakariya to Multan, but he chose to be critical of Sheikh Zakariya, who 'He once said that nothing had been cooked at his place for thirty years'. Here was a Qadria being boldly critical of the Suharwardiya icon.

Qadria Silsilah and Punjab

Sheikh Baha-ud-Din Zakariya was a companion saint of Baba Farid during the thirteenth century. He was equally renowned and credited with establishing a centre of distinguished learning and of spiritual life in Multan of the Suharwardiya Silsilah. His school of thought was fundamentalist in its worldview and part of the establishment. It was no part of the liberal tradition, growing spectrally in that part of the world. In contrast, the Chishti Silsilah and Baba Farid set different standards of austerity and denial of symbols of power and authority. Chishtis visualized society more in cultural than in religious terms. They chose the path of spirituality without, however, questioning the tenets of the Shari'a. They went about their task quietly. Sufism was a way of life for them. They avoided confronting the state and the law. They were, however, rooted in the soil. They were also engaged in a serious attempt to adopt indigeneous cultural values.

The Chishti Silsilah was gentlemanly in actual practice. They were, however, no part of the radical liberal establishment like the Qadria Silsilah, which made its late appearance in the 16th century. It was very much aligned to the indigeneous ethos and culture. At one time, it had a wide appeal among the masses. It was unorthodox and non-conformist and proclaimed it from the top of the house. It had pronounced iconoclastic Qalandari tendencies. Muhammad Ghous (1492-1517) was its original founder. He established his khanqah at Uch. Mian Mir, Bulleh Shah, Shah Husain and Shah Inayat were of Qadiri Silsilah. Its centre gradually moved away from Uch to Lahore, the cultural and intellectual centre of the Punjab, where pantheistic ideas were actively promoted. The foundation for a serious dialogue between Hindus and Muslims was laid on a sound footing for the first time.

Prototype Sufi

Baba Farid was the Mahatma Gandhi of his days. He has been called a great humanist of all times. He was a role-model Sufi. Baba Farid had the greatness of a morally perfect man, who was deeply immersed in his spiritual experience. He was emotionally successful in establishing the proposition that 'Muslim mysticism is, in its essence, a message of love. It created harmony in the descendant elements of society. True to these words, Baba Farid strove day and night to create that atmosphere of love and goodwill which was, and is even today, the greatest desideratum of human society. A healthy social order–free from divisions, conflicts, discriminations, hatred and jealousy–was the thing he loved. In love, faith, toleration and sympathy, which even included the enemy, he found the talisman of human happiness'.[9]

He was thus an early propounder of nonviolence. Considering his Central Asian links, a Buddha connection cannot be ruled out. However, there was much spontaneous activism and social awareness and social reform in the Bhakti movement rather than in Sufism. Baba Farid was in search of a total spiritual experience by establishing the Kingdom of Heaven on earth. His God was an all-encampassing personality, 'present in his ethical, intellectual and aesthetic experience and furnishing the inspiration for creating an ideal realm of values, the kingdom of heaven–in a distressed and struggling world'.[10]

Sufism and Vedanta

Akbar is believed to have said, 'the wisdom of Vedanta is the wisdom of Sufism'. The two cults had entirely different historical background. There was an implicit danger of a gigantic clash of civilizations. Luckilly, it was avoided and there were serious attempts towards conflict resolution. It was happily found that both the socio-religious movements had the common objective of divine love binding them together: Al-Biruni was one of the few earliest observers to note, '... because in their (Sufis') notions regarding the transformation of souls and the pantheistic doctrine of the unity of God with creation, there is much in common between these systems.'[11] Al-Gazali proclaimed, 'For him whose heart is with love of God', his love is increased multifold through samaa (literally means music), 'because the fire (of love) is increased by it' and accordingly, the Sufis 'appreciated the Sanskritic poetic language of emotion and devotion from the sects devoted to the worship of Krishna and incorporated much of the philosophy of Yoga'.[12]

Devotional mysticism caught the eye of the Sufis very early because it became the handiest spiritual fodder to attract droves of native audience and helped in broadcasting their ideas and their rapid-fire acceptance in general. Here the Chishti Silsilah contributed to the greatest and widest acceptability. The 'come-one-and-all' situation suited them the most in a caste-ridden and hierarchical society. Thus, pantheism was accepted by the Sufis with open arms. So far as the other concept of 'the unity of all beings', was concerned, it was also accepted with an equal enthusiasm. This concept was inherent in Hindu spirituality. It was also accepted by the Sufis, who became the greatest advocates of transcendental culture. Their doors were thus open to one and all. Logically its acceptance went against the grain of the Shari'a. In practice, such inconvenient contradiction was sought to be overlooked for practical gains. What was gained in numbers was lost over the premises of basic ideology of Islam. Thus a dialogue had begun in right earnest between the Sufis and Sants of India. The foundations for this dialogue was laid during the times of Baba Farid. He was the first IndianMuslim saint who started the practice of regular dialogue with religious thinkers. Especially the Hindu 'Jogis' were frequent visitors to his khanqah.

There was much give-and-take between Hinduism and Islam. Both of them, Sufism and the Bhakti movement, were based on institution. While devotional mysticism may have been the legate of Bhakti, 'for instance, the idea of "surrender" (prapatti) so important to the Shri Vaishnava tradition of south India, may have been influenced by Islam (the very name of which means surrender)'. No wonder, two of the most permanent legates of Chaitanya Mahaprabhu had assumed Muslim names before their conversion to the Vaishnava cult. In fact, the Bhakti movement in its initial stages, was confined to south India, and may have received a great deal of accelerated momentum, when it came into contact with foreign ideas and men of foreign faith. The results must have been obvious. The law of nature takes over of its own volition and the things begin to move of their own accord. 'More generally, the presence of people of another faith, raising awareness of previously imagined religious possibilities, may have inspired the spread of these new, more ecstatic forms of Hinduism and predisposed conventional Hindus to accept the more radical teachings of the Bhakti poet'.[13] There were parallel developments taking place simultaneously. It was too early in the day for the Bhakti movement, during Baba Farid's days in northIndia; it was also too early in thc day for the Sufi movement in south India. At both the levels, contacts must have been informal, but their significance cannot be ignored.

Jogi Connection

The practioners of yoga are popularly known as 'Jogis' in northIndia; they are the followers of Siva as opposed to the Sants who largely follow the Vaishnava cult. They are mavericks and equally unorthodox, always on the move and communicating with all castes and creeds, as well as followers of other faiths without hesitation. Like Malangs and Qalandars among Muslims, they take hashish and bhang to forget the worldly things altogether. They hardly get on with the followers of Vishnu, whose great favourite is the playful Krishna. Traditionally, they have been the intermediaries between Sufism and the Bhakti movement. Guru Gorakhnath, believed to be the founder of the Jogi cult, is a household name in northIndia. Their mobility gives them an advantage. They feel no inhibition in conducting dialogue with all and sundry. During the medieval times, they kept the channels open by communicating with religious leaders of all brands. They also did not distinguish between Hindus and Muslims. Ranjha, the famous hero of Heer, chose to be a Jogi and had the blessings of the highest guru of the Jogi cult. The fire that blazes nonstop around the four walls of Shah Hussain's tomb during Mela Charaghan (Lahore) has all the hallmark of dhuni (blazing fire) associated with the Nath Jogis. At some shrines, these fires have been kept burning for centuries together.

Jogis played a much bigger role than a mere symbolic one. They were the agents of peace between two communities. They conveyed messages and, remember, the exchange of messages was too frequent. Jogis were not mere 'pigeon-carriers' but active agents in working out solutions. In the initial stages, there was an urgent need for sympathetic mutual understanding, which eventually resulted in terms of agreement between the Sufis and the Sants. The Jogis had universal appeal to 'the Indian-Muslim culture'. Not only did the Sufis trust them, they were highly respected among the common people. They had also access to the ruling class. Ibn Batuta writes at length of the frequent meetings Muhammad Tughlak had with the Jogis, to understand them. It came to such a pass that the Sufis and the Jogis felt very comfortable in sharing the same platform. Both of them, along with the Sants of the Bhakti movement, had a status on par in society. It did not matter that they were considered being outside the pale of Hindu and Muslim orthodoxies. The Sufi movement would have been at sea without the Jogis providing the link language. In all probability, the Jogis have a long history rooted in the Vedic tradition. Then they were known as *Vratyas* ('People who have taken vows') 'the long-haired ascetic'. The Rigveda has a romantic picturization of them by describing them as 'Long Hair holds fire, holds the drug, holds sky and earth… These ascetics swathed in wind [i.e. naked], put dirty rags on. "Crazy with asceticism, we have mounted the wind … Our bodies are all you mere mortals can see … Long-Hair, drinks from the cup, sharing the drug with Rudra (Rigveda: 10.1.36)"'.

Social Reform

The Sants were on the warpath from day one. They were up in arms against Brahminic domination. They were even prepared to question them at the ideological level. They had succeeded in cornering Brahmins, where it hurt them the most by questioning the efficacy of Hindu ritualism. Luckily for them, the Sants had arrived on the scene at the right time. The political hold of the Brahmins had weakened considerably after the Muslim intrusion. Considerable demolition of rituals had also been done by Buddhism. Especially the moral authority of the Brahmin was being questioned successfully. Brahmanism was in retreat and the Sants were right on the spot to do the next cleanup. Indirect support to the Sants was provided by the Sufis in confronting the Brahmanic hierarchy. It was virtually a war of nerves between the upper castes and the lowest hierarchy. The west wind had begun to prevail slowly and steadily over the east wind. Here, the message of equality of Islam worked as a catalytic agent for the Sants.

In the framework created by the Sants, the message of the Sufis received wide favourable response. The common people were attracted in droves to the Sants and the Sufis alike, who practically acted as twin brothers. The Sufis were, however, handicapped in one respect. They were confronted with the might of the Shari'a ('the Law') and state power. They were no longer adventurous after the execution of al-Hallaj, the Sufi saint. Here the Sants scored over the Sufis. In a nutshell, the Sufis were no less effective than the Sants in actual results. Both of them refused to accept either the Brahmins or the fundamental Islam coming in their way by questioning their respective sanctity. Medieval India was, thus, a melting pot, but by no means a reformed society. Reformation in fact was a distant goal and dream. It actually took place in Europe and not in India.

Rise of the Unprivileged

The fifth caste at the bottom was an amorphous group, but it constituted the majority of the total population. The marginalized groups were considered outside the pale of society. They had, however, specific names like Chandals, Chamars and Pulkasas. They had odd names like Apasadas ('low and excluded'), Antyajas ('Born Lost') and Siva-Pakas ('Dog Cookers'). Much later, the British addressed them by a variety of names like the Untouchables, Criminal castes, Scheduled castes, Depressed classes, Outcastes and, the last but not the least, the Pariahs. Gandhi called them Harijans and Ambedkar addressed them as the Dalits. Whatever name you call them by, they were excluded from the four-caste hierarchy of Hinduism. They were the cursed of the earth. They were artisans, workers and artistes who lived in wretched slums on the periphery of villages. They had their mud huts outside and beyond the city and town walls. They were not allowed to live within the four walls. The Sufi khanqahs proved to be heavens on earth for them. They came in droves to listen to the messages of love and egalitarianism of the Sufis.

The Sants were also not far behind. Many of the Sants came from the underprivileged class and their message went home. Man, however, does not live by spiritual slugging alone. The material world is concrete and not merely abstract. The marketing world provided the answer. The material condition of the country had changed, after the new class had arrived on the scene. They had different tastes and demands. They had a surplus economy. They felt no particular sense of discrimination against the unprivileged. There was a upsurge in demand for artisans and artistes and their products. They had a taste in manufactured goods. They had no inhibitions in coming into direct contact with those who chose to come into contact with them on a day-to-day basis. The artisans who lived on the periphery of cities and towns moved within the four walls. They had a direct channel of communication with the ruling class. The Sants and the Sufis had also instilled much confidence in them. They were conscious of their rights for the first time and decided to exercise the privilege.

Balanced Perspective

Of all the four prominent Sufi Silsilah, Chishtis had opened channels of communication with other communities. There was a change in social order, but no large scale social transformation for the better was anticipated. The changes were mere cosmetic. While Baba Farid maintained a respectful distance from the symbols of state power, others were not so circumspect during his lifetime and in following him. 'Chishti Sufi masters were powerful figures in the cultural and devotional life of the Delhi sultanate (where their followers were often influential members of the court), despite the fact that they regarded 'going to the Sultan' an equivalent of 'going to the devil'.[14] There is also much exaggeration in crediting them with establishing an environment of 'supra-or cross-religious spirituality'. It is equally hyperbolic to assert, 'The Muslim mystics, however, rose to the occasion and released synergetic forces which liquidated social, ideological and linguistic barriers between the various culture groups of India and helped in the development of a common cultural outlook'.[15] Sufis had, however, the best of times during the days of Akbar. He was obviously searching for political space, which was conveniently provided to him by the Sufis. He decided to employ the resources of the empire in the cause of pluralism. His multi-religious theological salon was a replica of the khanqah with open discussion and debate taking place among theologians of various hues and colours, and in the following picturesque words is to be discovered the King Emperor expounding his faith: 'He sought for truth amongst the dust-stained denizens of the field of reflection and consorted with every sort of weavers of pitched garments such as [Jogis, renouncers, and Sufi mystics] and other solitary sitters in the dust and insoucient recluses'.[16] Akbar the Great sought to marry the wisdom of Vedanta with the wisdom of the Sufism, thus marrying the seemingly incompatibles.

The Doctrine of Unity (Wahdat)

The Baghdad school discovered divine love as the primordial urge of human beings. It raised the battle cry of 'La-Ilaha-ll-al-Ishq' ('There is no God but ishq'). The doctrine of unity was proclaimed defiantly by al-Husain ibn Mansur al-Hallaj in his *Ana-al-Haqq* ('I am the creative truth'), for which he had to pay a heavy price. He was executed in 922 A D for heresy. He had visited the lower Sindh valley in 905 A D. He had many admirers among Sufi poets, like Bulleh Shah, Shah Husain, Shah Abdul Latif and Sachal Sarmast. Especially Bulleh Shah was a forceful advocate, who had asserted that truth must be stated whatever the cost. For him, the slogan Ana al-Haqq was no more than the word of God underlying the essential unity of God and man. This theorem went against the very grain of fundamentalist Islam, whereby man required the services of the intermediary to reach them. The Sufis had put their faith in the Hallaj thesis, but they lacked the will to assert their faith openly. In other words, the Sufis did not pronounce what they professed and chose to express their faith in muted terms. The concept of unity of man and God had come to be increasingly accepted.

The Sufis had hardly any choice in the matter in the Indian context. The concept of unity was integral to the propagation of the Bhakti movement among the large masses. The Sufi acceptance spread fast and quick due to their muted acceptance of the Doctrine of Unity. This adoption was singularly responsible for their reach beyond the Islamic framework. The Doctrine of Unity was the only language, in which they were able to communicate with the leaders of the Bhakti movement in northIndia. Ultimately, the Sufis saw light at the end of the tunnel. The Sufis, especially the Chishti and Qadria sisilahs, adopted the Doctrine of Unity wholesale with the flux of time. Divine love came to be regarded as 'the backbone of the mystic experience' in the Sufi tradition in India. It was variously propagated as 'the restless love of God', 'love for love's sake', 'love of God', 'pure love of God', 'divine love as summum bonum', 'overflowing love of God', 'ishq' and la- Ilaha-Illa-al-ishq ('There is no God but ishq'). The Sufis ultimately fell in line with the Bhakti movement: "Bhakti has been defined as the worship of a personal deity in a spirit of love, as personal faith in personal God, love for him as for a human being, the dedication of everything to his service, and the attainment of 'moksha'".[17]

Pantheistic Undercurrents

The doctrine of the 'Unity of all Being' is very much inherent in the Vedanta thinking. It constitutes the core of Hindu spirituality. Pantheistic mysticism is a mantra common to Sufi and the Bhakti movement and it has turned out to be a paying proposition for the Sufis: 'The pantheistic mysticism of the Upanishads, the devotional mysticism mainly in the Vaisnavite line and Sahajiya movement offered Sufism a ready field and this will account for the speedy growth and spread of Sufistic faith in India'.[18] Sufis were equally admirers of the Sanskritic poetic language with its special stress on 'emotion and devotion'. It was equally true of the worshippers of Krishna and the philosophy of devotion. The dance and music component with the kirtan as the essential ingredient of the Krishna philosophy, coupled with the yoga practices of Jogis of going high, fascinated the Sufis no end.

The Islamic mysticism of the love of God also had parallels in the Bhakti tradition. It was next to impossible to keep pure and simple love away from the erotic emotion. Divine love logically leads to the theory of aesthetic emotions (rasa) in which Shringara rasa (erotic emotions) tend to predominate. It is vividly reflected in the association of the gopis with Krishna. There is, thus, difficulty in drawing a line of demarcation between the divine and the erotic love, because those express emotions of devotion and emotion similar in actual practice: 'In court literature, the Sanskrit theory of the aesthetic emotions (rasa), particularly the erotic emotions' is fused with the Islamic metaphors of the love of God to produce a Sufi narrative simultaneously religious and erotic, the romance made their hero a Jogi and their heroine a beautiful Indian woman.'[19]

The best of the Sufi literature in northIndia is in poetic form, as in romances like Heer, wherein divine love is best expressed in erotic love of man longing for an ideal woman. It is actually a symbolism for divine love. Sufis have, thus, followed in the ancient Indian tradition by their utter commitment to emotion and devotion.

Indian Roots

Sufism in India had a deep Indian connection, The Chishti cult is said to be essentially Indian in spirit. Its stress on devotional music and mystical poetry ranked it along with the Nath Jogis,Buddhist mystics and Vaishnava Bhaktas. The Qadria cult is said to be still much more Indian, Dara Shikoh had translated the Yoga Vashista and the Upanishad, his was the first translation in Persian of the Upanishad. Even Baba Farid did not perform in vaccume, he was preceded by the Siddhacharyas, followers of the Buddhist Sahajiya cult and the Nath Jogis who employed local dialects for versification in order to express extatic love for the Absolute. Sufis were influenced by Central Asian Buddhism too.

17

The Aesthetics of Sufism

MADHO Lal Husain was a Sufi with a difference. He danced, sang and drank. When drunk, he would dance, sing his compositions and preach the virtues of his brand of the Sufi cult. He was usually drunk and also brimful of divine love. He was not conventional, but always purposeful and in control of the situation: 'Doubt vanished and doubtless is established, therefore I, devoid of qualities, dance. If I play with the Beloved (God), I am ever a happy woman. The liar's face has been blackened and the lover's word proved right. Because doubt has vanished and doubtlessness is established, therefore, I, devoid of qualities, dance'.[1]

Dance and Music

Dance and music were integral to the Sufi practices throughout the centuries. The Sufis practiced *samaa*, which means hearing of music. This is the essence of Sufism al-Gazli said, 'For him whose heart is with the love of God, Samaa is momentous... because the fire increased by it.'[2] Bhakti movement was equally inspired and took to kirtan in a big way. Sikhism followed suit. Gurudwaras usually recruited a band of musicians called rahababis of Muslim descent. This tradition was followed religiously generation after generation. Sikh gurus were specially fond of music. The Indian classical music had a new lease of life through the practice of samaa and kirtan. The result was new forms of musical practices. The rahababis who were the principal singers of the Darbar Sahib sang on the pattern of the qawals. Indeed, the Sufis invented the qawali and popularized it. Qawalis have been immortalized by Amir Khusraw, whose name has become synonymous with it. Qawals are particularly fond of Amir Khusraw's qawalis. They and the audience never have enough of it:

> *'Thou have taken away from identity by a single glance,*
> *By making drink from the cup of love,*
> *Thou has intoxicated me by a single glance'.*

Equally, dance is integral to the Sufi tradition. The combination of samaa and mystical dance is integral to divine love. Swirling dance of the order of Meveleviyah, The Dancing Dervishes, is purposeful. It induces the mystical theifiyar, i.e. 'the Enchanted State'. Maulana Jalal-ud-Din Muhammad Rumi (b. 1209) is the founder of the order of Dancing Dervishes. The orthodox Sufi felt uncomfortable with the *samaa*, because it went against the spirit of the Shari'a, but they were equally reconciled to it, because the music had come to be associated in the popular mind, as the very essence of Sufism. 'Of new religions and social attitudes among those standing outside the orthodox communities: attitudes which, on consideration, found expression in the 14th century in a vigorous popular literature.'[3]

Revivalism and Sufism

Islamic spirituality in India was undoubtedly imported from Persia and Central Asia, but it had incorporated elements from Buddhism. After all, Buddhism was the dominant religion in large parts of Central Asia before the advent of Islam. It is a concept of the monastic order and was appropriated by the Sufi orders. It also got contaminated when it came into contact with the indigenous spiritual traditions, and equally made a counter impact on them. Buddhism, Nath Jogis and Sants were not organized and formal religions, but a way of life with considerable degree of flexibility. The Islamic spiritual tradition in India also made note of flexibility in Indian spiritual tradition and also adopted it in confronting the fundamental tendencies inherent in Islam. At another level, there was a considerable interplay between the two of them. Buddhism emphasized the democratic order of things. It also emphasized the preaching of religion through the medium of popular languages. All this must have been noted by the early Sufis.

There was also an exchange of ideas, expressions and practices. The Sufi *dhiky*, that is repetition, vocal or oral, of the divine name, is at the heart of the Sufi practices. It has been adopted by Nath Jogis and Sants and named jap or japa. Its higher stage leads to ajapajapa, the silent or interiorized remembrance. This state is described as that of *smarna* or *samirana*. These terms were also taken up by Sikh gurus in a big way. Equally, the Sants lapped up these concepts. In no time, Hindus and Muslims alike in north India were following the Sants and Sufis without any sense of discrimination. Indeed, the entire north India was speaking the same language. The *namo* or *nama* was threatening to replace Allah and Ishwar. In the words of Vaudeville, 'The Supreme importance of sumiran or nam-sumiran, as means of merging with God, is constantly emphasized by Kabir himself and by the Sant poets, as well as the whole Sikh tradition beginning with Nanak'.[4]

Universal Appeal

The universal appeal of the Jogi in the Indan-Muslim culture is truly phenomenal. They functioned as the linkmen between Sufis and the Bhakti movement. They were presumed to have a degree of objectivity due to their Saivite background, contrasted with the Sants who were largely of the Vaishnava adherence. There was also a degree of underlying hostility and competition that continued to nag their relationships. The Sufis and the Jogis, however, got along famously. At one time the entire north India and large chunks of Central Asia were the land of Buddhist converts. In fact, Jogis and Sufis filled the vacuum left by the decline of Buddhism. Undoubtedly they shared common ground on several scores, but they have also functioned as countermanding forces. At another level, the Jogis have been successful in checkmating the inroads of Indian Islam by offering similar packages to the popular mass. Jogis truly formed a bridge between Islam and Hinduism, but they also functioned as a block by offering similar packages. They were eminently successfully in packaging religion as spirituality. Rituals had no place in their scheme of things, or, at least, their practices like shaving of head, wearing of ring in ear, or putting on saffron clothes and carrying a begging bowl and musical instrument was intended for a mere identification of the brand.

Indeed the Jogi brand was a landmark in the spiritual history of India. There was a great deal of commonality between them, especially in their belief in one God, burying the dead, and opposition to caste being the most outstanding common feature. Vaudeville has observed that the Jogis were able to form a bridge between Muslim and non-Muslim interpretations, because of their monotheism, non-conformism, their opposition to caste distinctions and their rejection of rules of ritual purity. 'Their conception of the all-prevailing Godhead of Parama-Shiva or the invisible guru', continues to 'make them more acceptable to Muslims than to average smarta Hindu'. However, it is important to remember that for these common grounds, Nathism not only paved the way for Islam in India, but also, on the other hand, checked its greater expansion by enlarging the spectrum of indigenous spirituality'.[5] The checkmating was equally done by the Shakti movement. Jogis played a greater role than merely checkmating Sufi and Bhakti movements. They were the symbosis of three great traditions of India: Yoga, Buddhism and the Upanishads.

Nathpanthi Jogis

Very little is known about the life of the legendary Gorakhnath, believed to be the founder of the Nanthpanthi sect, which is also known as Gorakhnathis or kanphata-the slit-eared Jogis. The rise of Nathpanthis coincided with the demise of Buddhism in India. It filled the vacuum, in competition with Brahminism. Thus, Buddhist and Tantric influences are apparently very much there. Nathpanthis must have been ranked as the overflow from the Buddhist mainstream. It has an obvious Buddhist overload. Significantly they were headquarted at the Kanpatha monastery at Tilla, in the district of Jhelum (Punjab) in the land of Buddhist Gandhara. Its head is called mahant or pir, indicating the Sufi connection. In fact, Sufis and Jogis began to come together from the 14th century onwards.

Yoga practices fascinated the Sufis, who came to adopt some of them. They equally fascinated the masses. The Jogis' mobility also gave them an enormous advantage over others. They must have been in direct competition with the Dancing Dervishes. Folk literature is full of praise for them. The Sufi poets of Sindh, Saraiki and Punjab adopted the Nath cult and helped to propagate it on a nondenominational basis. Sufis and Jogis communicated often and thus helped to develop new ideas common to them. Obviously, such healthy contacts helped to develop thoughts outside the framework of fundamentalist religion. Both of them were monotheist, which also influenced Sikhism during its formative days. Spiritual beliefs rather than formal religion provided a common ground and platform to Hindus, Muslims and Sikhs alike. The spirit of the sentiment was expressed in a doha attributed to Gorakhnath:

'The Hindus call on Ram
The Muslims on Khuda.
The Jogi calls on the Invisible One,
In whom there is neither Ram nor Khuda'.

The resonance of the same expression is to be heard in Nanak and numerous Sufi poets of Punjab and Sindh. There is so much commonality between the Sufis and the Jogis, it overwhelms you. 'The Nath Jogis and Sufis shared some points of view, and also a comparable status outside the pale of Hindu and Muslim orthodoxy. The two groups appear to have found a degree of stimulus and support in each other from the time when they first came into contact in north India, and to have influenced each other's practices and view point Both won reputation among the common people for the sanctity of some of their members or for their supposed magical power. Nath ideas continue to have an impact on Sufi thought in later centuries.

The existence of common ground between Naths and Sufis encouraged liberal thought.

Two Icons

Baba Farid shinning light of Sufism in India, believed in a just political order. He had healthy doubts about organized religion. He expressed his doubts in aphorisms like, 'Fasting is half the way, and other things such as prayer and haj are half the way'. He was an ascetic who was sensitive to the needs and wishes of the people, and their service was his lifelong mission. His khanqah was a refuge from injustice. He was a morality free person. Prof. Mujeeb was to note that he arose above all the 'theological limitations' and he further noted that Baba Farid chose 'not to mention the Shari'a or Tariqah in this context'. For him Sheikh Fariduddin was more of a social reformer than religious leader. That was the essence of Sufism for him. The major role played by him was reconstructed in a new system of values with emphasis on moral and spiritual values in the Indian context. His philosophy of life is contained in the following words:

> *'Poverty, rejection of any political or social support, constant conflict with the needs and the sorrows as well as the weaknesses and vices of the people were the anvil on which the Sufi's personality was hammered out. From whatever aspect he is viewed, he stands out as an example'.*[6]

Baba Farid was not equally matched by those who followed him except for Mian Mir, who had little enthusiasm for Haj. He also emphasized the spirit rather than the form of the Shari'a. His was a model of spiritual life. In addition, he was a celibate. Dara Shikoh was his pupil. This enabled him to spread his teachings wide and fast. Since Lahore was the cultural capital of Punjab, it enabled him to influence the subsequent Sufi movement in north India. Baba Farid and Mian Mir talked in undertones, questioning the compatability of the Shari'a with spirituality. Those like Shah Husain, Sultan Babu and Bulleh Shah, who followed them had no such inhibitions. They were more poets and less philosophers and thinkers. They were, however, ingrained in spirituality and equally they were Sufis at the grassroots level. They were inclined to fall in line with Sheikh Sa'd' who said, Allah 'the life in the world is nothing but sport'. Shah Husain viewed life as play. He must have been inspired by the playful Krishna, engaged in *krida* (play) with his Gopis. Thus, play is 'play since it offers joy and joy is the chief expression of human freedom with his spiritual endeavour with which Husain employed himself.'[7] Religion, faith, beliefs, morality, playfulness, pleasure, human freedom and spirituality get together in the same chain.

Debating the Shari'a

'To be or not to be' is the famous Hamletian dialogue. This is also the dilemma that has confronted the Islamic world throughout the centuries. Those who swear allegiance to the Shari'a, are inclined to be vocal against those like Sufis, Dervishes and Qalandars, inclined to deviate in varying degrees. The deviants have been termed *be-shar*. They have deviated in thought and practice from orthodox Islam. The law had the support of the state. The results have been very devastating in extreme cases like Timur crossing the Indus in December 1398. "He had 100,000 Hindus slain with the sword of Holy War, and Maulana Nassiruddin, one of the chief ecclesiastes, who in all his life had never slaughtered a sheep put 15 Hindus to sword".[8] It should be interesting to recapitulate the antecedents of Saiyid Nur-ud-Din Mubarak Ghaznavi, an important khalifa of Sheikh Sihab-ud-Din Suhrawardi. Ultimush appointed him Shaiku'l-Islam, and he was called by the people of Delhi, Mir-I-Dehli (Lord of Delhi). He advocated the enforcement of Shari'a to be entrusted to officials. His definition of Muslims excluded non-Sunnis. He had definite and authoritative views on every subject on earth:

> *'The (rulers) should promote Islamic customs, promulgate the commands of the Shari'a, enforcing what is endowed and prohibiting what is forbidden by it, and uproot kufra (infidelity), shirk (polytheism) and idolatry. If they cannot fully uproot kufr and shirk they should make every effort to disgrace and humiliate Hindus, mushriks (polytheists) and idolaters, for they are inveterate enemies of God and the Prophet Muhammad. They should not tolerate the sight of Hindus, and in particular, they*

> *should exterminate the Brahmins, who are leaders of heretics and disseminators of heresy. They should not allow kafirs (infidels) and mushriks to lead an honorable life or assign to their high office.'*[9]

Progressive Currents

While the ulemas were arranged on one side, the Sufis and the mystics denounced them as ignorant of the underlying spirit of the Shari'a. Even the Sufis were not united on this score. Naqshbandis and Suhrawardis were in the drivers' seat as upholders of the law, but the Chishtis and Qadrias had begun to move away from the formalist position. 'There came a time in the later half of the 16th century, when the Qadrias increasingly turned unorthodox and unconformist. The Chishtis equally began to shift their position, with leads provided by Khwaja Mu'in-ud-Din Auliya and Baba Farid, with emphasis on the concept of an ecstatic love for God, with no 'differenciation between the lover, the beloved and love itself'.[10]

The Khwaja was in the opposite camp, confronting Nur-ud-Din Mubarak. His philosophy of life is summed up in one of his famous saying: 'The Hajis walked around the Ka'ba, but the '*arifs* (spiritualists) circumambulated the heart'. Equally the following aphorism enunciated his philosophy of life: 'The most superior kind of worship was to assist the helpless and to feed the hungry. All those possessing the following three virtues were friends of God: munificence, like an ocean, kindness like the sunshine and humility like the earth'.[11] The Chishtis had begun to move away gradually. They were more concerned with the moral character of human beings, rather than observance of religious practices. The Khwaja was equally backed by Baba Farid. He had moved away from the law and the state as the pillars of Shari'a. Here was an upright moral man who set an example to be emulated. This attitude began to pay dividends to the Chishti Sufi saints. They kept the door ajar by talking in the native language. The established faiths in India were less of formal religions, and more a way of life. Spiritualism appealed to them. The Chishti Sufi had also adopted the native language. It was like talking heart to heart. The Chishtis had discovered a magic world. They logically had more adherents than believers.

Ideological Wars

The historic fight was ideological in nature. Initial skirmishes and battles are bound to lead to unending wars. There are no pauses in ideological wars due to the fundamental incompatibilities; violent resistance is bound to come to pass, due to the churning of several spiritual traditions developing within the larger Islamic tradition. Differences arise due to dichotomy between 1) the very conception of Sufism, 2) the relationship with the state, 3) on responses to local cultures, and 4) in defining the place of law. While Qadiriahs and Chishtis are closer to the Persian tradition, the *Naqshbandis* and *Suhrawardis* are nearer to the Sufi Arab tradition. The liberal tradition of Sufism has emanated from Iran. It is essentially the Shia tradition. The differences go back to the days following the death of the Prophet. The Arab school emphasises the unity of the state and religion. This was actually the classical idea of the community in which the rulers and ruled were partners. Such an enunciation would not work in the Indian context. The Muslims are a minority, hence unable to make the majority community fall in line except temporally. The numbers are against them. Thus the Chishtis and Qadrias were farsighted in bowing to the reality gracefully.

Akbar's Plural Order

The see-saw battle between the ruling elite and the common man was actually the running battle between the conservatives and liberals, between status quoists and changers, and, finally, between closed minds and reformers. Eventually the battles were won and lost through state intervention. Emperor Akbar was a breath of fresh air. He massacred 20,000 noncombatants after the battle of Chitor. He, however, realized soon that winning the battle of the heart was a greater achievement than winning wars. He decided to lay the foundations of a pluralistic society. In the words of his chieftain, Abu'l Fazil, 'He sought for truth amongst the dust-strewn denizens of the field of reflection and consorted with every sort of wearers of packed garments such as [Jogis, renouncers, and Sufi mystics] and other solitary sitters in the dust and insouciant recluses'.[12] To Akbar is attributed the following saying: 'all religions are equally true or equally illusory'.[13] It helped because Islam was no longer the state religion. The diktat of the Shari'a no longer prevailed. The Ulema and the Quazi had been choked. Interreligious dialogue between Hindu and Muslim intellectuals and thinkers was encouraged. He used to hold a series of multireligious theological salons at his capital Fatehpur Sikri in which Sunni, Shia, Ismaili, Sufi, Saiva, Vaishanava, Jews, Christian and Jain thinkers participated. He even used to invite non-believers like Charvakas or Lokayatis to present their point of view. He equally invented a new religion called Din-e-Ilahi.

Those were the best of times for liberal tradition. Especially the Sufis had their day. With Akḥar's death, this space came to an end. The fundamentalist forces were bound to react and assert themselves. Ahmed Sirhindi was the father of new orthodoxy. He denounced Suffism as unIslamic. He once again reaffirmed the unity of the state and religion. He pronounced the classical idea of the community in which the rulers and ruled were partners. Dara Shikoh, like Akbar, was a breath of fresh air, but he was physically eliminated by his younger brother, Aurangzeb. Liberalism had been smothered and the Shari'a was the order of the day. The debate, however, did not end with Aurangzeb and it shall continue interminably. Liberal tradition is a way of life and practiced widely. It shall not die in Islam. After all, it has the sanction of eminent Sufis like Baba Farid and is totally backed by a whole range of eminent Sufi poets of the Punjab. Baba Farid had pronounced definitively that the Shari'a in the hands of the fundamentalists was an instrument of coercion.

New Literature

'From the twelfth century A D, the history of India represents a history of contact, conflict and compromise – political, cultural and religious. In this period of contact, Sufiism is transformed in India, could very well serve as a medium of compromise and it is this possibility that may be held responsible for the wide-spread popularity of the Sufiite thoughts' writes S Dasgupta. Sufism shall live, survive and flourish so long as men long for freedom. Liberal values are the cherished values of mankind. Both Sufism and Bhakti movements are points of the same transition and thus shape common heritage and history. Indeed, the Bhakti movement provided the impetus to the liberal Sufi movement. The other fact that favoured Sufism was the natural religiosity of the Indian people. Sainthood has a special place of honour in their scheme of things. They thronged the khanqas to listen to the words of wisdom, uttered by Sufi saints. Very soon, the Sufis came to recognize that, the best form of communication was through the local dialect. The Sufis not only adopted the medium to convey their message, but also set the ball rolling by creating an entirely new genre of literature. Thus they were destined to give a new forum of literature to the moribund Prakrit all over the country. Things began to happen, exactly coinciding with the rise of parallel Sufi and Bhakti movements. The Sikhs were the first to adopt the local languages, Punjabi and Saraiki. The actual ferment occurred subsequently. The 15th to the 18th centuries transformed the situation all over India. The Sufis and Bhaktas were together responsible for the transformation, and they also gave filip to new literature that emerged during the post-colonial period of the nineteenth century.

Indian Languages

Kabir is believed to have said, 'Sanskrit is like water in a well, the language of the people is a flowing stream'. He was speaking on behalf of the entire Sant community. Socially, the Sants belonged to the lowest strata of Indian society. Some of them were even atishudras, ranked at the lowest bottom. They were illiterates and had no Brahminical training and education. They were poor. They had no acquaintance with Sanskrit and they were totally ignorant of the Brahminical texts. They were, however, iconoclasts critical of the social and cultural establishment. They spoke only in local languages. They found buddies in the Sufis, who were equally anxious to communicate in local languages. The Sants were possessed of native talent. They were willing to experiment. They were also anti-establishment. They were the pioneers. They opened up vistas of new literary forms. The Sufi saints and Sants had come to a similar conclusion simultaneously. The new Indian languages were born with new literary formats.

Baba Farid (1173-1265) also composed in Persian. The local language Saraiki had a new birth under his inspiration. His Sufi poetry gave the language a formal status. Along with Saraiki, its sister languages, Punjabi and Sindhi, had a new birth. He may also have presided over the birth of Hindavi, the forefather of modern Hindi and Urdu. Hindavi must have been born on account of compulsions of communicating with visitors to his khanqah. His poetry also gave expression to this compulsion to communicate in the local lingo. His poetry is recited widely and its inclusion in the *Guru Granth Sahib* is a standing tribute to its sterling quality.

Amir Khusraw

The other name which comes to mind after the name of Baba Farid is that of Amir Khusraw. Nearly a century separates both of them. He also wrote in Persian and Hindavi. He was the most loyal disciple of Shaikh Nizam-u'd-Din Auliya. He is also the most famous poet of Hindavi. He was totally devoted to his master, who returned the compliment equally. The Sheikh paid the highest tribute to his disciple by asserting, 'There are few comparable to Khusraw in poetry or prose'. His favourite phrase about his favourite disciple, 'What more, Oh Turk'. Khusraw's love of Indian fauna and flora and its *tehzib* is wellknown. He invented the musical instrument, the *sitar*. He also invented several popular Indian music forms like the Qawali. His poetry is most melodious and has a natural rhythm about it. No Qawali session is complete without a Khusraw verse. His most famous verse is about mourning the death of Sheikh Nizam- u'd-Din Auliya:

> *'The beloved sleeps on her couch with her face*
> *covered with her curled back,*
> *Oh Khusraw! Return to your home*
> *for the entire world is now covered by night.'*

Khusraw lost his voice after the death of his master, and died after six months.

Along with Baba Farid and Amir Khusraw is to be ranked Saiyid Muhammad, Yusuf al-Hussain (1321-1422), more popularly known as Saujed Gisu Darazi and Khwaja Banda Nawaz. The recitation of Hindawi music at *samaa* at all Sufi centres became popular during his lifetime. This was indeed his forte. The combination of Hindavi songs of Baba Farid,

Amir Khusraw and Shaikh Hamidu'd-Din Nagauri used to be recited at *samaa* gatherings. Saiyid Gisu Darazi discovered the talisman of Indian verse and music in unison. He wisely recognized that 'each language was endowed with a characteristic of its own' and to him none was as effective as Hindavi for through it esoteric ideas could be clearly expressed, Hindavi music, the Saiyid believed, was also subtle and elegant, penetrating deeply into the heart and arousing greatness. When hearing it people became aware of their faults and therefore, it was natural, to the Saiyid that Hindavi music was becoming increasing popular.[14]

Unfortunately most of the songs have been lost and only a few are available. The tyranny of Persian literature was a closed chapter. Not only because the Indian languages were communicable, but they had the rhythm and subtlety that touched the tenderest chords of the human heart, and also gave the message clear and strong. The age of Indian languages had arrived. This also initiated the Hindu interest in Sufism, as it had evoked much interest in the Hindu faith among the Sufis. It was only a matter of time when the Sufi poets adopted the Hindu beliefs, philosophy and thought, some of them being accused, in turn, by their contemporaries as the propagators of the Vedanta.

Female Renaissance

Love and devotion are very special to mysticism, described often as the message of love. Passion and Devotion are keynotes of Bhakti and Sufi cults. Passion and devotion are special to womanhood. Baba Farid employs the female voice in his verse. His example has been followed by most Sufi saints of India. He sings of love and separation at the same time. Though he was the foremost legate of Sufi tradition in the subcontinent, he had worthy female predecessors abroad. One of them was Rabi'ah Adwych (d A D 801) who was popularly known as Rubiah Bussi. She preceded Baba Farid by four centuries. She sang of 'love for love's sake'. Closer home, Jayadeva, of *Gita Govinda* fame (a contemporary of Baba Farid) celebrated devotion and love of the lovelorn Gopikas for Krishna. Radha, the married Gopika, epitomises the idealisation of womenhood. In the words of Shrivatsa Goswami, Radha was the ultimate 'personification of love', equally the 'cultural symbol of woman in love' and indeed the ultimate tribute, the 'quintessence of all that is finest in human existence'. Bhakti has been defined by him as 'the highest state of love'. No wonder, the Vaishnavites greet eachother to this day with 'Sri Radhe'.

Baba Farid was no lone voice in the cause of womanhood. His Saraiki successor Sufi poets like Bulleh Shah, Shah Husain and Warris Shah, no less eminent in their own right, followed his tradition in the cause of womanhood. *Trinjan* (spinning wheel) became a woman's social motif, to express her freedom. Gandhiji's *charkha* became many things to her at the same time. The economy of the spinning wheel enabled her to be an active participant in the household economy. It also became a symbol of collectivity. a social club and window to the world which was otherwise closed to her during medieval times. Above all, the spinning wheel became a symbol of her spirituality, similar to the Buddha's wheel. Who can forget Shah Husain's famous verse:

'Main Bairagan
Main Bairagan Brindaban ki'
(I am a devotee and I have come from Vrindavan.)

Bulleh Shah's Albeli (maverick) gives a hint of radical feminism in her defiance:

'Na main vihai na main kunwari
beta god kedanvang'
(Neither am I married nor am I unmarried
I shall bring up my child as a single mother)

Baba Farid does not seek to romanticise womanhood. He presents a rational image by empowering her. This is cause for celebration as his woman is a role model for the future generation. She is empowered to take decisions by herself.

Womanhood Celebrated

Hats off to Shah Abdul Latif Bhita'i, who, in his classic *Risalo* has paid the finest tribute to womanhood. It has been said of Shakespear that he has heroins in his plays but no heroes. This is equally true of the Sindhi poet, whose heroines reflect the 'vastness and solitariness of the desert' and equally represent the true spirit of turbulent Sindhu or Mihran in their genes. *Risalo* is said to be the *Bible* of the Sindhis, cutting across caste, religion and community and a tribute to the pan-Indian spirit underlying it.

Shah's language and conception are 'almost pure Prakrit'. The work is a celebration of womanhood. His seven heroins are the 'Seven Queens of Sindh'.They invariably hail from common stock and are women of heroic proportions asserting their right to decision-making by seeking their own destiny, defying social order and consequently meeting their tragic ends heroically. Their constant quest for love is equated to man's constant and relentless endeavour to reach out to the personal God in one-to-one cosy relationship. The seven women Shah Abdul Latif has immortalised are Maruyi, Mumal, Sasui, Noori,Suhini, Heer and Leela. Contrast them with their lovers:Umar,Rano,Punhoon, Jam Tamachi, Meher, Ranjha and Chanesar who pale into insignificance as side actors, especially when contrasted with their high-profile lovers.

Bhakti and Sufi movements owe a great deal to women thinkers. The most distinguished among them was the Sufi saint Ŗabi'ah Adwych, who lived in the eighth century. Mirabai, the princess of Marwar (1462-1546), has contributed a great deal to the cause of the Bhakti movement and its renaissance. She was the Radha of medieval India, singing passionately, her devotion to Krishna. She was versatile in several languages, as the pioneering poet. She sang in old western Rajasthani, Brajbhasha and Khariboli, thus triggering the growth of several Indian languages. Lal Ded (14th century), who preceded Mira, was a pioneer in the Kashmiri language. If there was no Lal Ded, there would not have been any Kashmiri language as we know it today.She was definitely more profound, with 'a much wider knowledge and experience than Mira'. Lal Ded bridged the gap between Rabi'ah and Mira, This is unique as Lal Ded preceded Kabir and had no one to show her the way.

Lal Ded

The 14th century Kashmiri mystic still remains the most important spiritual and literary figure in the pan-Indian context. She is also known as Lalleswari or Laila Jogini. The Muslims call her 'Lal-arifa'. Lal Ded or Grandmother Lal, literary means 'Lal the womb', evoking the Mother Goddess connection. Kashmir is known to be the home of the Saivite cults and here was a woman literay figure who sought to bridge the gap between the Jogis and Sufis by speaking the language of poetry. The very fact that her poems are dear to both, the Hindus and the Muslims, is also a great tribute to her. Kashmiri as a modern language, owes her a great deal. She, singlehandedly, ensured the smooth transition of the Apabhransha-Prakrit tradition to the common man. At the same time, the language of her poetry maintained a link with mother Sanskrit, and her poetry is called *Vakh*. It resonates with the word 'Vak' and or sppeech or voice, and can be used in singular or plural. Ranjit Hosekote upgrades her by asserting, "Lalla's Vakhs bear the imprint of an ongoing linguistic and cultural change, which is recorded at the level of form, imagery, concept and vocabulary. Some archak words and phrases remain embeded in these poems, clues attesting to an earlier structure of the Kashmiri language. We find Sankrit terms and phrases and that have Hindu-Buddhist universe of meaning. These Sanskrit elements share conceptual and linguistic phrase, in the Vakhs, with more Arabic and Persianistic literature". (The Speaking Tree, June 12,2011). Here are the Bhakti, Jogi and Sufi movements seamlessly joined together.

In the Driving Seat

From the 14th century, the Sufi poets were largely free of the tyranny of Persian language and had opted for Indian themes and wrote masnavis in Hindi and other Indian languages. To their credit, the Sufis were first to adopt local and regional languages for the propagation of their beliefs. They were, thus, able to put across new ideas in the local jargon. They were confronted with an entirely new environment. Kabir, Guru Nanak and other Sants had prepared the ground for themselves and the Sufis found it convenient to walk into the vacuum.

The lead was also provided by the Chishtis of Bijapur during the 15th and 16th centuries. They were the precursors of Urdu language via Deccani. Earlier, Amir Khusraw had popularized the Hindavi, which was the precursor of modern Hindi and Urdu. Baba Farid was, however, the pioneer who wrote and spoke Saraiki. The Sikh gurus provided the helping hand by pronouncing the formal birth of Punjabi. The Sants on their part were working overtime for the revival of the Prakrits elsewhere as modern Indian languages. New forms of literary expressions emerged. Those had all to do with the poetic verse. Those included *kafi, baramah, athvara, quissa* (story), *dohra/doha* and *var* (ode). The dohra remains the most popular verse form in the Punjab and other regions of India. Dohra was popularized by Baba Farid, who employed the indigeneous dialects as the vehicle of expression of divine reality. The byproduct was the universalization of the Sufi legacy. It became a preeminent vehicle of poetic expression in Sufi and Sant literature. The Sikh gurus preferred dohra as the vehicle of expression.

Kabir-The Charismatic

Kabir stands out prominently among the Sants.. He stood out as a poet for his mystical experience in local dialects, and for the quality of the lyrical content in his poetry. He was not bound by any conventional literary traditions of the Sanskrit language. He experimented with new forms like dohas, sakhi and doctrinal poems. He was critical of ritualism and priest-craft. He was proud of being a julaha (weaver). Very little is known about his life. It is also difficult to single out his genuine output of poetic work with much certainty. Guru Granth Sahib contains a large body of his work. Its authentic authority is thus beyond doubt. His own saying 'No Hindu, No Turk' explains the man. Kabir was fully accomplished to be a Sufi or a Sant, or Bhakt, or all at the same time. Kabir has been called a muwahhid (follower of the Wahdat-ul-Wajud), which, in other words, means that he was a believer in the concept 'Unity of Being' and a believer in Islamic pantheism.

When Shaikh Sa'du' Allah (d. 1522), a contemporary of Kabir, was asked whether Kabir was a 'Muslim or Kafir', the reply was that he was a *muwahhid.* 'The Sheikh was then asked whether a muwahhid differed from both. Shaikh Sa'dullah replied that "the truth was difficult to understand and such knowledge could only be acquired gradually".[15] There was also no peace for his dead body. It was claimed by both the Hindus and Muslims. Doniger has no doubt that Kabir 'consciously rejected both Hinduism and Islam, nevertheless built his own religious world out of what he would have regarded as the ruins of Hinduism and Islam, as did many of the great Sufi saints at whose shrines many Hindus continue to worship'.[16] Obviously Kabir had a larger purpose in his mind. He was attempting to build an alternative infrastructure. On the one hand, he was trying to dismantle the superstructure of both the religions, but at another level he was trying to bring them together. There is a band of Kabirpanthis, who have existed to this day, 'with the social identity of a Muslim and both the earlier family background and the belief system of a Hindu, being a weaver, he weaved the woof of Islam into the warp of Hinduism (or, if you prefer the reverse) to produce a religion of his own that emphatically distanced itself from both.[17] There is a mention of Kabir twice in the Ain-i-Akbari. He is described as muwahhid on these occasions.

But there is another side of the picture. He was actually a Vaishnava *bairagi* (mendicant) and a follower of Ramananda. He was not a founder of the *Niraguna* Bhakti cult, but he happened to be its major exponent in northern India. The Nameless God without any attributes was adopted by the Sikh gurus via the Nirguna philosophy in a big way, as compared to the *Saguna* bhakti, which was adopted by the followers of Vishnu in different incarnations (avatars). Kabir was influenced by the concept of Absolute Reality expounded by the Naths. Its compatability with the Wahdat al-Wajud is to be noted. He says:

> *'As the bubbles of the river are accounted for water and*
> *blend with the water of the Ocean,*
> *So the man who looketh on all with an equal eye, shall become*
> *pure and blend with the infinite'.*[18]

Kabir was a multi-personality, impossible to classify. He was a Sufi, because he has been designated muwahhid. To the same extent he was an iconoclast to the Islamic fundamentalist. He was a Vaishnav bairagi, but refused to be a follower of saguna Bhakti. He was an exponent of the opposing concept of niraguna Bhakti. He was also close to the Nath *bairagis*, on account of his pantheistic beliefs. It brought him very near to the Wahdut ul-Wajud world view. Kabir was here, there and nowhere.

Kabir is one of the most charismatic personalities of medieval India. He also continues to be an enigmatic personality, about whose personal life still little is known. His parentage is obscure. His religious background is debatable. His date of birth is a subject of dispute. Whether he started as a Sufi and then turned to Bhakti, or he was both at the same time, is merely conjecture. He is believed to be a disciple of Ramanuja, the famous saint who also inspired Guru Nanak, equally Kabir influenced the Sikh gurus. There is, however, no evidence to support it. He spent most of his life at Benaras and thus there are landmarks associated with him that would establish his identity. The verses in the *Adi Granth*, the Kabir *Granthavali* and the *Beijak* (Treasury) are the only testimony that he ever exsisted. Then there are distinguished Hindi scholars who argue that there is no evidence to establish that he ever wrote a single line in his entire life. There are the Kabirpanthis who claim to be his followers. There was even no place for him after his death. Both Hindus and Muslims laid claim to his body. Abu'l Fazal, in his Ain-i-Akbari, refers to two of his tombs, one at Puri and the other at Rahaipur (Avadh). He was, however, secular to the core. Thus he was ahead of his times. The common terminology he employed was to express that the Ultimate Reality was essentially secular. He used words like Brahma, Om, Niranjan, Kahna, Vishnu, Rama, Krishna, Hari, Govind, Murari, Visambhar, Gopinath, Jagannath, Madhava, Sain, Allah, Rahim, Karim and Khuda.

This much is, however, certain. He denounced ritualism and priest-craft. It was ditto for idol worship. To this extent he was an iconoclast Hindu advocating reformation. He goes on to say: 'Better than that stone is a hand-mill which grindeth corn for the world to eat'.[19] He had little respect for Hindu and Muslim faiths alike. He extended autonomy to all, urging thinking human beings to chalk out a separate faith for themselves:

'The Muslamans accept the Tariqat;
The Hindus, the Vedas and Puranas;
But for me the books of both religions are useless.
A man ought to study divine knowledge
To some extent to instruct his heart'.[20]

Collective Leader

Kabir was one of the most prominent spiritual leaders of medieval India. Like Husain Shah, he was a julaha (weaver), whose community was the earliest converts to Islam, but who continued to retain their Hindu identity substantially. Again, like Husain Shah, he retained his composite personality in his upbringing and equally in his world view. His being was reflected in his lifetime accomplishments. He is counted among the Sufis, Sants and Bhakts (of the Sikh brand). He still remains a giant literary figure. He inspired Sufi poets of Punjab like Farid Sani, Sultan Bahu, Husain Shah, Bulleh Shah and Warris Shah. Doha in his hands was a strong literary weapon, as dohra was a strong weapon in the hands of Baba Farid. Both of the pioneers fashioned a trend that turned out to be universal. Kabir was embedded in the Hindu tradition, but he was opposed to its deifiecation. He was a reformist advocate, ready to free spirituality from its bondage. Like the Buddha he adopted the Middle Path. He also related to Sahajiya Buddhism by referring to *sunya* or *sahaja*, considered an extreme state of mind representing the concept of the Ultimate Reality. Kabir was the most fascinating personality, who could relate to Sufism, Sikhism, Mahayana Buddhism and Bhakti simultaneously. He was a Sufi, Bhakt and Sant at same time, as he was of Hindu and Muslim vintage simultaneously.

Punjab Connection

Kabir (1440-1518) and Guru Nanak (1469-1539) were contemporaries. 243 dohas of Kabir are included in the *Granth Sahib*. It was through this medium that several eminent Saraiki/Punjabi Sufi poets like Farid Sani, Sultan Bahu, Husain Shah, Bulleh Shah and Warris Shah were greatly influenced by Kabir. Guru Nanak was, like Kabir, a monotheist and his main interest was in the Unity of Being (or the Wahdat ul-Wajud), which was translated into Nanak's teaching of Ek Onkar ('The One Indivible Absolute Being'). There was, however, a distinct difference in their style. Kabir had no hesitation in denouncing the idolatry of the Pandit and the bigotry of the Mulla openly and brazenly. Guru Nanak did not denounce Hinduism and Islam, but he would not accept anything that was violative of his Niraguna philosophy. The supreme importance of sumiran or namsumiran, besides the Niraguna philosophy, joins Kabir, the other Sant poets and Guru Nanak in the closest bond. The importance of sumiran through kirtan is particularly rated, 'as means of merging God is constantly emphasized by Kabir himself and by the Sant poets, as well as by the Sikh tradition beginning with Nanak'.

Saraiki Poets and Kabir

Guru Arjun Dev was so much taken up with him that he incorporated the largest chunk of his dohas in the Adi Granth. A whole range of Punjabi Sufi poets were simply charmed by Kabir. They were equally obliged to him for his philosophy of life and poetic content. Kabir was like the Pole Star guiding them on the right path. Farid Sani (1550-1594) was one of the earliest Punjab Sufi poets to be impacted by Kabir. The task of introducing the Upanishadic thought to Sufi poets was accomplished at the instance of Farid Sani successfully. Bhakti cult thus made inroads via the Sufi poets, adopting Vedantic pantheism. The rest followed when Bhakti concepts like God as redeemer of the sinful, wifely devotion, latitudinarianism, practice of humility and the Doctrine of Grace were also accepted. Farid Sani is indebted to Kabir for many ideas including the poetic style and his borrowing of the terminology of Bhakti tradition literally. At times Farid Sani looks a bad copy of Kabir, lifting his ideas and words. The later Sufis like Husain Shah and Bulleh Shah were independently impacted by the Bhakti movement. The reason is obvious. Bhakti movement had made deep inroads among the Sufi poets of Punjab, thanks to the Qadiri order having embarked on the study of Upanishads and allied literature. Farid Sani was the pioneer who showed the path.

Husain Shah (1538-1599) represented the spirit of his times. He was attempting to free spirituality from the confines of formal religion. He lived in the times of Akbar, when the Shari'a had ceased to be the law of the land. He questioned the validity of the Shari'a and formal religion and was inclined to advocate universal spirituality. He was a believer in the Koran, but in his verse, he was as good as a Hindu Sant. His poetry indicates the influence of Bhakti thought reaching its peak. There is enough evidence to establish that Husain Shah borrowed ideas from Kabir, whose fame spread far and wide. He was considered the mentor of all liberal-minded Sufis of north India. There is no doubt that Kabir 'speaks abundantly' in the compositions of Husain Shah through his similies, metaphors, terminology and ideas. The eighteenth-century Sufi poet Farid Faqir (1720-90) has noted: 'Though there have been many learned men from amongst this profession, Hussain Shah and Kabir were those who reached to the threshold (of the Lord)' His poetic verses includes the influence of Vaishnava Vedanic Bhakti poets. It should be noted that Husain Shah, like Kabir, was a julaha (weaver) by caste and that also shows in his poetic content. His poetry is permeated with the spirit of Lahore as Kabir's was with his loving city Benaras. He,like Kabir, was an iconoclast, rebellious and of independent liberal spirit, the qualities that come naturally to born leaders. Vaudeville is hundred per cent correct in attributing that [Husain Shah's] independence of spirit is indeed reminiscent of the rebellious character of the Shudra artisan castes or weavers, which attracted them to Islam.... against the rigid social hierarchy of Hinduism'.[21] This is equally true of Kabir.

Sultan Bahu (1639-91), Bulleh Shah (1680-1757)

Sultan Bahu was a forerunner of Bulleh Shah, though he was no patch on him. Bulleh Shah was not a great poet, but in his thinking he was ahead of his times. Those were disturbed times in the Punjab. Orthodoxy had played havoc with the situation on the ground.. He was an advocate of Islamic spirituality and its autonomy from orthodox Islamic establishment. He took sustenance from Kabir in questioning the absolute authority of Shari'a. He is equally polemical and rhetorical in his political expression. This is a quality that he also shares with Kabir, who has made a great impact on the development of Sufism in the Punjab. Shah was essentially a reformer, a trait that he must have inherited from his mentor Kabir.

It must be said to the credit of the Sants that they had done an effective job of demolishing Hindu ritualism. Many of the saints were of Shudra origins, who were in fact social reformers, and who had consciously undertaken the task of demolishing Hindu orthodoxy. The Sufis had been cautious in confronting the Shari'a. Bulleh Shah had no hesitation in confronting the Shari'a's tradition. He was prepared to fight Islamic law, clergy and the state simultaneously. He was not a Vedantist. He was very much rooted in the Koran. He was like Kabir who was very much rooted in the Hindu tradition. Both of them were essentially social reformers. In Bulleh Shah, Sant and Sufi movements seemed to be working in tandem. Both of them were in line with the spirit of spirituality crossing all religious borders. Here we owe so much to Guru Arjun for thoughtfully selecting the Kabir verses for inclusion in the *Adi Granth.*

Exagerated Notions

Sufism and Bhakti movements were the breath of fresh air, but made no revolutionary impact. Khanqahs no doubt generated a town-hall spirit, and their impact was purely local and temporary. Things went back to normal. The depressed felt elated within the premises of khanqahs, but were completely deflated when they returned to their normal and routine dull and oppressive existence. No economic or social reform happened. The attempts to build bridges between Hindus and Muslims failed. The result was the partition of India in 1947. In reality, the Sufis failed to dare the orthodoxies, which were usually backed by the state. The depressed classes have continued to maintain their status quo for centuries altogether. Many social scientists and historian have remained skeptical about the lasting impact of Sufi and Bhakti movements. Prof R C Majumdar is categorical about the matter: '...the role of both medieval mysticism and Sufism in the history of Indian culture is often exaggerated beyond all proportions. Whatever might have been the value of either as a distinctive phase of Hinduism and Islam, from moral, spiritual and philosophical points of view, their historical importance is guaged by the fact that the number of Indians directly affected by them, even at their heyday, which was short-lived, could not be very large. The number dwindled very appreciably in (the) course of time, and the two orthodox religions showed no visible signs of being seriously affected by this sudden intrusion of radical elements. They persued their even tenor, resembling the two banks of a river, separated by the stream that flows between them.

Attempts were made to build a bridge connecting the two, but ended in failure. Even if there were any temporary bridge, it collapsed in no time'.[22]

The only real beneficiaries are the keepers of the khanqahs, which they were fortunate to inherit generation after generation. The other beneficiaries were the residents of urban centres like Uch, Multan, Ajmer, Nagour and Pakpattan. The third category who were beneficiaries were Quawals and beggars. The poor, the disposed and the discriminated have continued to remain stationery since the times of the Vedas.

Section - IX

Responsive Bhakti Movement

18

Pan-Indian Bhakti Movement

RELIGION is more a direct experience than a code of conduct in India. This explains the popularity of Bhakti and Sufi movements in this country. That is why Bhakti is defined as worship, love and devotion. The supreme deity has got to possess the qualities of a sakha or friend to qualify as God. Passionate devotion to God has to be reciprocated in equal measure. There are three paths to salvation including karma ('works' and 'rituals') and jnanana ('knowledge' and 'gnosis'). The third one, bhakti, is the preferred road to salvation for an overwhelming majority. It touches the deepest chords of the heart and talks the language of the people. This also explains the extraordinary appeal of Vaishnavism throughout the country. It is exclusively a religion of Bhakti. Vaishnavism has truly humanized God. The Radha-Krishna cult epitomizes the true spirit of the Vaishnava ethos. There is an instrinsic link between dance, drama, music and devotion. Devotion to God is to be viewed in concentric circles, with the following sequences representing the intensification of love. In Vaishnava tradition, the ascending order of devotion and intensification of love views God as the devotees' parent, master, friend, husband or sweetheart. The extent of intimacy grows proportionately in the following sequences. From formal relations with parents one transits to less formal and more intimate conjugal relations. That explains the saga of life viewed through the perspective of Bhakti, pure and simple.

The Bhakti movement is a product of south India. It is anti-Brahmin in its intent. Paradoxically, it is also an incidental bye-product of Brahmins reaching out to the Dravidian world. They introduced Sanskrit into the Tamil mainstream. The result was an amalgam of two cultures, and in the creation of the Tamil 'local Puranas' (Sthala Puranas), which, in turn, contributed to the contents of the Bhagvata Purana, the basic text of Vaishnava movement in north India. The Bhakti movement in south India began about 600 C E. It spread through the wandering poets and saints of the Siva and Vishnu cults. The former were known as the Nayanmars, numbering sixty-three, the later numbering twelve, were known as the Alvars, who in turn were devotees of Krishna-Vishnu. Thus Nayanmars and Alvars dominated the Bhakti scene in south India. They were also the pioneers of Bhakti movement in India.

People's Movement

Tamil, like Sanskrit, received royal patronage. It was equally a literary language. Both of them had parallel development and grew independently of each other. Sanskrit, however, made its mark on Tamil via the Bhakti movement. It heralded its entry via oral tradition. Bhakti movement skirted the royal and literary routes and instead took the route of folk and oral tradition. Both Vaishnava and Siva Bhakti traditions in Tamil Nadu made their entry via folk religion. They expressed themselves as folk poetry. Many of the folk poets were illiterate. Many of them were women. The Bhakti movement in Tamil Nadu absorbed Hindu mythology, though it had a distinctly Tamil substratum, it was inspired by classics like Ramayana and Mahabharata at the popular level. Brahmins, who were marginal to the Bhakti movement, had actually introduced the north Indian mythology to south India. It was subsequently taken over by popular folk tradition. Bhakti poets of Tamil Nadu were poets with a difference. No longer was the poetry of impersonal genre. They wrote about themselves and their life experiences. They were indeed autobiographical. They had an identity of their own. They had a distinct identity which could not be missed.

Equally the populace identified itself with the poetry. Songs were heard with great attention. They were sung individually and in unison. The word passed from one mouth to another repeatedly and eventually became the people's property. The Bhakti poets and poetry were thus a new literary gene. Thus, poetry became the vehicle of the Bhakti movement. Formal religion consisted of mumbo jumbo of diktats from above. Thus Bhakti movement, poetry and folk religion were located on the same plane. The God of Bhakti tradition was totally accessible and spoke the folk language. It was possible to have dialogue with him on par.

That explains the popularity of Krishna in Tamil Nadu. He is indeed the favourite God of the Bhakti movement, both in the north and south India. The thundering and awesome gods of the Vedas were thus marginalized. The folk heroes of Tamil Nadu sparked a prairie fire, torching the entire subcontinent from Kashmir to Kerala and Gujarat to Kamrup. The Bhakti movement in Tamil Nadu was an objective necessity. It was in response to multifarious challenges facing Vedic Hinduism. The result was, 'Both Saivite and Vaishnava Bhakti movements incorporated folk religion and folk songs into what was already a rich mix of Vedic and Upanishadic concepts, mythologies, Buddhism, Jainism, conventions of Tamil and Sanskrit poetry, and early conceptions of love, service, women and kings, to which after a while they added elements of Islam'.[1]

Secular Perspective

The totality of poems have a generic name of Caukam or Sangam (assembly) poetry. It is embedded deep in the Tamil tradition. It is essentially secular in its character and has to do with the theme of love in its multifarious dimensions. It is also known as the 'inner' (*akram*) world, as contrasted with the'outer' (*puram*) world, which has to do with the world of politicking and state craft. This contradiction has brought about the dialectical situation. In reality, akram poetry is a byproduct of puram poetry, but with a marked difference. The folk poetry bows to the royal tradition, but at the same time the resemblance is purely fictional. In reality Bhakti or oral/folk tradition is to be viewed as a distinctive landmark in pan-Indian cultural history. It has been compared to a banyan tree spreading its branches wide and far, as well as sinking deep its roots into the earth and multiplying into trunks of new trees with new branches. Bhakti movement in Tamil Nadu is to be credited with multiple births.

Tamil traditions travelled beyond the confines of south India. Puri, Varanasi, Mathura and Vrindavan became centres of pilgrimage attracting pilgrims from all over the country. The practice of darshan actually had its origin in south India and subsequently travelled to north India. Bhakti movement also shifted its focus from royal courts to temples, which also performed secular functions like promoting trade and commerce. Temples were convenient intersections as meeting points for social gatherings. Contrary to the widespread impression of cultural invasion of south India from the north, it was actually a two-way traffic. It came to pass, thanks to the innovative traditions of the south Indian Bhakti movement.

There were also a number of other innovations to be credited to the south Indian Bhakti tradition. Women were acknowledged. The Alvar, named Andal, was a noted musician and poet. Gender and sexuality were brought to the fore, through the work of the female Alvars. The male poets adopted the women's point of view by singing in the female voice. Here were attempts made to state the female's point-of-view objectively. Women thus strode the stage without being present there. There was a recognition that Bhakti tradition had female nuances and these were expressed in the same format. In any case, the Bhakti tradition had exclusively to do with the theme of love. The akram poetry distinguishes seven types of love, of which the place of primacy is given to 'love in separation' (*viraha*), which in fact unites Bhakti movement (both of south and north India) and Sufi tradition in Baba Farid's compositions. Here is a secular theme which has been adopted to suit the theological dimensions of both Bhakti and Sufi movements.

Guru Parampara

Bhakti movement in Tamil Nadu had its beginnings in about 600 B.C. The wandering poets and saints of both Nayanmar and Alvar sects spread the gospel of Bhakti over a millennium. There was a spurt in the Bhakti movement. The logjam was broken with the advent of Ramanuja (1017-1137) and Madhava (1139-1217). There was not only a spurt but qualitative transformation in the character of the Bhakti movement in Tamil Nadu, which still continued to provide the leadership. The institution of the Guru had by then come into being. The doctrines became more specific and philosophical. Soon, the gurudom became a threat to the institution of Brahminism by questioning its social relevance. The Guru was not necessarily a Brahmin. Even the pariahs and Shudras could lay claim to gurudom.

The Bhakti cult followers and groups cut across caste, class, gender and professions. The Bhakti movement was a great leveller. It had assumed a transformational character. It had assumed the spirit of reform from the Alvars. It was equally inspired by Buddhism and Jainism. The gurus had begun to dominate the scene and assumed, according to Bhandarkar, the role of *'Ekantika Dharma'*, or the religion of a single-minded love and devotion to one. They dominated the psyche of Hinduism, which, to its great credit, had shown a degree of resilience in response to challenges faced by it. The songs of the Alvars had made Vaishnava dharma popular. Similarly the doctrine of prapati (surrender) had a mass appeal in Tamil Nadu. Vaishnavism simply appropriated both of them to its advantage. The Buddhist challenge was also met half way, in the words of Monier-Williams, by the wonderful capacity for assimilation of this 'all-tolerant, all-compliant, all comprehensive, and all-absorbing religion'.

The Bhakti movement was essentially secular in character and emerged as a reform movement in reaction to the ritualist religion of the Vedas. The result was the birth of the Vedanta doctrine. In challenge-and-response situation, the Buddhist challenge was met by recognizing the Buddha as an incarnation of Vishnu. Even the Muslim challenge was met half way both at conscious and subconscious levels, as seen in the teachings of Namadeva, Kabir and Nanak, who were 'impressed by the simplicity of the Muslim creed and its insistence upon the oneness of God, those reformers denounced idolatry and caste, and preached that true religion consisted neither in the sophistries and dogmas of philosophers and divines in the practice of meaningless rituals, but in Bhakti, or a passionate feeling love of God'.[2] The great teachers or gurus dominated the religious soul and mind of India during the medieval history. Ramanuja was the progenitor and presiding deity of the medieval Bhakti movement. He was the crucial link between south and north India. Those influenced by him included Ramananda, Kabir, Nanak and Tulsidas. His spiritual guru was Nathamuni. He became closely associated with a devout Shudra. He had his initial lessons in Vaishnavism from the Shudra soulmate. He admitted Jains, Buddhists, Shudras, even the Untouchables to his fold. Ramanuja was truly the forefather of Vaishnavism, come south, north, east and west.

Expanding Frontiers

Now Vaishnavism was getting ready to leapfrog. Nimbarka, a Telang Brahmin, provided the opening. No precise dates are available about him. He certainly followed Ramanuja and Madhava. He lived somewhere between the twelfth-fourteenth centuries. While Vaishnavism had already made inroads into Tamil Nadu, Nimbarka expanded the frontiers of Bhakti movement beyond south India. It is for the first time that Krishna, the cowoherd, comes into prominence as the supreme lord of the universe. Thus, for the first time that the element of krida (sport) was introduced and it has continued to retain its doctrinal supremacy in Vaishnavism since the times of Nimbarka. Thus Vaishnavism was given a coherence which it lacked before. Now Vaishnavism was ready to spread its wings in all directions. Bengal and Orissa were the first to be impacted. The tenth century Sanskrit classic *Gita Govinda* is one of the most important texts of the Vaishnava cult. The love story of Radha and Krishna has become a household word, thanks to poet Jayadeva.

Gita Govinda also perpetrate the myth of Vishnu transforming into the Buddha, out of compassion for animals. Jayadeva was equally supported by Chandidas and Vidyapati Thakura through their powerful poetic compositions in perpetuating the Bhakti movement of the east. They were also responsible for preparing for the grand entry of Chaitanya Mahaprabhu at a later date. The ground was prepared successfully for Vaishnavism in Maharashtra by Namdeva and Eknath in the fourteenth century. Both of them were followed by Tukaram (1608-1649), who is considered the heart and soul of the Marathi Bhakti cult with marked preference for Lord Rama than Krishna. The locale of Bhakti movement was gradually shifting to north India with two pulsating centres at Nabadweep in Bengal and Mathura/Vrindavan in the sacred land of the Brajbhumi.

Moving Northwards

The locale of the Bhakti movement began to shift northwards, steadily reaching the climax during the sixteenth century. The roll call of honour is most impressive. It consists of founders of major sects of Vaishnavism, its philosophers and giant literary figures. All of them truly constituted the community of the most distinguished Sants of the Bhakti movement in north India. Among the founders are to be included Guru Nanak (1469-1538), Vallabhacharya (1479-1531) and Chaitanya (1483-1563). Each one of them has left his mark on the Sant tradition. The Bhakti movement has also left a blaze in transforming the 'prakrits' into contemporary Indian languages. The development of Indian literary genre is owed to the Bhakti movement. The pioneers of Bhakti movement were the founders of the various Sant sects. Among the literary giants are to be included Kabir (1448-1510), Surdas (1483-1563), and Mirabai (1486-1534). They sang the songs of Bhakti moment as well as went on to create a distinguished literary traditions.

Here in the ranks of founders and literateur stand apart the person of Jia Goswami (1517-1596), who can truly be designated as the philosopher of Vaishnavism. He is to be ranked along with his two uncles, Rupa and Sanatana, who laid the foundations of the Chaitanya version of Vaishnavism. There are times when it becomes virtually impossible to distinguish the founders from the literateur. Tulasidas is definitely an instance of the kind. He was not a founder of any sect like Guru Nanak, but he has millions of loyal followers in north India. The influence of the Ramacharitramanasa matches, if not exceeds, the impact of the *Granth Sahib*. Both of them are considered sacred works and treated with as much reverence as the Bible and the Koran. Both the sacred books could enter in a match to count the nember of times the name of Rama is mentioned therein. The Bhakti movement is truly a unifier of the country.

Ramananda

It is a long road from Kanchi of Ramanuja to Benares of Ramananda, spanning several centuries, but Vaishnavism is the link that binds them together. They are equally distinguished for being the pioneers in south and north India respectively. They are the landmarks and measuring rods in different parts of the world. Ramanuja was a mover and shaker in south India. So was Ramananda in north India. It is remarkable, considering that not a written word attributed to Ramananda is on record except a solitary verse recorded in the *Granth Sahib*. '... the guru revealed that Brahmin was in my own heart. Wherever I go, I see only water and stones (worshipped) but it is Thou who had filled them all with Thy presence. They all seek Thee in vain among the Vedas. My own true guru, Thou has put an end to all by failures and illusions. Blessed are Thou. Ramananda is lost in his master (swami) Brahmn, it is the word of the guru that destroys all the million bonds of action'. It was indeed brave of Ramananda to make such a defiant assertion in the Holy City (Varanasi) dominated by the Brahmin community. He also stood out, because he was making an important social statement. Ramananda was primarily a social reformer. Especially Kabir and Guru Nanak were very much impacted by his underlying philosophy. This is also an unusual statement stressing the extraordinary importance of the guru as in the Sufi tradition. His definition of the importance of the role of Brahmin has a Sufi tinge. The underlying unity between Bhakti and Sufi movements thus becomes meaningful.

Ramananda must have been a larger-than-life personality to have such a large impact, although hardly any writings are to be credited to him, excluding a mere scrap discovered in the *Granth Sahib*. His reputation has been built by his twelve disciples, of whom Kabir (a weaver), Pipa (Rajput princely chief), Sena/Sain (barber), Dhanna (Jat peasant) and Ramdas (cobbler) are wellknown. His disciples and devotees belong to all castes, creeds and classes. He was himself a Brahmin, but he had no hesitation in breaking bread with all of those professing to be Vaishnavas. His most revolutionary contribution lay in reviving the moribund Indian languages. Hindi and its various local versions like Avadhi, Braj and Magadhi had a great revival. These languages became the media of religious literature.

Sanskrit was no longer the sacred cow. The Vedic rituals were totally downgraded. The literature had become comprehensible to the common mass. Brahmins were no longer in demand as the intermediary between the God and his devotees. God had suddenly become accessible through one-to-one dialogue by dispensing all the intermediaries. Ramananda had also struck at the roots of the caste system. That the caste was no longer valid was the message he was conveying to all and sundry. His disciples carried on where he left. He lived long and survive most of his disciples. He is believed to have lived for more than a hundred years.

Kabir – the Man for All Seasons

Kabir lived in the 15th century. It was a time of great political upheavals. His life was centered around, Kashi or Banares (Varanasi). He became legendary during his lifetime. He was believed to be a follower of Ramananda. His lifespan and his origins are shrounded in mystery. He was brought up in a class of low-caste julahas (weavers), who were recent converts to Islam. One account mentions that Kabir had earlier worshipped the Goddesss Shakti.. There are others who believed that the weaver community of Varanasi were converts from a Jogi sect, most probably related to the Shaktas, such as the Naths. Kabir belonged to the lower strata of society. He is counted among the most distinguished of Ramananda followers. He was the composer of numerous pithy, biting and sarcastic sayings. All the establishment of religious hues and colours were under his constant and unrelentless scrutiny. He is believed to have started his career as a Sufi, but he is equally accepted as the tallest among the Sant bhakts. He is thus the man for all the seasons. Abu'l Fazl has singled him out for his 'catholicity and lofty vision'.

It should be in order to consider him to be a *muwahhid*. At the same time, he was in constant touch with Hindu Sants and felt increasingly comfortable with them with the passage of time. His concept of love as a path of suffering reminds one of Baba Farid. He definitely owed a debt to the Sufis.. He composed a large number of Hindi verses devoted to Tawhid (Wahdat al-Wajud) or the Unity of Being, a primordial belief in the ultimate nature of unity. Thus, his concept of ultimate reality is beholden to the Unity of Being. Here the terminology employed by Kabir in describing God is also of much interest. He employed at least twenty terms including Allah, Rahim, Karim, Khuda and Sain. The most often-used term employed by him to describe God is Rama, the favourite term of his guru, Ramananda. It also proves that his favourite god was Rama and not Krishna. While Rama is the favourite god of Banares, Krishna has also his empire carved out in Brajbhumi around Mathura and Vrindavan.

Wahdat al-Wajud or the Unity of Being owes as much to Nirguna Bhakti, as it does to the Wajud. Sufis and Sants are beholden to these concepts. Actually Nirguna Bhakti was made widely popular through the thought of Ramananda, who borrowed it from Maharashtra, the home of Rama Bhakti, and supplanted it in north India. Kabir was one of the earliest exponents of Nirguna Bhakti. The climax was, however, reached with Guru Nanak. His Nameless Supreme was the sole object of worship. He called him Nirguna Brahma. To Nanak, God was the source and essence of all living. He was absolute, with no further question.

Guru Nanak and Kabir

Sufi mysticism influenced the north Indian tradition of abstract aspect of God without qualities (nirguna). Especially Kabir and Nanak were much impacted. Kabir may have influenced Nanak greatly in this connection. Some have even described Kabir as the preceptor of Guru Nanak. It seems logical, because Kabir had preceded Nanak.The largest contribution in the Bhagat Baani, the generic name given to the Sant contributions, is that of Kabir. He also appears at the head of Bhagat Baani. There are 227 padas in 17 ragas and 237 slokas of Kabir contained in the *Adi Granth*. Kabir has been truly described as the parent of Sikhism. There is also another striking similarity between the thought of Sikhism and Kabir. Both of them are beholden to the Naths. There is in the *Guru Nanak baani*, a wealth of Hath Yoga terminology, and it has striking resemblance to the thought of the Naths at the structural level. In other words, Kabir, Guru Nanak and the Nath Jogis are in line with each other. In a manner of speaking, the Naths carry Kabir's Kabir's genes, considering the fact that the julahas were probably converts to Islam from the Nath tradition.

There are several other similarities which place Kabir, Guru Nanak and the Naths on the same plane. All of them welcomed the admission of lower castes like Chandals and sweepers to their ranks with open arms. All of them practiced non-hierarchical order. In other words, there were no class and distinctions in their ranks. They were also vehemently hostile to the Hindu caste system and thus in direct confrontation with the Brahmin hierarchy, by accepting the Untouchables and the Pariahs to their fold. The Naths also stand out distinctly in several other respects. The Nath doctrine was based on the trinity of Siva, Matsyndra Nath and Gorakhnath. The Naths also emphasized the discipline of the body and the mind through vigorous Yoga exercises. These were only inner variations.

What brought Guru Nanak, Kabir and the Nath together once again was the Nirguna Bhakti. It also united them with the Sufi movement. The Rudauli pirs identified Sufi beliefs based on the Wahdat-al-Wajoud with the philosophy and practices of Gorakhnath, and, by implication with the basic trends of Nirguna Bhakti. In fact, the Nirguna Bhakti philosophy had its deep roots in the movement initiated by the Alvars of Tamil Nadu. It travelled to the north with the thought of social reformer, Ramananda, who was also the mentor of Kabir, and, by implication, of Guru Nanak. It is a long-winding chain from the Alvars, travelling to the Deccan and reaching out to north India, with Ramananda, Kabir and Guru Nanak providing the helping hand, and with Sufis performing the role of the foster mother. His plurality was his strongest point. Kabir was a true cosmopolitan medieval Indian. He was born before his times. He invoked the concept of cultural nationalism, before Indian nationalism was actually born. He sang, 'There is no Hindu, no Turk', and lived by this maximum. Sufism and Bhakti movement are the liberal face of India. Kabir is the genuine and true ambassador of humanism. At heart, he was a true Vaishnavite and one of the foremost Sant bhakts. He was indeed a co-founder of a new faith and religion. He was a Nath Jogi, a Şavite, a Vaishnavite, a Sikh, a liberal Hindu and a Sufi at the same time. You name it, he represented the soil of India.

Chaitanya Mahaprabhu (1486-1534)

The sixteenth century was truly the century of the Bhakti movement. There was a jamboree of Bhakti saints that included Vallabhacharya, Nanak, Kabir, Surdas, Mirabai and Chaitanya crowding the century. Chaitanya was the Grand Old Man of Bhakti movement, whose influence spread fast from Puri to Peshawar and Udaipur to Manipur in no time. He has been called the symphony of India. There is a popular song that depicts the man:

'Look how Chaitanya goes to Vrandavana',
A torn rag at his back,
His head shaven, and,
A begging bowl in hand'.

There is no sharper description of the physiogonomy of Chaitanya, after he made his appearance in Vrindaban for the first time, than by an astute observer:

> 'A sanyasi has come from Jagannath, whose glory and power cannot be adequately described. Big of limbs, fair as the purest gold, long-armed, lotus-eyed, clad in all the marks of Godhead, as one can see. Oh, marvel! The sight of him convinced one that he is Narayan. Whosoever beholds him chants Krishna's sankirtan. All the marks of a great Bhagvat as described in the Bhagavat Puran are evident in him. Even ashis tongue sings Krishna's name. his eyes run tears like the Ganges stream. Now He dances, now laughs, now sings and now weeps, or at times roars like a lion. The world's benefactor is He, named Krishna-Chaitanya. His name, appearance, and virtues – all are matchless. To see Him is to know Him as fashioned in God's world. Hearing will not make one credit this marvelous tale'.[3]

His popularity is phenomenal, considering he did not write anything, except for a series of verses known as 'eight verses of instruction; believed to contain the complete philosophy of Gaudiya Vaishnavism in a condensed form. He was born in Navadvipa in Nadiya, West Bengal, to a Brahmin family. His original name is known as Vishambhra Misra. He is known by the nickname of Nimai. He is known also as Chaitanya Mahaprabhu, Shri Krishna Chaitanya and Lord Gauranga. He stands out for qualities that are special to him. A passionate religious emotion is his distinctive hallmark. No other Sant Bhakt can match him in this respect. This emotion has been called the 'subconscious of the refined man'.. There is sheer poetry in his religiosity. He has added warmth and colour to religion. At the same he is a protest against barren and boring ritualism of religion. He is overwhelmingly opposed to rigid religious doctrines and dogmas. Chaitanya directs his appeal to the heart and it works wonders. It is possible to strike a bond with him instantaneously.

Radha-Krishna cult

Nimbanka introduced Radha and Krishna as cult figures. Chaitanya brought them into prominence and got them identified with Vaishnavism. Every other god identified with Vishnu was put into shade. His followers believed Chaitanya to be an incarnation of Radha and Krishna. They saw both of them in one body. The Sahajiya sect of Bengal went a step further by identifying them not only with Chaitanya, but in every man and woman. Chaitanya brought about the miracle of placing the ordinary devotee not only at par with Chaitanya, but also with Radha-Krishna. Bhakti had played the extraordinary trick, of building into every ordinary man and woman the compability to upgrade themselves spiritually. Thus, all devotees were twice blessed. Each of them was apparently rollicking in the Radha-Krishna consciousness. Here was a step forward in 'helpyour spirituality'. It was not necessary to seek god outside, because he was within you. The next logical conclusion was now possible. Krishna was born once again as Chaitanya in order to teach the Bhakti dharma and relieve his devotees of all worldly troubles through the direct intervention of god himself. While Islam had a Messenger to intervene with God Almighty, Vaishnavism was an advance because the very God had appeared amidst us.

The culture of emotion had arrived amidst us. Chaitanya was its master. He would lose consciousness in no time. He would full flat on the ground at the height of his 'emotional felicity'. His audience would inevitably identify itself with him by sharing his agony and increased tension. He would thereby convey his message in no uncertain terms. It enabled him to establish perfect rapport with his audience. He would not only make his point besides winning the sympathy. He would set his audience thinking. Thus he was a master trickster. It would be wrong to consider him 'a phantom figure' or a magician who would fade away or be forgotten. His apparent behavior of 'an unbalanced one' was to make a point.. He was 'a definite historical personage' and no ghost. He had arrived on the scene at the right historical moment and indeed claimed to be an avatar to remind us of a destiny awaiting us. He was there to shepherd his stock. There was little that could be credited to him in written text, but he was an erudite scholar in his own right.

He was determined to teach the lesson of Krishna to one and all. Here he made no distinction between any creed or class. His doors were open even to the Chandals. He denounced the caste system. He was overwhelmingly opposed to ceremonial rites. The Brahmanical practices were 'no, no' for him. He had declared the universal brotherhood of man. He was committed to the practice of Bhakti alone. The Worship of Hari and singing of his name were the only panacea for him. He must have been an apt master of psychology, showing the road to salvation. He practiced what he preached in public. He recited verses and sang with tears in his eyes. He was not a master of yoga, but his body movements were as tangible as his soulful singing. The exalted emotions were his hallmark. It was a spiritual experience to watch him. The ecstasy of joy and 'the enhanced psyhological experience' have continued to be communicated to his followers generation after generation. That explains the inherent strength of the Gauranga Vaishnavism renewing itself generation after generation.

Spiritual Experience

Emotionalism and sentimentality were the distinctive brands that distinguished Chaitanya from the rest of the Bhakti Sant community. *Kirtans* were the physical expression of mystical rupture that overwhelmed him frequently. He had a handsome personality and bearing, but he dressed to the bare minimum. He had a strip of cloth to cover the lower part of his body. He moved from town to town, village to village and street to street, barefooted, dancing in rhythm, with the crowd dancing in unison with him, joining him by repeatedly reciting Hare Krishna, and thus generating an atmosphere of communal frenzy led by Chaitanya. His body would be covered with dust. Only his face had a glow which kept the participating audience spellbound. The whole atmosphere is best described in his own words:

'I crave only to repeat your name
So that – my eyes shall overflow with tears,
My mouth utters only broken syllabus,
And my breath be suffocated with emotion,
My soul fill with wound, my body covered with horrification'.

Thus, with raised hands and dancing, Chaitanya went from one locality to another singing. Public *kirtan* or walking *kirtan* came to be associated with Chaitanya as his distinctive brand. God blessed him because he breathed a new life in the Bhakti movement now full of endless glow and pulsation.

Goswami Associates

Chaitanya was very fortunate in his associates, several of his companions were poets and high-powered intellectuals. Several of them were aesthetics of the highest order. His main disciples were the reunciants called Goswamins. He was mostly stationed at Puri in Orissa, but the chief Goswamins were stationed at Vrindavan, which eventually became the headquarters of the Gaudiya Vaishnavs. He had actually done the ground work himself, so that the whole of India had turned Vaishnav. He had danced, wept and laughed his way through the heart and mind of ordinary people. He had prepared the ground himself for the Goswamins to walk in. There were six main Goswamins who were personally influenced by him and in some instances, they were his direct pupils or disciples. His influence extended much beyond his main disciples. Swami Haridas, the noted musician and guru to Tansen, were also his disciples. He spent most of his life in Nidhiban, the so-called garden in Vrindavan associated with the Gaudiya Vishnavism.

In Vaishnav tradition, the term 'Goswami' has very little to do with the ownership of cows, which is indeed its literal meaning. The term has actually to do with functions of different order. In this particular context, the term 'Goswami' is a hallmark of identification. The term also refers to a master of senses, or an acharya (teacher).

The main six Goswamis were as follows: 1) Rupa (d. 1534), 2) Sanatana (d. 1553), 3) Jiva Goswami (1511-1596), 4) Gopal Bhatta, 5) Raghunatha Bhatta, and 6) Raghunath Das Goswami. Rupa and Sanatana were Karnataka Brahmins and Jiya Goswami was their nephew. The elder two had come in contact with Chaitanya while in Bengal. At that time both of them were ministers in the court of Alauddin Hussein Shah who ruled Bengal during 1493-1519. They were respectively known by their Muslim names of Sabar Mallik and Dalbir Khan, but they never embraced the Muslim faith in their personal lives. Rupa and Sanatanta were the main pillars of the Gaudiya Vaishnav cult after they were established in Virandavan. Their nephew, Jiva Goswami, is considered to be a philosopher. Rupa, Sanatana and Jiva Goswami have left their strong mark on Gaudiya Vaishnavism–as strong as Chaitanya himself. The rough edges were straightened and they gave shape to Vaishnavism through their extensive writings and skillful management. Furthermore, they were eminently successful in making Vaishnavism a way of life. They succeeded in pronouncing passionate love as their mission of life. Thus Bhakti, and not austerities to be practiced in life or rituals to be exercised, wasplaced in the central scheme of things.

Prema Bhakti

Bhakti is viewed by Chaitanya in the light of classical *rasa* theories. Bhakti (*prema*) is considered a supreme *rasa* by itself. Rupa has enunciated the theory of bhakti *rasa*. He has delineated five primary modes (bhavas) for relating to the supreme god Krishna. Those are *sara* (contemplature adoration), *dasya* (humble servitude), *sakhya* (companionship), *vatsalya* (parental affection) and *madhurya* (passionate love). For Rupa, Radha is the ideal devotee of Krishna, the supreme lover. Madhurya is thus considered the supremest rasa denoting prema or love. It remains an unfulfilled love with viraha (separation) being its theme song. Radha is nothing but the idealization of love. It remains an unfulfilled love thus intensifying it. Love was also the main passion of Chaiatanya. He has passed on his legacy to the rest of the community. Love is the exclusive watchword of the Chaitanya cult. Indeed it is considered the supreme principle of universe by him. Prema bhakti has the potential to sublimate the sexual love. It transforms love into a passionate religious emotion. Chaitanya is on record over the subject. Sexual love has not only to be suppressed but discounted totally for opening the doors to prema bhakkti, ultimate in the life for the bhaktas. *Prema bhakti* is an enhanced psychological experience. Thus it differs materially from several Saivite cults advocating sex in the central place.

Worldwide Impact

The 19th century renaissance in Bengal is associated with the modernization of India. There are some scholars who attribute another kind of renaissance in Bengal in the 16th century to Chaitanya. It had broader impact than limiting to religious thought. Its influence extended not only to literature and culture, it had also elements of social reform in it. Salimullah Khan, a noted linguist, believes, 'Sixteenth century is the time of Chaitanya Dev, and it is the beginning of modernism in Bengal. The concept of humanity that came into fruition is contemporaneous with that of Europe'. He goes still further by asserting, 'History says that the Bengali people experienced the renaissance not only once but also twice in the course of history. Bengalis witnessed the first renaissance in the 16th century when Husain Shah and Sri Chaitanya's idealism influenced a sect of upper class of people'.[4]

The Baul movement is one of the finest byeproducts of the Gaudiya Vaishnavism. This tradition of spiritual music is alive and kicking to this day. The repertoire of Indian music shall be incomplete without it. Baul music is essentially based on the Chaitanya perspective of Bhakti, but it is also a fine instance of composite culture, in which Hindus and Muslims are joined together. The Bauls have developed a distinct culture and way of life which marks it distinctly from the rest of the community. Theyare indeed the Jogis of the Bengal variety. The Sufi and Bhakti culture are joined in them, yet they exude the Chaitanya stamp prominently. Chaitanya has become relevant for modern times also. His ideas have equally proliferated in the West. This has become possible due to the vision of A.C. Bhaktivedanta Swami Prabhupada, who has founded the movement known as the International Society for Krishna Consciousness (ISKCON). The followers of ISKCON have danced their way through the world. The Krishna way has thus become a way of life abroad beyond the confines of India. Krishnalogy has now become an academic discipline in its own right. Bhakti has also come under scrutiny by a tribe of distinguished psychologists. Mind reading is no longer an art, but is also become a science to be studied under laboratory conditions. Sri Chaitanya has thus travelled a long way.

Baul Fakiri Music

Baul music has another enrichened dimension in Baul Fakiri music sung by the wandering ministrels of Nadia, Birbhum, Bankura and Murishabad districts of West Bengal. The Baul Fakiri *gaan* is a devotional form of folk music, drawn from quawali sung in Benagli. It is extremely popular among ordinary folk, so much so that it is performed in more than 500 dargahs in Nadia district alone. In contrast, the original version of north Indian *quawali* is sung in Saraiki, Punjabi and Urdu alone. This genre of music employs the dhol and khal (percussion instrument), instead of the tabla as in the original Nnorthern style. Fakiri music praises both Allah and Krishna by singing *juge juge Mohammad Krishna prochar* as the typical refrain. It is however, less known, but quite distinct in presentation and language. It resorts to several phrases, lifted from Arabic quoting from the Holy Book and Hafiz. In the words of Shreya Roy Choudhury, it has generated *Menabiti dharma*, a cult based on the unorthodox faith that regards human beings as gods and their philosophy is in tune with their music, which draws all its vocabulary and imagery from religious discourse but at the same time it is secular'. We have the authority of Karl Marx about progressive ideas during medieval times being interpreted in religious jargon. Even Rabindranath Tagore has been influenced by Baul Fakiri music.

Dhrupad Style

The Dhrupad style of classical Hindustani music is one of the richest byproducts of the Vaishnava movement. It owes origins to the devotional music traditionally performed in the Vaishnava temples of northern India. Literally speaking, the term Dhrupad had its origins in 'Dhruva', meaning immutable or fixed.It also means 'pada', hymn or verse. It is an unhurried and austere style.The phrasing is melodic, based on poetic compositions, treated with sanctity. It was the rage during the 15th and the 16th century. Mian Tansen was its most renouned exponent. There is a recent revival of this particular genre of music. The major gharana of the Dhrupad genre of music include the following: 1) the Dagar gharana, 2) Darbhanga gharana, 3) Battiya gharana, 4) Talwandi gharana, and 5) Mathura gharana. The classical Indian music thus owes a great deal to the Bhakti movement.

Classical Tradition

The old tradition of classical music has its roots deep in the soil of Sapta Sindhu, going as far back as to the Vedic Age. Ragas were revealed by the rishis. Sound is inherent in all creation, and it first manifested itself in the primeaval sound 'Om'. Different ragas were different manifestations of sound., and it is believed 'music has affinity with nature and each of the swaras (notes) has been inspired by the call of a particular bird or animal – the note sa with the peacock, re with the dove, ga with the goat, ma, the crane, pa with the cuckoo, dha with the frog, ni with the elephant.' 6

Sangeet (music) is the flavour of the *Gurubaani* and indeed, *Adi Granth* has music in its essence. Guru Arjan set most of the baani to the musical descipline of ragas and raginis.The land of the Five Rivers has contributed four famous gharanas to the Dhrupad gayaki.Khayal gayaki is a modified version of the Dhrupad without compromising with its rigours and is a true ligate of sufi and Bhakti movements. Khayal bandishes based on Saraiki verses are sung all over the country.Multani ragas were ode to the genious of Suhrawardi Sufi Sheikh Baha-ud-Din Zakaria. Kafi tones have a Bulleh Shah connection. Tappa (meaning jumping), which is considered most intricate style of classical music was owed to the genious of a camel trader; He constantly gazed at stars in clear desert nights, while travelling tirelessly with his caravan, with jingling bells and sounds in their steady steps. All this establishes the truth of ordinary turning into exteraordinary, like *paras* turning stone into gold by mere touch.

19

Bhakti Aesthetics

The Epicurian Vaishnav (1479-1553)

Chaitanya and Vallabhacharya were Vaishnav faces in north India. Both of them emerged on the scene about the same time. Both of them were headquartered in the Brajbhumi. Both of them were worshippers of Krishna. Both of them had spread their wings in southwest Punjab and had followers scattered in the tribal lands of Afghanistan and north-West Frontier Province. The similarity ends here. Vallabhacharya and his sect have been described as the Epicurean Vaishnav. His locale of operations covered Sindh, Rajasthan and Gujarat. In contrast Chaitanya had his strongholds in the entire Gangetic belt.

Vallabhacharya was a Telang Brahmin from Andhra Pradesh. He eventually settled in Gokul near Mathura. Like Chaitanya, he was regarded as an incarnation of Krishna in his life time. He had seven sons. He was succeeded by his second son Vitthalnath (d. 1586). He had the leadership of the sampradaya divided among his seven sons. He had also an adopted son, Tulsidas, nicknamed Lalaji, who was asked to look after the Punjab and Sindh. He was headquartered at Dera Ghazi Khan, situated on the western bank of the Indus river. Vallabhacharya left behind 84 followers to spread the mission throughout India. Thus the powerful combination of 84 followers and eight sons heading the sampradaya functioned as missionaries of the cult. While Chaitantya had left no progeny to head the Gaudiya Vaishnav cult, Vallabhacharya had taken care to leave the affairs of the cult in familiar hands. His successor acquired the title of Maharaja. They were also known as Gosains, a substitute for Goswamins, that is 'the lord of cows', 'an epithet of Krishna' title that was again shared with the leadership of the Gaudiya Vaishnavas.

Liberal Faith

Vallabhacharya and his sons were very liberal in opening their doors not only to untouchables and Shudras, but even to persons of the Muslim faith. Here they were in line with the Chaitanya cult. They, however, differentiated from them in their concepts of Bhakti and attitude toward Krishna. Bhakti was developed by the sect through stages in ascending order of *bhava, prema, pranaya, sneha, raga, anuraga* and *vyasana* (passion) for Krishna. While Chaitanya completely rules out the place of passion in his Bhakti scheme of things, the Vallabhacharya cult places passion pure and simple as the entire focus in its view of Bhakti. Thus, Chaitanya and Vallabhacharya were placed in the opposition camps in their view of Bhakti. Logically, the distinguishing feature of the Vallabha faith remains the absence of asceticism. It is not denial but fulfillment of passion that is celebrated by Vallabhacharya. He proves to be more of a Shakta than a Vaishnav. There is also another marked difference with Chaitanya. Krishna without Radha is inconceivable by the Gaudiya Vaishnavas. Indeed Radha and Krishna are two-in-one. Even Radha is placed above Krishna in actual practice. The Krishna of Vallabh a concept is a different god. There is no Radha in a supporting role in his scheme of things. Krishna remains supreme. In the Vallabha sect temples, Krishna is worshipped along with his consort. She is by no means Radha. His consort is usually referred to as Swamiji, or the

Lady. She is the subject of Krishna's Shakti and plays second fiddle to him.

The father figure of the Krishna Bhakti, Nambarka, succeeds in uniting Chaitanya and Vallabhacharya in viewing Krishna, the cowherd, as the supreme Lord of the Universe. Thus, for the first time, the element of *krida* (sport) is introduced in Vaishnavism. Vallabha was careful in laying stress upon the sports of Krishna's childhood. Chaitanya extended the play to the entire adulthood of Krishna. It reminds you of a Krishna with a flute being playful with the gopis on the banks of Yamuna. The Vallabhacharya followers had no hesitation in breaking the barriers, with practically no holds barred for them. The path of Bhakti or devotion propagated by Vallabhacharya was the path of acquiring the grace of God, but it was turned upside down by his followers, who forget all about Krishna's childhood and acquiring Grace through fasting, prayer and similar pious acts. By sanctifying all human players in his service 'according to the pure Vaishnava faith, Krishna's love for Gopis is to be explained allegorically but the followers of Vallabhacharya interpreted it in a material sense.'[1]

Erotic Mysticism

Bhakti rasa, also called *Madhurasa* or *Madhura Rasa*, has been designated as Pushti-marg in the Vallabhacharya school of thought. It is best expressed in the call of the *rasa lila* by women and young girls of Braj in their love for Krishna, comparable to 'divine madness' of Chaitanya: Their conduct violate social norms and conventions of traditional Indian society. It was pure and simple illicit longing for Krishna, and expression of apparent licentious behavior. The licentious behavior of Gopis was justified by their status as ideal Bhaktas. There were compensations to be had by devotees, who are called *sevaks* in the Vallabhacharya vocabulary. There were pleasures of union, the pain of separation, the longing of wanting and expectations of the unexpected. The sevaks were prone to surrender, which was bound to be subjected to exploitation. It was liable to get down to crude earthly passion in reality. The Vallabhacharya doctrine of devotional Bhakti has been subjected to severe criticism. It has been variously called, 'erotic contemplation', 'emotional debauchery', and 'psychological and ethical aberration'. Thus, erotic mysticism has come under severe criticism. The undesirable practices of the sect led to the puritanical movement of Swami Narayana of the 19th Century.

The Vallabhacharya cult has, however, continued to grow right and left especially in Gujarat and Rajasthan. The fact remains that even the pontifs of the cult have also come under scrutiny on this account. Eroticism as a devotional principle has been sought to be justified on the specious plea that the behavior does not take place in the real world, but it is enacted in the 'sacred or *alukik* realm'. Apparently it makes mockery of principles of self-denial and self-mortification associated with Bhakti practices. No wonder, the Vallabhacharya School has been called the 'Epicurean School of Vaishnavism'. It is named the 'Epicureanism of the East', and more specifically, it has earned the title of the 'Epicureans of India'. Monier-Williams has called *ashti-marga* 'the way of eating, drinking and enjoying oneself; that is to say, worshipping the deity, not with fasting, self-denial, self-mortification, and penitence, but with indulgence of the natural appetite and enjoyment of the good things of the world'.[2] While Monier-Williams has passed strong strictures over the resultant state of the Vallabhacharya cult, Dr RG Bhandarkar has presented a more cogent case based on ethical grounds: 'The spirit of this system, therefore, seems to be sportive enjoyment and it cannot but be expected to influence the ordinary life of its followers. Moral rigidity culminating in indifference to worldly enjoyments and self-abrogation does not appear to be a characteristic of this school'.[3] It is not surprising as to what has come to pass the spirit of Vallabhacharya's doctrines with the flux of time. Real intentions were forgotten and the gross externals edged out the core content. There is, however, much to be credited to Vallabhacharya and his associates.

Suradas – The Vallabha Poet

The Krishna cult in north India owes so much to Vallabhacharya. Braj Bhasha owes a debt of gratitude to the cult. Two great Brajbhasha poets, Surdas and Parmananda, were not only major poets, but were great exponents of the Vallabhacharya cult. The cult spread like wild fire in north and west India because of the lyrical quality of the poetry. The Parmananda and Surdas songs were on the lips of the common man. Even Brajbhasha has become richer due to its association with the Vallabhacharya cult.

The Vallabha cult got a boost with the poets Suradas and Parmananda taking over as its literary exponents. Both of them were contemporaries of Vallabhacharya and his successor son. Both of them were poet-saints in the real sense of the term. Parmananda was in fact one of Vallabha's eight companions of his sampradaya (doctrinal community). Parmananda was also designated as a saint of the Vallabha cult. He has been called the poet-saint of 'morality beyond immorality'. The followers of Vallabha, called *sewaks*, were devoted to praise Krishna's childhood life in Vrindavan. One has to marvel at the richness of detail and Parmananda's sensitivity to the theme of Krishna. His *padas* were extremely popular throughout north India, because those helped in creating the necessary bond between the common man in the street and his god. His padas were sung in homes, in temples and on the streets of Brajbhumi. His themes were built around *raslilas* performed by the *gopis*, the cowherding women and young girls of Braj. The Vallabh tradition contrasted the *laukik* with the *alaukik* world, 'the world of the profane realm' contrasted with the 'realm of the sacred'. The gopis were no ordinary mortals, because they were of the *alaukik* and of beyond the world. Parmananda is a master of sensual perceptions and hence the real and the unreal world are joined together in his framework.

Parmananda, however, pales into insignificance when compared with Suradas. (1479-1584). Both of them were, however, contemporaries. Suradas was placed a notch lower in the cult's hierarchy. Suradas was physically handicapped due to his blindness. It was no handicap to his creativity. He is considered one of the brightest luminaries in the Hindi literary firmanent. He fell under the spell of Vallabha in his younger days, but he was not his direct disciple unlike Parmananda. He was a disciple of his son, Vitthalnatha, who was largely responsible for inspiring Suradas. Like Parmananda, he also adopted Braj as the medium of his literary expression. Brajbhasha thus owes a debt of gratitude to Suradas. Actually, Suradas and Tulasidas are to be placed in the same class. They have been compared to the sun and the moon of Hindi literature. While Tulasi praised Rama in Avadhi language, Suradas's ideal was Krishna and he spoke in his tongue, Braj. Both of them Hindi literary traditions. In fact, Tulasidas and Suradas are in the same class as several other poet-saints of the Bhakti movement and they are to be ranked accordingly as the pioneers of devotional lyrics.

Indian Literary Tradition

'The most famous authors of this school were Mira, Vidyapati, Chandidas and Narasimha Mehta. Of course, all their songs have deep religious and spiritual significance. Rabindranath Tagore once wrote a poem inquiring whether it was really so, would it be wrong in tracing in these love lyrics 'ordinary human elemental passion'.[4] 'Rabindranath has succeeded in probing the depth of the Bhakti movement. It is the elemental passion that motivates ordinary human beings, which, in turn, inspires saint-poets of the Bhakti movement. Thus it explains the popularity of the Krishna cult. Radha and Krishna's love comes down to love between ordinary man and woman in literal terms. The ideal love of Rama and Sita is no match for it. Not surprising, the main expression of Vaishnava thought in the heartland, from the plains of the Punjab to the Bengali hinterland, is related to Krishna Bhakti for four centuries. While Chaitanya and Vallabha are to be credited with giving the momentum, the poets have been singing of Radha and Krishna love in preceding and succeeding centuries'.

Transformational Brij Bhasha

Krishna-bhakti, Brajbhasha literary tradition and Vaishnava thought are closely allied. They emerged on the scene simultaneously. While Vaishnava thought was centered on Mathura, Vrindaban and Gokul Krishna Bhakti and Brajbhasha literary tradition were well spread over north India. Brajbhasha is a continuum of sister dialects and languages like Punjabi, Avadhi, Bhojpuri, Magadi and Rajasthani. All these languages are collectively the foster mother of modern Hindi. There is even a concoction language called 'Braj boli'–the speech of Braj–employed by the Bengal Vaishnavas as the language of devotional poetry. This is an admixture of literary Bengali joined with Brajbhasha–a compelling tribute to the magic quality of Krishna's mother tongue. The Krishna-bhaktas have no difficulty in identifying themselves with god's own tongue.

Brajbhasha has a literary tradition which goes back to the 15th century, a century or so before Chaitanya and Vallabha. This development also predates the emergence of distinguished poet-saints on the scene. The emergence of Chaitanya and Vallabha on the scene must have accelerated the process. Brajbhasha actually progressed by leaps and bounds due to its spontaneity. Vaishnava Bhakti had a high degree of spontanaity; the common people had identified themselves with it. Brajbhasha was thus the people's language. Vaishnava Bhakti and Braj Bhasha devotional poetry expressed in the language of the common people their innermost yearing. Radha and Krishna had an empathy with them and thus won over their trust completely.

Here was a living language, the vehicle of expression by Krishna during his own times, and decidely the sacred language of Vaishnava thought. What were the Krishna bhaktas looking for? The answer was a logical response, 'They needed a language through which the *bhava* (feelings) of their Bhakti might be understood by and familiar to, the ordinary masses. as well as by those of higher social status. Braj Bhasha served their requirement perfectly'.[5] Brajbhasha, like Punjabi and Saraiki, was by no means distinguished for its literary content. Primacy was given by sant-poets to *bhava* of Bhakti in their kirtans. Above all, they encouraged mass participation. Devotional poetry was expected to be down-to-earth. It must have retained its rusticity since the times of Krishna. Thus, it was possible to identify with Krishna by speaking and singing in his mother tongue. Brajbhasha had a transformational effect on other north Indian dialects too. Indeed Bhakti literature is the beginnings of modern Indian literary tradition. The transition from the Prakrits was smooth. Brajbhasha has inspired the rest to follow. Vaishnav thought opened the path to social transformation of the entire subcontinent.

Gita Govinda and Afterward

Brajbhasha had a prominent place in promoting Bhakti movement in north India. Bhakti movement had a previous history. Brajbhasha came at the fag end. The chain of poet-saints of the Bhakti movement had its roots in the religious life of Tamil Nadu, influenced by the Vaishnav Alvars and the Saiva Nayanars from about the 6th century A D. The next spurt occurred with Jayadeva's *Gita Govinda* in about the 12th century. The locale of Bhakti movement also shifted from Tamil Nadu to Orissa. Jayadeva was the court poet of the ruler Laksmansena (1179-1203). He preceded Chaitanya by several centuries, but *Gita Govinda*, literally known as The Song of [Krishna] the Cowherd, is considered the Bible of Gaudiya Vaishnavism. Jayadeva has continued to inspire the following generations of north Indian poet-saints since then. He has also inspired the following generations of poet-saints of eastern India like Vidyapati and Chandidas. *Gita Govinda* has been called 'an unfailing and rich source of literary inspiration as well as religious emotion'. *Gita Govinda* is also considered a landmark for several other reasons. It is a sociological landmark for its feminine outlook. Radha and not Krishna is placed in the centre of things. Radha, the lover, is more powerful than Krishna, who is forced to play second fiddle to her.

It is through *Gita Govinda* that Vaishnavism has introduced the erotic tendency into Bhakti. It could be explained due to the influences of Buddhist Tantrism and the Nath cult in eastern India. *Gita Govinda* has also a different imagery by emphasizing the separation (viraha) rather than union, longing, fulfilment or renunciation of love. It looks odd to find Krishna bending before Radha and she, in turn, placing her foot on his head. Here is a powerful depiction of woman power. Thus Krishna, 'may do the whole work of building the world, but Radha sits as Queen. He is at best her Secretary of State'. Jayadeva has inspired a generation of poet-saints like Chandidas and Vidyapati of the 14th and 15th centuries, who also wrote from the standpoint of a Radha dominating Krishna. The biggest impact of *Gita Govinda* was on the Gaudiya Vaishnavism. *Gita Govinda* and worship of Radha became central to the theology, doctrine and rituals of Gaudiya Vaishnavism. The Goswamis took it to Vrindavana and popularized the cult in north India. *Gita Govinda* singing is popular in temples all over India. It has also made a major impact on the performing arts, especially on dance drama. The Radha-Krishna theme has been adopted by Kathak dancers. Literature in eastern India has also been greatly impacted by Jayadeva. He has become immortal.

Pan-Indian Revival

Jayadeva ignited the fire and it spread from one corner of the country to other in no time. The echoes of Orissa and Bengal were heard in Kashmir, the farthest north. Kashmir has always been a stronghold of the Saivite cult. Hence the Bhakti movement in Kashmir assumed the Shaivite format. Its spokesman was the 14th century Kashmiri poetess. Lala Ded. She was a *Sivadvaitavadini.* Her poems happen to be the earliest specimen of Kashmiri literature. She was thus a pioneer of Kashmiri language. Even today, her writings are popular and quoted and sung extensively. At the other end, Chandidas and Vidyapati Thakur were engaged in a commendable job of promoting Bhakti through the Bangla and Maithili verses respectively.

Chandidas who emerged on the scene in the 14th century was distinguished for his love for a low-caste washerwoman named Rani. He saw Krishna's Radha in his Rani. His Radha was a domineering character. So was true of Radha of Vidyapati's conception. Vidyapati was a Maithili. He was a contemporary of Chandidas. He emerged on the scene in the initial stages of the spread of the Bhakti movement in north India. He is believed to have flourished between 1350-1450. His lyrics of Radha and Krishna laid the foundations of Maithli literature. Vidyapati was an important link in the chain of Vaishnav poet-saints of north India. His poetry was taken to heart in Bengal. The Brajboli language is a hybrid cross between Maithili and Bengali. He had thus a pan-Indian vision linking Brajbhasha with the Bengali language. Brajboli had a stranglehold on the mind of Bengali intelligentsia, so much so that Rabindranath Tagore wrote one of his earliest works in Brajboli, detailing the romance of Radha and Krishna in the Bhakti format.

With time, the scene moves west and the region comes under the grip of the Bhakti movement. Mirabai (1492-1546) emerges on the scene. She is believed to be the greatest poetess of north India of the medieval times. She wrote in old western Rajasthani, the source language of Rajasthani and Gujarati. Her passion was like that of Lala Ded, genuinely feminine. Like Vidyapati, she cut across her native language. She has been recognized as a poetess of Gujarati, Rajasthani and Hindi. She was also a link between Khariboli and Brajbhasha. It shall be in order to call her the link woman. She has the feminine quality of being sentimental, but her poetry lacks much philosophical depth, compared, for instance, to Kabir. Her poetry is substantially devoted to Krishna and, no surprise, she has substituted

Radha in her lyrical poetry. Narasimha Mehta (popularly called Narsi Mehta) was her contemporary, somewhat staid and serious, who combined two influences, Bhakti and Jnana (knowledge) in his poems distinguished by his inimitable language. He composed the famous song, 'Vaishnav jana tere kahiye' which Gandhiji has helped to popularize. Tukaram (1608-49) was in contrast socially sensitive. He was a Shudra who challenged caste through his poetry. His god is called Vitthal. Tukaram's poetry is extremely popular in Maharashtra.

Tulasidas's Ramacharitamanas

The late Prof AK Ramanujam is of the view, "In India… no one ever reads the Ramayana or the Mahabharata for the first time, the stories are 'always there'".[6] Prof Ramanujam is both right and wrong. Ramayana is fed with mother's milk to babies in India. It is also impossible to escape the resonance of daily recitations of Tulasi's Ramayana in north Indian homes. The preferred title of the Holy Book by Tulasidas himself is The Holy Lake of the Acts of Rama. Alternatively, it is known as Ramacharitamanas. Tulasidas was no prophet. He also left behind no cult after him. He lived by the sheer power of the pen. His antecedents are doubtful. He was probably born in 1532 and is believed to have died in 1623 at the age of 91. He may have belonged to the Ramananda sect. Again this is a matter of speculation. He was thus a prophet without any organizational backing, but he had millions of admirers who simply adored his version of the Ramayana. Wonder of wonders, he is recognized as one of the main architects of north Indian Vaishnavism.

In one of the finest tributes to him, his Ramayana has been called the common man's Upanishad. Here his version calls for comparison with Valmiki's Ramayana which preceded him. The Ramayana is written entirely from the Bhakti perspective. Thus, the Holy Book is one of the finest tributes to the Bhakti tradition. In a nutshell, it has both the flavor of Bhakti and devotion to Rama. It is not Krishna but Rama, who is his ishta deva. Tulasidas must be a very jealous bhakta. There is no scope for any other option in selecting his Personal God. He was a strict monotheist and, like Ramananda, his personal god was Rama joined by Sita, his consort as his Shakti. For him Rama was an incarnation of Brahman and Sita his

Shakti. In his worldview he had substituted the 'Rama-and-Sita' duo for the more popular Krishna-Radha combination. There is no other god in his scheme of things. He refuses to recognize the possibility:

Rama I have no special abilities,
I do not practice Yoga.
I am unable to mediate,
I have no possessions.
I have only love to offer to you.
You please guide me to the shore with only my love for you.[7]

He practiced what he preached from a high moral pedestal. His Ramayana is in Avadhi and not in his native tongue Bhojpuri. His poetry is sonorous. His Ramayana is set in Chaupais meter compromising five syllables.

Musical Muse

Indian classical music has roots deep in Bhakti and Sufi traditions. Both Hindustani and Karnataka music are rooted deep in Indian spirituality. Indian music is the universal language. There are believed to be 999 ragas constituting the entire corpus of Hindustani music. Hindustani music is unique, constituting as it does a bridge between Hindu composers and Muslim musicians. One of the greatest musicians-cum-composer, Tansen, was born Hindu and was a converted Muslim. The popularity of Vaishnavite themes was a remarkable feature in Sufi 'samaa' rituals. Hindustani music was equally an unifying chord between two major communities of India. It was the Bhakti movement that provided so much acceleration to Hindustani music, and, which in return, provided momentum to it. Two basic and intrinsic aspects of Bhakti are devotion and love. There is also an intrinsic link between music and devotion. Thus Bhakti, devotion, love music constitute one integral entitity. Bhakti is drawn from the stem bhaj, which is, in turn, linked to another term, bhajana, denoting a specific type of music. It is intimately concerned with devotional music in the tradition of Indian spirituality, thus 'music and devotion form one single metaphysical entity'.[8] Music remains the active agent with devotion responding to it. Here devotional poetry comes into the picture by interacting with music to include ecstasy. Thus the ultimate aspect of Bhakti is to induce a state of ecstacy through love, devotion, poetry and music.

There are no two opinions about the spiritual roots of Hindustani music. It is through music that the saint relates his mystical experience through public kirtan. It enables him to identify himself with the collective It is bound to generate mass hysteria so essential to generate ecstasy. To rational minds it may uppear bizarre and incomprehensible, but to the devotee, it is divine music and celestial music melody, transcendent, beyond the senses and intellect. At times it is hard to quantify either creativity or ecstasy, but Bhakti sants are left with no doubt on this score. Kabir and Mira mention *Anhad Naad*, the intrinsic sound or naad, as the music heard within the depths of one's being. *Anhad Naad* has been described as unsung and unheard, but it can be felt in the depths of the being. Tagore in his essay 'the Poet's religion' talks of bonds between music, harmony and creativity. He describes the relation as 'spiritual union between the finite and infinite, of the union which is the prime cause of joy, of all music, of all creativity'.

Musical Essence

The concept of rasa in Indian culture and music is considered a profound principle of life. Rasa is the spiritual life force. The noted musician Pandit Amar Nath views rasa as the essence, underlying the abstract quality of the raga. He is also categorical in linking rasa, Hindustani music and Bhakti tradition. 'There is basically one essence or rasa in all of Hindustan music, and that is the Bhakti rasa'. There are in fact nine rasas expressing varying bhavas (feelings), which comprehend the whole range of human emotions. Every musical piece in this scheme of things, as well as in every rasa related to it, constitutes some aspect of Bhakti. Bhakti rules the roost, because every underlying rasa is always and inevitably Bhakti. In fact, the ragas of Hindustani music have been categorized into nine rasas. To repeat, nine rasas represent bhavas or emotions. *1) Sringara (lovee), 2) hasya (humour), 3) raudra (anger), 4) vira (valour), 5) abdhuta (wondrous), 6) vibhatsa (odious), 7) karuna (compassionate) 8) bhayanaka (fearful),* and *9) shanta (peaceful).*

Among these rasas, Sringara rasa has a place of primacy in relations between Krishna, Radha and his gopis. Thus considerable number of ragas are devoted to this particular rasa. The highest space, however, is devoted to the nineth rasa, Shanta rasa reaching the state of niravana. Some of the finest ragas are actually devoted to it. The highest state of Bhakti is also achieved in this ultimate rasa. Bhakti is thus all-comprehending in enveloping the entire range of rasas. It is through music that great saints like Chaitanya, Kabir, Surdas and Mira narrate their mystical experience and thus succeed in communicating it to the common man.

Music aligned with devotional poetry is unbeatable, and reaches its ecstatic height as the convenient instrument in the hands of Bhakti saints. Truly speaking, Bhakti saints have created modern languages, but, in fact, music has created them. Literature is the language of the mind, and music is the language of the heart. Heart and mind thus function in unison to create a mass movement. Bhakti movement spread wide and fast in north, south, east and west of India by combining devotional poetry with music. The popularity of *Geet Govinda* testifies to the fact. It is not only a great literary piece of work, it is equally great a work of musical excellence comprehending different ragas, talas and chhandas. It also merits as a great piece of dance drama.

Sufi Connection

Bauls are a popular group of Muslim and Hindu singers of Bengal. They are always on the move like bairagis. They follow the tradition of Chaitanya. There is also a marked difference between Muslim and Hindu Bauls. The Muslim stick to Sufi traditions and Hindu Bauls conduct themselves as Vaishnavites. The Bauls as a whole are regarded as the 'Men of the Heart'. Sufi, Bauls however incorporate the Vaishnavite themes in their Sama practices. The Vaishnav rituals were adopted by Sufi Bauls to induce ecstasy. The process of indigenisationmust have been adopted to broaden the appeal beyond the Muslim circuit. To their credit, the Muslim Bauls have helped to open other channels for Vaishnavism. It has also been the beginnings of dialogue with the Sufis. The Muslim Bauls are the best ambassadors that Vaishnavism had ever had for its wide propagation. To their credit they have helped to expand the frontiers of the Bhakti movement. The Sufis have maintained interest in the development of Vaishnavism and Bhakti movement going as far as back as the sixteenth century.

In 1566 Mir Abdul Wahid Bilgrami compiled a Persian dictionary of Hindu devotional songs familiar to the Sufis. It was entitled Haqa-I Hindi. The songs were connected with the Vaishnav Bhakti movement. It was divided into three sections: 'The first section gives a mystic explanation of Hindi words used in Dhrupad songs. The second section allegorically explains the words used in Vaishnavite songs used in Brajbhasha, the dialects of the Mathura region. The Mir Justifies the popularity of the names of kafirs, used in Sufi samaa on the grounds that the Quran itself uses the names of both kafirs and enemies. The third section gives the Sufi explanation of the words used in Hindi Sufi poetry'.[9]

This goes to show several things. The Vaishnav thought had already made a major impact on Sufis through incorporation of devotional poetry in the practice of samaa. There was a regular dialogue between the two cults. They were competing for the same audience. The Sufis had begun to make a systematic study of the thought of the Bhakti movement. The Sufi movement had decided to adopt indigeneous practices. Thus, there is also no doubt it was a two-way traffic.

Personal God

Personal God is one of the greatest inventions of human ingenuity. Bhakti and Personal God are twin sisters. Bhakti represents the spirit of India.. It is a tribute to the wisdom of the crowd. It speaks of the uncanny collective wisdom of Indian masses. It is also the revolt of the masses. The Bhakti movement made its appearance in the form of a religious reform movement. It was a revolt against the ritualist practices of the Vedas. Here it was in line with Buddhism and Jainism, which preceded it and equally inspired the Bhakti movement. It was especially inspired by democratic nature of Buddhism, broader participation of suppressed groups like women and Shudras and its use of popular languages for communication purpose. It is women who receive special consideration under the benign regime of the Bhakti movement. One of the Alvars and three of the Nayanmars were women. Prof Ramanajun was perceptive enough to note, 'It is more common for a married woman saint to get rid of her husband than to endure him'.[10] Again, the very concept of Personal God was due to no other than the ingenuity of the Alvars, who considered God as father, son, brother and master. This theme song was taken over by Gaudiya Vaishnavism as its chief motive. They considered Krishna as a master (dasya), a son (vatsalya), a friend (sakhya), or a beloved (madhuriya).

The proper acceleration to the Bhakti movement was provided by Nimbarka. Supreme God begins to take concrete shape in the person of Krishna, the cowherd. He has been raised to the status of the Supreme Lord of the Universe. The element of the concept of Grace is introduced as an additional bonus. The element of sport comes into picture at the same time. Vaishnava Bhakti now begins to take concrete shape and structure. It has now to await the arrival of Chaitanya to complete the picture. Dialectical transformation became possible with the arrival of Chaitanya on the scene. For him love or premabhakti was enunciated as the regulating principle of the universe. He was a cosmopolitan Bhakti saint who was beyond caste and class distractions. His instructions to his disciples were to 'teach the lesson of faith in Krishna to all men down to the Chandals and freely preach the lesson of love and devotion'.

Simultaneously Sufism had begun to make its impact from the fourteenth century onwards. It had begun to make conscious and unconscious, subtle and not so subtle, impact on the philosophical minds of Bhakti thinkers. The influence of Islam is clearly manifested in the thought of Bhakti saints like Kabir, Namdev and Guru Nanak. Guru Nanak was fundamentally a Vedantist in his worldview. He was also one of the few Sant Bhakts who attempted a serious synthesis of Islam and Hinduism in his unified doctrine. Finally, Bhagvata Purana seems up the history of Bhakti movement in one sentence: '[Bhakti] was born in Dravida and grew up in Karnataka. I live here and there in Maharashtra, and became weak and old in Gujarat. There, during the terrible Kali Age, I was shattered by heretics and I became weak and old along with my sons. But after reaching Vrindavana I became very young and be united again'.[11]

Love and Devotion

Above all, love (prema) is the cementing force in Bhakti tradition. It is also a religion of devotion and worship. Bhakti constitutes the triad of love, devotion and worship. It is pure and simple emotional aspect of religion. It relates to the heart and not the mind. It is dedicated to a Personal God involving person-to-person relationship. Human beings, by their very nature, feel insecure. The Personal God fills up the gap and provides the psychological protection and security. In a nutshell, 'the natural desire of humankind is to be happy, to get rid of all suffering, and the search leads finally to the discovery of a state in which the very duality of happiness, pleasure and pain, is abolished'.[12] This is a plain and simple but very specific and pinpointed description of the ultimate objective of Bhakti. At the highest plane, Bhakti would result in the state of pure bless. It is a worship of Personal God, exclusive devotion to him, resulting in unblemished love. In return, it seeks grace from the Personal God.

The net result is *moksha* or spiritual liberation of the self. It is not class or caste bound. Its doors are open to one and all. Bhakti promises a mystical union with the Personal God, who is also prepared to play the other side of the game. Bhakti as a religion of love and devotion is motivated by a Personal God, divine and full of grace, self-dedication, and with love of the devotee, promising liberation to all, irrespective of caste and sect, and finally arriving at the mystical union. Bhakti is not confined to Hinduism alone. It had a parallel development in Buddhism of the Mahayana kind, thereby elements of Tantra also crept into the Bhakti movement.

The *Bhagvad Gita* has delineated three paths (margas) to liberation from human bondage. They are also termed three Yugas: Karma (works and rituals), Jnana (knowledge and gnosis), and Bhakti (love and devotion). Each one of the three yogas operates in a broader framework. While Karma functions as the equivalent of dharma, Jnana operates within the framework of moksha, Bhakti bridges the conflicting gap between Karma and Jnana. The religion of knowledge is confined to the learned, the intellectual and philosophically- inclined, constituting a small coterie. The religion of ritual is based on the moribund Brahmanic rituals, or equally antediluvian animistic practices. Bhakti follows the Middle Path by bridging the gap in providing binary opposition to Karma (ritual) and Jnana (faith and knowledge).

Metaphysics of Bhakti

The strong advocates of Bhakti like Shrivatsa Goswami assume Bhakti corresponds to the 'whole of human nature', to a worldview subsuming Karma and Jhana Yogas within its framework. However, it must be said in favour of Bhakti that it has no prerequisites and preconditions to be fulfilled. Bhakti is pure joy and it requires no prediscipling. The Bengali poet Chandidas has said the last word on the subject, 'Man is the highest reality; nothing else is higher'.[13] So the Mahabharata asserts, 'Nothing is superior to being human'.[14] Bhakti places man in the centre of things. Even his Personal God is man's replica in an ideal situation. In other words, his Personal God is what he would like to be in the best of the circumstances. The ideal situation is reached by aiming at the achievement of the aesthetic experiences, the alternative name for it being rasa, in the Gaudiya Vaishnav jargon. The state of rasa is another name for pure bliss, which is hard to quantify but it is an essential prerequisite of Sant baani. The appeal of Bhakti is universal. Its roots lie in love (prema) and its climax is reached in a supreme ecstacy (mahabhava), which translates into aesthetic experience (rasa).

The nearest approximation to this state of being is sensuality, the common adult experience of all human beings. The Gaudiya Vaishnava have long recognized that 'the nearest counterpart to such aesthetic experience, rasa, in the human setting is that of sensual pleasure in the context of an amorous relationship', And as the *Taittiriya Upanishad* explains it succinctly in a famous passage: 'That (the ultimate reality), verily is rasa (aesthetic experience), and it alone causes improve bliss.[15] Kama, thus, makes an intrusion in the practice of Bhakti. This sensual relationship is depicted at its finest in Jayadeva's *Gita Gobinda* in love-making between Radha and Krishna. Vaishnava Bhakti rasa has to be viewed as an psychological state of being. It has been described as an erotic emotion, transmitted into 'a deep and ineffable devotional sentiment', further transformed into 'a mental condition of disinterested joy'. Thus the Personal God has been described as the highest, conception of human nature wrapped in sensuality. Krishna's gopis were the ones to comprehend the essence of Bhakti contained in pure and simple love: 'The only thing they understood was that he was infinite love, that was all the gopis understood Krishna as–only as the Krishna of

Vrindavan.... A great landmark in the history of religion is here, the ideal of love for love's sake, work for work's sake, duty for duty's sake...'[16] This was undoubtedly the greatest of spiritual experiences. The fear of religion and its institutions was gone. The common man was on top of the world, thanks to the munificence of the Bhakti movement.

Ideological Foundations

The Gita sets out a paradigm of three paths, namely, Karma, Jnana and Bhakti. While the dialogue between Arjuna and Krishna revolves around the performance of Karma (duty) as obligatory, Gita's religion is a compromise between the intellect and populism. Bhakti has, however, scored over the rest. Bhakti was preached as a doctrine for the first time in the *Bhagavad Gita*. Ramanuja and Madhava gave concrete shape to doctrinal matters and helped to popularize it. The medieval Bhakti movement was merely in the nature of a 'restatement of values' afresh. The roots of Bhakti lie deeper, beyond the Gita. The beginnings of Bhakti may be traced to several hymns scattered in the Rigveda, with Indra being praised, or addressed as a sakha or friend, via longing prayers addressed to him. At the most it can be said that the germ of Bhakti was merely implicit in the Rigvedic hymns. It began to take shape subsequently in the Upanishads. The doctrine of Grace was developed, though implicitly, in *Katha Upanishad* (II, 23). Significantly it rejects the concept of Jnana (knowledge), 'Nor by intellect, nor by much learning'.

The two scriptures, the *Srimad Bhagavad Gita* and the *Srimad Bhagavad Purana* are the very foundations of Bhakti philosophy. *Bhagavad Gita* has discovered the very essence of Hindu tradition and thereby created Bhakti from nowhere. It had only to await for the medieval times to catch the imagination of the populace and electrify them, that the necessary ground had been prepared by the *Bhagavad Gita* with supporting assistance from *Bhagavad Purana*. The *Bhagavad Gita* very cleverly combined 'various theories into one system, by interweaving so to speak, threads from the Sankhya, Yoga, and Vedanta, so as to form a many-coloured wool of thought' which is shot across a stiff warp of doctrine of love (bhakti) for Krishna, and of stern devotion to caste duties (dharma). The maximum kickstart was, however, provided by *Bhagavad Purana* riding on the shoulders of the

Bhagavad Gita. It provided the necessary vibrant emotionalism. Bhakti constitutes the very foundations of the Sant tradition. There are four dimensions to Bhakti provided by its four background traditions of different dimensions, historical impact and background. The four dimensions which helped to form the Sant tradition include Vaishnavism, Shaivism, Tantra and Sufism. They have interacted fruitfully with Bhakti movement with varying results.

Bhakti and Pandits

The Bhakti movement was a distinctive landmark in the cultural history of India for a variety of reasons. It was an act of assertion on the part of the suppressed classes. The true spirit of Bhakti rested on its etymological sense of participation and not devotion. It was accepted universally, being expressed in the local dialect. It had sought to humanise the abstract idea of supreme divinity by direct one-to-one relations with God. It was also an assertion of creative feminity by imaging Godhood in the form of a woman (Sri Radhe).

Poetry became the main instrument of communication. The imagery used by the poets was born of their immidiate experience and environment. The poetry was simplyfied and complex.Familiar, profound and sublime at the same time. This genre of literature was simultaneously romantic (with a tinge of erotic flavour), spiritual but secular, and had an open and shut social message. It was a revolution which shed no blood and conveyed the message of universal love. This transformation in the environment of the ancient land was beautifully summed up in the words of Kabir (The true midwife of Bhakti and Sufi sangam),

'whoever learns one word 'love' becomes a pundit.

Section - X

Progressive Khalsa

20

Sikhism and the Sant Tradition

THE Bhakti Age had its origins in the south, inspired by mystics, poets and reformers. It had a long innings beginning in the seventh century to the end of the Vijayanagara empire. It was inspired by the Bhagavad Gita. Yet it was essentially an indigeneous movement, which was subsequently to spread like wildfire throughout the entire country. Religion had come to be entirely focused on love and yearning (expressed as viraha or separation). There is a great divide between Tamil Nadu and the Punjab in terms of history and geography. The Bhakti movement, however, united them. Bhakti is a blanket term which has different connotations in different cultural contexts. There is a bond that inextricably unites the devotees of Bhakti movement, whether in north, south, west or east. Even Tamil Nadu and the Punjab bonded together on basic issues concerning the ideology of Bhakti. Both of them are located in the periphery of the subcontinent. The orthodox ideas have never occupied permanent stage in Tamil Nadu and the Punjab. Liberal thoughts have always predominated in the two distant geographical territories. Vedic Brahmin traditions have had a weaker hold on the mind of the common man. Ascetism in these two geographic locales was not as popular as it was in middle India.

Tamil and Sikh Bhakti tradition has always highly regarded the institution of family. Here there is a great deal common between Guru Nanak and Tiruvalluvar, who has greatly influenced the Tamil religious thought. Thiruvalluvar's classic *Thirukural* has been held in equal reverence as the *Adi Granth* in the Punjab. There is a great deal common between the two masters and faiths united by a separation of great distance, but joined together in spiritual bonds, 'Both Guru Nanak and Thiruvalluvar were house-holders-cum-teachers. Domestic virtue, truth, purity, humility and charity form the favourite themes of some of their finest verses couched in simple and straightforward manner in their respective languages. Again, their views about vast variety of themes such as good and bad actions, love, truthfulness, virtue, humility and good conduct etc., have been expressed without entering into dogmatic or doctrinal controversies. While trying to lead men from darkness to light, from evil to righteousness and from mortality to immortality, neither of them posed as a prophet or law giver'.[1] Mysticism was also not a strong point with Guru Nanak. He was very practical. In fact, he reflected the ethos of the Land of the Five Rivers. Even the prophets are born to reflect their own times. Sikh Bhakti movement thus reflected the local ethos in the context of the pan-Indian Bhakti movement.

Mainstream Sant Tradition

The Bhakti movement is comparable to Hinduism. It is a many-headed hydra with no focus. It is everywhere and nowhere. Vaishnaism is so different from Saivism, as the Nath tradition is from Sikhism. Similarly, Guru Nanak is so different from Chaitanya, as Ramanuja is distant from Ramananda. The *Nirguna* philosophy is equally counterpoised with the *Saguna* way of life. What is the focus of the Bhakti tradition? None, comes the prompt reply! For millions to be electrified spontaneously by the magic of Bhakti, by this 'diversity in unity', the movement speaks of the under-currents of intra-religious and inter-religious spirituality underlying it. Bhakti is innately an Indian bye-product. It cuts across the geographical, historical and cultural barriers. What brings together Bhakti movements is the magic of the Sant tradition. Guru Nanak undoubtedly ranked high in the Sant tradition of Northern India. Sikhism was definitely a variant from the rest of the Bhakti mainstream. Subsequently, it was proclaimed a separate religion. Guru Nanak's thought possessed a high degree of distinctive coherence to pronounce its distinctive identity. His thought was a part of the mainstream Bhakti movement. He ranked equally along with other Sants in their distinguished hierarchy. He was inspired by other Sants and he, in return, inspired several generations of the Sant community. He was a new synthesis of the Bhakti theme, but the system developed was 'essentially a reworking of the Sant pattern'.

It remains to be emphasized that the Bhakti movement and the Sant tradition had a dissenting character. They reflected the revolt of the masses against the oppressive Brahminic ritualization. The Sant tradition was born as a result of interaction with three dissenting movements: Vaishnava, Nath and Sufism. Guru Nanak was greatly influenced by these three dissenting movements. The influencing took place during the lifetime of Guru Nanak. Punjab was the fertile ground for arriving at a rapport between the Bhakti and Sufi movements. Sufi poets like Baba Farid and Shah Husain had been the pioneers in this connection. There are however several critics like W H McLeod who disavow any influence of Sufi thought on Guru Nanak except in the extreme fringes.

The other two dissenting movements interacting with the thought of Guru Nanak were Vaishnava Bhakti and the Hatha-Yoga of the Nath Jogis. The Vaishnava movement was the primary agent of Bhakti movement. The concept of love was its distinctive contribution. Bhakti movement spread far and wide, as the vehicle of love. Guru Nanak's *baani* is saturated with love. Nath influences had previously persisted in the Punjab as seen in folk and oral tradition and Saraiki/Punjabi literature. The Nath Jogis were also headquartered in the province. Nath influences emerge prominently in the basic terminology employed by Kabir (and subsequently by Guru Nanak). The principal concept of Sahaj employed in *Adi Granth* was derived from the Nath tradition. Sikhism is to be credited with major social reforms like the rejection of class distinctions and ritual practices. Credit is sure to go to the Naths. Nevertheless, the Bhakti influence retained its primacy.

Kabir Again

The concept of love has a universal appeal. It cuts across most barriers. It does not burden the mind. It directly appeals to the heart. It stirs the subconscious. No wonder, Bhakti spread like wild fire in north India with the twinkling of the eye. It spoke the language of the people. Khariboli had been adopted as the lingua franca of north India. It supplemented and substituted the local languages. Bhakti became coterminous with the Vaishnava Bhakti due to the magic mantra of 'love'. Guru Nanak felt enchanted by the concept. The impression that he also adopted it in no time was, however, wrong. Guru Nanak and other Sikh gurus adopted the term with their kind of interpretation. There were considerable reservations about the philosophy and practices of Vaishnavism. Some of the differences were of fundamental nature. In fact, Sikh gurus were much more comfortable with the Nath influences, thanks to the close association of Kabir with Guru Nanak and his thought. There is no proof that they ever met personally. That Kabir influenced Sikhism greatly is no secret. Indeed Kabir has been called the co-founder of Sikhism. Kabir was a julaha (weaver) by caste, who were believed to be converts to Islam from the Nath tradition. Nath influences were in his blood, he pumped these influences in the mainstream of Sikhism.

Nath tradition had been, in its turn, influenced by Mahayana Tantric Buddhism. Guru Nanak rejected totally the Tantric emphasis on sex, but he accepted wholesale the Tantra rejection of Vadic rituals, class distinctions and Brahmanic dominance. Kabir and Guru Nanak were certainly aligned on the same platform. As it has been pointed out, 'Nath influence emerges in much of basic terminology, used by Kabir (and later by Guru Nanak), in a rejection of all interior forms, ceremonies, caste distinctions, sacred languages, and scriptures, in a strong emphasis upon unity as opposed to 'duality', and in the concept of a mystical union which destroys this 'duality'. It is not without significance that the commonest of all terms used by both Kabir and Guru Nanak to express this experience of union is *sahaj*, a word which at once carries us back into Nath theory and beyond the Nath tradition into the earlier world of tantric Buddhism'.[2] This goes to prove that Sikhism did not fall from the heavens. It has a past which planted it in the mainstream of the Bhakti movement. It had roots not only in Vaishnavism (as explained earlier), it had also a part in Mahayana Buddhism and Nath traditions. Contradictory as it may seem, while Guru Nanak rejected Vedic ritualism, he seemed to subscribe to the Vedanta (end of the Vedas) which emerged as the predominant system and gained wide currency through *Bhagavad Gita*. It reflects unity in diversity in Indian tradition and Sikhism was no exception to it.

Sufi Influences

There was another dimension to Kabir. He was a Vaishnavite, being the follower of Ramananda. He was under considerable influence of the Nath tradition. His reformist streak came from this particular background. He had also another dimension to his personality. He was presumably born a Muslim. Bhagat Kabir Julaha has been claimed to be a follower of Tauhid (*Wahdat-al-Wajoud*). His search for reality straight led him to Nirguna, the core of the philosophy of Guru Nanak. It speaks highly of inter-religious spirituality, shared equally by Guru Nanak and Kabir. Sufi mystics had contributed their might in strengthening the foundations of the Bhakti movement. Sufi traditions helped greatly in broadening the outlook. It also sharpened the edges of the Bhakti movement in fighting its battles against the orthodox Brahminic practices. The Nirguna tradition of Guru Nanak was considerably strengthened by example. The Islamic faith in oneness of God and social equality dazzled the thinking minds in the subcontinent. There were strong currents underway in the Punjab for reconciliation between Bhakti and Sufi movements. Several distinguished Sufi poets were in the frontline.

Guru Nanak could not help but be impressed by the Sufi undercurrents. The writings of Baba Farid are prominently displayed in the *Adi Granth*. Kabir was a Vaishnavite, but he substituted Suguna for Nirguna God. So, had Guru Nanak done the same? Kabir was been called 'the Child of Ram and Allah'. Guru Nanak has been called the symbol of Sant synthesis.

The synthesis was essentially between the different streams of the Bhakti movement. There was also another kind of synthesis that was taking place at another level. This was a relationship of subtle conflict and its resolution between clanging Hindu and Muslim traditions. Alternatively it had to be viewed in terms of reconciliation between Bhakti and Sufi movements. There was a considerable element of competitiveness, because both of them were competing for the same audience. Strategies and tactics were strikingly similar. The stress on love and devotion, open-house policy to attract large audience, emphasis on simple living and high thinking, the fondness of collective singing and music, the respect given to the guru, and, last but not the least, exclusive attention devoted to the Personal God, were, astonishingly enough, common denominations of both Bhakti and Sufi movements. The thought of Guru Nanak epitomizes the spirit of genuine synthesis at various levels.

Variant Bhakti Tradition

In north India Bhakti tradition was synonymous with the Vaishnava cult. Its overwhelming dominance had to do with its stress on populist love and devotion. It turned out to be a mass movement. Vishnu's human incarnations like Rama and Krishna were concrete manifestations of the personal God. The appeal was widened when the manifested God came to be associated with his consorts like Radha, Rukmini and Sita. Images of these deities and their consorts were installed and worshipped in the temple. God was not merely an abstract *Nirguna* manifestation, but a reflection of the human family. He could be directly approached and supplicated. Post-Chaitanya Vaishnavism had deviated from the path laid down by the Master. Brahminic ritualism had been adopted wholesale after the death of Chaitanya. The doors to Bhakti were shut to the lower castes by designing the path of propatti (unquestioned self-surrender) for them. Singing and dancing formed an essential part of the worship. Every devotee was expected to join in this activity with gay abandon. No intermediaries were required, but the path of propatti had placed an hurdle in direct communication with the personal God. Similarly, music and dance had become a specialized activity. The deva-dasis took over the propiation of God inside the temples.

The devotee had thus become a mere spectator. The devadasis, who were literally speaking 'female slaves of the deity', were also designated *nagarbadhus* (public wives).

Bhakti was in danger of losing its purpose and rationale. Bhakti movement had broken class and caste distinctions and had brought religion at the door step of the discriminated and unprivileged classes. Primarily, it was a social reform-movement bringing economic and social benefits to the peripheral classes. At some stage, Bhakti was no longer loving devotion, but emotion and frenzy for the mere sake of it. The dominant Vaishnava Bhakti had gone into reverse gear. It had also come under Tantric influences. This was probably due to the influences emanating from the Mahayana and Nath traditions. The traditional Vaishnava Bhakti had to be challenged at some stage. The response came from Ramananda, whose disciples included Kabir and Ravidas. He challenged the basic tenets of Vaishnava Bhakti including avtarvad, idol worship, religious rituals and caste distinctions. Ramananda is to be credited with saving Chaitanya, the founder of Vaishnavism, from post. Chaitanya influences. Kabir was Ramananda's most outspoken spokesman. More importantly, Kabir was the linkman and the most effective salesman of the Bhakti movement. His ideas had travelled extensively far and wide during his lifetime. He had a questioning mind. He was a linkman between Sufi and Bhakti movements. His ideas had the largest acceptability in the Land of the Five Rivers. His lifetime coincided with the emergence of Sikhism in the Punjab. He helped to shape the thought and philosophy of Guru Nanak. The *Adi Granth* is as much a tribute to Kabir as to the Ten Gurus.

Ideological Foundations

Vaishnavism flourished unchallenged in North and East India, but it did not have a free hand in the Punjab. There was considerable interplay of religious ideas in that part of the world. Sufism had also made a great headway. There was also considerable scope for dialogue between Sufi and Bhakti movements. There was much scope for mutual give-and-take. In the circumstances, the Punjab could ill-afford to be ill-liberal in exchange of ideas, beliefs and social behavior. Dialogue was possible only in non-conformist and protestant environment. Vaishnavism made only a limited headway in the Punjab on that account. Several distinguished Saraiki Sufi poets made good use of Vaishnava concepts in their poetic works. Krishna emerges as a prominent character in those writings. There is, however, no comparable locally-bred Bhakti poet to be found. The reason is crystal clear. Vaishnava cultists never communicated in either Saraiki or Punjabi, the local dialects of the Land of the Five Rivers. Brajbhasha had a limited use among the local devotees of the Bhakti movement. There was, thus, a vacuum that remained to be fulfilled. Sikhism had addressed itself to these ideals. It was waiting to fulfill the gap in the spiritual life of the people. Then there appeared Guru Nanak to walk into the vacuum. He was a non-conformist and protestant in his worldview. He was sensitive to the criticism emanating from the contemporary society. He was, thus, a bridge between Vaishnavism on the one side, and Sufism on the other. He, however, continued to maintain his Sant identity.

Guru Nanak and Sikhism stand out distinctly in several respects, even though they were in line with the basic tenets of Bhaktism. Sufism laid much stress on renunciation of the world as a spiritual pursuit. So did several Sants of the Bhakti movement. Sikhism was totally opposed to such a pursuit. It was very much of the world. It has always had dual ideals in life. It found no contradiction between the other worldly (piri) as well as this worldly (miri). In fact, both of them stand cheek-by-jowl, supportive of each other in the Sikh tradition. It has the distinction of being the religion of the householder. Fortunately, for Sikhism, the Punjab was a favourable ground to function freely. The hold of Brahmanism had weakened considerably due to persistent invasions from the north. Earlier Buddhism had strongholds in that part of the world. It proved to be a double whammy in weakening the hold of Brahmanism. Guru Nanak's ideology was founded on three strong pillars of positive social content, spiritual and ethical principles. Sikhism lays so much stress on moral values. The followers of Sikhism had come to have a distinctive identity in the course of time. This process had begun during the time of Guru Nanak himself. The Punjabi language and the Gurmukhi script also gave a sharpeningly distinctive edge to Sikhism, even though it has to be admitted that the *Adi*

Granth speaks the language of Khariboli. Thus Sikhism has a pan-Indian and regional character simultaneously.

Sant Ideologue

Guru Nanak has been called a Sant ideologue. He functioned within the framework of the Sant ideology. While its contours were understood, it was hard to define precisely. Its flexibility was its greatest advantage. Guru Nanak must be placed within the framework of Sant thought. He was, however, an ideologue with a difference. He was nearest to Kabir, but he was not his copy. He had chalked out a separate path for himself and his creed. Punjabis are said to be pragmatic and practical. Guru Nanak was a direct image of his people. He understood their psyche well. He did not believe in renunciation, but believed like his own people, that life had to be lived and lived well. Suffering was no part of his life. Labour was an obligation and honour. He used to say, 'He who eats what he has earned by his own labour, and gives some to (others)–Nanak, he it is who knows the true way' (Vat. Sar. Moh I). His earliest followers came from the Khatri and Arora stock. Guru Nanak himself was Khatri by birth. The trader in him must have calculated in terms of loss and profit. Religion was thus translated in terms of profitable commerce. He must have also realized that armies do not fight on an empty stomach. It must be said to the credit of the Sikh community that no beggars are found among them, thanks to the foresight of the founder of Sikhism. It had also another major fallout. Sikhism became a religio-social movement with the definite purpose of reforming society.

In the ultimate analysis, Sikhism is the product of its environment. The Punjab had a dominant Islamic environment. Guru Nanak had to come to terms with it. He chose the middle path because the intellectual elite of medieval Punjab were dominated by liberal Sufi poets. The middle path thus fitted the boots of Guru Nanak. However, Sikhism is not a blend of Hinduism and Islam. Punjabi Sufism was of a home-grown variety. It was so different from the classical model of Arab and Persian Sufism. It worked on the simple principle of 'I teach and you teach me'. Guru Nanak reminds you of the Buddha, who followed the Middle Path. Logically it leads to the synthesis born out of several permutations and combinations: 'He received a synthesis and he passed it on, but he did so in a form which was in some measure amplified, and in considerable measure clarified and integrated. This applied in particular to his understanding of the manner of divine communication with man. Guru Nanak's concept of the Sabad, the Nain, the Guru, and the Hukum carry us beyond anything that the works of earlier Sants offer in any explicit form. It is Sant thought which we find in his works, but it is Sant's thought expanded and re-interpreted'.

Sikhism and Terminology

Guru Nanak and his successor nine Gurus employed the terminology of the Sant movement without apologies. It goes to prove once again that Sikhism was a part and parcel of mainstream Bhakti tradition. Nirguna, Saguna, Omkara, Sabd', Guru and Sahaj are concepts basic to Indian spiritual tradition. These concepts are interpreted differently in different environment, but their essential meaning has remained the same. Several of these terms trace their origin to the Vedas, or, at least, to the Vedanta (End of the Vedas). Some of the terms have remained unchanged for millennia together. Others have been twisted: and turned to suit the local conditions. Several of the concepts prevalent in Sikh tradition have been drawn from the Nath tradition. These are no longer purely Nath concepts, because they belong to the Sants who have owned them as their own. Similarly, ONKAR, generally written as Oankar in Sikh scriptural writings, is derived from the Upanishadic word Oankara (Om kara). It is a synonym of the Om word employed in Vedic literature, as well as the Upanishads, as a mystic concept of great weight in Indian tradition. It also happens to be of utmost significance in the Sikh tradition, being equated with Brahman, the Supreme Spirit. These concepts have been interpreted valiantly in the Sikh tradition, but the variation is only marginal and basically it is aligned with the Sant tradition.

Another important concept basic to Sikh mystical thought is *Sahaj*–a state of mental and spiritual equilibrium. This concept was drawn from the leftist Tantric cults, in whose vocabulary Sahaj signified a protest against the formulism of all orthodox religious traditions like class and caste distinctions and religious ritualism. It indicates the Nath influences in the thought of Sikhism. It also underlines the close connection of Guru Nanak and Kabir, and through him, to the Nath tradition. The Sikh concept of Sahaj includes the (1) rejection of formal rituals, (2) rejection of priesthood, (3) due recognition of the guru, and (4) recognition of the Supreme Deity. The State of Sahaj has been called a state of freedom and peaceful equilibrium of mind. In fact, the state of Suhaj is widely practiced among the Bauls, the Naths, Sahyojana Vaishnavism and several sects of Mahayana Buddhism. It is of Tantric origin and logically leads to the state of *maithuna*, the sexual union, to achieve the highest state of *nirvana* resulting in physical union between man and woman. This logically leads to licence, and the degeneration of society. The merit of Guru Nanak lies in obviating the path of *maithuna* and observing and practicing high moral standards in personal life.

Guru Granth Sahib

The *Guru Granth Sahib* is a pan-Indian religious classic. It was planned under inspiration of the fifth Guru, Guru Arjan Dev (1563-1606) and executed under his direction by Bhai Gurdas. It represents four centuries of Indian religious thought. It contains about 6,000 verses, of which about 5,000 have been contributed by the first five gurus including Guru Nanak and Guru Arjan Dev. The rest are the contributions of the Bhaktas, Sufis, Bhatts or bards (attending the courts of the gurus). They number 15 saints or Bhagats, 11 Bhatts and three other Sikhs. The entire collection is divided into 31 classical ragas. *Guru Granth Sahib* is also called as Pothi Sahib. The Holy Book was formally consecraled on August 16, 1604. The gurus emphasized the path of the worship of the Name (*Namamarga*). Such ragas that raised passion of any kind were eschewed. Ragas like Jag and Dipak were likewise omitted for their melancholy atmosphere. Megh and Hindol were welcomed for their spontaneous ebulience.

Guru Granth Sahib is not a monolithic text. It is a compilation of teachings of saints from the entire northern India. South and east India Sants are omitted for obvious reasons of language. Bhakti movement in north India was a major achievement. It began to talk in the same language.

Suddenly, the language barriers gave away. Everyone began to talk in the same language. It is not merely that the Sants were communicating with each other. The devotees were able to communicate with each other. The language of the *Guru Granth Sahib* was no hurdle. The Sacred Book was certainly not communicating in the native Punjabi. It was talking in the language of the Sant Bhasha. It was also known as Khariboli. In Sufi circles it came to be known as Hindwi. It was a text of Espranto which had emerged from nowhere, but it planted itself everywhere in no time. It coined its vocabulary by itself. Its appeal came from its extensive use in writing of religious verse. It was a language of the common people. Most of the Sants belonged to the lower classes. In several instances they happened to be illiterate. The *Guru Granth Sahib* was non-esoteric in expression and its content was its greatest asset. Its simplicity is its strongest point. It is also a book of record. It has the stamp of authenticity on the *Sant baani* contained in it. It provides the stamp of approval over the verse of great Sufis and Sants like Baba Farid and Kabir, besides the baani of six Sikh gurus.

Various Recensions

The late Prof Pyar Singh made a comprehensive study of various compilations and granths, also known as *birs* throwing light on the history and evolution of the *Adi Granth*. He was able to compile a list of 44 recensions or birs on the basis of available manuscripts of rare and ancient pothis and birs in Gurumukhi script. The original Granth Sahib prepared under the direction of Guru Arjan Dev is known as Kartarpuri bir. It is known so because it is deposited at Kartarpur and happens to be in the custody of the Sodhi family of Kartarpur. It is to be recalled in this connection that the last six Gurus hailed from this very Sodhi family. It attained the present eminent status during the regime of Maharaja Ranjit Singh. The said family has refused to part with it, in spite of the persistent efforts of the Shiromani Gurdwara Prabandhak Committee. Even the law courts have been involved in the dispute. Access to the Kartarpuri bir is rarely granted.

The Sikh Holy Book compromises writings based on two streams – the sayings of the Gurus, six of them, and those of Bhagats (bhaktas or saints). The baani of the Bhagats is a unique feature of the sacred book, unparalleled in sacred scriptures of other religious faiths. It draws upon the writings of leaders of the *Nirgundhara* bhakti and the Sufi movements from all parts of north and west India. *Guru Granth Sahib* is the only sacred book, which secular though it is a religious text. Furthermore, 'They all, the writings of the Gurus, as well of Bhagats, constitute one single text. On any point of percept and doctrine both will have equal validity.... In fact, the notion of 'Two' does not exist.... The Sikhs have believed through the centuries that they embody one single moral and spiritual maxim'.[3]

The other historically famous bir is known as Bannomal bir, compiled in 1642, so called because the said bir belonged to Bhai Banno, one of Guru Arjun's disciples, which he got prepared from the original text. It has been termed as khari (brakish) and hence not acceptable. Subsequently the tenth and last guru, Guru Gobind Singh, added briefly to the *Gurbaani* by incorporating the baani of the ninth guru, Guru Tegh Bahadur. It is popularly known as the Damdama bir (having been dictated at Damdama Sahib). The authenticity of particular birs has been a subject of much speculation and controversies, as Guru Arjan Dev incorporated the hymns of Ravidas and Dhanna in the Santbaani portion of *Adi Granth*, subsequently to placate the followers of the Jats and cobblers, who were getting attracted to the new faith in larger numbers. It has also been alleged that the sants from other regions of India have only a 'token representation'. Such criticism does not detract from the historical importance of the Holy Book in its grand conception.

Pan-Indian Language

Sikh gurus had a pan-Indian vision. At one level, Sikhism had its lower sight in reforming the Punjabi society, but, at another level, their vision was set higher beyond the Land of the Five Rivers. The *Adi Granth* had a broader vision. It was addressed to a larger audience. Punjabi language would not serve the purpose on account of its limited appeal. Khariboli was in the process of evolution. The answer was to construct the *Santbhasha*, a kind of model for all religious compositions. It was called Hindwi, a sort of precursor of the modern Hindi language. The medieval times in which the Sikh gurus lived were the age of transition. Sanskrit language was no longer in use. Prakrits were in the process of dying. The modern Indian languages like Punjabi, Hindi, Marathi and Gujarati, etc. were in the process of being born. The Sikh gurus adopted Hindwi as their convenient vehicle. They, however, discarded the local tongue. They adopted Hindwi by modifying it with the local dialect. You find an admixture of Saraiki, Punjabi and Hindwi in their writings incorporated in the *Adi Granth*. Guru Gobind Singh went very much beyond. He made use of pure Hindwi in his religious writings. He is said to be nearly unintelligible to his Punjabi/Sikh audience.

The Sikh gurus were pioneers in the right sense of the term. They had totally discarded the Sanskrit meter. They had no use for rules and practices of Sanskrit poetry. They were adventurers exploring new avenues. They had some use for old Prakrit meter, but they also did not hesitate to explore new avenues. Logically, the grammatical forms of the language were in a state of transition. New structures were in the process being invented. The Prakrits were being revived to a great extent. *Guru Granth Sahib* was a great laboratory for grammatical forms and new prosody. Local dialects were thus being revived and those were recognized as modern Indian languages. *Santbaani* was a great leveler and, at another plane, the most creative ideas were also born in the medieval times. Perhaps it is for the first time after Ashoka the Great and Shankar that the idea of India as a unit took concrete shape. The idea of unity took definite shape in the mind of the ordinary people for the first time ever. Ernest Trump has called the Sikh Granth as 'the treasury of the old Hindwi dialectics', or 'grammar of the Prakrit of the Middle ages' (or the old Hindwi). In order to fill the gap which exists between the neo-Indian languages and the old Prakrit, 'then we shall be able to survey the development of the Aryan idom in India, beginning with the old Vedic Sanskrit, up to our days .... (letter dated the 23rd May, 1873)'.[4]

Bhatras-The Chroniclers

The term *bhatra* is a diminutive of the Sanskrit term bhutta, a bard, an endogamous and tightly-knit community among the Sikhs. The Bhatts are hereditary panegyrists, generalogists or family bards. The Bhatts recorded events of the lives of the Gurus and of the members of their families in their scrolls called Vahis. Bhatts are poets who celebrate the lives and times of the gurus in spiritual terms. They are also called Sarasvat, i.e., the learned Brahmins. They used to live on the right bank of the river Saraswati. They specialized in recording the bansavalinama or generalogies of their patrons. Being professional generalogists since ancient times, they utilized their association with the Sikh Gurus to the best of their advantage. Some of the vahis are preserved to this day. Vahis are useful sources of information on Sikh religious history and still await to be full explored. It is possible to cull out valuable information regarding dates, places, events and personalities of the period. Actually, they are secularized Brahmins who felt equally at home in the courts of princes and deras of Sikh gurus. They have been ranked the highest as chroniclers, so much so as to be addressed as 'the Vedas incarnate', in other words, the walking encyclopedias of Sikh religious history.

They have earned a name for themselves in Sikh religious history for an important reason. Bhatt Baani is recorded under the title of Savaiyye, the name popularly given to the compositions of the Bhatts, as included in the *Guru Granth Sahib* (pl. 1389-1409). Bhatts are known to sing in chorus. 17 Bhatts find their baani included in the Adi Granth. They are thus placed on par with sant baani, indeed the highest tribute to them in the circumstances. The total number of compositions included in the Bhatt Baani is 123 savaiyye. Bhatts are responsible for perpetuating one of the most significant tenets of the Sikh faith. The Bhatts see the gurus as one light or spirit passing from the other. Equally the *Bhatt Baani* has as much significance for the common Sikh as the word of the guru. Bhatts have thus travelled a long way from being mere chroniclers. The Gurus, the Sants and the Bhatts are placed on par in certain respects.

Vedanta and Sikhism

There is a close connection between Hindu mystical tradition, Sikhism and Sufism, as there is an intimate relation between Kabir and Guru Nanak. The popularity of the Nath-Jogic philosophy among Muslim Sufis had increased immensely, especially among the *muwahhids* (believers in the unity of Being). In the meanwhile the channels of communication were opening up fast with the availability of Persian translations of the Sanskrit *Bhagavad Gita* and the *Yoga Vashishtha*. The similarities between the Wahdat ul-Wujud and the Yoga philosophy and Vedanta were so remarkable as to result in their universal acceptability. Even the Emperor Jahangir and many others were fond of quoting the following verse of the Sufi poet, Baba Fighani (d. 1519) of Shiraz, 'epitomized' in the teachings of both the Vedanta and Sufism. The Baba wrote:

There is one lamp in this house, by whose rays,
Wherever I look there is an assembly.[5]

The similarities between Vedanta and Wahdat ul-Wajud are so striking as to place Bhakti, Sufism, Kabir and Guru Nanak in the same rank. Extended further in time, similarities can also be found with Greek philosophers as well as Jogis and Brahmins. These links are very deep. According to one source, 'Nanak acknowledged Kabir as his spiritual guide'.[6] Guru Nanak was also very much aligned with the spirit of Vedanta. Nanak says:

Hear ye, the meaning of the Word OM,
Which, indeed, is the Essence of the three worlds

He further added:

When there is no form, no sign, no indoctrination, then the Word,
in its Essence, abided in the Absolute God.[7]

Khushwant Singh, in his article on Sikhism in Encyclopaedia Britanica (vol. 17, edn. 15), has clinched the matter, but in the process raised a controversy. His views on Guru Nanak and Vedanta are definitive: 'Sikhism was a historical development of the Vaishnava Bhakti movement – a devotional movement among followers of God Vaishnava that began in Tamil country and was introduced to the north by Ramanuja (traditionally 1017-1037).'

In the same article, he elaborated his thesis of Sikhism being in the mainstream of the Bhakti movement, 'Sikhism is an offshoot of Hindus and is only distinguishable by the external symbols of the Khalsa faith. The theology is Hindu (and) almost nine ttenths of the *Granth Sahib*, composed largely by Guru Arjun, is in fact Vedanta, and an essence of all that you read in *Upanishads* and the *Gita*'.[8]

Guru Nanak is the shining light of Sikhism as well as of the Bhakti movement. His times were great times for Bhakti, considering he had the company of the greats like Kabir (1448-1510), Haridas (1478), Vallabhacharya (1479-1531), Surdas (1483-1563), Chaitanya (1483-1563), and Mirabai (1486-1534). Two of them, Chaitanya and Vallabhacharya, were founders of the Vaishnava cult built around them. Mirabai and Surdas were great Hindi lyrical poets, who fired the imagination of the entire north India. Swami Haridas, the guru of the famous singer Tansen, was a great classical composer and singer of all times. Kabir was the most versatile thinker of medieval times, who is also believed to be an architect of Sikh faith along with Nanak. Guru Nanak, the founder of Sikhism, was in the same tradition as the Alvars and Nayanmars of Tamil Nadu, going back to about 600 B C, who spread the gospel of Bhakti in the Punjab. He was no philosopher like Jia Goswami (1517-1596), but he was the most logical of Sant-Bhagats, consistent in his thought, and he was a man of principles. The nine Gurus who followed him were all of the Khatri caste. Sikhism is thus associated dwith the revival of Hinduism in the Punjab. The Khatri revival ended with the Jat one, closely linked to the upsurge of Sikhism. The second phase of upsurge coincided with the birth of the Khalsa.

Family Connection

The *Guru Granth Sahib* is the holiest of the holy book for the Sikhs. It is their Vedas, the Puranas, the Mahabharata, the *Bhagavad Gita* and the Ramayana, all combined into one. It has evolved over a period of time. In its first version it was known as the *Pothi Sahib*. It contains the baani of the first four Gurus consisting of 1622 hymans, which works out to be more than one fourth of the final version of the *Guru Granth Sahib*. At this stage it did not contain the Santbaani. Each one of the Gurus had made a distinctive contribution to broadening the socialization process of the Sikh community. Guru Angad had lived under the shadow of Guru Nanak all his life, but made the path-breaking contribution by introducing the Gurumukhi script to the Punjabi language. Guru Amar Das introduced the practice of community kitchen (langar) and thus breaking the caste barriers and in introducing the communal living. The fourth Guru Ram Das built the sacred tank in Amritsar, around which the golden Temple took shape subsequently. Guru Ram Das was the first Guru belonging to the Sodhi (Khatri caste). He was followed by Guru Arjan Dev, the fifth Guru, who was also a Sodhi himself. The remaining five gurus were also

Sodhis and belonged to the same family.

The fifth Guru Arjan ranks the highest along with Guru Nanak, as does the tenth Guru, Guru Govind Singh (Original name: Gobind Ram), who laid the foundations of the Golden Temple. Guru Arjan Dev is also the author of the Granth, with Bhai Gurdas providing the necessary editiorial assistance in the task. Now the Pothi Sahib had transformed itself into the *Guru Granth Sahib* by incorporating the baani of Guru Arjan Dev, as well as the Santbaani for the first time. The sixth Guru Har Gobind was the son of Guru Arjan Dev, and the next Guru Har Rai was the grandson of the Sixth Guru, as was the next Guru, Hari Krishan, the eighth Guru, son of Guru Har Rai. The sixth, the seventh and the eighth Gurus are not represented in the *Guru Granth Sahib*, the successor volume of the Adi Granth. The tenth Guru Gobind Singh chose not to incorporate his prolific contributions to the Holy Book, but he decided to incorporate 115 hymns of his father Guru Tegh Bahadur into it.

Fugures at a Glance

The *Guru Granth Sahib*, the Holy Book of the Sikhs, has passed through three stages of *Pothi Sahib*, *Adi Granth* (Kartarpuri Bir) and the Damdama Bir. It consists of 1,430 pages and contains about 6,000 verses. It contains the baani of the first five Gurus and the ninth Guru, Guru Tegh Bahadur, with the total of hymns numbering 5,110. It works out to 80% of the entire corpus contained in The Holy Book. The rest of the hymns are devoted to 15 Sants or Bhagats, 11 Bhatts and 3 other Sikhs. The *Guru Granth Sahib* was installed formally in the Golden Temple in 1604 AD, thus starting a new chapter in the history of Sikhism. The maximum number of hymns incorporated in the Holy Book are to be credited to Guru Arjan Dev. The next three Gurus have made no contribution whatsoever. Guru Gobind Singh decided to incorporate 115 hymns of his father and the nineth Guru, Guru Tegh Bahadur, thus transforming the *Adi Granth* into the Damdama Bir. The baani of 15 Sants or Bhagats continued to incorporated to give The Holy Book a pan-Indian coloration. It works out to 775 hymns, of which 758 hymns are attributed to four saints, namely Kabir (541 hymns), Baba Farid (116 hymns), Namdev (61 hymns) and Ravidas (40 hymns). It also contains the baani of Bhai Mardana, the lifelong companion of Guru Nanak, classed with his other companion, Guru Angad.

A bare 17 hymns are to be attributed to the remaining Sants. Only one each hymn is to be attributed to Pipa, Parmananda, Surdas, Sadhna and Sain. The scarce numbers take away somewhat from the merit of its pan-Indian character. The *Guru Granth Sahib* is of historical character in another respect. It places the stamp of authenticity upon the hymns contained in it. It is especially true of the hymns attributed to Kabir, Namdev, Ramdas and Baba Farid. The controversy, however, continues about the hymns attributed to Baba Farid. Indeed The Holy Book is the encyclopaedia of Indian linguistics and literature in the right sense of the term. It is by no means a treasure house of Punjabi language and literature. The Holy Book speaks the language of Hindwi, the predecessor of Khari boli.

Guru Gobind Singh was a wise man. He saw trouble in the plethora of unending streams of Gurus to follow him in future. He took the Damdama Bir to Huzur Sahib in Maharashtra. He decided to cease the tradition by passing on his *gaddi* to The Holy Book. Now the *Guru Granth Sahib* was totally complete and no additions were possible in it in future. Nothing could be added or subtracted from it. The last seven Gurus had come from the Sodhi family and no more it was possible to add to the figure. The Holy Book was declared as the Guru in 1708. Priority to it in 1678, Guru Gobind Singh had taken the historical step of establishment of the Khalsa. Thus the identity of the Sikh community was established for the first time.

Appendex

Table 1: Chrolology of Successor Gurus

S.No.	Name	Chronology	Caste	No. of Hymns
1.	Guru Nanak	1469-1539	Bedi	974
2.	Guru Angad	1504-1552	Trehan	62
3.	Guru Amar Das	1479-1574	Bhalla	407
4.	Guru Ram Das	1534-1581	Sodhi	679

5.	Guru Arjan Dev	1563-1606	Sodhi	2281
6.	Guru Har Gobind	1595-1644	Sodhi	-
7.	Guru Har Rai	1630-1661	Sodhi	-
8.	Guru Hari Krishan		Sodhi	-
9.	Guru Tegh Bahadur	1621-1695	Sodhi	115
10.	Guru Gobind Singh	1661-1708	Sodhi	-

Notes:

1. AlL the ten Guru belonged to Khatri sub-castes.

2. Refers to the number of shabads/dohas included in the *Guru Granth Sahib*

Table II : Chronology of Sants/Bhagats

S.No.	Name	Chronology	Profession	Caste/ Religion	No. of Shabds/ dohas	Region/ State
1.	Baba Farid	1173-1265	Sufi saint	Muslim	4+112	Punjab
2.	Trilochan	1267		Vaishya	4	Maharashtra
3.	Namdev	1270-1350	calico painter	Dalit	61	-do-
4.	Ravidas		tanner	Dalit	40	Uttar Pradesh
5.	Ramananda	1300-1410		Brahmin	2	-do-
6.	Dhanna Bhagat	1415?	agriculturist	Jat	3	Rajasthan
7.	Pipa	1425?	prince	Rajput	1	-do-
8.	Kabir	1448-1570	julaha	Muslim	541	Uttar Pradesh
9.	Parmananda	1483?		Brahmin	1	
10.	Surdas	1529	Amin	Brahmin	1	Uttar Pradesh
11.	Dadu	1544-1603	cotton card-ing (julaha)	Muslim		Gujarat
12.	Beni				3	
13.	Bhikan			Muslim		
14.	Sadhna		butcher	Dalit	1	Sind
15.	Sain		barber	Dalit	1	

21

People's Religion, Protestant Movements

SANTBAANI consists of fifteen per cent of the total hymns contained in the *Guru Granth Sahib*. Sants and Bhagats hailed from the Punjab, Uttar Pradesh, Rajasthan, Gujarat, Sindh and Maharashtra. Only two of them were Brahmins and one more of upper caste belonged to the Vaishya community. At least four of them were Muslims, provided Kabir is considered of the same community. While Rajputs and Jats were represented by singular numbers, Dalits had an impressive tally of at least four on the roll of honour. It was impressive for Sants or Bhagats of Dalit background to have reached the upper ladders of their respective movements. The greatest by any standards were Baba Farid and Kabir, both belonging to the Muslim community. Ravidas has forty hymns to his credit and stands out for inspiring entire generations of *mazhabi* Sikhs. His followers were leaders of the dissident movement among the Dalit Sikhs. All this has been represented graphically in Table II: 'Chronology of Sants/Bhagats' in the preceding Chapter. Some eleven of fifteen Sants have taken representation by mere one or two hymns. It certainly detracts from the pan-Indian image of the contents of *Guru Granth Sahib.* The picture is however, encouraging when viewed in the context of the professional background of Sants and Bhagats. They were barbers, chamars/cobblers, butchers, julahas, cotton workers, calico printers, mirasis, tanners, Brahmins, Vaisyas, Muslims and Sufis/mystics. Evidently there was a social upsurge, thanks to the mass movement inspired by Bhakti surge in north India.

Baba Farid (1173-1265) stands the tallest among the Sants and Bhagats ranked in the Guru Granth Sahib. Guru Nanak, Guru Amar Das and Guru Arjan have acknowledged their inspiration from Baba Farid in their hymns. It speaks very highly of him, considering that he was essentially a poet of Saraiki, a language marginal to the corpus of modern Indian languages. He was also a recluse who shunned publicly. He was, however, a humanist of the highest order. His language has been called the 'authentic idiom of the countryside'. He was a pioneer, who dominated and inspired coming generations. The voice of human suffering finds expression in his shlokas. He was also one of the founding father of the Chishti Sufi order in India. He was an extraordinary Sufi poet, who fitted perfectly in the gallery of Sants and Bhagats. There are still doubts about the authenticity of his poetic work. Did he write or whether his successor Sufi poets were the real authors? There is however, the unity of content and its uniform high quality that is never doubted. He was a Sufi who could pass for Sant or Bhagat, or the other way around.

'Sparrows to Hawks'

Guru Gobind Singh, the tenth Guru, was the last in the chain of ten Gurus. He left a mark on Sikh religion as remarkable as Guru Nanak, the founder of Sikhism. Under him Sikhism had radically transformed itself. Largely it was an affirmation of the tenets enunciated by Guru Nanak, but it was also a substantive departure from the norms. Equally Guru Gobind Singh affirmed his Hindu and Khatri identity openly, but his affirmation of the *Khalsa* resulted in a clear departure from the beliefs of traditional Hinduism. There was also a turnover in the character of Sikh sangat.

So far the Khatris had dominated the scene. All the ten Gurus were of Khatri origin. In fact, the consecutive chain of last six Gurus belonged to the Sodhi Khatri subcaste. The locale of Sikhism had gradually begun to shift to the eastern districts of the undivided Punjab. The Jat community had began to play a more dynamic role in the affairs. Comparatively, the Khatris had now gone on the defensive. These changes had been brought out consciously by Guru Gobind Singh. The times had changed. The tenth Guru had decided to ride them out. Thus, he was traditional on the one hand, radical on the other.

Gobind re-defined the basic tenets of Sikhism, expanded it geographically and transformed the sociological base of Sikhism. In line with others and, especially, Guru Arjan Dev, Guru Gobind Singh had a pan-Indian vision. He was born at Patna. He had done his intense tapasya in the enchanting Himalayan locale of Hemkunt, and he was to establish the Holy Scripture as the Guru in Maharashtra during his last days in 1708. He denounced several social practices like the use of Junao, the distinct division of castes and classes in the Hindu system. He invited one and all to join the Khalsa and his watchwords were kritnash, kulnash, dharamnash and karamnash, meaning thereby 'Forsake occupation, family, ritual and ceremonies'. It was indeed a war against the Brahminic practices. Guru Gobind was also very conscious of the Hindu identity. He, for instance, advocated and practiced *brahmacharya,* a major Hindu convention, and thus preceding Mahatma Gandhi by several centuries. His third wife, Sahib Deven, was taken under his protection, but he never consummated his relationship with her. Her marriage is described as the kunwara dola (virgin wedlock). She was also designated as the Mother to the five men baptized by Guru Gobind Singh, as he was known as their father.

Biachitra Natak

Guru Gobind Singh had a special fascination for Hindu mythology. The goddesses Chandi and Durga were his special deities. *Sarabok Granth*, for instance, is a poem narrating the mythological story of the gods and the demons fighting it out. So are his other two works *Chandi Charitra* and *Vir Durga Ki* on the same theme. The authenticity of these works and authorship attributed to the Tenth Guru is, however, doubted in certain Sikh circles. *Bichitra Natak*[1] (bachitra = marvelous, wondrous + natak = drama, play) is a work of different order. It is assembled in his work, the *Dasam Granth*, (i.e. Book of the Tenth Master). The *Dasam Granth* is to be distinguished from the *Adi Granth* (first, primary or original), now known as *Sri Guru Granth Sahib*. It is also equally considered as sacred as the *Adi Granth*. The *Bichitra Natak Granth* is the collective name given to *Bichitra Natak* itself, some of the other being, *Ukti Bilas, Chandi Charitra, Var Sri Bhagauti Ji Ki* (or *Chandi de Van), Gian Prabadhi* and *Chaubis Autar.*

The *Bichitra Natak* is a religious work with a difference. It is essentially autobiographical in nature. It opens with an invocation to Bhagavati, i.e. several hymns embodying the divine principle of justice. Guru Gobind Singh conceived Sikhism embodying the fighting spirit of the community. It was difficult for him to forget that his father, Guru Tegh Bahadur, had sacrificed his life to save the sacred symbols of Hinduism in an act 'deeply unparalled for heroism in the Kali age'. While Guru Nanak preached 'love thy neighbour', Guru Gobind singh did not hesitate to raise his sword in defence of his faith and country. The special significance of the *Bichitra Natak* lies in its autobiographical character. The Bedi/Vedi lineage of Guru Nanak and the Sodhi lineage of Guru Arjan Dev and Guru Gobind Singh are traced to the house of Lord Rama and his two sons Lava and Kusha. He also goes to the extent of tracing his previous life in which he practiced intense meditation and austerity on the Hemkunt mount in the Himalaya. Guru Gobind Singh conceived God as the embodiment of the fighting spirit. He was essentially a romantic human being with a pan-Indian vision. He was born in Bihar, spent his active life fighting for the cause of the Punjab, retired to spend his last days in Maharashtra and traced his lineage all the way to the Ramayana.

Birth of the Khalsa

Guru Gobind Singh established the Khalsa in 1699 and indeed it was a turning point in Sikh history. Govind Ras was suddenly transformed into Gobind Singh, the founder of the Khalsa. He baptized five persons, who were in no time transformed into one family of 'Singhs'. Gobind Singh was their father and they adopted his third wife Sahib Deven as their mother. The Guru was no longer their superior. He was one of them. He and others now belonged to the family of the Khalsa. After administering the oath, he greeted the converts with a new form of greeting:

Vah guru ji ki Khalsa,
Vah guru ji ki Fateh.

The Khalsa are the chosen of God,
Victory be to our God.

Thus did Gobind 'trained the sparrow to hunt the hawk and one man to fight a legion'.

'The Khalsa shall rule [*Raj Karega khalsa*]
Their enemies will be scattered.'
Only they that seek refuge will be saved.

His predecessor Gurus had worked out a formula whereby *piri* (sainthood, and *miri* (rule), were to be combined. The sixth Guru had also appealed to arms, but the tenth Guru raised an army to fight their enemies.

Guru Gobind Singh had not forgotten his pan-Indian vision in all this local skirmishing. The first initiates of the Guru were five men of different castes and regions of India. They were a barber of south India, a Khatri of the Punjab, a Kahar of Jagannath, a Jat of Hastinapur (UP) and a Chipha of Dwarka in Gujarat. None of them was a Brahmin. These were precisely the castes which had been attracted to Sikhism. Historically and sociologically, the birth of the Khalsa was a turning point for Sikhism. Sikhs had now an identity of their own, which was distinct from those practicing Hinduism. Non-militant urban Hindus, mostly of the Khatri caste, were no longer in the driving seat. There was now a line of demarcation between *Keshadharis* (wearing turban and those keeping hair) and *Sahajdharis* ('those who took time to adopt'). Later on, the Sikh by definition had to be a *Keshadhari* and thus the doors were shut on Sahajdhairis. The rural Jat had taken off where the Hindu Khatris had left.

Guru Gobind Singh took the first step by manifesting the Khalsa in 1699. He took another historic step by installing the Holy Scripture as Guru during 1708. Before his end came, he asked the Sacred Book to be brought to him. He called the Sangat to be invited in his presence. 'The

Guru', he said, 'will henceforth be in the Granth and the Khalsa, where the Granth is with any five Sikhs, representing the Khalsa, there will Guru be'. The institution of the Khalsa and its formal installation is described most picturesquelly in the *Bhatt Vahi Talauda Parganah Jind* in the following manner. 'The Guru placed before [the Sri Granth Sahib] five pice and a cocoanut and bowed his head before it. He said to the Sangat, 'It is my commandment: Own Sri Granth Ji in my place. He who so acknowledges it will obtain his reward. The Guru will rescue him. Know this as the truth.[2] The solemn ceremony took place at Nanded, on the Godavari bank in Maharashtra. Sri Gobind Singh is described herein as the great grandson of Guru Arjan Dev of Surajhanu Gosal clan, Sodhi Khatri, resident of Anandpur. You can take the Guru out of the Sodhi, but it shall be next to impossible to take the Khatri out of the Sodhis.

Music in Sikhism

Sikhism, following in the Vedic tradition, gives due significance to the arts. It follows in the footsteps of Bhakti and Sufi movement. Special significance is attached to poetry and music in unison. Music enhances the value of poetry, which is the truth shared equally by the Vedic tradition, Bhakti and Sufism. All the Sikh Gurus followed in the same tradition. The Guru Granth Sahib is an ideal model in which poetry and music are entwined. Guru Nanak set the pattern which is followed to this day. Dr. Surjit Patra, the wellknown poet, has put it succinctly: 'Sikhism as a religion recognized the power of art as medium for thought and culture. In a religion where Guru is baani and baani is Guru the importance of music and poetry is also very evident. Guru Nanak, whose poetry was a medium to convey his message, for this was and is the only medium which could vary the intensity of his thoughts. Guru Nanak's poetry is not only about the divine Revelation, but also reflects the intense pathos of contemporary life'.[3]

Guru Nanak and the following Gurus were talking the people's language. There is, however, a dialectical situation confronting us. The Guru Granth Sahib does not speak the Punjabi language. Guru Arjan Dev spoke and wrote in the language common to all the saint poets of north India. They had a common lingua france called the Sant-bhasa. It was the common language for writing religious verses. It cut across the geographical boundaries. It was spoken and understood across the frontiers. The Sant-bhasa was distinguished for its non-esoteric character and its utter simplicity. It was equally true of the *Guru Granth Sahib*. The Sant-bhasha was famously accepted by the entire Sikh community, which kept expanding due to the appeal of the Sacred Book. Guru Angad is to be credited for inventing the Gurmukhi script, which was also adopted by the *Guru Granth Sahib*. The script has played a significant role in Sikh faith and tradition. It has been an instrument of introducing literacy among the Sikh masses. The Sikh religion has, thus, performed a useful social role.

Poetry and Music

Baba Farid is in a class of his own. His poetry is sheer music. He wrote in Saraiki and not Punjabi. The *Guru Granth Sahib* contains four of his sabdas (hymns) and 112 slokas (couplots). Guru Nanak, Guru Amar Das and Guru Arjan were equally enraptured by him and employed his ideas and words in their poetic work. It is surprising, considering the fact that the entire range of ten Gurus eschew any tragic thoughts. Baba Farid, is however, known for his tragic thoughts and distinguished for the fatalist view of human existence: 'The voice of human suffering finds in him an expression heard seldom and only in the greatest poetry. His language is the authentic idiom of the countryside of south western Punjab, where he spent the major part of his life. Yet by a miracle of poetic creation this language has become in his hands full of subtle appeal, evoking tender emotions and stimulating the imagination'.[4] The main theme of Baba Farid's baani is what in the Indian, religious terminology would be called *vairagya*, that is dissension towards the world and worldly goods. Even though his main philosophy runs contrary to the worldview of the Gurus, they were enchanted by his intellectual and imaginativie prayers. His baani has been set to music in the *Guru Granth Sahib*, and it is sung with deep intensity in the gurudwaras all over the world.

Guru Nanak calls himself a *dhadhi* (ministrel) and *shair* (poet). The new forms of poetry and poetical compositions gained currency in medieval India. They chanted and sang their hymns in verse. The communal chant of poetical verse became a powerful instrument in communicating with the masses. The word was spread and communicated widely though the fakirs and sadhus. There was a special verve in them. They were possessed of the spiritual and mystical experience. Guru Nanak was the pioneer in this respect. He was also a versatile human being and equally leader in his own right. Besides being a master of poetry, he was equally versatile in folk and classical music. This could be equally said of other gurus and many Sikh leaders of the community. His immediate disciple, Mardana, was known to be a master of *rabab* or Indian *rebec.* Guru Nanak is believed to have invented the instrument. Guru Amardas is believed to have invented *saranda* or the Indian violin. He was followed by Bhai Kahan Singh, the court musician of Patiala, who invented the *tadoos* or Indian peacock-faced guitar. Thus, Sikh religious came to be associated with the invention of several folk musical instruments. Guru Nanak also followed the example of Sufis by introducing several Persian melodies like Kafi, Tukkari and Dakhni in the Sikh tradition. Guru Nanak is to be credited in integrating Saraiki and Punjabi languages, folk and classical music, and integrating and developing numerous musical instruments, besides experimenting with new poetic forms.

Sacred Music

Music has been regarded as a sacred art since ancient times in India. Its roots lie in the Vedic tradition of simple chants, nuanced in a singing manner. The rhythmatic manner of the chants is enchanting. Later on followed the Gandharva music, 'seen by the creator in his contemplation and afterwards performed by seers and saints'. Thus music and poetry were god-given gifts. That is how sacred music came to be born in the Land of the Bharata. It was to be contrasted with secular music. While the one was called Marga Sangeet, the other came to be known as Desi Sangeet. Sacred music comprised of devational songs led to the development of classical music. The *Guru Granth Sahib* inherited the same tradition. Incidentally, the first five Sikh gurus represented in the Sacred Book were also knowledgable and accomplished musicians. It is perhaps the largest ever collection of the sacred hymns of the first five Gurus, 15 saints and 15 bards compiled by Bhai Gurdas under the guidance of Guru Arjan Dev. These sacred hymns are set to classical ragas specified chapter-by-chapter in the *Adi Granth*. It is also commendable on account of its pan-Indian character.

There were also other influences at work. Devotional and classical music were also very much inspired by the Vaishnava Bhakti. Sikh Bhakti movement had a direct liaison with the Vaishnava tradition. Jayadev Goswami's *Geet Govinda* is a classical example of devotional music and it left its mark on Sikh devotional music. No wonder, Guru Arjan Dev has commented, 'Gurbaani is the treasure of the jewels of Bhakti. By singing, hearing and acting up to it, one is enraptured'. One must however go back to the beginnings to comprehend the psychology of sacred music. In Vedic hymns and chants are the beginnings of the religious poetry of mankind. The ancient Vedic scholars developed a sophisticated branch of Vedic learning called Chants, i.e. prosody or science of matercial composition. The Sama Veda is a collection of materical rhymes. Since the Vedas belong to the oral tradition, the science of metrical rhymes has been developed as a sophisticated art over centuries. Guru Nanak comes at the tailend of this tradition. Guru Arjan Dev fully understood the ancient tradition. The *Guru Granth Sahib* is a shining example of this instance of ancient tradition. At the conclusion of the Sacred Book is *Ragmala*, a classification of ragas listing 84 measures, as a guide to music. The Holy Book contains only 31 ragas. Then there are ragas and its off-springs, raginis (female ragas) and putras (offsprings) to classify and retain the individual character (mood) of each raga.

People's Religion

Religious music became integral to Sikhism as a formal service or worship. Kirtan, bhajan, Sufiana kalam and quawali were popular forms of religion in the Punjab on the eve of Sikhism joining the scene. These forms of religious music gained popularity among the masses. The sound was as important as the meaning of the verses. Poetry also scores for another reason. It is so rhythematic that it appeals to the ear. Community singing makes it a collective effort. The participant is no longer an observer. He is in the midst and centre of it. The Gurus were conscious of this. To them the music was not played for the sake of it. It should help to comprehend the underlying meaning. So many of the hymns contained in the *Guru Granth Sahib* are in the mould of folk poetry. The instructions to ragis who recited from the Sacred Book was to avoid exposition of the raga for the sake of it, but to sing it in a manner as to make the meaning of the content crystal clear. The hymns of the Granth are divided into 31 ragas or musical modes into which they are to be sung.

The Sikh Gurus had opted for the Bhakti Marga (devotion) rather than the Karma Marga (action or good deeds) or Gyan Marga (knowledge). Bhakti Marga was translated into 'the Path of Worship of the Name' (Nama Marga) to simplify it. Nama Marga at its best was collective singing of hymns popularly known as kirtan, that is music directed to the expression of collective devotion 'Kirtan is an invaluable jewel, bringing bliss, treasure of qualities' (GG, 893), so sayeth the Holy Book. Guru Arjan Dev sings poems to the beauty and harmony of music to induce the mood of devotion. 'When performed, all desire then ends' (GG, 958). It is not merely arousing emotion through musical devotion, its objective is also to enhance the intellectual content of the participants. Thus Sikhism is truly a people's religion. It has also been called for this reason the householders religion (grihastha dharma). Accordingly asceticism, austerity, penance and celibacy have no place in the scheme of things of Sikhism. That is why its three mottos are kirt karo (work), nam japo (worship) and vand joko (give in charity) are practical to the extreme.

Sufism

There is no doubt that Sufism had made a freat impact on Guru Nanak and other Sikh Gurus. The very fact that the baani of Sheikh Farid is given so much prominence in the Granth is enough proof of it. The Punjab has been called the homeland of Sufi movement in north India. It should not be forgotten that Bhakti movement was impacted by Sufism throughout the centuries. It was actually a two-way traffic. Kabir has been called the linkman between Sikhism and Sufism. It shall not be wrong to say that Sikhism being an integral part of Sant tradition was impacted by Sufism and it influenced the Sant tradition as a whole. It was also recognized that the Sant tradition was a synthesis of 'the three principal dissenting movements, those being the Vaishnava Bhakti, Tantric Yoga and Sufism in the descending order. Islam impacted Sikhism to the extent it influenced the Sant tradition, the influence was marginal and of no fundamental significance. The basic concepts of Sikhism are essentially traced to Vedanta and any parallel with Sufism is merely coincidental.

This is a view held by most scholars of Sikhism and also those with expertise on Sufism in India. 'It would indicate that Guru Nanak, through his own meditation, arrived at the same conclusion as had already been reached by Sufis such as Rumi, Sa'di, Iraqi, Jami and Hafiz. Guru Nanak presents his thoughts with remarkable consistency. Although some hymns in the Adi Granth had like portions of the Masnavi of Maulana Rumi, which some called 'The Qur'an in Persian', 'there is nothing to indicate that Guru Nanak was imitating the great poet. The spiritual life of India discussed in this chapter bears out the Rig Vedic assertion'.[5] There are reasons embedded in history that explain the great divide between Islam and Sikhism, more correctly, the religious wars between the Sikhs and the Mughals. 'Gradually the Sikhs came to see themselves as a reformed Hindu sect, tracing the source of their beliefs chiefly from the Vedas, the Upanishads and later Sanskrit classics.... Even in sober works, Islam and Sufism were referred to contemptuously'[6] It is also incorrect to assert that Sikhism was an attempt at an ideal synthesis between two contrasting religions. The following conflict is quoted in support of the contrary construction: 'Neither the Veda nor the Kitab know the mystery'. It is interpreted wrongly. Guru Nanak was actually attempting to point out the irrelevance of both of the sacred beliefs. He was pleading for a new synthesis. Sikhism is indeed a new synthesis, but nothing of the kind to claim it as the synthesis of Hinduism and Islam.

Miracle Saints

For much of the 19th century and early 20th century, Hindus and Sikhs were involved in the worship of miracle saints and undertook regular pilgrimages to these shrines, generally of Muslim pirs. Among these saints Sakhi Sarwar, was widely worshipped by Hindus and Sikhs. The popular name of the miracle saint is associated with the name of Sayyid Zamulabidin, a resident of Baghdad, who migrated to India in 1126 C E. The main shrine as located at Nigah in the dry and barren foothills of the Suleiman mountains, at a distance of 32 kilometers from Dera Ghazi

Khan on the right bank of River Indus. The Sikh connection is apparent by names like Sarwar Panthi, Guru Sultania and Ramadasia Sultania. There were several shrines built on the spot including a shrine devoted to Guru Nanak towards the east. There was also a temple, besides the main shrine built on the tomb of Sakhi Sarwar.

Here was a movement centred around a Muslim pir, a gurudwara, and a temple to Bhairva, who in the present instant was a messenger of the saint instead of Lord Siva as the tradition goes. These seemingly religious festivals had a distinct secular character. The major festival in honour of Sakhi Sarwar was, however, held at Nigah annually. The companies of pilgrims travelled from all parts of the Punjab on well-established ancient routes. In the 1911 census of 79,085 registered as followers of Sakhi Sarwar. Apparently the number of the followers was much larger than indicated. The real reason for the popularity of miracle saints lay elsewhere, and 'Part of the answer to popular faith in saints like Sakhi Sarwar, even among their Muslim followers may be found in cognitive frameworks of illness and healing'.[7] People worshipped the pir to get cured of physical and psychological ailments by harnessing his supernatural povers.

Protestant Movements

Guru Ravidas has forty of his shabads and one of his shloka included in the Granth. He is thus honoured by his inclusion in the Santbaani. He is a Dalit Sant who is believed to be compared with Sant Namadeva of Maharashtra for his eminence. He is believed to have spent several years in the Punjab. He is a favourite hero of the Dalits in the Punjab and their role model and his spirit is expressed in the hymn described as Begumpura, 'The spirit of verse [incorporated in the Guru Granth Sahib] is: Begumpura is the name of the city where there is no place for sorrow / There is no suffering or anxiety; no sovereignty of God/ Where there is lasting place and safety for all / All are equal, no one is second or third in Begumpura / Ravidas the Shoe maker is a friend of all who are citizens of Begumpura'. The hymn truly expresses the underlying desire of Dalits to break their centuries-old shackles. Dalits living in the Sikh homeland have been anxious to make their presence felt in the state's religio-cultural sphere. Sikhism had been initially promised a classless society. The upper caste domination of Sikh institutions like Khatris had occured gradually. Sikh Jats had replaced them, but there was no place for Sikh Dalits in this scheme of things. The Dalit feel discriminated by 'higher caste' Sikhs.

This sense of resentment resulted in a mass social movement in the 1920s. It was no longer a matter of attention of the Sikh community alone. The Dalit community got due recognition by the British Government and they were registered as *ad-dharmis* in the census of 1931, affirming their assertion that they were neither Hindu nor Sikh; they also claimed to be 'original inhabitants of India'. Dalits are divided into Ravidasias, Mazhbis and Valmikis. Ravidasias are the most vocal and wield power due to their wealthy status. Dalits have begun to build their separate gurdwaras. Many villages have both upper caste and Dalit gurdwaras. The Dalit gurdwaras have begun to be called *gurughars*. Parall to the separate Gurudwara movement is another movement for establishing exclusive Dalit *deras* and sects. A dera is technically the headquarters of a group of likeminded devotees who follow the teachings of a particular spiritual guru equally revered. The guru is usually anointed by their predecessor. Since the institution of living guru has been discontinued in the Sikh tradition, it is the cause of constant conflict with orthodox Sikhs. Moreover, *deras* do not discriminate between Hindus and Sikhs. While membership of the deras is open to one and all, those are the virtual gurudwaras of the Dalit community.

Ravidasia Cult

Obviously, the Dalits of the Punjab are making their influence felt. The action is moving from the gurdwaras to the Dalit deras. The Dalits are in conflict with orthodox Sikhs with their conflicting interpretation of the Sikh religion. Deras are an open house to Sikhs and non-Sikhs alike. The protestants have taken over from orthodox Sikhs. Dalit consciousness, in fact, has emerged against the backdrop of the teachings of Ravidas (the dera's patron saint), an untouchable saint-poet of the north Indian Bhakti movement. He was no Punjabi, but the native Dalits have adopted him, as Dr. Ambedkar has been adopted by contemporary Dalits all over India. Ravidas is the beloved of the Punjabi Dalits.

Ramdasis are another cult. You have necessarily not to be a Sikh to be a Ramdasi. Being Dalit is the only requirement. Belief in Sikh faith is secondary. Deras have been turned into gurudwaras with a difference. They break from the Granth, but equal importance is given to the baani of Sant Ramdas. In fact most of the Ramdasis are Scheduled Caste Hindus, who are clean shaven and pay only ritual attention to the *Adi Granth*.

Ideally speaking, the Ramdasi are Sikhs of pre-Gobind Singh times, when there was no distinction between *Keshdhari* and *non-Keshdhari* Sikhs. Dalit deras are catching up fast, and they seem to be performing as substitutes for traditional gurdwaras. Obviously there is a caste conflict waging intensely between upper and lower castes Sikhs. Equally there is implicit tension between the deras and the gurudwaras at the institutional plane. Sikhism was born to abolish caste distinctions. In actual fact, the caste conflict has intensified. Dera Sachkand Ballan was established about seventy years ago is a symbol of this malaise. Its founder believed in the teachings of the 15th century saint philosopher, Guru Ravidas, who was also one of the followers of the Bhakti movement. He presented a middle path between assimilation and radical separate Dalit identity. Things don't work out in real life. There are inherent conflicts of the order of class conflict between upper and lower castes, between haves and have nots, which are bound to go-out-of hand. Sikh gurus worked out a perfect mechanism, but, unfortunately, it is not working out in real life. The models are ideals, which don't work in real life.

Looking into Future Prism

Sikhism is the youngest religion and possibly the highest expression of Sufi-Sant samagam that has extended over a millennium. It is also an expression of its inability to meet challenges implied in widespread social discontent of contemporary times of the Ravidasi age. These are challenges of different kinds by a different class of people, poor, discontented and disfranchised who refused to abide by the rules of the game. The battle of the mind has little meaning for the hungry and discriminated against general mass refusing to be content with mere spirituality of the secular kind.

Footnote

Chapter – 1

1. Fairley, Jean. The Lion River: The Indus. John Day, 178, 1978
2. Masson, Charles. Narratives of various journeys in Baluchistan, Afghanistan and the Punjab, including residence in those countries from 1826 to 1838. V.I., London, Richard Bentley, 1842
3. Aitzaz Ahsan. The Indus Saga and the Making of Pakistan. Oxford, Karachi, 1997, 78
4. Ibid
5. Cunningham, Alexander. Ancient geography of India, ed. By Surendranath Majumdar Sastri. Calcutta, Chackervertty, Chatterjee, Calcutta, 1924, 269.
6. The Mahabharata, tr. by Bibek Debroy, New Delhi, Penguin Books, V.1., 2010, XXVIII
7. Ibid, 220
8. Op.cit., 221
9. Op.cit., 246

10. Op.cit., 311
11. Xuanzang, Si Yu Ki. Buddhist records of the western world, tr. Samuel Beal. Landon, 1884 (2000)
12. Bruce, R.J.B. Notes on the Dera Ghazi Khan district, N.W.Frontier and its border tribes. Lahore, Civil Secretarial Press, 1871, 130
13. Ibid.,
14. Pakistan. Lok Visa. Dera Ghazi Khan field staff report (RC-81-1). Islamabad
15. Conan, W.L. and Craik, H.D.Eds. Chiefs and families of note in the Punjab. Rev, edn. V.2 Lahore, 1910, 362
16. Dames, H. Longworth. The Baloch race: A historical and ethnological sketch, London, Royal Asiatic Society, 1904, 47
17. Gilmartin, David. "Irrigation and the Baloch frontier" in Haider, Mausura, ed. Sufis, Sultans and feudal orders: Professor Nurul Hassan commemoration volume. New Delhi, Manohar, 2004, 377
18. Pakistan, The Pakistan gazetteer: Dear Ghaze Khan district. V.6.Ed.2.2000, 177-78
19. Gilmartin. Op. cit., 377, Footnote

Chapter – 2

1. Roseberry, III, J. Royal. Imperial rule in Punjab: The conquest and administration of Multan, 1888-1881, New Delhi, Manohar, 1987, 78
2. Ibid.
3. Cunningham, Alexander. History of the Sikhs
4. Punjab, Gazeteer of the Dera Ghazi Khan district. Printed at the Calcutta Central Press Company, 1883-84, 35
5. Ibid.
6. Roseberry, Op.cit., 78
7. Op.cit., 75
8. Op.cit
9. Maisson, Op. cit., 21
10. Op. cit., 30
11. Punjab, Appendix to Multan Gazetteer, 1883-84, 165
12. Roseberry. Op.cit., 62
13. Ibbetson, Denzil and Maclagan, Edward. Glossary of the tribes and castes of the Punjab and North-West Frontier Province, comp by H.A. Rose, New Delhi. Amar Prakashan, 388

14. Kevalarama, The Rasa Mana ke Pada of Kevalarama, ed. By Alan William Entwistle. Vrindavan, Vrindavan Research Institute, 6.
15. The Encyclopaedia of Sikhism, ed. By Harbans Singh, V. 4 S-Z Patiala. Panjabi University, 1998, 50
16. O' Brien, Aubrey, The Mohammedan Saints of the Western Punjab. Journal. (Royal Anthropological Institute), 42, 1911, 519
17. Ibbetson, Op.cit., 568
18. Op.cit., 569
19. Oberoi, Harjot. The construction of religious boundaries: Culture, identity in the Sikh tradition
20. Doniger, Wendy, The Hindu: An alternative history. New Delhi, 2009, 104
21. Kuegi, Adolf. The Rigveda : The oldest literature of like the Indians. Boston, Ginn , 1866, 12-13
22. Sachdev, Ram Nath. Dera phulan da sehra; A history of Dera Ghazi Khan. Printed at Shadeed Prakashan, New Delhi, 194

Chapter – 3

1. Kaegi, Adolf. The Rigveda: The oldest literature of the Indians. Boston, Ginn, 1886, 12
2. Doniger. Op. cit., 155
3. Max Müller, Friedrich. Collected works, V. 3. London, 1903
4. Griffith Ralph T, tr. The hymns of the Rigveda, ed. By J. L Shastri. Delhi, Motilal Banarasidas. 1973, 587
5. Albinia, Alice. Empires of the Indus: The story of a river. London. Murray, 2008, 130
6. Wilson, John. Indian caste. V.2. K.K. Books
7. Max Muller, F. Collected works. V.3. Anthropological rivers, London, 1903
8. Hamilton, Alexander. A new account of the East Indies. Edinburgh. 1727
9. Fairlay, Op.cit., 1978, 134
10. Xuangzang. Op.cit., 200
11. Burton, Richard F. Sindh and the races that inhabit the valley of the Indus. Karachi, Oxford University Press, 1973, 327-28

Chapter – 4

1. Fairlay. Op.cit., XIV
2. Hamidi, Tasvir Husain. Indus Valley Civilization: New interpretation, in

Meadows, A and P.S., The Indus river: Biodiversity, resources humankind. Oxford University Press, Pakistan, 1999

3. Albinia. Op.cit., 306
4. Fairley. Op.cit., 65
5. Op.cit., 127
6. Trevelyan, Humphrey. The Indus we left. Macmillan
7. Ibid.
8. Ahmed, Mohammad Farooq. The world life of the Indus in Merdows, Op.cit., 4.
9. Fairley, Op.cit., 97
10. Wilson, J comp. Grammar and dictionary of Western Punjabi as spoken in the Shahpur district, etc. Lahore, Printed at the Punjab Government Press, 25
11. Mushabir Hasan. Birds of the Indus. Oxford University Press, 2001, XIV
12. Albinia. Op.cit., 100
13. Mahabharata, V.2, tr. By Bibak Debroy. Penguin, New Delhi, 2011, 459
14. Ibid., 140
15. Op. cit., 223
16. Cunningham, Alexander. Op. cit.
17. Albinia. Op.cit., 257
18. Hamidi. Op.cit., 331
19. Schemmel, Annemarie. Indus-The River of poetry. Meadows, Op.cit

Chapter – 5

1. Liddchi_Grassi, Magi. The great golden sacrifice of the Mahabharata. Random House India, Noida, 2011, 649
2. Ibid., 651
3. The Mahabharata of Krishna Dvaipayana Vyasa, tr., by Kisori Mohan Ganguli. Book 14. Ashwamedhika Parva. Ed. 5. Munshiram Manoharlal, Delhi, 1991, 132
4. Doniger, Wendy. Op.cit.42
5. The Mahabharata of Vyasa, tr. By P.Lal Vikas, New Delhi, 1990, 3

Chapter – 6

1. Debroy. Op. cit., 158
2. Liddchi-Grassi. Op.cit, 601
3. Op. cit.

4. The Mahabharata, tr. By Bibek Dehroy, V.2,Penguin Book, New Delhi, 2010, 226
5. Ibid., 207
6. Op.cit, 213
7. Op.cit, 214
8. Liddchi-Grassi, Op.cit, 649
9. Op.cit.
10. Debroy. V.1, Op.cit, 158
11. Liddchi-Grassi, Op.cit, 502
12. Op.cit., 601
13. Debroy. Op.cit., 14
14. Liddchi_Grassi, Op.cit, 329
15. Op.cit
16. Op.cit., 207
17. Op.cit., 165
18. Op.cit
19. Ganguli, Op.cit., V. 3, Harana Parva, 523
20. Op.cit.
21. The Mahabharata of Krishna Dwairpayana Vyasa, V. 6. Drona Parva, Orcental Publishing House, Calcutta. Ed.2, P.217
22. Lal. Op.cit., 166

Chapter – 7

1. Liddchi-Grassi. Op.cit, 528
2. Debroy, Op.cit. V.1, P.295
3. Op.cit., 296
4. Op.cit., V.2, P.208
5. Lal, Op.cit, 262
6. Liddchi – Grassi, Op.cit., 739
7. Op.cit., 626
8. Ganguli, Op.cit, V.14, Ashwamedha Parva, 134
9. Ganguli, Op.cit, 133
10. Op.cit. V.1. Adi Parva, 272
11. Op.cit. V.7. Stree Parva, 83
12. Roy, Op.cit., V.6. Dvona Panva. Ed.2. p.217
13. Ganguli. Op.cit, Ashwamedha Parva, 135

14. Liddchi – Grassi, Op.cit, 638
15. Op.cit, 654
16. Gurcharam Das. The Difficulty of being good etc., Allenlance, 2009, 91
17. Ibid
18. Op.cit.,92
19. Lal. Op.cit, 33

Chapter – 8

1. Dames, M. Longworth. Op.cit., 47
2. Gilmartin. Op. cit., 336
3. Op. cit., 338
4. Fryer, F.W.R. Final report of the first regular settlement of the Dera Ghazi Khan district, (1868 to 1874). Lahore, Central Jail Press, 1876, 66
5. Pehrson, Robert N. The social organization of the Marri People, comp by Frederick Barth, New York, Wenner–Green Foundation for the Anthropological Research, 1966, 4
6. Gilmartin, Op.cit., 332
7. Bruce, Richard Issac. The forward policy and its results. London, 1900, 224.
8. Ibid.
9. Op.cit., 225
10. Hittu Ram. Sandeman in Baluchistan. Calcutta, Government Printing Calcutta, 1916, 82
11. Thornton, Thomas Henry. Colonel Sir Robert Sandeman: His life and work on our Indian frontier. Karachi, Oxford University Press, 1979, 87
12. Ibid., 303
13. Dames. Op.cit., 47
14. National Archives of India, Foreign Department. Proceeding (Pol. A), June 1863, No. 123-25, Martin, 277
15. Roberts, Frederik. Forty one years in India, 372-73
16. Thornton, Op. cit., 304
17. Gilmartin, Op. cit., 362-63
18. Thornton, Op. cit., VI
19. Op. Cit., 184
20. Op. Cit., 187
21. Op. Cit., 51
22. Op. Cit., 50

Chapter – 9

1. Thornton, Op. cit., 100
2. Op.cit., 244
3. Bruce, op.cit., 241
4. Hittu Ram, op.cit., 82
5. Op.cit, 8.
6. op.cit., 225.
7. Op.cit., 226.
8. Op.cit., 227.
9. Hittu Ram, op.cit., Reface, V
10. Bruce, Op.cit., 100
11. Hittu Ram, Op.cit.,
12. India, Foreign Department, Future administration of the Kalat State, Ap. 1894.
13. Thoronton, op.cit., 264-65
14. Op. cit., 266
15. Hittu Ram. Op. cit., Preface, VI
16. Thoronton, Op. cit., 245
17. Op.cit., 246
18. Op.cit., 256
19. Op.cit., 257
20. India. Foreign Department. Agent to the Governor-General (H S Barnes) May 17, 1898
21. Ibid, Jan 26, 1898
22. Op. cit.
23. Op.cit., Acting AGC (Col. Henry Wylie), March 16, 1898
24. Op. cit., May 25, 1898
25. Op.cit.
26. Op.cit., May 17, 1898
27. Op.cit.
28. Op.cit.
29. Op.cit., AGG (H S Barnes), Jan 20, 1898
30. Op.cit., Jan 28, 1898
31. Op. cit., Acting AGG, Feb 24, 1898

Chapter – 10

1. Ibbetson and Maclagan. V.2. Op.cit., 507

2. Op. cit., 505
3. Op.cit., 504
4. Op.cit.,
5. Singh, S.K. Indian communities. V.1., New Delhi
6. Puri, B.N. The Khatris--a socio-historical study. New Delhi. M.N. Publications and Distributors, 1988, 43
7. Rose, Op. cit., 509

Chapter – 11

1. Shearing, M.B. Hindu tribes and castes, etc. V. 2. Calcutta. Thacker Spink, 1879, 78-79
2. Ibbeston, Op. cit., 512
3. Wilson, J. comp. Op.cit., 21
4. Quoted in Ibbeston, Op.cit., 506
5. Op.cit., 19
6. Op.cit.
7. Op.cit., 251
8. Op.cit.
9. The Mahabharata, V.I., Op. cit, 275
10. Op. cit.
11. Op.cit.
12. Op. cit., 159-60
13. Op.cit., 160

Chapter – 12

1. Grierson, G.A. Linguistic Survey of India. V. 8. Pt.1. Indo-Aryan family. North-Western group, specimens of Sindhi and Lahnda. Low Price Publication, Delhi, 1919, 1
2. Shackle, Christopher. From Wuch to Southern Lahnda; A study of Saraiki studies in English. Multan, Saang-e-Mehal
3. Kohli, S.G. A critical study of Adi Granth, New Delhi, 1961
4. Smirnov. V.A. The Lahndi (Saraiki) language. Saraiki Adbi Board, Multan, 2006, 28
5. Ibid
6. Grierson. Op. cit., 2
7. Shackle, C. Hindko in Kohat and Peshawar, Bulletin (School of Oriental and

African Studies), 43, 1980, 486.
8. Ibid
9. Smirnov, Op. cit., 36
10. Op.cit., 38
11. Grierson, Op.cit., 359
12. Op. cit

Chapter – 13

1. Grierson, Op.cit. 4
2. Smirnov. Op.cit, 53
3. Bahri, H. Lahndi phoetics. Allahabad, 1963
4. Shackle, C. 'South-western' elements in the language of the Adi Granth Bulletin (School of Oriental and African Studies), 40, 1977. [36]
5. Encyclopedia of Sikhism, ed. By Harban Singh. Patiala, Punjabi University, V.2, 1992, 181-83
6. Op.cit., 181
7. O'Brien, E. Glossary of the Multani Language
8. Ibid., 28
9. Smirnov, Op. cit., 32

Chapter – 14

1. Shuja a shlaq. A forgotten vision: A study of human spirituality in Islamic tradition, Vikas, New Delhi, 1997
2. Mohammed Habib. Hazrat Amir Khushrau of Delhi, 31
3. Nizami, Khaliq Ahmed. The life and times of Shaikh Farid-ud-Din Gunj-I-Shakar. Aligarh Muslim University
4. Shuja A shlaq, Op. cit
5. Op. cit
6. Baxi, Lochan Singh. Prominent mystic poets of Punjab. New Delhi, Publications Division (Govt. of India)
7. Shuja A shlaq, Op. cit., 189
8. Op. cit., 191
9. Sharda. S. R. Sufi Thought. Etc. Delhi, Munshiram Manoharlal, 106
10. Ibid
11. Shuja A shlaq, Op.cit., 184
12. Sharda, Op.cit., 107

13. Op.cit., 138

Chapter – 15

1. Shuja Ahlaq. Op.cit., 375
2. Kohli, Surinder Singh. History of Punjabi literature. Delhi, National Book House, 69
3. Chattar Singh and Jeevan Singh. Heer Waris Shah (Gurmukhi).
4. Ajwani, L.H. History of Sindhi literature, New Delhi, Sahitya Akademi, 75
5. Ibid., 73
6. Schimmel, Annemarie. Sindhi literature. Wiesbaden, to Harrasowitz, 1974, 17
7. Ajwani, Op. cit., 75
8. Schimmel. Op. cit., 17
9. Advani, Kalyan B.Sachal–The Dervish, New Delhi, Sahitya Akademi, 1971, 5
10. Op.cit., 21

Chapter – 16

1. Nizami, Op. cit
2. Hamid Husain. Sufism and Bhakti movement. External relevance. New Delhi, Manak, 2007, 155
3. Hamid Husain. Impact of Sufism on Sikhism. Special reference to Baba Faird in Hamid Husain, bid. 121
4. Schimmel, Annemarie. Islam in the Indian Subcontinent. Lahore, Sange-Meal, 2003, 24
5. Mujeeb, Muhammad. Islamic Culture, April 1940, 140
6. Schimmel. Op. cit
7. Mujeeb. Op. cit., 108 (footnote)
8. Shuja Ashlaq, Op. cit., 218-19
9. Nizami. Op. cit., 1-2
10. Op. cit., 3
11. Al-Biruni. India, tr. By Edward C. Sachau., Ed. By Qujammdin Ahmed. Nationa Book Trust, New Delhi, 1983, 6
12. Doniger, Wendy. The Hindu: An alternative history. Penguin/Viking 2009, 46
13. Ibid, 368
14. Op. cit., 460
15. Nizami, Op. cit., 105
16. Keay, John. India, A history. New York, Grove Press, 2000. 312

17. Tara Chand quoted in Hamid Husain, Op. cit., 23
18. Dasgupta, S.Obscene religious cults. Ed. 2. Calcutta
19. Doniger. Op. cit., 460

Chapter – 17

1. Mujeeb, The Indian Muslims, New Delhi, Munshiram Manoharlal, 1985, 306.
2. Al-Gazali, Kunuja-e-sa'dat, 370
3. McGregor, R.S. Hindu Literature, from its beginnings to the nineteenth century. Wiesbaden, 1984
4. Vaudeville, Ch. Granthad valu, 140
5. Shuja Alhaq. Op.cit., 328
6. Mujeeb, Op.cit., 145
7. Shuja Alhaq. Op.cit., 224
8. Schimmel, Op.cit., 36
9. Rizvi, Athar Abbas. History of Sufism in India. V. I. New Delhi, Munshiram Manoharlal, 1978,194
10. Ibid, 124
11. Keay. Op.cit., 312
12. Das Gupta. Op.cit., 168
13. Doniger. Op.cit., 532
14. Rizvi. Op.cit., v.2, 326-27
15. Rizvi., Op.cit., 373
16. Doniger. Op.cit., 45
17. Op.cit., 463
18. Macauliffe, M.A. The Sikh religion. V.6. Oxford, 1969, 141
19. Ibid., 182
20. Vaudeville, Op. cit., 140
21. Shuja Alhaq. Op.cit., 397-98
22. Rizvi, Op.cit., 397-98

Chapter – 18

1. Doniger. Op. cit., 344
2. Ishwari Prasad, History of Medieval India. Allahabad, Indian Press, 1940, 559.
3. Ibid., 558-59
4. Kaviraj, Krishnadas, Chaitanya's life and teachings, tr. By Jadunath Sarkar. Orient Longmans, 1988,158

Chapter – 19

1. Ishwari Prasad. Op. cit., 565
2. Monier-Williams. Hinduism. Delhi, Rare Books, 1977, 144
3. Ishwari Prasad, Op. cit., 566
4. Mujumdar, AK Bhakti renaissance.Bombay, Bharatiya Vidya Bhavan, 1965, 43.
5. Ishwari Prasad, Op.cit., 981
6. Ramanujam, A.K. The collected essays of A.K. Ramanujam, ed. By Vijay Dhaiwadher, New Delhi, O.U.P., 188
7. Thielman, Selma. The spirituality of music. New Delhi. APH, 1969, 201, 69
8. Ibid., 147
9. Rizvi, Op. cit. V.1., 359
10. Ramanujam, Op. cit., 274
11. Ishwari Prasad. Op. cit., 568
12. Goswami, Shrivatsa. Radha, ect. In Hawley, John Stratton and Wolg, Donna Marie. The divine consort. Motilal Banarasidas, 1984, 72-73
13. Op.cit., 76
14. Op.cit.
15. Op.cit., 74
16. Monier-Williams, Op.cit., 208

Chapter – 20

1. Ahluwalia, M.G.Reflection on the Bhakti movement in Tamil Nadu and Punjab. Sikh Spectrum Com quarterly, 19, 2005
2. McCleod, W.H. Guru Nanak and the Sikh religion. Oxford, 1968, 153
3. Encycloaedia of Sikhism, V.I. Panjabi University, Patiala, 1992, 12-13
4. Schimmel, Annemarie. Pearls from the Indus: Studies in Sindhi Literature. Sindhi Adabi Board, Hyderabad, 1986
5. Rizvi, Op.cit. V.2., 391
6. Das, Sunil Kumar. Sri Chaitanya and Guru Nanak, A comparative study of Vaishnavism and Sikkhism. Calcutta, Rabindra Bharati University, 1984, 48
7. Ibid., 44
8. Girja Kumar. The book on trail: Fundamental and censorship in India New Delhi, Har-Anand, 1997, 382

Chapter – 21

1. Encyclopedia of Sikhism; V.1, 243, 1998

2. Ibid, V.2., 1992
3. Chaudhry, Amrita. Divine verses. Indian Express, Now. 13, 2008
4. Muzaffar Ali, Ed. The Sufis of the Punjab. Rume Foundation, 2012
5. Rizvi. Op. cit., V.2, 396
6. Op. cit., 395
7. Oberoi, Harjot. Op.cit., 154

INDEX

A

Abdul Latif (Shah) 68, 100, 254, 313, 316, 333, 342, 358, 359
Abhimanyu 123-125, 136
Abu'l Fazal 363
Adyasthana 88
Aesthetics 268, 270, 385
  Bhakti 30-34, 63, 73, 249,272-444
  Sufi 17, 18, 33-93, 244-444
Ain-i-Akbari 218, 362, 363
Ajodhan 8, 229-234, 278-284
Akbar (Emperor) 4, 6, 30, 145, 157, 214, 224, 293, 307-364
Aror or Alor 121
Alvars 372-427
Amir Khusraw 281, 346-360
Ana-al-Haqq 342
Arjuna 14, 15, 86, 236, 407
Aror 12, 104, 121, 122, 144, 201, 226, 227, 247
Arora 23-39, 122, 153, 187, 201-257, 278, 308, 334, 419
Ashvapati (king) 111
Aswamedha Yajna 108
Attock 10,16,47,61-90,120,145,248

B

Baba Farid 31, 93, 214, 267, 277-311, 329-361, 374, 380, 413
Baha-ud-Din Zakariya 37,330,335,389

Bahawalpur 17, 27, 34, 75, 77, 227, 228, 248, 250-259, 278, 279, 298
Bairagis 31, 362, 402
Bahlika (Kingdom) 10, 15, 98, 106, 109, 110, 111, 122, 123
Balmiki 36
Baloch 18-33,63,74,87,101,144-444
Balochistan 4, 5, 19, 21, 34, 74, 87, 101, 121, 144-201, 251-257, 316
Bari 74, 215, 218, 230-238
Barnes (H S) 154, 192, 193, 195
Bauls 387, 402, 421
Bedi (sub-caste) 210, 222, 223, 434
Bhagvad Gita 405
Bhakti (Movement) 30-34, 63, 73, 249, 272-319, 336, 337-444
Aesthetics 82, 268, 270, 385
Bakhtiyar Kaki 281, 282, 329
Bheeshma 10, 102, 110, 118, 120, 123, 127, 197, 235
Brahmin 12, 14, 31, 32, 57, 59, 60, 97, 99, 100, 112, 122, 129, 202, 203-240, 324, 332, 339, 352, 372, 376, 390, 412, 435
Brahui (Tribe) 143, 169, 174, 176, 177, 183, 190
Braj Bhasha 33, 393, 396
Buddha 9, 15, 46, 107, 205, 244, 336, 358, 364, 375, 419
Buddhism 46, 47, 64-112, 208, 219, 262, 264, 339, 344, 346-375, 403, 405, 414-421
Buddhist 6, 69, 77, 87-93, 104, 121, 204-211, 240, 344-376, 397
Bulleh Shah 93, 279, 289, 291, 294-367, 389
Burton (Richard) 67, 246

C

Camel 20, 75-85, 172, 190, 272, 389
Campbell (George) 228, 229
Canals 17, 20, 21, 25, 30, 41, 63, 144-173
Chaitanya Mahaprabhu 30, 31, 33, 337, 377, 382, 383
Chatterji (S K) 253
Chishti Silsilah 63, 281, 282, 329, 333, 335, 337

D

Dalit (Sikh) 202, 237, 340, 341, 442-444
Dara Shikoh 6, 300, 334, 344, 350, 354
Dera Ghazi Khan 3-42, 73, 391
Dera Ismail Khan 19, 27, 28, 34, 35, 79, 143, 251, 254, 255, 285
Dharma 12 , 99, 102, 116, 119, 133, 137, 139, 148, 203, 375, 383, 388, 405, 407, 440
Dhritarashtra (King) 10, 103-137
Dhrupad 388, 389, 403
Dipalpur 3, 31
Dodai (Baloch Tribe) 18, 144
Dodai, Sohrab Khan 23, 143
Dohra 228, 286, 290, 331, 361, 364
Dolphin (Indus) 79, 83, 84, 85
Doniger (Wendy) 362
Draupadi (Queen) 105, 106, 116, 119, 124, 128, 131, 139
Dronacharya (Guru) 108,118,123,125
Duroyadhana 110, 111, 118-129

Dushala (Queen) 10, 123, 136, 137

E

Edwardes (Herbert) 29, 151

F

Farid Sani 278,287,288-293,364, 365
Farishta 333
Fauna and Flora 49, 79, 85, 356
Flyway No. 4 81, 82

G

Gandhara 10, 13, 15, 90-139, 208, 262, 265, 270, 349
Gandhari (Queen) 10, 101, 102, 103, 113, 115, 119, 120-139, 306
Ganjamali (Krishandas) 31
Ganpat Rai (Diwan) 30,154,176,195
Gaudiya Vaishnavism 382, 386, 387, 397, 404
Gazetteer 26
Ghazi Khan (Mirrani) 4, 30, 33, 144, 153, 155
Ghulam Farid (Khwaja) 63, 278, 279
Gilmartin (David) 23, 147, 163
Gisu Darazi (Saiyid) 356, 357
Gita Govinda 357, 376, 396, 397
Goswami 30, 31, 357, 377,385, 386, 391, 397, 406, 427, 439
Gotra 202, 205, 207, 211, 212, 213, 214, 215, 220, 222, 223, 224, 239
Gujrati Muslim Khatri see Muslim Khatri 224, 225
Guru Granth Sahib 28, 210, 256, 278, 331, 356, 361, 421, 422, 423-442
Guru Nanak 37, 209, 222, 226, 245, 267, 269, 270, 280, 322, 360, 363, 365, 377, 378, 380, 381, 404, 412-442
Guru Arjan Dev 268, 284, 421-440
Guru Angad 222, 269, 270, 427, 429, 437

H

Habib (Mohd.) 332
Hakim 39, 40
Hastinapur 6, 9, 99-137, 435
Heer Damodar 307, 308
Hindko 249, 251, 255
Hindwi 422, 423, 424, 429
Hittu Ram (Rai) 30, 154, 176-189
Horse
  Kamboja 10, 12, 98, 106-108, 135
  Saindaha 100-135
Husaini Brahmins 237, 332

I

Ibn-e-Batuta 75
Indraprastha (Delhi) 6, 9, 99, 138

J

Jacob (John) 151, 163, 164, 165
Jokes (A) 273
Jayadeva 357, 376, 396, 397, 406
Jayadratha (King) 10,98-106,113- 137
Jhulelal 64, 333
Jia Goswami 377, 427
Jogi (Movement) 97, 111, 279-444
Julaha 361, 364, 366, 379, 381, 414, 432

K

Kabul (River) 3,34,48,52,53,71,81

Kaikeyi 12, 14
Kandahar 3, 63, 127, 132, 148, 187, 251, 280
Kane (V.P.) 207
Karna 103,111,118,119,123,125,137
Kauravas 9, 10, 103-139
Kekaya (Kingdom) 10,14,15,98-122
Kewalarama 34, 35, 281
Khan of Kalat 17, 148, 151, 166-196
Khanqah 63, 278, 281, 285, 316, 331, 333-368
Khatri 23-59, 153, 187, 196, 419, 427-436
Khetaran (Tribe) 145
Khosa (Tribe) 18, 145, 146, 176
Kirar 25, 28, 233-39, 266
Kirakki (Script) 266
Konkan Brahmins 234
Koran 93, 301-321, 365-378
Kshatriya (Caste) 12, 14, 30, 97-137, 201-237

L

Lahndi 245-273
Lal Ded 359, 360
Lalji (Maharaj) 30-35
Leghari (Tribe) 18, 22, 145-177
Lion's Mouth 46, 67, 69, 70
Lohana (Sub-caste) 225, 232, 237

M

Maclagan, Edward 208
McLeod (W.H.) 473
Madra (Kingdom) 10, 12, 15, 104, 109, 110, 111, 120, 122
Masnavi 360, 441
Max Müller (F.) 50, 52, 60, 68, 88
Morewerther, William 166, 167, 168, 176, 177, 178
Mian Mir 298, 300, 334, 335, 350
Mirabai 359, 377, 382, 398, 427
Mithankot 17, 47, 77, 78, 150, 167, 174, 175
Mithankot Conference (1871) 150, 167, 174
Mohenjodaro 87, 88, 91, 92
Moin-ud-Din Chisti (Khwaja) 281, 282, 311, 329, 330, 333
Mul Raj (Diwan) 29
Multan 3-93, 121, 144, 180, 201, 208, 209, 211, 216, 218, 224-315, 329-335

N

Nambarka 284, 392
Namdeva 377
Napier (Sir Charles) 172
Naqshbandi 352
Naths 350, 362, 379-318, 414, 421
Nayanmar 372, 375, 403, 427
Nigaha 36, 37
Nirguna Bhakti 380, 381
Nizamuddin (Hazrat) 281

O

O'Brien (E) 246

P

Pakpattan 3, 31, 73, 248, 267, 278-284, 311, 329-334
Pandavas 6, 9-15, 86, 87, 98, 101-137
Panis (Rigvedic Tribe) 104

Panini 90, 104, 110, 203-205, 252
Parasuram 203, 207, 208, 234, 235
Pashto 247, 255
Peshawar 10, 34, 37, 47, 102, 121, 208, 211, 247-260, 382
Potohar 68, 74, 87, 98, 201, 208, 211, 214, 218, 220, 252-266

Q

Qadria Silsilah 335

R

Ramananda 362, 376, 378-381, 399, 412, 415-430
Ramanuja 283, 363, 375, 376, 378, 399,407, 412, 426
Ranjit Singh 27-29, 422
Rasa 35, 53, 202, 219, 343, 386, 392, 401-406
Ravidas (Sant) 210, 417-444
Rumi 93,297,301,314,319,349,441
Runn of Kutch 74, 100, 315

S

Sachal Sarmast 254, 279, 320, 323, 324, 342
Saguna Bhakti 362
Sakhi Sarwar (Sultan) 3, 21, 35, 36, 37, 73, 441, 442
Sandeman (Robert Groves) 4, 21, 30, 144-197
Sanjay 60, 119, 132
Saraiki Language 33, 80, 81, 244, 250, 256, 262, 266, 271, 277, 285, 307, 332
Sarasvati (River) 38, 47-64, 87, 99, 109, 207, 219, 234
Sauvirah see Sindhu Kingdom 100-103, 121
Schimmel (Annemarie) 67,93,325,333
Shackle (Christopher) 299, 442, 251, 252, 261, 287
Shah Husain 277-296, 303-311, 334, 335, 342, 350-358, 413
Shakuni 10, 86, 98-139
Shalva (Kingdom) 10, 98, 104, 111
Sibi 19, 101, 121, 171, 254
Shyamji (Maharaj) 30-35
Sikhism 32, 33, 36, 73, 209, 210, 223, 267, 346, 364, 380, 411-444
Soubala (King) 86, 103, 105, 113, 115-130
Souvira see Sindhu (Kingdom) 101-107, 121
Sufism 36, 63, 89, 93, 244, 279, 299, 302, 304, 316, 319, 327-368, 381, 404, 408, 413, 417-441
Silsilah 63, 281, 282, 329-341
Suhrawardi Silsilah 330
Sultan Bahu 334, 364, 366, 279
Surdas 377, 382, 393, 402, 426-430
Swat 46, 48, 71-93, 208, 209

T

Tagore (Rabindranath) 388, 395-401
Takshasila 102
Talpur (Mir) 18, 77, 146
Taxila 7, 10, 47, 87, 90, 91, 98, 103, 121, 201, 208, 252
Todar Mal (Raja) 214, 224
Trinjan (Spinning Wheel) 358
Trumpp (Ernest) 258, 313, 424
Tulsa 33, 34

Tulsidas (Goswami) 376, 391
Tumun 18, 20, 21, 145, 152, 159,
Tumundar 18-27, 146-165, 176, 196, 197

U

Uddiyana see Swat 46, 77, 92, 93
Uluka (Prince of Gandhara) 115-138

V

Vallabhacharya (Vithalnath) 30, 377, 382, 390, 391, 426
Vidura 119, 123, 129, 130-133

W

Wahdat al-Wajoud 362, 380
Warris Shah 63, 93, 279, 291, 303, 306, 313, 334, 358, 364

Z

Zakariya Baha-ud-Din 330, 333, 335
Zindapir 64, 84, 333